THE PHILOSOPHY
OF THE BODY

THE PHILOSOPHY
OF THE BODY

REJECTIONS OF
CARTESIAN DUALISM

EDITED WITH AN INTRODUCTION BY

STUART F. SPICKER

CHICAGO

QUADRANGLE BOOKS

Library of Congress Catalog Card Number: 70–101074

Grateful acknowledgment is made to Harvard University Press for permission to reprint a selection from *Collected Papers of Charles Sanders Peirce*, ed. C. Hartshorne and Paul Weiss, copyright © 1934, 1962 by the President and Fellows of Harvard College, and to The Macmillan Company for permission to reprint a selection from *Philosophical Investigations* by Ludwig Wittgenstein, trans. G. E. M. Anscombe.

For Richard M. Griffith and
the American Committee to Keep Biafra Alive

PREFACE

This book is an attempt to resolve a teacher's frustration. During the last few years, I have been disappointed with the paucity of published material dealing with the philosophical conception of the human body available to students of philosophy, psychology, and medicine. To be sure, there is a plethora of literature published under the rubric of "philosophy of mind" and "philosophical psychology"; but thus far only a small fraction of the finest philosophical literature deals primarily with the philosophy of the body.

The materials contained in the following pages are not readily available to the university student; they are even less accessible to the general reader with intellectual interests. All the papers in this collection are related to a central theme and set of problems; this in itself should serve to dispel the myth that philosophical speculation regarding the concept of the body is only sporadic and therefore reflects no thematic development within the history of Western philosophy.

The subtitle of this anthology, *Rejections of Cartesian Dualism*, presupposes that the reader is familiar with the philosophy of René Descartes (1596–1650). Since this is to some degree the strategy of the collection, I explicate in the Introduction what I consider to be the essentially important theses of Descartes' philosophy of the body, while at the same time distinguishing the philosophy of Descartes from "Cartesian" thought in general. I have purposely avoided including excerpts from Descartes' writings, since his work is already reprinted in many places and need not be reprinted once again. However, the following five references to the works of Descartes may prove worth reading in combination with the materials from this collection:

(1) *Meditations on First Philosophy*, 1641. See especially Meditations I, II, and VI.

(2) *Objections and Replies,* 1642. Especially Hobbes, Arnauld, and Gassendi, respectively.

(3) *The Principles of Philosophy,* 1644. Especially Principles 40, 41, 48, 51–54, and 60.

(4) *The Passions of the Soul,* 1649. See especially Articles 23, 24, and 30–34.

(5) *Correspondence with Princess Elizabeth,* 1643.

I wish to express my appreciation to the Research Council of the University of Wyoming for its financial assistance in making the first compilation possible for student use prior to the actual publication of this book. During the time this collection was in preparation, many colleagues and associates gave concrete, constructive criticisms and suggestions. My personal thanks are extended to Professors Forrest Williams, Vere Chappell, Manfred Frings, Herbert Spiegelberg, and Erling Eng. To those many friends whom I encountered at the 1968 Council for Philosophical Studies I also extend my gratitude for their suggestions. I am especially indebted to James M. Edie for his critical suggestions pertinent to the selection and publication of the essays. I am most appreciative of my secretary, Mrs. Judine Drayer, whose indefatigable effort and competence were invaluable in the completion of this book. I close this list of benefactors with a special testimony of appreciation to my teachers, Erwin Straus and Hans Jonas, companions of my thought, and to my wife, Judith, companion of my life.

S. F. S.

Cambridge, England
November 1969

CONTENTS

PART III
TOWARD A PHILOSOPHICAL ANTHROPOLOGY

Descartes is the father of modern philosophy, and the spirit of Cartesianism—that which principally distinguishes it from the scholasticism which it displaced—may be compendiously stated as follows:

1. It teaches that philosophy must begin with universal doubt; whereas scholasticism had never questioned fundamentals.

2. It teaches that the ultimate test of certainty is to be found in the individual consciousness; whereas scholasticism had rested on the testimony of sages and of the Catholic Church.

3. The multiform argumentation of the middle ages is replaced by a single thread of inference depending often upon inconspicuous premisses.

4. Scholasticism had its mysteries of faith, but undertook to explain all created things. But there are many facts which Cartesianism not only does not explain but renders absolutely inexplicable, unless to say that "God makes them so" is to be regarded as an explanation.

In some, or all of these respects, most modern philosophers have been, in effect, Cartesians. Now without wishing to return to scholasticism, it seems to me that modern science and modern logic require us to stand upon a very different platform from this. . . .

—Charles Sanders Peirce

THE PHILOSOPHY
OF THE BODY

INTRODUCTION

"The human body is the best picture of the human soul." This oft-quoted sentence from Ludwig Wittgenstein's *Philosophical Investigations*[1] has, according to current philosophical literature, lost its portentous character and achieved prominence among philosophical clichés. This sentence appears whenever a philosopher discusses some problem under the rubric "philosophy of mind." It is generally believed that Wittgenstein's sentence expresses a truth which anyone upon the slightest reflection would comprehend and unhesitatingly repeat. But perhaps the "truth" expressed is not so readily accessible, even after philosophical reflection, as one would first believe. This is partially evidenced by a contemporary British philosopher's translation of "Körper" as *face*, thereby rendering Wittgenstein's sentence "The human face is the best picture of the human soul."[2] Since the phrase remains an enigma, perhaps the time has come to give it more serious consideration. Thus the remarks to follow, including the bulk of the text, are intended as gradual steps in formulating a novel conception of the human body. More specifically, one might hope to clarify the conceptual network behind Wittgenstein's sentence. This does not seem an unreasonable tactic, since his sentence is not fully intelligible to us, notwithstanding the competent analyses of numerous interpreters of Wittgenstein's writings. In brief, the time is appropriate for discussing the idea that the human body (*Leib*) is the best picture of the human mind, and this may well be achieved by turning our attention to a philosopher who offers us what some consider to be the only tenable conception of the soul: Aristotle.

II

It is well known that Aristotle distinguishes the human body from the human soul, where the term "soul" not only refers to the principle of life but to the form of a *particular* living body. He quite clearly states that "the body cannot be soul";[3] the body is the matter, not what is attributed to it.

We are reminded that the body of a living animal is an *organized* body, the soul being the actual organization of this body. With this qualification, Aristotle advances the analogy of the human eye to an animal. We now realize that sight is analogous to the soul of the animal.[4] The eye itself corresponds to the matter or material substratum, and the power of sight corresponds to the essence or formal substratum. When the power of sight is absent, the eye is no longer an eye in the proper sense, but an "eye" in name only. That is, it is no more an actual human eye than is the "eye" of a statue. Generalizing this analysis to include the entire human body, the living organism, we come to appreciate the fact that all the senses require both a material and formal principle for their operation. It would appear, then, that Aristotle is proposing more than a body-soul dualism, except that he suggests that the human soul can act without involving the human body. If this is possible, then one might well be more inclined to accuse Aristotle of propounding a dualistic conception of man. We are therefore compelled to face the question of whether the human soul can act or be acted upon without involving the human body.

Aristotle takes the initial stance in Book One that ". . . there seems to be no case in which the soul can act or be acted upon without involving the body," that is, without a concurrent affection of the body.[5] In general, it seems that the affections—e.g., anger, appetite, passion—of any soul are inseparable from the material substratum of animal life. In particular, this is the same with respect to the human soul's relation to the human body. The question, then, whether the soul is capable of separate existence can only be determined if there is at least one activity of the soul which does not require a concurrent connection to the human body. It is, of course, well known that Aristotle maintains that "thinking seems the most probable exception."[6] He warns, however, that if thinking ". . . proves to be a form of imagination or to be impossible without imagination it too requires a body as a condition of its existence."[7] Aristotle appears certain that both perception and imagination require a connection with a body, but he has not yet drawn the same conclusion with respect to "thinking" (the manipulating of abstract concepts of, say, science, mathematics, and philosophy). At this point it appears to be an open question whether the body and the soul of a man are one.[8]

But in Book Two of *De Anima* Aristotle suggests that thinking is to the affections as that which is eternal is to that which perishes.[9] That is, thinking, as one specific activity of the human soul, is capable of separate and independent existence from any connection to a body. So "when mind is set free from its present conditions it appears as just what it is and nothing more: this alone is immortal and external. . . ."[10] At this point Aristotle generates a classical *aporia* or impasse created by the dual theses that (1) reason, being a kind of imagination, forms a unity with and is inseparable from the body, and (2) there is at least one activity of the soul (reasoning) that can exist independently and separately from any connection to a body. Rather than discuss this classical *aporia* which is the definitive Aristotelian position, it might prove more profitable to discuss Aristotle's remarks regarding the significance of the living body's relation to the soul (or mind) in his evaluation of Plato's and his predecessors the Pythagoreans' views.

In Book One of *De Anima* Aristotle says:

> The view we have just been examining [Plato's], in company with most theories about the soul, involves the following absurdity: they all join the soul to a body, or place it in a body, without adding any specification of the reason of their union, or of the bodily conditions required for it. Yet such explanations can scarcely be omitted; for some community of nature is presupposed by the fact that the one acts and the other is acted upon, the one moves and the other is moved; interaction always implies a *special* nature in the two interagents. All, however, that these thinkers do is to describe the specific characteristics of the soul; they do not try to determine anything about the body which is to contain it, as if it were possible, as in the Pythagorean myths, that any soul could be clothed upon with any body—an absurd view, for each body seems to have a form and shape of its own. It is as absurd as to say that the art of carpentry could be embodied in flutes; each art must use its tools; each soul its body.[11]

It is evident from this passage that although the soul generally requires connection to a body—while it cannot *be* a body but something relative to a body—it is *in* a body of a definite kind. That is to say, each particular *kind* of soul necessarily requires a particular *kind* of body; and this is a matter not of physical but of logical necessity. That such a connection is not merely a matter of physical impossibility is what is so difficult for Aristotle (and others as well) to prove to the satisfaction of all.

On the basis of what has been said thus far, it is clear that it is not sufficient that we explicate the various activities of the soul of the horse,

dog, fly, or man; what is required for a satisfactory analysis of the connection of each particular kind of soul and its particular kind of body-
accompaniment is that we give serious attention to the nature of the
body to which a particular kind of soul is related. The classical over-
simplification of this consideration is the Pythagoreans' doctrine of the
transmigration of souls where there is no logical necessity connecting
certain souls to certain bodies. This is obvious in a reading from
Xenophanes of Colophon.[12]

Xenophanes reports that Pythagoras was said to have been passing
by when a puppy was being beaten. Pitying it, he said, "Stop! Cease
your beating, because this is really the soul of a man who was my
friend: I recognized it as I heard it cry aloud!"[13] This particular an-
ecdote suggests that souls could be reincarnated in the form of living
things other than man, a doctrine sometimes referred to as "metamorphosis" or "metempsychosis." The doctrine maintains that a soul or mind
might animate a human and even a non-human body at various times.
Herodotus supplies us with a further account of the doctrine of transmigration:

> . . . the Egyptians are the first to have maintained the doctrine that the
> soul of man is immortal, and that, when the body perishes, it enters into
> another animal that is being born at the same time, and when it has been
> the complete round of the creatures of the dry land and of the sea and of
> the air it enters again into the body of a man at birth; and its cycle is com-
> pleted in 3,000 years.[14]

Aristotle, extremely critical of the doctrine of transmigration, thinks
it is a mistake to do as these former thinkers did, that is, to fit the soul
into a body without adding a definite specification of the *kind* and
character of that body. Serious reflection requires the conclusion that
the actuality of any given thing can only be realized in what is already
potentially that thing. In brief, Aristotle rejects the doctrine of the
Pythagoreans which claims that the soul can clothe itself in different
sorts of bodies. Rather, a particular soul is the entelechy or formative
force of a particular body and the individuality of the particular man.
As a result, every living body appears to have a distinct form and
character. It is unknown, Aristotle concludes, for any chance thing to
admit any other chance thing; no casual subject appears capable of
undergoing any casual or haphazard effect.

In his *Commentary* on Aristotle's *De Anima,* Thomas Aquinas interprets Aristotle's stress on the *"kind"* or *"character"* of the body which is besouled as a mere reference to the need for "some definite and appropriate material."[15] According to Aquinas, Aristotle is merely saying that living beings are composed of one *kind* of material substance and non-living beings of another *kind* of material substance. Given Aquinas' view it would follow that living beings are composed of a physical-organic substance whereas non-living beings are composed of a merely physical substance. But this, I think, is not quite the distinction Aristotle is drawing. Rather, Aristotle is arguing that a human soul is actualized "in a matter of its own appropriate to it."[16] For Aristotle, "matter" refers to the *particular* organic totality which is besouled. So he is not merely concerned with all the species of living beings as such, but with each particular living being that is generated within any species. The correct doctrine is based upon careful description of bodily comportment and physiognomy, and suggests that every particular soul requires a connection to a particular organic whole. Thus the soul of a particular horse is not contingently related to a particular horse physiognomy expressive of a unique comportment; similarly, each human soul is non-contingently related to a particular and unique human physiognomy expressive of a specific comportment. This is the case for each and every living being. Hence no longer must one be satisfied with any conception of a person which views him as a member of a species, class, or set. Each living being is unique. The suggestion that souls or minds are interchangeable in different bodies—even two bodies within the same species—is, according to Aristotle, absurd. It is the epitome of understatement to consider such an incoherent fantasy a "mistake" or spurious suggestion. But this is the danger awaiting those who fall into the trap "that yawns for all who use fantasy in philosophy."[17]

No use of fantasy is found in Aquinas' commentary on *De Anima*. He observes that with the Pythagorean fable any soul can enter any body;

> . . . the soul of a fly for instance might perchance enter the body of an elephant. This cannot in fact happen; for the body of each particular thing, and especially of living things, has its own form and species and type of movement; hence there are great differences between the bodies of a worm, a dog, an elephant and a gnat. When we say that any soul can enter any body, it is as if one were to say that the art of weaving could enter flutes, or that the art of the coppersmith could enter a weaver's loom. If it was in the power of these arts to enter bodies or instruments they would not

do so indiscriminately, but the art of playing the flute would enter flutes, and not lyres, while the art of playing stringed instruments would enter stringed instruments and not flutes. In the same way, if there is a body for every soul, *any* soul does not enter *any* body; rather the soul shapes the body fit for itself; it does not enter a ready-made body. Plato and others who speak only about the soul are too superficial; they fail to define which body answers to which soul, and the precise mode of existence of each in union with the other.[18]

Thus Plato is the perpetuator of a "savage superstition"[19] in supposing that a man's constitution includes a wholly immaterial mind or soul such that the body is extrinsic to the person, like one's coat or shoes. Furthermore, Plato and the Pythagoreans were mistaken in another important respect—they all join the soul to a body, or place it in a body, *without adding any specification of the reason for their union*. Yet such explanations can scarcely be omitted; for some continuity of nature is presupposed by the fact that the one acts and the other is acted upon, the one moves and the other is moved; interaction always implies a special nature in the two interagents.[20] Unfortunately, Aristotle's admonitions have gone unheeded. The genius of Plato before him and Descartes after him have served to perpetuate the savage superstitions.

The philosopher who some eighteen centuries after the writing of *De Anima* addressed himself to the problem posed so succinctly by Aristotle was, of course, René Descartes. In offering a rational explanation of the nature of the union of the human soul and body, he delved into the nature of the two interagents. Since this anthology assumes a posture in opposition to Cartesian dualism—a thesis which supposes that man consists of two essentially distinct substances, body and soul, which separate at death—it is necessary to consider Descartes' conceptualization in some detail as it pertains to our theses, always keeping in view what his antagonist, Julien Offray de la Mettrie, said of him: ". . . it is none the less just for me to make an authentic reparation to this great man for all the insignificant philosophers—poor jesters, and poor imitators of Locke—who instead of laughing impudently at Descartes, might better realize that without him the field of philosophy, like the field of science without Newton, might perhaps be still uncultivated."[21]

III

In the remarks to follow I shall not mean by "Cartesian philosophy" that philosophical doctrine identical with the philosophy of Descartes.

Rather I shall henceforth use the term as a referent to those who are disciples of Descartes' philosophy and who tend to believe they think like him. For it is my conviction that "Cartesian philosophy" is not quite applicable as a description of Descartes' own position. It is simply one of the ironies of the history of European philosophy that Descartes is not a "Cartesian." That is, if one considers the generally acknowledged dualistic view attributed to Descartes as a consequence of the argument in his *Meditations*, then one will surely come away with the standard interpretation of his metaphysic of mind and body; but if one can come to appreciate Descartes' other penetrating insights expressed in the *Meditations* and in writings regarding the phenomena of human embodiment, then one is compelled to view Descartes' philosophical stance in a radically new way which is sharply distinguishable from Cartesian philosophy. It therefore becomes necessary to de-emphasize the standard interpretation of the mind-body dualism that is frequently stressed in most textbooks and to stress those heretofore neglected insights which reveal that Descartes was often his own most severe critic. This strategy suggests a specific interpretation of the subtitle (*Rejections of Cartesian Dualism*) of this anthology. For I am in no way attempting to be critical of Descartes' philosophy in order to dispose of his view; on the contrary, I hope to show that a rejection of what has come to be called "Cartesian" would be quite consistent with Descartes' own position.

In his private notebook Descartes wrote "*larvatus prodeo*," "I come forward in a mask."[22] Could it be that the mask was the dualism personified by Descartes' self in the activity of meditation? Again his antagonist, La Mettrie, penetrates that mask: "For after all, although he extols the distinctness of the two substances, this is plainly but a clever trick, a ruse of style, to make theologians swallow a poison, hidden in the shade of an analogy which strikes everybody else and which they alone fail to notice."[23] In order to defend the novel approach of La Mettrie it is necessary to consider the metaphysic of mind and body generally attributed to Descartes, and to follow this exposition with a discussion of those insights which clearly indicate that Descartes did not in fact subscribe to what we currently understand as his general and, I regret to say, popular philosophy.

IV

In Descartes' earlier meditations, man is viewed as a composite of two essentially distinct substances, and when we refer in any way to a person we are actually referring to one (and sometimes both) of these separate substances. Each of these substances is describable in terms of a given set of properties which are mutually exclusive or "disjoint." That is, there are properties of mind and properties of body, and none of the properties of either can be a property of the other. Moreover, any two substances differ in kind rather than degree if there is some defining characteristic of one that is not shared by the other and if there are no intermediaries between them. Descartes, to be sure, maintains that these two substances are radically different both in kind and degree; and the ensuing analyses in the *Meditations* revolve around this point.

In his "Dedication" to the Faculty of Theology of Paris, Descartes writes that he intends to establish once and for all the "real distinction of mind and body." This "intention" La Mettrie considered a "clever trick" and "ruse of style." And apparently the "ruse" was worth prolonging for those of clerical persuasion, for in the "Synopsis" of the *Meditations* he tells the theologians that "we are not able to conceive the half of a mind, as we can of any body, however small, so that the natures of these two substances are to be held, not only as diverse, but even in some measure as contraries." And in Meditation Six it appears that the last word has been said: ". . . there is a vast difference between the body and mind, in respect that body, from its nature, is always divisible, and that mind is entirely indivisible."[24] The *Meditations* makes it quite clear that the human mind is not extended in length, breadth, or depth, and participates in none of the properties of body.[25] For a body is an extended and unthinking thing and entirely distinct from a mind. In distinguishing mind from body it is necessary that there be nothing included in the concept of body that belongs to the mind; and nothing in that of mind that belongs to the body. Furthermore, Meditation Three seems to suggest that Descartes views himself as pure mind which merely happens, quite contingently, to be "enclosed" in matter.[26] But even if we grant that pure mind is identical to Descartes' ego, the "I," we must, with Thomas Aquinas, recognize that it in no way follows that pure mind is identical to the *person*. In his commentary on I Corinthians 15, Aquinas says that "my soul is not I; and if only souls are saved, *I* am not saved, nor is any man." We now come to appreciate the fact that a man, a person, is a "composite whole" of the mind in its union with the body.

Princess Elizabeth of Bohemia (1616–1680) discloses the confusion which occurs should Descartes' dualism be taken seriously; he himself, in fact, does not maintain the truth of the "professed" dualism. When she questions Descartes about the union of soul and body and how the soul has the power of moving the body, Descartes replies that in his *Meditations* he said "almost nothing" of the first fact "for my main object was to prove the distinction of soul and body."[27] But now that her Highness "sees too clearly for dissimulation to be possible," Descartes consents to discuss the union of soul and body. Not satisfied with the content of Descartes' reply, Elizabeth writes another letter almost a month later. In his second response Descartes makes a few startling remarks. First, Elizabeth is told that the soul is conceived only by the activity of the pure intellect; second, the union of soul and body can be understood only in an obscure way by pure intellect or when the intellect is aided by imagination, but is understood very clearly by means of the *senses*. Consequently, in the course of ordinary life and conversation, by *abstaining from meditating and studying,* her Highness—and the rest of us as well—is able to perceive the union of soul and body. Although she does, in fact, find more obscurity in the notion of the union of soul and body, she is courteously reminded that she forms such a conception primarily by experiencing it in her own case. And it is therefore Descartes' position that the unity of the self is absolutely indubitable; this is an empirical truth having its basis in the activity of sense, and not in the activity of the pure intellect. One might expect Descartes to ground all claims of absolute indubitability on acts of pure intellect, but we now know this is not a requirement in his search for apodictic knowledge. After such a reading one can no longer dismiss Descartes' conception of the role of the senses. To stress this point, Descartes writes the Princess that "everybody always [has the awareness of the union of soul and body] in himself without doing philosophy. . . ."[28]

It is soon apparent that Elizabeth is not at all satisfied with his response; for she is keenly aware of the fact that Descartes contradicts himself when he admits that the body can act on the mind: How can sensations, which we are told require the activity of the body, arise in a mind whose essence (so we are told) consists in pure thought[29] which exists independently of all activity of the body? For the union of the spirit[30] and the body is made evident by sense; whether or not we comprehend it, it still remains sensed. This union, then, which is found only in man (this is not the case for other animals), is beyond the comprehension of finite intellects; we can have no genuine conceptual knowledge of their union whether we think on the level of metaphysical, medical, or ordinary knowledge. The union of body and mind, moreover, rests on the omnipotent decree of Divinity and is only disclosed to finite minds through sense experience, thereby becoming a matter of natural belief, since the mind and body differ *toto genere*.

V

Having completed our discussion of the general doctrine which is usually adduced from a reading of Descartes' comments on the nature of the union of the mind and the body of man, as well as his conclusion that finite minds are unable to fully comprehend the nature of that unity, it is important to consider the specific theses which are the basis of his general conclusions.

The human mind is capable of three cognitive faculties: pure intellect, sense, and imagination. The essence of the mind consists in pure intellection apart from all sense and imagination. Although intellect can be conceived apart from sense and imagination, these two faculties cannot be conceived apart from the body in which they are active. There are, then, no body processes involved in acts of pure intellection, whereas brain activity is required for the occurrence of sense and imagination. In short, Descartes has to some extent modified his dualistic thesis when he argues that sensations and images can only arise in a mind through its union with a material body. Earlier he had argued that the "I," the mind, that by which he is what he is, is entirely distinct from his body, and may even exist without it.[31] But we should not be confused by this assertion. As Peter Geach points out:

> . . . if a man can bring himself to doubt whether anything material exists, but cannot bring himself to doubt his own existence . . . then all that follows is that in this state of doubt he does not know that he himself is a material being, not that he is not one.[32]

Descartes is still able to maintain that he *is* a body as well as a mind; his difficulty is to prove that he can (in his technical sense) *know* it. This is already prefigured in Meditation Two when he remarks that he "was somewhat astonished to find such faculties [as the power of self-motion, perceiving, thinking] in some bodies."[33] From this remark we are compelled to conclude that the inanimate material object is

Descartes' paradigm of *body;* and the human body is thereby viewed as a peculiar modification of the inanimate external world of objects. This accounts for his "astonishment." This is more clearly illustrated in his analysis of a piece of wax as the exemplar of body-as-such. For, he adds, "what is here remarked of the piece of wax, is applicable to all the other things that are external to me."[34] This, of course, necessarily includes one's own body—namely, Descartes' body! Returning to our earlier point, the exercise of the pure intellect requires no brain, i.e., body processes, and is, as Aristotle had already suggested, entirely independent of the body; however, sense and imagination are essentially conditioned by brain and other neurological activity, such that in the absence of these activities sense and imagination would not in fact occur. The result of this *aporia* is the thesis that the mind and the body constitute a quasi-substantial unity. Whereas the faculty of pure intellect is the activity of mind contemplating itself, the faculties of sense and imagination demand that the mind activate the body. Descartes offers us a stringent mechanical explanation of the manner in which images and sensations arise in us. In *The Passions of the Soul* Descartes says:

> When we wish to image something we have never seen, this volition has the power of causing the [pineal] gland to move in the manner required in driving the spirits toward the brain-pores on the openings of which the thing can be represented. Thus, too, when we wish to hold our attention fixed for some little time on some one object, this volition keeps the gland bent in this direction. And lastly, when we will to walk or to move the body in any manner, this volition causes the gland to impel the spirits toward the muscles which bring about this effect.[35]

In order for images and sensations to arise in us, the body is required; but, we are told, the body is the "not-I." And the "I" in the total absence of any relation or activity of the body has no power of imagery or sense. Descartes apparently leaves us with a completely spiritualized conception of the "I." Perhaps the solution to the problem is that the "I" is not strictly identifiable with the "self" or the "person." When Descartes refers to the self he is usually referring to the composite whole of the mind and the body.[36] And when he speaks of the composite whole, the unity, he frequently refers to his "nature." Thus in Meditation Six we find him using such phrases as "dictates of nature," "necessary to my nature," "nature seemed to incline me," "nature teaches me," and only later does he inform us that he must "accurately define" what he properly understands by "being taught by nature." But unfortunately no such clearly presented definition is ever offered. We simply discover that we can pervert the order of our nature, which is not omniscient, and which can be corrupted because it necessarily involves (and perhaps *is* identifiable with) the activity of the body. These passages in Meditation Six indicate that Descartes has not yet decided to confront the crucial role which the human body plays in clarifying the concept of man, person, self. At the close of the six meditations Descartes has not advanced sufficient evidence toward proving that the self is an embodied self; yet he does not hesitate to point out that he was not altogether wrong in believing that the body which "by a special right I called my own pertained to me more properly and strictly than any of the others."

> . . . for in truth, I could never be separated from it as from other bodies:
> I felt in it and on account of it all my appetites and affections, and in
> fine I was affected in its parts by pain and the titillation of pleasure and
> not in the parts of other bodies that were separated from it.[37]

But in spite of this insight Descartes must still account for the union of the mind with the total physical organism, and he proceeds to do this in such a way that one cannot help believing with La Mettrie that the dualism was merely a "clever trick" or ruse put forth as a philosophical disguise behind which stood the serious philosopher.

V I

Descartes "clearly discerns" that he is a composite whole, and the possible relation between the mind and the body might be expressed by suggesting that (1) the whole mind is united to the whole body;[38] (2) the mind is in the brain; or (3) the mind is in some place intermediate between the foot and the brain.[39] He proceeds to reject (1) and (3) because "when a foot, an arm, or any other part is cut off, I am conscious that nothing has been taken from the mind." He argues for (2) on the basis of evidence brought forth from anatomical observations which include the structure of the pineal gland and the brain. An infirmity to certain areas of the brain will, to be sure, inhibit sense and imagination, if not pure intellect as well.

In the closing paragraph of Part Five of his *Discourse on Method,*

Descartes says of the pure intellect that it would not suffice to place it in the human body as a pilot in a ship, but that it must be more intimately conjoined and united with the body in order to have feelings and appetites like ours, and so constitute *a real man*. In *De Anima*[40] Aristotle had already raised the question of whether the soul may not be the actuality of its body in the sense in which the sailor is the actuality (actuator) of his ship. Aristotle mentions this in the wake of Plato's earlier view that the soul is the act of the body not as its form but as its mover. But Aristotle never asserts that the soul is the mover of the body as the sailor is the mover of his ship, and Descartes implies his agreement with Aristotle on this point:

> Nature likewise teaches me by these sensations of pain, hunger, thirst, etc., that I am not only lodged in my body as a pilot in a vessel but that I am besides so intimately conjoined, and as it were intermixed with it that my mind and body compose a certain unity. For if this were not the case, I should not feel pain when my body is hurt, seeing I am merely a thinking thing, but should perceive the wound by the understanding alone, just as a pilot perceives by sight when any part of his vessel is damaged.[41]

This significant observation serves to illuminate the fact that Descartes' analysis of pain after an injury conflicts with his dualistic thesis; for we have already noted that this dualism fails to account for the interaction of body and mind in acts of (1) sensing and imaging, (2) volition, and (3) emotion, e.g., feeling pain. But one must not pass too quickly over the fact that it is Descartes who offers us the illustration of the pilot and his vessel! Descartes is surely not unaware that pain and other emotional phenomena demonstrate unquestionably the intimate relation between the human mind and the human body. It is his view that the feeling of pain is "nothing more than certain confused *modes* of thinking arising from the union and apparent fusion of mind and body."[42] For sensing and imaging are modes of thinking, and they are modes because of the bodily activity involved in these faculties.[43] Notwithstanding this point, Descartes retreats to the realm of physiology, and what had begun as a significant insight terminates all too abruptly, and we are left without further clarification of phenomena such as pain. In Meditation Six we find the following:

> . . . I have sometimes been informed by parties whose arm or leg had been amputated, that they still occasionally seemed to feel pain in that part of the body which they had lost,—a certain circumstance that led me to

> think that I could not be quite certain even that any one of my members
> was affected when I felt pain in it.[44]

With this remark Descartes' method fails him, and he is even led to
doubt that the pain in his leg is, strictly speaking, *in* his leg. This interpretation implies that there is nothing organic about pain. In his
response to Regius' Sixth Article he remarks that "Certainly I remember
hearing in the Schools that the *mind is an activity of the organic body*,
but till this day I never heard the mind itself termed 'organic'."[45] He
understands Regius to mean by the mind being organic "that it does
not act of itself, but is used by the body as though it were something
that strengthened its members and other corporeal modes. . . ."[46] Regius
had maintained that the mind is nothing other than a mode of the
body and that man consists of body alone; Descartes denies that he is
the assemblage of members called the human body. As early as Meditation Two, Descartes, for methodological purposes, was willing to say
that he *thought* that he possessed a countenance, hands, arms, and all
the fabric of members that appear in a corpse, and which he called by
the name of body,[47] but this is not the way he speaks at the close of
the *Meditations*. Nevertheless, this remark would lead one to believe
that for Descartes there is no significant difference between the living
body of a person and a corpse. Yet on the other hand, he never believed
this for an instant. Certainly, the earlier meditations seemed to prove
conclusively that all bodies, all external, physical objects (including
human bodies) have been reduced to a single substance, *res extensa*,
and no special or privileged place need be found for persons, embodied selves. On the other hand, he observes that although he certainly does "possess" a body with which he is closely conjoined, he
does not possess it as one possesses a suit of clothes. Although one *has*
a body one does not *have* it in quite the same sense as one has a coat or
hat. Yet Descartes is apparently unwilling to say that he, the "I," *is* his
body, for this thesis is not only too strong but quite flagrantly in
conflict with the entire drive (or should we say ruse) of the *Meditations*.
Perhaps further clarification of this philosophical conflict is possible if
we consider Descartes' conception of animal existence in contradistinc-
tion to his analysis of human existence.

VII

What precisely is the difference between the brute animals and man,
since both animals and men possess bodies?

According to Descartes, animals are mere automata lacking consciousness. "Life," he once wrote, "I deny to no animal; except in so far as I lay it down that life consists simply in the warmth of the heart."[48] Whereas human beings are conscious and combine body and mind, body and consciousness, animals do not. It is not merely that "animals have less reason than man, but that they have none at all."[49] This is evidenced in part by the fact that they do not talk.

> It is . . . unbelievable that a monkey or a parrot which was one of the best of its species should not be equal in this matter of talking of one of the most stupid children, or at least of a child infirm in mind, if their soul were not of a wholly different nature from ours.[50]

It is evident that the *soul* of man is of a wholly different nature from that of the brute animals, but unfortunately Descartes did not choose to thematize his own observation concerning the nature of the *bodies* of these animals, just as he failed to do so with the body of a man. Conceptual difficulties arise at this point regarding the concepts of *body, physical body, external object. Living bodies* are not *bodies* in the same sense in which a block of wax is a *body,* as a consequence of which these concepts lose their applicability when connections are broken with other concepts. Just such a breakdown or collapse occurs when we try to think of *living body* merely in terms of predicates like "weighs 180 pounds," "is 67 inches long," "contains none of its original molecular parts but wholly new parts," etc. Although these predicates can be ascribed to living bodies when living bodies are considered mere physical bodies, they alone do not suffice to sustain the concept of *living human body.* When Regius remarked that "the human mind, though it is a substance really distinct from body, is nevertheless, so long as it is in a body, organic in all its activities,"[51] he had begun to reinstate the early truth first articulated by Aristotle. For it is absolutely essential, in my view, to retain the organic nature of mind if we insist on using *mind* or *soul* in any meaningful way. Even the modest position of Regius would have led to an alternate doctrine superior to the Cartesianism which predominates not only in the *Meditations* but in *our* ordinary language as well. But once again there is the Descartes whose views do not (as is now to be expected) coincide with the Cartesianism of the *Meditations.* In a letter to Regius he writes:

> It is not accidental to the human body to be united to the mind but its very nature; because, as the body has all the dispositions requisite for receiving the mind, and without it is not properly the human body, it

could not without a miracle happen that the mind should not be united to it.[52]

In spite of the dualism, then, Descartes does not intend that man is merely a spirit that makes use of a body. His view is that mind is "substantially united" with a body.[53] As Descartes indicated, the "bridge" that permits mind and body, thought and extension, to meet rests in the animal spirits in the pineal gland. But this incoherent view, as Peter Bertocci points out, is strictly a "technical howler."[54] Descartes apparently persists in arguing that the mind is so dependent upon the humors and the condition of the organs of the body that if it is possible to find some way to make men wiser and more clever than they have been so far, it is in medicine that it should be sought.[55] Descartes is fully aware of the fact that the entire human organism operates as a totality, the study of this totality generally being the prerogative of the physician. Philosophers might well profit from the wisdom of the classical physicians. It is no mere historical accident that philosophers misunderstand the subtle position of La Mettrie. In his *Man a Machine* (admittedly a misleading title), La Mettrie does not advocate a naïve materialism. He writes:

> Man is not moulded from a costlier clay; nature has used but one dough, and has merely varied the leaven. . . . The soul is therefore but an empty word, of which no one has any idea, and which an enlightened man should use only to signify that part in us that thinks. . . . I believe that thought is so little incompatible with organized matter, that it seems to be one of its properties. . . . Let us then conclude boldly that man is a machine, and that in the whole universe there is but a single substance differently modified.[56]

VIII

Although the readings in this anthology generally share in their mutual rejection of Cartesian dualism, it would be misleading to conclude that all philosophers agree that Cartesian dualism is justifiably and appropriately rejected. The dualistic thesis generally credited to Descartes is by no means rejected by all contemporary philosophers. One such advocate of the Cartesian stance is Jerome Shaffer. In "Persons and Their Bodies"[57] Shaffer admits at the outset that the view he defends "will be considered by many to be shockingly reactionary, for it consists in a defense of a theory very much like that of Descartes."[58]

For Shaffer a person is a "nonphysical entity," a "nonbodily thing," and it is a contingent matter that a person has *that* body which he calls *his*. Somewhat later in the same article Shaffer clarifies his view even further:

> . . . a person does not *necessarily* have the body which in fact he has—that is, that a particular body is only contingently the body of whatever person it is the body of. It does not follow from this that it is a merely contingent fact that a person has any body at all.[59]

Thus Shaffer claims that (1) it is not a contingent fact that a person has a body and (2) it is a contingent fact that a person has the particular body *that* he has. These two claims are, of course, based upon the distinction between a person and his body, a distinction which Shaffer maintains is "perfectly legitimate."[60] In Shaffer's view it is correct to say that "persons have bodies";[61] moreover, it is appropriate to say that "a person must be something which *could* have a body although it is only a contingent fact that any particular person does have the body he has."[62]

From the above it is possible for Shaffer to conclude that this body which is mine (1) could (logically) have been the body of someone else, (2) can someday be the body of someone else, and (3) can someday no longer be the body of some person. To be sure, (3) is indisputable if one considers the case of my body becoming a dead body or corpse. But cases (1) and (2) imply that two persons can switch bodies, that is, that this is logically possible. For according to Shaffer, " a body which belongs to a person just *happens* to belong to *that* person."[63] Shaffer is surely correct that "if we are willing to admit the possibility that persons could switch bodies, then it follows that the fact that any one has the body he has is a *contingent* fact, in that he just happens to have the body he does and might, in the next instant, suddenly find himself with some other body." This, we are reminded, is because "the identity of the body is logically independent of the identity of the person whose body it is."[64]

Almost every article within this collection takes issue with one or more of Shaffer's claims. As a group, these readings defend the following claims:

(1) a person is not a nonphysical or nonbodily entity;

(2) the distinction between a person and his body is not perfectly legitimate;

(3) it is not merely a contingent fact that a person has *that* body which he calls *his;*

(4) a person *necessarily* has *that* particular body which he calls his;

(5) this body which is mine could not (logically) have been the body of someone else;

(6) this body which is mine cannot (logically) someday be the body of someone else;

(7) no two persons can (logically) be said to exchange or switch bodies;

(8) the identity of the body is not logically independent of the identity of the person whose body it is;

(9) although it is correct to say that a person *has* a body, it is more precise to say that a person *is* his body.

The general problem, then, is to demonstrate that the possibility of two persons' switching bodies is not only impossible in this world but logically impossible as well. Such a demonstration would suffice to prove that the body which one has is not a contingent fact at all, and that the identity of one's body *is* logically dependent on the identity of the person whose body it is. And thus the conclusion: a person *is* his body.

I X

In closing this introduction in order to permit the reader to turn his attention to the selections which follow, I should like to repeat that one of the aims of this book is to enable the reader to reject Cartesian dualism for cogent reasons. One would hope that the old dualistic notion of mind and matter, soul and body, so prominent in Cartesian philosophy will find no defenders by the end of this century. By rejecting Cartesian dualism as a "savage superstition" one might in all likelihood be driven to some form of "spiritual materialism," which seems a self-contradictory doctrine at best, but which might, if carefully rendered, differ radically from the crude materialisms or elegant spiritualisms disclosed in the history of philosophy. Moreover, a thorough examination of this development reveals that the concept of the *living human body* remains unclarified in spite of the marked advances in our knowledge of the anatomical body, knowledge, it should be noted, which has come to us from the genius of medicine and the care of the physician. For the physician, then, as well as the philosopher, the words of

Nietzsche are also germane, since they serve to indicate the new direction in which philosophical thought must advance: "Body (*Leib*) am I, and soul"—thus speaks the child. And why should one not speak like children?

"But the awakened and knowing say: body am I entirely, and nothing else; and soul is only a word for something about the body."[65]

NOTES

1. (New York: Macmillan, 1953), Part IV, Section 178: "Der menschliche Körper ist das beste Bild der menschlichen Seele."
2. Anthony Flew, ed., *Body, Mind, and Death* (New York: Macmillan, 1964), "Introduction," p. 24.
3. *De Anima*, 412^a [17]
4. *Ibid.*, 412^b [19]; see 413^a [3-4]
5. *Ibid.*, 403^a [5-7]
6. *Ibid.*, 403^a [8]
7. *Ibid.*, 403^a [9-10]
8. *Ibid.*, 412^b [6]
9. *Ibid.*, 413^b [25-26]
10. *Ibid.*, 430^a [23-24]
11. *Ibid.*, 407^b [13-25]
12. Fragment 7.
13. G. S. Kirk and J. E. Raven, *The Presocratic Philosophers* (Cambridge: Cambridge University Press, 1960), pp. 222–23.
14. *Ibid.*, p. 222.
15. *Aristotle's De Anima in the Version of William of Moerbeke and the Commentary of St. Thomas Aquinas* (New Haven: Yale University Press, 1959), p. 195.
16. *De Anima*, 414^a [20-26]; see *Metaphysica*, 1035^b [14]
17. Peter Geach, *God and the Soul* (London: Routledge & Kegan Paul, 1969), p. 14.
18. *Aristotle's De Anima in the Version of William of Moerbeke and the Commentary of St. Thomas Aquinas*, p. 114.
19. Geach, *God and the Soul*, p. 38.
20. *De Anima*, 407^b [13-25]
21. *Man a Machine* (LaSalle, Ill.: Open Court, 1961), p. 142.
22. Elizabeth Anscombe and Peter Geach, eds., *Descartes: Philosophical Writings* (London: Thomas Nelson and Sons Ltd., 1966), p. 3.
23. *Man a Machine*, p. 143.

24. *The Meditations and Selections from the Principles of René Descartes*, trans. John Veitch (LaSalle, Ill.: Open Court, 1966), *Meditations* VI, 99. Hereafter *Med.*

25. *Med.* IV, 63.

26. *Med.* III, 60.

27. *Descartes Philosophical Writings*, p. 275.

28. *Ibid.*, pp. 274–286. The correspondence between Descartes and Princess Elizabeth was dispatched during May and June 1643.

29. Lat. *Cogitatio;* Fr. *Pensée.*

30. The term "spirit" (Fr. *l'esprit*) is synonymous with "mind" when Descartes is speaking of the mind as if it were in fact unconnected to body. The term "soul" (Fr. *l'âme*) is Descartes' term for mind when it is considered in union with the body. Hence "spirit" and "soul" are not always interchangeable, *salva veritate.*

31. *Med.* VI, 91.

32. P. Geach, *God and the Soul*, p. 8.

33. *Med.* II, 32.

34. *Med.* II, 40.

35. Article 43.

36. *Med.* VI, 95.

37. *Med.* VI, 88–89.

38. *Med.* VI, 100.

39. *Med.* VI, 102.

40. 413[a] [9]

41. *Med.* VI, 94.

42. We will not take the time here to enter upon Descartes' concept of "mode" except to point out that it is this notion upon which the problem of the unity of mind and body is to be resolved should one consider the dualism a tenable thesis.

43. Norman Kemp Smith, *New Studies in the Philosophy of Descartes* (London: Macmillan, 1963), p. 293. Cf. N. K. Smith, *Studies in the Cartesian Philosophy* (New York: Russell & Russell, 1962), pp. 126–128.

44. *Med.* VI, 89–90. Cf. pp. 101–103.

45. *The Philosophical Works of Descartes,* trans. E. S. Haldane and G. R. T. Ross, 2 vols. (Cambridge: Cambridge University Press, 1911–12, reprinted, 1931–1934; also Dover Publications, New York, republication of the 1931–1934 edition) I, 440.

46. *Ibid.*, I, 437–438.

47. *Med.* II, 31.

48. N. K. Smith, *New Studies in the Philosophy of Descartes*, pp. 126–127. Letter to Henry More (February 5, 1649). Cf. *Oeuvres de Descartes*, ed. C. Adam and P. Tannery, 12 vols., Paris (1897–1910), V, 278.

49. *Discourse on Method* (New York: Liberal Arts Press, 1956), Part V, p. 37.

50. *Ibid.*

51. *The Philosophical Works of Descartes*, Haldane and Ross, eds., I 432: Article VI.

52. *Ibid.*, II, 102; Reply to Objections IV. Cf. *Oeuvres de Descartes*, VII, 227–228.

53. "Descartes and Marcel on the Person and His Body: A Critique," read at the meeting of the Aristotelian Society (March 25, 1968), p. 212.

54. *Ibid.*

55. *Discourse on Method*, Part VI, p. 40.

56. *Man a Machine*, pp. 117, 128, 143–144, 148.

57. *Philosophical Review*, XXV, No. 1 (January 1966), 59–77.

58. *Ibid.*, p. 59.

59. *Ibid.*, p. 70.

60. *Ibid.*, p. 63.

61. *Ibid.*, p. 64.

62. *Ibid.*, p. 76.

63. *Ibid.*, p. 67.

64. *Ibid.*, p. 65.

65. "Thus Spake Zarathustra," trans. Walter Kaufmann in *The Portable Nietzsche* (New York: Viking, 1967), First Part, "On the Despisers of the Body (*des Leibes*)," p. 146. The original text reads: " 'Leib bin ich und Seele'—so redet das Kind. Und warum sollte man nicht wie die Kinder reden? Aber der Erwachte, der Wissende sagt: Leib bin ich ganz und gar, und nichts ausserdem; und Seele ist nur ein Wort für ein Etwas am Leibe."

PART I

THE HUMAN

ORGANISM

OF THE NATURE AND
ORIGIN OF THE MIND

Benedict de Spinoza

DEFINITIONS

I. By *body* I mean a mode which expresses in a certain determinate manner the essence of God, in so far as he is considered as an extended thing.

II. I consider as belonging to the essence of a thing that, which being given, the thing is necessarily given also, and, which being removed, the thing is necessarily removed also; in other words, that without which the thing, and which itself without the thing, can neither be nor be conceived.

III. By *idea*, I mean the mental conception which is formed by the mind as a thinking thing.

Explanation.—I say *conception* rather than perception, because the word perception seems to imply that the mind is passive in respect to the object; whereas conception seems to express an activity of the mind.

IV. By *an adequate idea*, I mean an idea which, in so far as it is considered in itself, without relation to the object, has all the properties or intrinsic marks of a true idea.

Explanation.—I say *intrinsic*, in order to exclude that mark which is extrinsic, namely, the agreement between the idea and its object (*ideato*).

V. *Duration* is the indefinite continuance of existing.

This selection is extracted from Spinoza's *Ethics* in *The Chief Works of Benedict de Spinoza*, translated by R. H. M. Elwes (New York: Dover Publications, Inc., 1951), II, 82–107.

Explanation.—I say *indefinite,* because it cannot be determined through the existence itself of the existing thing, or by its efficient cause, which necessarily gives the existence of the thing, but does not take it away.

VI. *Reality and perfection* I use as synonymous terms.

VII. By *particular things,* I mean things which are finite and have a conditioned existence; but if several individual things concur in one action, so as to be all simultaneously the effect of one cause, I consider them all, so far, as one particular thing.

AXIOMS

I. The essence of man does not involve necessary existence, that is, it may, in the order of nature, come to pass that this or that man does or does not exist.

II. Man thinks.

III. Modes of thinking, such as love, desire, or any other of the passions, do not take place, unless there be in the same individual an idea of the thing loved, desired, &c. But the idea can exist without the presence of any other mode of thinking.

IV. We perceive that a certain body is affected in many ways.

V. We feel and perceive no particular things, save bodies and modes of thought.

N.B. *The postulates are given after the conclusion of* Prop. xiii.

PROPOSITIONS

PROP. I. *Thought is an attribute of God, or God is a thinking thing.*

Proof.—Particular thoughts, or this or that thought, are modes which, in a certain conditioned manner, express the nature of God. God therefore possesses the attribute of which the concept is involved in all particular thoughts, which latter are conceived thereby. Thought, therefore, is one of the infinite attributes of God, which express God's eternal and infinite essence. In other words, God is a thinking thing.   *Q.E.D.*

Note.—This proposition is also evident from the fact, that we are able to conceive an infinite thinking being. For, in proportion as a thinking being is conceived as thinking more thoughts, so is it conceived as containing more reality or perfection. Therefore a being, which can think an infinite number of things in an infinite number of ways, is, necessarily, in respect of thinking, infinite. As, therefore, from the consideration of thought alone we conceive an infinite being, thought is necessarily one of the infinite attributes of God, as we were desirous of showing.

PROP. II. *Extension is an attribute of God, or God is an extended thing.*

Proof.—The proof of this proposition is similar to that of the last.

PROP. III. *In God there is necessarily the idea not only of his essence, but also of all things which necessarily follow from his essence.*

Proof.—God (by the first Prop. of this Part) can think an infinite number of things in infinite ways, or can form the idea of his essence, and of all things which necessarily follow therefrom. Now all that is in the power of God necessarily is. Therefore, such an idea as we are considering necessarily is, and in God alone.   *Q.E.D.*

Note.—The multitude understand by the power of God the free will of God, and the right over all things that exist, which latter are accordingly generally considered as contingent. For it is said that God has the power to destroy all things, and to reduce them to nothing. Further, the power of God is very often likened to the power of kings. But this doctrine we have refuted, and we have shown that God acts by the same necessity, as that by which he understands himself; in other words, as it follows from the necessity of the divine nature (as all admit), that God understands himself, so also does it follow by the same necessity, that God performs infinite acts in infinite ways. We further showed that God's power is identical with God's essence in action; therefore it is as impossible for us to conceive God as not acting, as to conceive him as non-existent. If we might pursue the subject further, I could point out, that the power which is commonly attributed to God is not only human (as showing that God is conceived by the multitude as a man, or in the likeness of a man), but involves a negation of power. However, I am unwilling to go over the same ground so often. I would only beg the reader again and again, to turn over frequently in his mind what I have said in Part i from Prop. xvi to the end. No one will be able to follow my meaning, unless he is scrupulously careful not to confound the power of God with the human power and right of kings.

PROP. IV. *The idea of God, from which an infinite number of things follow in infinite ways, can only be one.*

Proof.—Infinite intellect comprehends nothing save the attributes of God and his modifications. Now God is one. Therefore the idea of God, wherefrom an infinite number of things follow in infinite ways, can only be one.   *Q.E.D.*

PROP. V. *The actual being of ideas owns God as its cause, only in so far as he is considered as a thinking thing, not in so far as he is unfolded in any other attribute; that is, the ideas both of the attributes of God and of particular things do not own as their efficient cause their objects (ideata) or the things perceived, but God himself in so far as he is a thinking thing.*

Proof.—This proposition is evident from Prop. iii of this Part. We there drew the conclusion, that God can form the idea of his essence, and of all things which follow necessarily therefrom, solely because he is a thinking thing, and not because he is the object of his own idea. Wherefore the actual being of ideas owns for cause God, in so far as he is a thinking thing. It may be differently proved as follows: the actual being of ideas is (obviously) a mode of thought, that is a mode which expresses in a certain manner the nature of God, in so far as he is a thinking thing, and therefore involves the conception of no other attribute of God, and consequently is not the effect of any attribute save thought. Therefore the actual being of ideas owns God as its cause, in so far as he is considered as a thinking thing, &c.   *Q.E.D.*

PROP. VI. *The modes of any given attribute are caused by God, in so far as he is considered through the attribute of which they are modes, and not in so far as he is considered through any other attribute.*

Proof.—Each attribute is conceived through itself, without any other; wherefore the modes of each attribute involve the conception of that attribute, but not of any other. Thus they are caused by God, only in so far as he is considered through the attribute whose modes they are, and not in so far as he is considered through any other.   *Q.E.D.*

Corollary.—Hence the actual being of things, which are not modes of thought, does not follow from the divine nature, because that nature has prior knowledge of the things. Things represented in ideas follow, and are derived from their particular attribute, in the same manner, and with the same necessity as ideas follow (according to what we have shown) from the attribute of thought.

PROP. VII. *The order and connection of ideas is the same as the order and connection of things.*

Proof.—For the idea of everything that is caused depends on a knowledge of the cause, whereof it is an effect.

Corollary.—Hence God's power of thinking is equal to his realized power of action—that is, whatsoever follows from the infinite nature of God in the world of extension (*formaliter*), follows without exception in the same order and connection from the idea of God in the world of thought (*objective*).

Note.—Before going any further, I wish to recall to mind what has been pointed out above—namely, that whatsoever can be perceived by the infinite intellect as constituting the essence of substance, belongs altogether only to one substance: consequently, substance thinking and substance extended are one and the same substance, comprehended now through one attribute, now through the other. So, also, a mode of extension and the idea of that mode are one and the same thing, though expressed in two ways. This truth seems to have been dimly recognized by those Jews who maintained that God, God's intellect, and the things understood by God are identical. For instance, a circle existing in nature, and the idea of a circle existing, which is also in God, are one and the same thing displayed through different attributes. Thus, whether we conceive nature under the attribute of extension, or under the attribute of thought, or under any other attribute, we shall find the same order, or one and the same chain of causes—that is, the same things following in either case.

I said that God is the cause of an idea—for instance, of the idea of a circle—in so far as he is a thinking thing; and of a circle, in so far as he is an extended thing, simply because the actual being of the idea of a circle can only be perceived as a proximate cause through another mode of thinking, and that again through another, and so on to infinity; so that, so long as we consider things as modes of thinking, we must explain the order of the whole of nature, or the whole chain of causes, through the attribute of thought only. And, in so far as we consider things as modes of extension, we must explain the order of the whole of nature through the attribute of extension only; and so on, in the case of other attributes. Wherefore of things as they are in themselves God is really the cause, inasmuch as he consists of infinite attributes. I cannot for the present explain my meaning more clearly.

PROP. VIII. *The ideas of particular things, or of modes, that do not exist, must be comprehended in the infinite idea of God, in the same way as the formal essences of particular things or modes are contained in the attributes of God.*

Proof.—This proposition is evident from the last; it is understood more clearly from the preceding note.

Corollary.—Hence, so long as particular things do not exist, except in so far as they are comprehended in the attributes of God, their representations in thought or ideas do not exist, except in so far as the infinite idea of God exists; and when particular things are said to exist, not only in so far as they are involved in the attributes of God, but also in so far as they are said to continue, their ideas will also involve existence, through which they are said to continue.

Note.—If anyone desires an example to throw more light on this question, I shall, I fear, not be able to give him any, which adequately explains the thing of which I here speak, inasmuch as it is unique; however, I will endeavour to illustrate it as far as possible. The nature of a circle is such that if any number of straight lines intersect within it, the rectangles formed by their segments will be equal to one another; thus, infinite equal rectangles are contained in a circle. Yet none of these rectangles can be said to exist, except in so far as the circle exists; nor can the idea of any of these rectangles be said to exist, except in so far as they are comprehended in the idea of the circle. Let us grant that, from this infinite number of rectangles, two only exist. The ideas of these two not only exist, in so far as they are contained in the idea of the circle, but also as they involve the existence of those rectangles; wherefore they are distinguished from the remaining ideas of the remaining rectangles.

PROP. IX. *The idea of an individual thing actually existing is caused by God, not in so far as he is infinite, but in so far as he is considered as affected by another idea of a thing actually existing, of which he is the cause, in so far as he is affected by a third idea, and so on to infinity.*

Proof.—The idea of an individual thing actually existing is an individual mode of thinking, and is distinct from other modes (by the Corollary and Note to Prop. viii of this Part); thus (by Prop. vi of this Part) it is caused by God, in so far only as he is a thinking thing. But not in so far as he is a thing thinking absolutely, only in so far as he is considered as affected by another mode of thinking; and he is the cause of this latter, as being affected by a third, and so on to infinity. Now, the order and connection of ideas is the same as the order and connection of causes. Therefore of a given individual idea another individual idea, or God, in so far as he is considered as modified by that idea, is the cause; and of this second idea God is the cause, in so far as he is affected by another idea, and so on to infinity.   *Q.E.D.*

Corollary.—Whatsoever takes place in the individual object of any idea, the knowledge thereof is in God, in so far only as he has the idea of the object.

Proof.—Whatsoever takes place in the object of any idea, its idea is in God (by Prop. iii of this Part), not in so far as he is infinite, but in so far as he is considered as affected by another idea of an individual thing; but (by Prop. vii of this Part) the order and connection of ideas is the same as the order and connection of things. The knowledge, therefore, of that which takes place in any individual object will be in God, in so far only as he has the idea of that object.   *Q.E.D.*

Prop. X. *The being of substance does not appertain to the essence of man—in other words, substance does not constitute the actual being[1] of man.*

Proof.—The being of substance involves necessary existence. If, therefore, the being of substance appertains to the essence of man, substance being granted, man would necessarily be granted also, and, consequently, man would necessarily exist, which is absurd. Therefore, &c. *Q.E.D.*

Note.—This proposition may also be proved from I. v, in which it is shown that there cannot be two substances of the same nature; for as there may be many men, the being of substance is not that which constitutes the actual being of man. Again, the proposition is evident from the other properties of substance—namely, that substance is in its nature infinite, immutable, indivisible, &c., as anyone may see for himself.

Corollary.—Hence it follows, that the essence of man is constituted by certain modifications of the attributes of God. For (by the last Prop.) the being of substance does not belong to the essence of man. That essence therefore is something which is in God, and which without God can neither be nor be conceived, whether it be a modification, or a mode which expresses God's nature in a certain conditioned manner.

Note.—Everyone must surely admit, that nothing can be or be conceived without God. All men agree that God is the one and only cause of all things, both of their essence and of their existence; that is, God is not only the cause of things in respect to their being made (*secundum fieri*), but also in respect to their being (*secundum esse*).

At the same time many assert, that that, without which a thing cannot be nor be conceived, belongs to the essence of that thing; wherefore they believe that either the nature of God appertains to the essence of created things, or else that created things can be or be conceived without God; or else, as is more probably the case, they hold inconsistent doctrines. I think the cause for such confusion is mainly, that they do not keep to the proper order of philosophic thinking. The nature of God, which should be reflected on first, inasmuch as it is prior both in the order of knowledge and in the order of nature, they have taken to be last in the order of knowledge, and have put into the first place what they call the objects of sensation; hence, while they are considering natural phenomena, they give no attention at all to the divine nature, and, when afterwards they apply their mind to the study of the divine nature, they are quite unable to bear in mind the first hypotheses, with which they have overlaid the knowledge of natural phenomena, inasmuch as such hypotheses are no help towards understanding the Divine nature. So that it is hardly to be wondered at, that these persons contradict themselves freely.

However, I pass over this point. My intention here was only to give a reason for not saying, that that, without which a thing cannot be or be conceived, belongs to the essence of that thing: individual things cannot be or be conceived without God, yet God does not appertain to their essence. I said that "I considered as belonging to the essence of a thing that, which being given, the thing is necessarily given also, and which being removed, the thing is necessarily removed also; or that without which the thing, and which itself without the thing can neither be nor be conceived."

PROP. XI. *The first element, which constitutes the actual being of the human mind, is the idea of some particular thing actually existing.*

Proof.—The essence of man (by the Coroll. of the last Prop.) is constituted by certain modes of the attributes of God, namely, by the modes of thinking, of all which the idea is prior in nature, and, when the idea is given, the other modes (namely, those of which the idea is prior in nature) must be in the same individual. Therefore an idea is the first element constituting the human mind. But not the idea of a non-existent thing, for then the idea itself cannot be said to exist; it must therefore be the idea of something actually existing. But not of an infinite thing. For an infinite thing must always necessarily exist; this would involve an absurdity. Therefore the first element, which constitutes the actual being of the human mind, is the idea of something actually existing. *Q.E.D.*

Corollary.—Hence it follows, that the human mind is part of the infinite intellect of God; thus when we say, that the human mind perceives this or that, we make the assertion, that God has this or that idea, not in so far as he is infinite, but in so far as he is displayed through the nature of the human mind, or in so far as he constitutes the essence of the human mind; and when we say God has this or that idea, not only in so far as he constitutes the essence of the human mind, but also in so far as he, simultaneously with the human mind, has the further idea of another thing, we assert that the human mind perceives a thing in part or inadequately.

Note.—Here, I doubt not, readers will come to a stand, and will call to mind many things which will cause them to hesitate; I therefore beg them to accompany me slowly, step by step, and not to pronounce on my statements, till they have read to the end.

PROP. XII. *Whatsoever comes to pass in the object of the idea, which constitutes the human mind, must be perceived by the human mind, or there will necessarily be an idea in the human mind of the said occurrence. That is, if the object of the idea constituting the human mind be a body, nothing can take place in that body without being perceived by the mind.*

Proof.—Whatsoever comes to pass in the object of any idea, the knowledge thereof is necessarily in God, in so far as he is considered as affected by the idea of the said object, that is, in so far as he constitutes the mind of anything. Therefore, whatsoever takes place in the object constituting the idea of the human mind, the knowledge thereof is necessarily in God, in so far as he constitutes the nature of the human mind; that is the knowledge of the said thing will necessarily be in the mind, in other words the mind perceives it.

Note.—This proposition is also evident, and is more clearly to be understood from II. vii, which see.

PROP. XIII. *The object of the idea constituting the human mind is the body, in other words a certain mode of extension which actually exists, and nothing else.*

Proof.—If indeed the body were not the object of the human mind, the ideas of the modifications of the body would not be in God in virtue of his constituting our mind, but in virtue of his constituting the mind of something else; that is the ideas of the modifications of the body would not be in our mind: now we do possess the ideas of the modifications of the body. Therefore the object of the idea constituting the human mind is the body, and the body as it actually exists. Further, if there were any other object of the idea constituting the mind besides body, then, as nothing can exist from which some effect does not follow (I, xxxvi) there would necessarily have to be in our mind an idea, which would be the effect of that other object; but there is no such idea.

Wherefore the object of our mind is the body as it exists, and nothing else.   *Q.E.D.*

Note.—We thus comprehend, not only that the human mind is united to the body, but also the nature of the union between mind and body. However, no one will be able to grasp this adequately or distinctly, unless he first has adequate knowledge of the nature of our body. The propositions we have advanced hitherto have been entirely general, applying not more to men than to other individual things, all of which, though in different degrees, are animated.[2] For of everything there is necessarily an idea in God, of which God is the cause, in the same way as there is an idea of the human body; thus whatever we have asserted of the idea of the human body must necessarily also be asserted of the idea of everything else. Still, on the other hand, we cannot deny that ideas, like objects, differ one from the other, one being more excellent than another and containing more reality, just as the object of one idea is more excellent than the object of another idea, and contains more reality.

Wherefore, in order to determine, wherein the human mind differs from other things, and wherein it surpasses them, it is necessary for us to know the nature of its object, that is, of the human body. What this nature is, I am not able here to explain, nor is it necessary for the proof of what I advance, that I should do so. I will only say generally, that in proportion as any given body is more fitted than others for doing many actions or receiving many impressions at once, so also is the mind, of which it is the object, more fitted than others for forming many simultaneous perceptions; and the more the actions of one body depend on itself alone, and the fewer other bodies concur with it in action, the more fitted is the mind of which it is the object for distinct comprehension. We may thus recognize the superiority of one mind over others, and may further see the cause, why we have only a very confused knowledge of our body, and also many kindred questions, which I will, in the following propositions, deduce from what has been advanced. Wherefore I have thought it worth while to explain and prove more strictly my present statements. In order to do so, I must premise a few propositions concerning the nature of bodies.

Axiom I.—All bodies are either in motion or at rest.

Axiom II.—Every body is moved sometimes more slowly, sometimes more quickly.

Lemma I. *Bodies are distinguished from one another in respect of motion and rest, quickness and slowness, and not in respect of substance.*

Proof.—The first part of this proposition is, I take it, self-evident. That bodies are not distinguished in respect of substance, is plain from both I. v and I. viii. It is brought out still more clearly from I. xv, note.

LEMMA II. *All bodies agree in certain respects.*

Proof.—All bodies agree in the fact, that they involve the conception of one and the same attribute. Further, in the fact that they may be moved less or more quickly, and may be absolutely in motion or at rest.

LEMMA III. *A body in motion or at rest must be determined to motion or rest by another body, which other body has been determined to motion or rest by a third body, and that third again by a fourth, and so on to infinity.*

Proof.—Bodies are individual things, which (Lemma I) are distinguished one from the other in respect to motion and rest; thus each must necessarily be determined to motion or rest by another individual thing, namely by another body, which other body is also (Ax. i) in motion or at rest. And this body again can only have been set in motion or caused to rest by being determined by a third body to motion or rest. This third body again by a fourth, and so on to infinity.   *Q.E.D.*

Corollary.—Hence it follows, that a body in motion keeps in motion, until it is determined to a state of rest by some other body; and a body at rest remains so, until it is determined to a state of motion by some other body. This is indeed self-evident. For when I suppose, for instance, that a given body, A, is at rest, and do not take into consideration other bodies in motion, I cannot affirm anything concerning the body A, except that it is at rest. If it afterwards comes to pass that A is in motion, this cannot have resulted from its having been at rest, for no other consequence could have been involved than its remaining at rest. If, on the other hand, A be given in motion, we shall, so long as we only consider A, be unable to affirm anything concerning it, except that it is in motion. If A is subsequently found to be at rest, this rest cannot be the result of A's previous motion, for such motion can only have led to continued motion; the state of rest therefore must have resulted from something, which was not in A, namely, from an external cause determining A to a state of rest.

AXIOM I.—All modes, wherein one body is affected by another body, follow simultaneously from the nature of the body affected and the body affecting; so that one and the same body may be moved in different modes, according to the difference in the nature of the bodies moving it; on the other hand, different bodies may be moved in different modes by one and the same body.

AXIOM II.—When a body in motion-impinges on another body at rest, which it is unable to move, it recoils, in order to continue its motion, and the angle made by the line of motion in the recoil and the plane of the body at rest, whereon the moving body has impinged, will be equal to the angle formed by the line of motion of incidence and the same plane.

So far we have been speaking only of the most simple bodies, which are only distinguished one from the other by motion and rest, quickness and slowness. We now pass on to compound bodies.

Definition.—When any given bodies of the same or different magnitude are compelled by other bodies to remain in contact, or if they be moved at the same or different rates of speed, so that their mutual movements should preserve among themselves a certain fixed relation, we say that such bodies are in union, and that together they compose one body or individual, which is distinguished from other bodies by this fact of union.

AXIOM III.—In proportion as the parts of an individual, or a compound body, are in contact over a greater or less superficies, they will with greater or less difficulty admit of being moved from their position; consequently the individual will, with greater or less difficulty, be brought to assume another form. Those bodies, whose parts are in contact over large superficies, are called *hard;* those, whose parts are in contact over small superficies, are called *soft;* those, whose parts are in motion among one another, are called *fluid.*

LEMMA IV. *If from a body or individual, compounded of several bodies, certain bodies be separated, and if, at the same time, an equal number of other bodies of the same nature take their place, the individual will preserve its nature as before, without any change in its actuality (forma).*

Proof.—Bodies (Lemma I) are not distinguished in respect of substance: that which constitutes the actuality (*formam*) of an individual consists (by the last Def.) in a union of bodies; but this union, although there is a continual change of bodies, will (by our hypothesis) be maintained; the individual, therefore, will retain its nature as before, both in respect of substance and in respect of mode.   *Q.E.D.*

LEMMA V. *If the parts composing an individual become greater or less, but in such proportion, that they all preserve the same mutual relations of motion and rest, the individual will still preserve its original nature, and its actuality will not be changed.*

Proof.—The same as for the last Lemma.

LEMMA VI. *If certain bodies composing an individual be compelled to change the motion, which they have in one direction, for motion in another direction, but in such a manner, that they be able to continue their motions and their mutual communication in the same relations as before, the individual will retain its own nature without any change of its actuality.*

Proof.—This proposition is self-evident, for the individual is supposed to retain all that, which, in its definition, we spoke of as its actual being.

LEMMA VII. *Furthermore, the individual thus composed preserves its nature, whether it be, as a whole, in motion or at rest, whether it be moved in this or that direction; so long as each part retains its motion, and preserves its communication with other parts as before.*

Proof.—This proposition is evident from the definition of an individual prefixed to Lemma IV.

Note.—We thus see, how a composite individual may be affected in many different ways, and preserve its nature notwithstanding. Thus far we have conceived an individual as composed of bodies only distinguished one from the other in respect of motion and rest, speed and slowness; that is, of bodies of the most simple character. If, however, we now conceive another individual composed of several individuals of diverse natures, we shall find that the number of ways in which it can be affected, without losing its nature, will be greatly multipled. Each of its parts would consist of several bodies, and therefore (by Lemma VI) each part would admit, without change to its nature, of quicker or slower motion, and would consequently be able to transmit its motions more quickly or more slowly to the remaining parts. If we further conceive a third kind of individuals composed of individuals of this second kind, we shall find that they may be affected in a still greater number of ways without changing their actuality. We may easily proceed thus to infinity, and conceive the whole of nature as one individual, whose parts, that is, all bodies, vary in infinite ways, without any change in the individual as a whole. I should feel bound to explain and demonstrate this point at more length, if I were writing a special treatise on body. But I have already said that such is not my object, I have only touched on the question, because it enables me to prove easily that which I have in view.

POSTULATES

I. The human body is composed of a number of individual parts, of diverse nature, each one of which is in itself extremely complex.

II. Of the individual parts composing the human body some are fluid, some soft, some hard.

III. The individual parts composing the human body, and consequently the human body itself, are affected in a variety of ways by external bodies.

IV. The human body stands in need for its preservation of a number of other bodies, by which it is continually, so to speak, regenerated.

V. When the fluid part of the human body is determined by an external body to impinge often on another soft part, it changes the surface of the latter, and, as it were, leaves the impression thereupon of the external body which impels it.

VI. The human body can move external bodies, and arrange them in a variety of ways.

PROP. XIV. *The human mind is capable of perceiving a great number of things, and is so in proportion as its body is capable of receiving a great number of impressions.*

Proof.—The human body (by Post. III and VI is affected in very many ways by external bodies, and is capable in very many ways of affecting external bodies. But the human mind must perceive all that takes place in the human body; the human mind is, therefore, capable of perceiving a great number of things, and is so in proportion, &c. *Q.E.D.*

PROP. XV. *The idea, which constitutes the actual being of the human mind, is not simple, but compounded of a great number of ideas.*

Proof.—The idea constituting the actual being of the human mind is the idea of the body, which (Post. I) is composed of a great number of complex individual parts. But there is necessarily in God the idea of each individual part whereof the body is composed; therefore, the idea of the human body is composed of these numerous ideas of its component parts.   *Q.E.D.*

PROP. XVI. *The idea of every mode, in which the human body is affected by external bodies, must involve the nature of the human body, and also the nature of the external body.*

Proof.—All the modes, in which any given body is affected, follow from the nature of the body affected, and also from the nature of the affecting body (by Ax. I, after the Coroll. of Lemma III), wherefore their idea also necessarily involves the nature of both bodies; therefore, the idea of every mode, in which the human body is affected by external bodies, involves the nature of the human body and of the external body. *Q.E.D.*

Corollary I.—Hence it follows, first, that the human mind perceives the nature of a variety of bodies, together with the nature of its own.

Corollary II.—It follows, secondly, that the ideas, which we have of external bodies, indicate rather the constitution of our own body than the nature of external bodies.

PROP. XVII. *If the human body is affected in a manner which involves the nature of any external body, the human mind will regard the said external body as actually existing, or as present to itself, until the human body be affected in such a way, as to exclude the existence or the presence of the said external body.*

Proof.—This proposition is self-evident, for so long as the human body continues to be thus affected, so long will the human mind regard this modification of the body—that is (by the last Prop.), it will have the idea of the mode as actually existing, and this idea involves the nature of the external body. In other words, it will have the idea which does not exclude, but postulates the existence or presence of the nature of the external body; therefore the mind will regard the external body as actually existing, until it is affected, &c.   *Q.E.D.*

Corollary.—The mind is able to regard as present external bodies, by which the human body has once been affected, even though they be no longer in existence or present.

Proof.—When external bodies determine the fluid parts of the human body, so that they often impinge on the softer parts, they change the surface of the last named (Post. V); hence (Ax. II, after Coroll. of Lemma III) they are refracted therefrom in a different manner from that which they followed before such change; and, further, when afterwards they impinge on the new surfaces by their own spontaneous movement, they will be refracted in the same manner, as though they had been impelled towards those surfaces by external bodies; consequently, they will, while they continue to be thus refracted, affect the human body in the same manner, whereof the mind will again take cognizance—that is, the mind will again regard the external body as present, and will do so, as often as the fluid parts of the human body impinge on the aforesaid surfaces by their own spontaneous motion. Wherefore, although the external bodies, by which the human body has once been affected, be no longer in existence, the mind will nevertheless regard them as present, as often as this action of the body is repeated. *Q.E.D.*

Note.—We thus see how it comes about, as is often the case, that we regard as present things which are not. It is possible that the same result may be brought about by other causes; but I think it suffices for me here to have indicated one possible explanation, just as well as if I had pointed out the true cause. Indeed, I do not think I am very far from the truth, for all my assumptions are based on postulates, which rest, almost without exception, on experience, that cannot be controverted by those who have shown, as we have, that the human body, as we feel it, exists. Furthermore, we clearly understand what is the difference between the idea, say, of Peter, which constitutes the essence of Peter's mind, and the idea of the said Peter, which is in another man, say, Paul. The former directly answers to the essence of Peter's own body, and only implies existence so long as Peter exists; the latter indicates rather the disposition of Paul's body than the nature of Peter, and, therefore, while this disposition of Paul's body lasts, Paul's mind will regard Peter as present to itself, even though he no longer exists. Further, to retain the usual phraseology, the modifications of the human body, of which the ideas represent external bodies as present to us, we will call the images of things, though they do not recall the figures of things. When the mind regards bodies in this fashion, we say that it imagines. I will here draw attention to the fact, in order to indicate where error lies, that the imaginations of the mind, looked at in themselves, do not contain error. The mind does not err in the mere act of imagining, but only in so far as it is regarded as being without the idea, which excludes the existence of such things as it imagines to be present to it. If the mind, while imagining non-existent things as present to it, is at the same time conscious that they do not really exist, this power of imagination must be set down to the efficacy of its nature, and not to a fault, especially if this faculty of imagination depend solely on its own nature—that is (I, Def. vii), if this faculty of imagination be free.

PROP. XVIII. *If the human body has once been affected by two or more bodies at the same time, when the mind afterwards imagines any of them, it will straightway remember the others also.*

Proof.—The mind imagines any given body, because the human body is affected and disposed by the impressions from an external body, in the same manner as it is affected when certain of its parts are acted on by the said external body; but (by our hypothesis) the body was then so disposed, that the mind imagined two bodies at once; therefore, it will also in the second case imagine two bodies at once, and the mind, when it imagines one, will straightway remember the other.   *Q.E.D.*

Note.—We now clearly see what *Memory* is. It is simply a certain association of ideas involving the nature of things outside the human body, which association arises in the mind according to the order and association of the modifications (*affectiones*) of the human body. I say, first, it is an association of those ideas only, which involve the nature of things outside the human body: not of ideas which answer to the nature of the said things: ideas of the modifications of the human body are, strictly speaking, those which involve the nature both of the human body and of external bodies. I say, secondly, that this association arises according to the order and association of the modifications of the human body, in order to distinguish it from that association of ideas, which arises from the order of the intellect, whereby the mind perceives things through their primary causes, and which is in all men the same. And hence we can further clearly understand, why the mind from the thought of one thing, should straightway arrive at the thought of another thing, which has no similarity with the first; for instance, from the thought of the word *pomum* (an apple), a Roman would straightway arrive at the thought of the fruit apple, which has no similitude with the articulate sound in question, nor anything in common with it, except that the body of the man has often been affected by these two things; that is, that the man has often heard the word *pomum*, while he was looking at the fruit; similarly every man will go on from one thought to another, according as his habit has ordered the images of things in his body. For a soldier, for instance, when he sees the tracks of a horse in sand, will at once pass from the thought of a horse to the thought of a horseman, and thence to the thought of war, &c.; while a countryman will proceed from the thought of a horse to the thought of a plough, a field, &c. Thus every man will follow this or that train of thought, according as he has been in the habit of conjoining and associating the mental images of things in this or that manner.

Prop. XIX. *The human mind has no knowledge of the body, and does not know it to exist, save through the ideas of the modifications whereby the body is affected.*

Proof.—The human mind is the very idea or knowledge of the human body, which is in God, in so far as he is regarded as affected by another idea of a particular thing actually existing: or, inasmuch as (Post. IV) the human body stands in need of very many bodies whereby it is, as it were, continually regenerated; and the order and connection of ideas is the same as the order and connection of causes; this idea will therefore be in God, in so far as he is regarded as affected by the ideas of very many particular things. Thus God has the idea of the human body, or knows the human body, in so far as he is affected by very many other ideas, and not in so far as he constitutes the nature of the human mind; that is, the human mind does not know the human body. But the ideas of the modifications of body are in God, in so far as he constitutes the nature of the human mind, or the human mind perceives those modifications, and consequently the human body itself, and as actually existing; therefore the mind perceives thus far only the human body. *Q.E.D.*

PROP. XX. *The idea or knowledge of the human mind is also in God, following in God in the same manner, and being referred to God in the same manner, as the idea or knowledge of the human body.*

Proof.—Thought is an attribute of God; therefore there must necessarily be in God the idea both of thought itself and of all its modifications, consequently also of the human mind. Further, this idea or knowledge of the mind does not follow from God, in so far as he is infinite, but in so far as he is affected by another idea of an individual thing. But the order and connection of ideas is the same as the order and connection of causes; therefore this idea or knowledge of the mind is in God and is referred to God, in the same manner as the idea or knowledge of the body.   *Q.E.D.*

PROP. XXI. *This idea of the mind is united to the mind in the same way as the mind is united to the body.*

Proof.—That the mind is united to the body we have shown from the fact, that the body is the object of the mind; and so for the same reason the idea of the mind must be united with its object, that is, with the mind in the same manner as the mind is united to the body.   *Q.E.D.*

Note.—This proposition is comprehended much more clearly from what we said in the note to II, vii. We there showed that the idea of body and body, that is, mind and body, are one and the same individual conceived now under the attribute of thought, now under the attribute of extension; wherefore the idea of the mind and the mind itself are one and the same thing, which is conceived under one and the same attribute, namely, thought. The idea of the mind, I repeat, and the mind itself are in God by the same necessity and follow from him from the same power of thinking. Strictly speaking, the idea of the mind, that is, the idea of an idea, is nothing but the distinctive quality (*forma*) of the idea in so far as it is conceived as a mode of thought without reference to the object; if a man knows anything, he, by that very fact, knows that he knows it, and at the same time knows that he knows that he knows it, and so on to infinity. But I will treat of this hereafter.

PROP. XXII. *The human mind perceives not only the modifications of the body, but also the ideas of such modifications.*

Proof.—The ideas of the ideas of modifications follow in God in the same manner, and are referred to God in the same manner, as the ideas of the said modifications. This is proved in the same way as II, xx. But the ideas of the modifications of the body are in the human mind, that is, in God, in so far as he constitutes the essence of the human mind; therefore the ideas of these ideas will be in God, in so far as he has the knowledge or idea of the human mind, that is, they will be in the human mind itself, which therefore perceives not only the modifications of the body, but also the ideas of such modifications.   *Q.E.D.*

PROP. XXIII. *The mind does not know itself, except in so far as it perceives the ideas of the modifications of the body.*

Proof.—The idea or knowledge of the mind follows in God in the same manner, and is referred to God in the same manner, as the idea or knowledge of the body. But since the human mind does not know the human body itself, that is, since the knowledge of the human body is not referred to God, in so far as he constitutes the nature of the human mind; therefore, neither is the knowledge of the mind referred to God, in so far as he constitutes the essence of the human mind; therefore, the human mind thus far has no knowledge of itself. Further the ideas of the modifications, whereby the body is affected, involve the nature of the human body itself, that is, they agree with the nature of the mind; wherefore the knowledge of these ideas necessarily involves knowledge of the mind; but (by the last Prop.) the knowledge of these ideas is in the human mind itself; wherefore the human mind thus far only has knowledge of itself.   *Q.E.D.*

PROP. XXIV.—*The human mind does not involve an adequate knowledge of the parts composing the human body.*

Proof.—The parts composing the human body do not belong to the

essence of that body, except in so far as they communicate their motions to one another in a certain fixed relation (Def. after Lemma III),
not in so far as they can be regarded as individuals without relation to
the human body. The parts of the human body are highly complex
individuals (Post. I), whose parts (Lemma IV) can be separated from the
human body without in any way destroying the nature and distinctive
quality of the latter, and they can communicate their motions (Ax. i,
after Lemma III) to other bodies in another relation; therefore the idea
or knowledge of each part will be in God, inasmuch as he is regarded
as affected by another idea of a particular thing, which particular thing
is prior in the order of nature to the aforesaid part. We may affirm the
same thing of each part of each individual composing the human body;
therefore, the knowledge of each part composing the human body is
in God, in so far as he is affected by very many ideas of things, and not
in so far as he has the idea of the human body only, in other words, the
idea which constitutes the nature of the human mind; therefore the
human mind does not involve an adequate knowledge of the human
body.   Q.E.D.

PROP. XXV. *The idea of each modification of the human body does
not involve an adequate knowledge of the external body.*

Proof.—We have shown that the idea of a modification of the human
body involves the nature of an external body, in so far as that external
body conditions the human body is a given manner. But, in so far as
the external body is an individual, which has no reference to the human
body, the knowledge or idea thereof is in God, in so far as God is regarded as affected by the idea of a further thing, which is naturally
prior to the said external body. Wherefore an adequate knowledge of the
external body is not in God, in so far as he has the idea of the modification of the human body; in other words, the idea of the modification of
the human body does not involve an adequate knowledge of the external
body.   Q.E.D.

PROP. XXVI. *The human mind does not perceive any external body
as actually existing, except through the ideas of the modifications of
its own body.*

Proof.—If the human body is in no way affected by a given external
body, then neither is the idea of the human body, in other words, the
human mind, affected in any way by the idea of the existence of the
said external body, nor does it any manner perceive its existence. But,

in so far as the human body is affected in any way by a given external body, thus far it perceives that external body.   Q.E.D.

Corollary.—In so far as the human mind imagines an external body, it has not an adequate knowledge thereof.

Proof.—When the human mind regards external bodies through the ideas of the modifications of its own body, we say that it imagines; now the mind can only imagine external bodies as actually existing. Therefore, in so far as the mind imagines external bodies, it has not an adequate knowledge of them.   Q.E.D.

PROP. XXVII. *The idea of each modification of the human body does not involve an adequate knowledge of the human body itself.*

Proof.—Every idea of a modification of the human body involves the nature of the human body, in so far as the human body is regarded as affected in a given manner. But, inasmuch as the human body is an individual which may be affected in many other ways, the idea of the said modification, &c.   Q.E.D.

PROP. XXVIII. *The ideas of the modification of the human body, in so far as they have reference only to the human mind, are not clear and distinct, but confused.*

Proof.—The ideas of the modifications of the human body involve the nature both of the human body and of external bodies; they must involve the nature not only of the human body but also of its parts; for the modifications are modes (Post. III), whereby the parts of the human body, and, consequently, the human body as a whole are affected. But the adequate knowledge of external bodies, as also of the parts composing the human body, is not in God, in so far as he regarded as affected by the human mind, but in so far as he is regarded as affected by other ideas. These ideas of modifications, in so far as they are referred to the human mind alone, are as consequences without premises, in other words, confused ideas.   Q.E.D.

Note.—The idea which constitutes the nature of the human mind is, in the same manner, proved not to be, when considered in itself alone, clear and distinct; as also is the case with the idea of the human mind, and the ideas of the ideas of the modifications of the human body, in so far as they are referred to the mind only, as everyone may easily see.

PROP. XXIX. *The idea of the idea of each modification of the human body does not involve an adequate knowledge of the human mind.*

Proof.—The idea of a modification of the human body does not involve an adequate knowledge of the said body, in other words, does not adequately express its nature; that is it does not agree with the nature of the mind adequately; therefore the idea of this idea does not adequately express the nature of the human mind, or does not involve an adequate knowledge thereof.

Corollary.—Hence it follows that the human mind, when it perceives things after the common order of nature, has not an adequate but only a confused and fragmentary knowledge of itself, of its own body, and of external bodies. For the mind does not know itself, except in so far as it perceives the ideas of the modifications of body. It only perceives its own body through the ideas of the modifications, and only perceives external bodies through the same means; thus, in so far as it has such ideas of modification, it has not an adequate knowledge of itself, nor of its own body, nor of external bodies, but only a fragmentary and confused knowledge thereof.   *Q.E.D.*

Note.—I say expressly, that the mind has not an adequate but only a confused knowledge of itself, its own body, and of external bodies, whenever it perceives things after the common order of nature; that is, whenever it is determined from without, namely, by the fortuitous play of circumstance, to regard this or that; not at such times as it is determined from within, that is, by the fact of regarding several things at once, to understand their points of agreement, difference, and contrast. Whenever it is determined in anywise from within, it regards things clearly and distinctly, as I will show below.

PROP. XXX. *We can only have a very inadequate knowledge of the duration of our body.*

Proof.—The duration of our body does not depend on its essence, nor on the absolute nature of God. But it is conditioned to exist and operate by causes, which in their turn are conditioned to exist and operate in a fixed and definite relation by other causes, these last again being conditioned by others, and so on to infinity. The duration of our body therefore depends on the common order of nature, or the constitution of things. Now, however a thing may be constituted, the adequate knowledge of that thing is in God, in so far as he has the ideas of all things, and not in so far as he has the idea of the human body only. Wherefore the knowledge of the duration of our body is in God very inadequate, in so far as he is only regarded as constituting the nature of the human mind; that is, this knowledge is very inadequate in our mind. *Q.E.D.*

NOTES

1. *"Forma."*
2. *"Animata."*

SPINOZA AND THE

THEORY OF ORGANISM

Hans Jonas

I

Cartesian dualism landed speculation on the nature of life in an impasse: intelligible as, on principles of mechanics, the correlation of structure and function became within the *res extensa,* that of structure-plus-function with feeling or experience (modes of the *res cogitans*) was lost in the bifurcation, and thereby the fact of life itself became unintelligible at the same time that the explanation of its bodily performance seemed to be assured. The impasse became manifest in Occasionalism: its tour de force of an extraneous, divine "synchronization" of the outer and the inner world (the latter denied to animals) not only suffered from its extreme artificiality, the common failing of such *ad hoc* constructions, but even at so high a cost failed to accomplish its theoretical purpose by its own terms. For the animal machine, like any machine, raises beyond the question of the "how" that of the "what for" of its functioning—of the purpose for which it had thus been constructed by its maker.[1] Its performance, however devoid of immanent teleology, must serve an end, and that must be someone's end. This end may (directly) be itself, as indeed Descartes had implied when declaring

This selection is reprinted from the *Journal of the History of Philosophy,* III, No. 1 (April, 1965), 43–57. Copyright by The Regents of the University of California and reprinted with the permission of the author and The Regents of the University of California.

self-preservation to be the effect of the functioning of the organic auto-maton. In that case the existence as such of the machine would be its end—either terminally, or in turn to benefit something else. In the former case, the machine would have to be more than a machine, for a mere machine cannot enjoy its existence. But since, by the rigorous conception of the *res extensa,* it cannot be more than a machine, its function and/or existence must serve something other than itself. Automata in Descartes' time were mainly for entertainment (rather than work). But the *raison d'être* of the living kingdom could not well be seen in God's indulging his mechanical abilities or in the amusement of celestial spectators—especially since mere complexity of arrangement does not create new quality and thus add something to the unrelieved sameness of the simple substratum that might enrich the spectrum of being. For quality, beyond the primitive determinations of the extended per se, is the subjective creature of sensation, the confused representation of quantity in a mind; and thus organisms cannot harbor it because as mere machines they lack mentality, and pure spirits cannot because they lack sensuality, or the privilege of confusion and thereby of illusion with its possible enjoyment. And as to their intellectual en-joyment, even that, deprived of the thrill of discovery by the same token, would pale in the contemplation of what to sufficiently large intellects is nothing but the ever-repeated exemplification of the same few, ele-mentary (and ultimately trivial) truths.

There remained, then, the time-honored—Stoic as well as Christian—idea that plants and animals are for the benefit of Man. Indeed, since the existence of a living world is the necessary condition for the exis-tence of any of its members, the self-justifying nature of at least one such member (= species) would justify the existence of the whole. In Stoicism, Man provided this end by his possession of reason, which makes him the culmination of a terrestrial scale of being that is also self-justifying throughout all its grades (the end as the best of many that are good in degrees); in Christianity, by his possession of an immortal soul, which makes him the sole *imago Dei* in creation (the end as the sole issue at stake); and Cartesian dualism radicalized this latter position by making man even the sole possessor of inwardness or "soul" of *any* kind, thus the only one of whom "end" can meaningfully be predicated as he alone can entertain ends. All other life, then, the product of physical necessity, can be considered his means.

However, this traditional idea, in its anthropocentric vanity never a good one even where it made sense, no longer made sense in the new dualistic and occasionalist setting. For man, the supposed beneficiary of living creation, i.e., of all the other organic mechanisms, was now himself an inexplicable, extraneous combination of mind and body—a combination with no intelligible relevance of the body for the existence and inner life of the mind (as also, of course, vice versa). Therefore, even if it was shown that the existence of the organic world was necessary for the existence of human bodies, as indeed it is, it could not be shown that the existence of this very body was necessary for the existence of "man" considered as the thinking ego. Furthermore, the very distinction of man's body within the animal kingdom, viz., to be at least partially an organ of mind—that distinction for the sake of which Descartes had been willing to brave the contortions of the pineal gland doctrine—was also nullified by the occasionalist fiction, in which the human body became no less completely an automaton than all other organisms. Thus, the existence of the entire living kingdom became utterly unintelligible as to purpose and meaning as well as to origin and procreative cause. A vast scheme of delusory "as ifs" superseded all question of real issue in the working of things.

All this amounts to saying that the main fault, even absurdity, of the doctrine lay in denying organic reality its principal and most obvious characteristic, namely, that it exhibits in each individual instance a striving of its own for existence and fulfillment, or the fact of life's willing itself. In other words, the banishment of the old concept of appetition from the conceptual scheme of the new physics, joined to the rationalistic spiritualism of the new theory of consciousness, deprived the realm of life of its status in the scheme of things. Yet, since sheer unrelatedness never satisfies theory, and since the irrepressible evidence of every one of our psychophysical acts obstinately contradicts the dualistic division, it was inevitable that attempts were made to overcome the rift.

For this there were in principle three ways open, each of which was in fact chosen at one time or another: to accord primacy alternatively to matter or to mind, or to transcend the alternative by a new concept of substance. The third choice was Spinoza's, in one of the boldest ventures in the history of metaphysics. Its important implications for a philosophy of the organism, only partially explicated by Spinoza himself, are seldom noticed.[2]

I I

Let us briefly recall the general principle of Spinoza's system. Its basis is the concept of one absolute and infinite substance, transcending those specifications (viz., extension and thought) by which Descartes had distinguished between different kinds of substance. Besides difference of kind, the oneness of Substance also excludes plurality of number: the infinity, being non-partitive, leaves no room for the existence of finite substances. Thus whatever is finite is not a substance but a modification or affection of infinite substance—a "mode." This is to say that individual being is not self-subsistent but inheres in the self-subsistent as a passing determination thereof. On the other hand, the infinity of the one substance involves an infinite number of "attributes" expressing the nature of that substance—each adequately insofar as it is itself infinite and in this conforms to the infinity of substance (as, e.g., the infinity of space does for the attribute of extension), but inadequately, namely incompletely, insofar as it expresses it only under this form. The sum of the attributes is the essence of substance itself, thus each attribute is "part" of the essence (or, the essence in one aspect) and as such complementary with all the rest. The same can also be stated by saying that the attributes all together "constitute" the essence, not however additively, but as abstract moments that are only abstractly separable. Individual existents, then (the "modes" mentioned before), are variable determinations of substance *in terms* of its invariable attributes ("*this* particular cube," "*this* particular thought"); and each individual affection of infinite substance as it occurs is exhibited, equally and equivalently, throughout all its attributes at once. Extension and Thought are two such attributes, the only ones of which *we* are cognizant. Thus, while the "modes" (affections) are what really happens to substance, the particular actualities of its existence, the "attributes"—e.g., extension and thought—are the universal forms in which such actualities manifest themselves and under which they can be conceived with equal truth by any finite mind that enjoys cognition of some of these forms. Since, in the human case, this is limited to the two indicated, our world consists in fact of body and mind, and nothing else.

The point for our context is that what to Descartes and to Cartesians like Geulincx were two separate and independent substances—as such requiring for their existence neither each other nor a ground common to both[3]—are to Spinoza merely different aspects of one and the same reality, no more separable from each other than from their common cause. And he stresses that this common cause—infinite substance or God—*is* as truly extension as it is thought, or, as truly corporeal as mental; but there is as little a substance "body" as there is a substance "mind." Now since both these attributes express in each individual instance an identical fact, the whole problem of interaction, with which Occasionalism had to wrestle, or of the interrelation generally between the two realms, vanished. Each occurrence (mode) as viewed under the attribute of extension is at the same time, and equivalently, an occurrence viewed under the attribute of thought or consciousness, and vice versa. The two are strictly complementary aspects of one and the same reality which of necessity unfolds itself in all its attributes at once. It would even be too disjunctive to say that each material event has its "counterpart" in a mental event, since what externally may be registered as a parallelism of two different series of events is in truth, that is, in the reality of God or nature, substantially identical. Thus the riddle created by Cartesian dualism—of how an act of will can move a limb, since the limb as part of the extended world can only be moved by another body's imparting its antecedent motion to it—this riddle disappears. The act of will and the movement of the body are one and the same event appearing under different aspects, each of which represents in its own terms a complete expression of the concatenation of things in God, in the one eternal cause.

III

Spinoza's central interest, it is true, was not a doctrine of organism, but a metaphysical foundation for psychology and ethics; but incidentally his metaphysical basis enabled him to account for features of organic existence far beyond what Cartesian dualism and mechanism could accommodate. In the first place, Spinoza was no longer compelled to view those complex material entities we call organisms as the products of mechanical design. The idea of a purpose, in analogy to man-made machines, was replaced by the eternal necessity of the self-explication of the infinite nature of God, that is, of substance, that is, of reality. Therefore, what mattered in the understanding of an organism was no longer its lesser or greater perfection as an independent piece of functioning machinery, but its lesser or greater perfection as a finite "mode," measured by its power to exist and to interact (communicate) with the rest of existence, or, to be a less or more self-determined part of the whole: on whatever level of such perfection, it realizes one of the intrinsic possibilities of original substance in terms of matter and mind at once, and thereby shares in the self-affirmation of Being as such. And the principle of infinite reality, involving infinity of possible determination, would account for the wealth and gradation or organic forms. The purpose, then, is not ulterior and certainly does not lie in man, but lies entirely in the infinite self-expression itself; and even this does, strictly speaking, not merit the term "purpose," since it is governed by the immanent necessity of the absolute cause.

Secondly, the very image of "machine" could be dropped. Here we must note one of the inherent limitations of that image, quite apart from the psychophysical question. The model—meant from the outset for animals and not for plants—provides: (a) for a connected *structure* of moving parts, such as levers, hinges, rods, wheels, tubes, valves; and (b) for the generation of *movement* from some source of power, such as the tension of a spring in a clock, or the heat of fire in a steam engine. Though the latter, or any combustion engine, was unknown to Descartes, he anticipated the model when he declared heat to be the moving force in the animal machine, and this heat to be generated by the "burning" of food. Thus the combustion theory of metabolism complements the machine theory of anatomical structure. But metabolism is more than a method of power generation, or, food is more than fuel: in addition to, and more basic than, providing kinetic energy for the running of the machine (a case anyway not applying to plants), its role is to build up originally and replace continually the very parts of the machine. Metabolism thus is the constant becoming of the machine itself—and this becoming itself is a performance of the machine: but for such performance there is no analogue in the world of machines. In other words, once metabolism is understood as not only a device for energy production, but as the continuous process of self-constitution of the very substance and form of the organism, the machine model breaks down. A better analogy would be that of a flame. As, in a burning candle, the permanence of the flame is a permanence, not of substance, but of process in which at each moment the "body" with its "structure" of inner and outer layers is reconstituted of materials different from the previous and following ones, so the living organism exists as a constant exchange of its own constituents, and has its permanence and identity only in the continuity of this process, not in any persistence of its material parts. This process indeed *is* its life, and in the last resort organic existence means, not to be a definite body composed of definite parts, but to be such a continuity of process with an identity sustained above and through the flux of components. Definiteness of arrangement (configuration) will then, jointly with continuity of process, provide the principle of identity which "substance" as such no longer provides.

On these lines indeed, Spinoza seeks to answer the problem of organic identity. Substance cannot by the terms of his ontology furnish such identity, because substance is not individual, and the organism is an individual. What is individual is a "mode," and so must be the organism as a species of individual. In fact, it is under the title of "individuality," i.e., in considering what makes an individual, and not under the title of "living things" in particular, that Spinoza treats the phenomenon of organism. Now *any* mode of universal substance, whether simple or complex, whether brief or enduring, is an individual (by definition, for to be a "mode" means just to be a distinct occurrence in the eternal self-unfolding of infinite being), and is this in all of the attributes if in any one of them. In that of extension this means to be a *body*, either simple or composite, *distinct* from other bodies. Since this distinctness cannot lie in its substance (by which on the contrary it is one with all), it must lie in its modal *determinations,* such as figure and motion, and in their interaction with other instances of determination in the same attribute. The continuity of determinateness throughout such interactions (a continuity, therefore, not excluding change) bespeaks the self-affirming "conatus" by which a mode tends to persevere in existence, and which is identical with its essence. Thus it is the *form* of determinateness, and the *conatus* evidenced by the survival of that form in a causal history, i.e., in *relation* to coexisting things, that defines an individual. All three—form, continuity, and relation—are integral to the concept of an individual and provide a clue to the meaning of its identity. The manner of "relation," i.e., of the causal communication with the environment in acting and suffering (affecting and being affected), depends on the given *form* of determination, i.e., on the kind of body involved: the affections of a simple body will simply reflect the joint impact of the environment, fusing the many influences into one, without discrimination of the various individual agents; whereas composite bodies of a certain kind, as we shall see, may embody the affections of the environment differentially in their condition and thus also act on the environment differentially. Here we note one divergence from the machine model, to be taken up later: the point of such compositeness, i.e., of degree of complexity, is not variety of mechanical performance by a self-contained automaton, but range and variety of reciprocal *communication* with things, or the manner of being part of the whole while yet being something apart from the whole.

IV

However, the interactional aspect (the being part of a whole) is based on the formal nature of the individual; and as this may be composite, and is so in all cases of higher relatedness, we have first to consider the meaning of compositeness as such, or, the manner in which an individual itself can be a "whole" of its own parts, a "one" of many. This—as the parts of a composite are in turn individuals—is the same as asking how a plurality of individuals may be so united that all together form a larger (and higher-order) individual. Now any union of individuals must be in terms of interaction, i.e., of mutual determination; and if it is more than a haphazard collection, the order of grouping may engender an *order* of interaction such that the *total* of mutual determinations will be a *form of determinateness* itself. But form of determinateness, as we have seen, is precisely what defines "individual," as it constitutes the distinctness of a mode: and thus a body composed of many and diverse bodies (which again may be "composite to a high degree") may truly be an individual—if this total *form* of multiple inner relations maintains itself functionally in the interactions of the compound with the outside world, thereby testifying to a common conatus of the whole.

The possible advantage of such compositeness in terms of the external relations of an individual has been provisionally indicated and is not our concern at present. What matters now is the new possibility of "identity" opened up by the concept of individual here expounded. If it is the (spatial and dynamic) *pattern* of composition and function in which the individuality of a composite consists, then its identity is not bound to the identities of the simpler bodies of which it is composed; and the preservation of that identity through time rests with the preservation of the pattern rather than of the particular collection presently embodying it. The identity of a whole is thus compatible with a change of parts; and such a change may even be the very means by which the identity of certain individuals is sustained.

This train of thought obviously permits an understanding of organism quite different from the Cartesian one and, we think, more adequate to the facts; and this even in terms of "extension" alone, i.e., without the full benefits of the doctrine to be reaped from complementing the physical facts with those in the attribute of "thought." The main propositions touching upon the physical side of organism are found in Part II of the *Ethics*, entitled "Of the Nature and Origin of the Mind" and thus preeminently dealing with the mental side. However, from Proposition XI onward, Spinoza deals with the soul-body problem, and in that context makes certain statements concerning the type of body that corresponds to a soul or mind, and the type of identity that pertains to it. They are Lemmata 4–7 after Prop. XIII—as follows:

LEMMA IV. If a certain number of bodies be separated from the body or individual which is composed of a number of bodies, and if their place be supplied by the same number of other bodies of the same nature, the individual will retain the nature it had before without any change of form.

DEMONSTRATION. Bodies are not distinguished in respect of substance (Lem. I);[4] but that which makes the form of an individual is the union of bodies (by the preceding definition).[5] This form, however (by hypothesis), is retained, although there may be a continuous change of the bodies. The individual, therefore, will retain its nature with regard both to substance and to mode, as before.—Q.E.D.

LEMMA V. If the parts composing an individual become greater or less proportionately, so that they preserve towards one another the same kind of motion and rest, the individual will also retain the nature which it had before without any change of form.

LEMMA VI. If any number of bodies composing an individual are compelled to divert into one direction the motion they previously had in another, but are nevertheless able to continue and reciprocally communicate their motions in the same manner as before, the individual will then retain its nature without any change of form.

LEMMA VII. The individual thus composed will, moreover, retain its nature whether it move as a whole or be at rest, or whether it move in this or that direction, provided that each part retain its own motion and communicate it as before to the rest.

Lemma 4 refers to metabolism, 5 to growth, 6 to movement of limb, 7 to locomotion. There follows an important scholium to this whole series of lemmata.

> SCHOL. We thus see in what manner a composite individual can be affected in many ways and yet retain its nature. Up to this point we have conceived an individual to be composed merely of bodies which are distinguished from one another solely by motion and rest, speed and slowness, i.e., to be composed of the most simple bodies. If we now consider an individual of another kind, composed of many individuals of diverse natures, we shall discover that it may be affected in many other ways, its nature nevertheless being preserved. For since each of its parts is composed of a number of bodies, each part (by the preceding lemma), without any change of its nature, can move more slowly or quickly, and consequently can communicate its motion more quickly or more slowly to the rest. If we now imagine a third kind of individual composed of these of the second kind, we shall discover that it can be affected in many other ways without any change of form. Thus, if we advance *ad infinitum,* we may easily conceive the whole of nature to be one individual whose parts, i.e., all bodies, vary in infinite ways without any change of the whole individual.

After this, a number of postulates deal with the human body in particular, of which we quote postulates 1, 3, 4, and 6.

> POST. 1. The human body is composed of a number of individual parts of diverse nature, each of which is composite to a high degree.
> POST. 3. The individual parts composing the human body, and consequently the human body itself, are affected by external bodies in many ways.
> POST. 4. The human body needs for its preservation many other bodies by which it is, as it were, continually regenerated.
> POST. 6. The human body can move and arrange external bodies in many ways.

V

If we ponder these statements in the total context of Spinoza's theory, we realize that, for the first time in modern speculation, an organic individual is viewed as a fact of wholeness rather than of mechanical interplay of parts. The essence of organic being is seen, not in the functioning of a machine as a closed system, but in the sustained sequence of states of a unified plurality, with only the form of its union enduring while the parts come and go. Substantial identity is thus replaced by

formal identity, and the relation of parts to whole, so crucial for the
nature of organism, is the converse of what it is in the mechanistic view.
There, the finished product, the complete animal machine, is the sum
of the component parts, and the most elementary of such parts, the
simplest units of matter, are the ultimate and the only true subjects of
individuality. Identity then, as identity of individual corporeal substances, comes down to the mere inert persistence of matter, and from
this basic type of individuality and identity every other individuality
and identity in the extended realm is derived. Conversely, identity in
Spinoza's theory of individuality is the identity of a whole which is so
little the mere sum of its parts that it remains the same even when the
parts continually change. And since the individual is a *form of union*,
there are qualitative grades of individuality, depending on the degree
of differentiated order, and quantitative grades, depending on the
numerical extent of inclusion (both scales, on the whole, tending to
coincide)—so that the All forms a hierarchy of individualities, or
wholes, of increasing inclusiveness culminating in the most inclusive
one, the totality of nature as such. Within a certain range along this line
are those grades of individuality, i.e., of complexity of organization,
which we term "organic": but this is a matter of degree only, and on
principle all nature is "alive." On whatever level of compositeness (but
the more so, the higher the level), the various orders of individuality
exist essentially in the succession of their states, i.e., in the continuous
series of their changes, rather than in any momentary structure which a
mechanical analysis into elements would reveal. The specifically
"organic" bodies, then, are highly composite minor totalities of subordinate individuals which again are composed of lesser ones, and so on.
In such a stratification, the variability of being which compositeness
enjoys as such is communicated upward cumulatively, and with each
supervening level is raised to a higher power, so that the uppermost
level representing the totality in question is the beneficiary of all its
subordinate members.

Thus the concept of organism evolves organically, without a break,
from the general ontology of individual existence. Of every such existence it is true to say that as a modal determination it represents just
one phase in the eternal unfolding of infinite substance and is thus
never a terminal product in which the creative activity would come to
rest.[6] While a machine certainly is such a terminal product, the modal
wholes, continuing their conative life in the shift of their own parts and

in interchange with the larger whole, are productive as much as produced, or, as much "natura naturans" as "natura naturata."

VI

So far we have dealt with the phenomenon of life in the attribute of
extension only, that is, with life as represented by organized bodies. If
we now turn to the inward aspect, the progress of Spinoza's monism
over Cartesian dualism becomes even more manifest. Extension as a
whole, as we have seen, represents but one attribute by which the infinite essence of substance is of necessity expressed. It is equally expressed, with equal necessity and equal validity, by the attribute of
thought. This means that to every *mode* of extension there corresponds
a mode of "thought" which is only another aspect of the same underlying
cause complementarily expressed in either way. Now since individuals
are modes of the one substance, and in each such mode substance is
affected throughout its attributes, it follows that *any* individual in the
world of bodies (and not just a certain class of individuals) has its
coordinate counterpart in an individual of thought. This principle dis-
cards two connected Cartesian ideas at once: that "life" is a fact of
physics alone, and that "soul" is a fact of man alone: according to the
first, life is a particular corporeal *behavior* following from a particular
corporeal structure which distinguishes a *class* of objects in nature, viz.,
the natural automata; according to the second, "soul," equated with
consciousness of any kind, be it feeling, desiring, perceiving, thought
(anima = mens = cogitatio), as such not required for physical function
of any kind *and thus not for life*, is absent in animals and present in
man, but is neither in *his* case a principle of "life," which remains a
purely behavioristic phenomenon in all cases. To Spinoza, soul still is
not a principle of life considered physically (as it was to Aristotle), but
neither is life itself mere corporeal behavior. The concurrence of out-
wardness and inwardness is here no longer a unique arrangement in the
case of man, nor even a distinctive mark of the whole class of things
normally called "animate": as the essence of substance, that concurrence
is the pervading trait of all existence. Yet the universality of the principle
by no means obliterates those distinctions in nature by which we speak
of animate as against inanimate things, of sentient as against merely
vegetative organisms, and of conscious and reasoning man as against
unreasoning animals. On the contrary, for the first time in modern

theory, a speculative means is offered for relating the degree of organization of a body to the degree of awareness belonging to it.

Let us recall that dualism did not offer such a means, i.e., did not provide for an intelligible relation between the perfection of a physical organization and the *quality* of the life supported by it: all it provided for was the relation between organization and observable behavior. The wealth of gradation in the animal world between the most primitive (i.e., simple) and the most subtle (i.e., complex) structure could not be overlooked but had to remain meaningless. Since no other kind of soul but the rational was recognized, all the mechanical perfection displayed in animal organisms amounted just to a gigantic hoax, as no higher type of experient life corresponded to greater excellence of mechanical performance. Thus the very perfection in terms of external construction and function mocks all justification in terms of lives and purposes. Even in man, as noted before, there is no intelligible connection between the excellence of his body and the uniqueness of his mind, as these two are only extraneously joined together. On materialistic premises such a connection was plausible enough, since mind, if it is a function of the brain, must needs be determined in its quality by the quality of the brain. But this plausibility is paid for by too heavy a price in difficulties concerning the nature of mind itself. Spinoza's psychophysical parallelism offered an ingenious theory of connection between grade of organization and grade of mentality without violating the principle of non-interaction between the two sides. That such interaction cannot be is no less axiomatic to him than to the whole Cartesian school: "The body cannot determine the mind to thought, neither can the mind determine the body to motion nor rest, nor to anything else, if there be anything else" (*Ethics*, III, Prop. 2). The positive complement of this negative rule is thus stated for the corporeal side: "A body in motion or at rest must be determined to motion or rest by another body, which was also determined to motion or rest by another, and so on ad infinitum" (*ibid.*, Lem. 3 after Prop. 13). At least in this application to the physical realm, the ontological rigor of the rule admits no exception; and we may add that none of the leading thinkers of the period down to, and including, Kant ever challenged the validity of it. The reasons for thus ruling out of court the most insistent evidence of common experience—that fear or love or deliberation can determine action and thus be causes of bodily motion—cannot be discussed here: we just note that they commanded overwhelming consensus. But if interaction is ruled out, the alternative need not be mutual independence or unrelatedness of the two sides. The Occasionalists, in their attempt to account for the prima facie facts of interconnection, acquiesced in a mere externality of correlation, which was no less miraculous a coincidence for the fact that God saw to its happening time and again. This unsatisfactory construction Spinoza replaced by an intrinsic belonging-together of mind and matter, which gave causal preference neither to matter, as materialism would have it, nor to mind, as idealism would have it, but instead rested their interrelation on the common ground of which they both were dependent aspects.

VII

Applying this formula to the doctrine of organism and the diversity of biological organization, of which man represents one, and perhaps the highest, degree, we have to ask more concretely in what the correlation of mental to physical modes consists. Spinoza answers that the "soul" is an individual mode of thought, that is, an "idea" in God, whose one and continuous object (*ideatum*) is an actually existing individual body. This "idea" of one determinate body, if it is as sustained as the existence of its object, must of course be a *series* of ideas, corresponding to, and concomitant with, the series of states in which the pertaining body exists; and it must at each moment be a *complex* idea, in accordance with the complexity of the body. What is represented in the idea is the total state of the body at each given instant. Now that state of the body is determined by two factors: (1) by what it is in itself, its own formal nature, that is, by the form or pattern of its composition; and (2) by its affection from outside, i.e., the influence of other bodies on its condition. Thus the state of a body represents at each moment itself *and* those bodies of the surrounding world which do affect it at that moment. And it does represent the latter insofar as they affect it, which they do again, not only in virtue of their own power or their own intrinsic nature, but also in virtue of the way in which the affected body can be affected: that is, its own organization determines the manner in which other things besides itself can be represented in its own state.

Now, clearly, degrees of organization can be understood precisely as degrees of the faculty of a body to be affected more or less variously, distinctly and thus adequately by other bodies individually (being in any case affected by them collectively). Thus a more differentiated, because more complex, organization—for instance, of the sensory apparatus—would make for a more perfect, that is, more differential way in which the body receives the affections from other bodies. In brief, degree of organization may mean degree of discriminatory sensitivity— both understood in strictly physical terms (as, e.g., in a camera). Now, since the soul is nothing but the correlate "idea" of an actually existing body, the degree of distinctness, differentiation, and clarity enjoyed by this idea is exactly proportionate to the state of the body that is its sole object. Thus, although the immediate object of the soul is only the coordinate body, which is the same mode of substance in terms of extension that the soul is in terms of thought, yet through this body's being affected by other bodies and affected in different degrees of perfection according to its own organization (and to circumstances), the corresponding mental state will have mediate awareness of the world— as represented through affections of the body—in different degrees of obscurity and clarity, of limitedness and comprehensiveness. Therefore "soul" is granted to animals and plants on exactly the same principle as to man, yet not the same soul. The soul, being the equivalent of the body in a different attribute, or the expression of the same mode (determination) of substance of which the body is the expression in extenso, must be completely conformal to the kind of body whose soul it is, and there are as many kinds and degrees of soul as there are kinds and degrees of vital organization.[7] The two are in each case just the two equivalent aspects of one and the same basic reality, which is neither matter nor mind, but is equally expressed by both.

The general principle is stated in the famous Prop. 7 of Part II, the *Magna Carta* of "psychophysical parallelism": "The order and connection of ideas is the same as the order and connection of things." With reference to the human mind, the doctrine is expressed in the following propositions of the same part:

PROP. XI. The first thing which forms the actual being of the human mind is nothing else than the idea of an individual thing actually existing.

PROP. XII. Whatever happens in the object of the idea constituting the human mind must be perceived by the human mind; or, in other words, an idea of that thing will necessarily exist in the human mind. That is to say, if the object of the idea constituting the human mind be a body, nothing can happen in that body which is not perceived by the mind.

PROP. XIII. The object of the idea constituting the human mind is a body, or a certain mode of extension actually existing, and nothing else.

SCHOL. Hence we see not only that the human mind is united to the body, but also what is to be understood by the union of the mind and body. But no one can understand it adequately or distinctly without knowing adequately beforehand the nature of our body; for those things which we have proved hitherto are altogether general, nor do they refer more to man than to other individuals, all of which are animate, although in different degrees. For of everything there necessarily exists in God an idea of which He is the cause, in the same way as the idea of the human body exists in Him [which idea is the human mind]; and therefore, everything that we have said of the idea of the human body is necessarily true of the idea of any other thing [being the "mind" of that other thing]. We cannot, however, deny that ideas, like objects themselves, differ from one another, and that one is more excellent and contains more reality than another, just as the object of one idea is more excellent and contains more reality than another. Therefore, in order to determine the difference between the human mind and other minds and its superiority over them, we must first know, as we have said, the nature of its object, that is to say, the nature of the human body. . . . I will say generally that in proportion as one body is fitter than others to *do or suffer many things* [*severally*] *at once,* in the same proportion will its mind be fitter to perceive many things at once; and the more the actions of a body depend upon itself alone, and the less other bodies co-operate with it in action, the fitter will the mind of that body be for distinctly understanding. We can thus determine the superiority of one mind to another; we can also see the reason why we have only a very confused knowledge of our body. . . .

PROP. XIV. The human mind is adapted to the perception of many things, and its aptitude increases in proportion to the number of ways in which its body can be disposed.

PROP. XV. The idea which constitutes the formal being of the human mind is not simple but is composed of a number of ideas. [This follows from the high degree of compositeness of the human body.]

PROP. XVI. The idea of every way in which the human body is affected by external bodies must involve the nature of the human body and at the same time the nature of the external body.

DEM. All ways in which any body is affected follow at the same time from the nature of the affected body and from the nature of the affecting body; therefore, the idea of these modifications necessarily involves the nature of each body; and therefore the idea of each way in which the human body

is affected by an external body involves the nature of the human body and
of the external body.

COROLLARY 1. Hence it follows, in the first place, that the human mind perceives the nature of many bodies together with that of its own body.

COR. 2. It follows, secondly, that the ideas of external bodies indicate the
constitution of our own body rather than the nature of the external bodies.[8]

VIII

The conclusion from these general propositions, regarding the question whether animals have souls, that is to say, whether they feel, strive,
perceive, even think in a way, is stated by Spinoza in no equivocal
terms. Since mind is not a species of substance, defined by fixed attributes like reason and intellect, but itself a total attribute of infinite
substance, and as such admits on principle of the same infinity of different modes as extension has in its own sphere, animals can obviously
enjoy a degree of mind congruent with their bodies without any prejudice to the distinctive characteristics of the human mind, as congruent
with its body. Thus we read in Part III:

PROP. LVII. The affect of one individual differs from the corresponding
affect of another as much as the essence of the one individual differs from
that of the other.

SCHOL. Hence it follows that the affects of animals which are called
irrational (for after we have learnt the origin of the mind we can in no
way doubt that brutes feel) differ from the affects of men as much as their
respective natures differ from human nature. Both the man and the horse,
for example, are swayed by lust to propagate, but the horse is swayed by
equine lust and the man by a human one. The lusts and appetites of insects, fishes, and birds must vary in the same way; and so, although each
individual lives contented with its own nature and delights in it, nevertheless the life with which it is contented and its joy are nothing else but
the "idea" or soul of the individual [body] in question, and so the joy of
one differs in character from the joy of the other as much as the essence of
the one differs from the essence of the other. . . .

The last scholium, in conjunction with that to Prop. 13 of Part II,
clearly establishes the principle of an infinite gradation of "animate-
ness," coextensive with the gradation of physical composition, for which
the entirely simple is merely a limiting case: even this would not be
devoid of a minimum of inwardness, since to its distinctness, such as it
is, there must correspond the idea "of" it in God—and this is its

"thought" or "soul." Note how in Spinoza's logic a *genitivus objectivus* —the idea of this body—turns into a *genitivus subjectivus*—this body's thought. On the lowest level, this "thought" will not be more than an infinitesimal feeling, but even this will be compounded of an active and a passive aspect: namely, on the one hand, self-affirmation, whose physical equivalent is the *vis inertiae* (both expressing the conatus for self-continuation), and on the other hand, experience of otherness, or, perception, whose physical equivalent is the subjection to outside forces (both expressing the integration into the sum of things). Each thing asserts itself, but all things around it assert themselves, and in the case of the very simple, low-grade individual (illustrated perhaps by the atom), completely at the mercy of external impingements, the compound assertion of all others in its dynamic condition all but submerges its self-assertion, so that the active aspect will be at a minimum; and correspondingly, the very experience of otherness (its "affects") will not rise beyond an indiscriminate fusion of mere passivity: its perception will be as indistinct as its selfhood. Only complex functional systems afford the inner *autonomy* that is required for greater power of self-determination, *together* with greater variety of inner states responding to the determinations which impinge on it from without. The mental equivalent of both is, on the active side, higher degree of consciousness with its affirmation and enjoyment of *self*, and, on the passive side, greater distinctness of perception with its understanding (and possible mastery) of *things*. The idea of *power* is fundamental in the evaluation of the corporeal as well as of the mental side and furnishes the standard of perfection: the power of the body to exist, persist, to do and suffer many things, to determine others and itself, is at the same time affirmation of that power by the mind which is the "idea" of that body.[9] And since degree of power is degree of *freedom*, it is true to say that higher organization of the body, and correspondingly greater complexity of its idea, mean greater freedom of the individual both in body and in mind.

The phrase "fitness to do or suffer many things" expresses Spinoza's insight into the essentially dual character of the organism: its *autonomy* for itself, and its *openness* for the world: spontaneity paired with receptivity. Their concurrent, indeed interdependent, increase is a seeming paradox, since openness in perception means exposure to affection, thus determination from without, contrary to the self-determination which autonomy of action would imply and all conatus must seek. Yet increase in *passive* power is asserted by Spinoza together with increase in active power to be the mark of higher fitness of an organism and thus of its perfection. Here is proof of his profundity. For this dialectic is precisely the nature of life in its basic organic sense. Its closure as a functional whole within the individual organism is, at the same time, correlative openness toward the world; its very separateness entails the faculty of communication; its segregation from the whole is the condition of its integration with the whole. The affectivity of all living things complements their spontaneity; and while it seems to indicate primarily the passive aspect of organic existence, it yet provides, in a subtle balance of freedom and necessity, the very means by which the organism carries on its vital commerce with the environment, that is, with the conditions of its continued existence. Only by being sensitive can life be active, only by being exposed can it be autonomous. And this in direct ratio: the more individuality is focused in a self, the wider is its periphery of communication with other things; the more isolated, the more related it is.

This dialectic of individual life in the world Spinoza has seen, and provided for in his system, as neither Descartes before him nor Leibniz after him did.

NOTES

1. The concept of "machine," adopted for its strict confinement to efficient cause, is still a finalistic concept, even though the final cause is no longer internal to the entity, as a mode of its own operation, but external to it as antecedent design.

2. Some excellent observations on the biological aspect of Spinoza's metaphysics, with special reference to modern developments in the physical and biological sciences, are found in Stuart Hampshire, *Spinoza* (Pelican Books, A253), pp. 75 ff.

3. They do require the latter in the extraneous sense of first having had to be created and then continuously to be confirmed in existence by God: but the *creative* (as well as preserving) cause is not an immanent cause; and insofar as those things were created *as* substances, they were precisely created as self-subsistent, however revocable that subsistence may be.

4. LEMMA I. Bodies are distinguished from one another in respect of motion and rest, quickness and slowness, and not in respect of substance.

5. DEF. When a number of bodies of the same or of different magnitudes are pressed together by others, so that they lie one upon the other, or if they are in motion with the same or with different degrees of speed, so that they communicate their motion to one another in a certain fixed proportion—these bodies are said to be mutually united, and, taken altogether, they are said to compose one body or individual which is distinguished from other bodies by this union of bodies.

6. That activity, being that of substance as a whole, can of course in its universal movement overrule any individual conatus, and inevitably does so sooner or later.

7. This, incidentally, is the first theory after Aristotle's to show why a human soul cannot be transposed into an animal or vegetable body, i.e., which excludes the *possibility* of metempsychosis. Leibniz's *Monadology*, while avoiding most of the pitfalls of Cartesian dualism, falls short of Spinoza on this point.

8. The following quotation from *Ep. 66* may here be added as a succinct summary of Spinoza's doctrine of mind: "The essence of the mind consists in this alone that it is the idea of an actually existing body; and accordingly the mind's power to understand extends to those things only which this idea of the body contains in itself or which follow from it. But this idea of the body involves and expresses no other attributes of God but extension and thought. Hence I conclude that the human mind cannot apprehend any attribute of God save these two."

9. Compare Spinoza's restatement of his principle of the degrees of mental perfection as *related* to, though not *causally* dependent on, degrees of bodily perfection, in the Explanation at the end of Part III: "Since the essence of the mind consists in its affirmation of the actual existence of its body, and since we understand by perfection the essence itself of the thing, it follows that the mind passes to a greater or less perfection when it is able to affirm of its body, or some part of it, something which involves a greater or less reality than before."

MAN A MACHINE *and* THE
NATURAL HISTORY OF THE SOUL

Julien Offray de la Mettrie

MAN A MACHINE

It is not enough for a wise man to study nature and truth; he should dare state truth for the benefit of the few who are willing and able to think. As for the rest, who are voluntarily slaves of prejudice, they can no more attain truth, than frogs can fly.

I reduce to two the systems of philosophy which deal with man's soul. The first and older system is materialism; the second is spiritualism.

The metaphysicians who have hinted that matter may well be endowed with the faculty of thought have perhaps not reasoned ill. For there is in this case a certain advantage in their inadequate way of expressing their meaning. In truth, to ask whether matter can think, without considering it otherwise than in itself, is like asking whether matter can tell time. It may be foreseen that we shall avoid this reef upon which Locke had the bad luck to make shipwreck.

The Leibnizians with their monads have set up an unintelligible hypothesis. They have rather spiritualized matter than materialized the soul. How can we define a being whose nature is absolutely unknown to us?

Descartes and all the Cartesians, among whom the followers of

This selection is excerpted from *Man a Machine* and "The Natural History of the Soul" (Chicago: Open Court Publishing Co., 1912), pp. 85–86, 128–49, and 153–61. These pages are reprinted with the permission of the Open Court Publishing Company and its editor, Eugene Freeman.

Malebranche have long been numbered, have made the same mistake. They have taken for granted two distinct substances in man, as if they had seen them, and positively counted them. . . .

But since all the faculties of the soul depend to such a degree on the proper organization of the brain and of the whole body, that apparently they are but this organization itself, the soul is clearly an enlightened machine. For finally, even if man alone had received a share of natural law, would he be any less a machine for that? A few more wheels, a few more springs than in the most perfect animals, the brain proportionally nearer the heart and for this very reason receiving more blood—any one of a number of unknown causes might always produce this delicate conscience so easily wounded, this remorse which is no more foreign to matter than to thought, and in a word all the differences that are supposed to exist here. Could the organism then suffice for everything? Once more, yes; since thought visibly develops with our organs, why should not the matter of which they are composed be susceptible of remorse also, when once it has acquired, with time, the faculty of feeling?

The soul is therefore but an empty word, of which no one has any idea, and which an enlightened man should use only to signify the part in us that thinks. Given the least principle of motion, animated bodies will have all that is necessary for moving, feeling, thinking, repenting, or in a word for conducting themselves in the physical realm, and in the moral realm which depends upon it.

Yet we take nothing for granted; those who perhaps think that all the difficulties have not yet been removed shall now read of experiments that will completely satisfy them.

1. The flesh of all animals palpitates after death. This palpitation continues longer, the more cold-blooded the animal is and the less it perspires. Tortoises, lizards, serpents, etc., are evidence of this.

2. Muscles separated from the body contract when they are stimulated.

3. The intestines keep up their peristaltic or vermicular motion for a long time.

4. According to Cowper, a simple injection of hot water reanimates the heart and the muscles.

5. A frog's heart moves for an hour or more after it has been removed from the body, especially when exposed to the sun or better still when

placed on a hot table or chair. If this movement seems totally lost, one has only to stimulate the heart, and that hollow muscle beats again. Harvey made this same observation on toads.

6. Bacon of Verulam in his treatise "Sylva Sylvarum" cites the case of a man convicted of treason, who was opened alive, and whose heart thrown into hot water leaped several times, each time less high, to the perpendicular height of two feet.

7. Take a tiny chicken still in the egg, cut out the heart, and you will observe the same phenomena as before, under almost the same conditions. The warmth of the breath alone reanimates an animal about to perish in the air pump.

The same experiments, which we owe to Boyle and to Stenon, are made on pigeons, dogs, and rabbits. Pieces of their hearts beat as their whole hearts would. The same movements can be seen in paws that have been cut off from moles.

8. The caterpillar, the worm, the spider, the fly, the eel—all exhibit the same phenomena; and in hot water, because of the fire it contains, the movement of the detached parts increases.

9. A drunken soldier cut off with one stroke of his saber an Indian rooster's head. The animal remained standing, then walked, and ran: happening to run against a wall, it turned around, beat its wings still running, and finally fell down. As it lay on the ground, all the muscles of this rooster kept on moving. That is what I saw myself, and almost the same phenomena can easily be observed in kittens or puppies with their heads cut off.

10. Polyps do more than move after they have been cut in pieces. In a week they regenerate to form as many animals as there are pieces. I am sorry that these facts speak against the naturalists' system of generation; or rather I am very glad of it, for let this discovery teach us never to reach a general conclusion even on the ground of all known (and most decisive) experiments.

Here we have many more facts than are needed to prove, in an incontestable way, that each tiny fiber or part of an organized body moves by a principle which belongs to it. Its activity, unlike voluntary motions, does not depend in any way on the nerves, since the movements in question occur in parts of the body which have no connection with the circulation. But if this force is manifested even in sections of fibers the heart, which is a composite of peculiarly connected fibers, must possess the same property. I did not need Bacon's story to persuade me of this.

It was easy for me to come to this conclusion, both from the perfect analogy of the structure of the human heart with that of animals, and also from the very bulk of the human heart, in which this movement escapes our eyes only because it is smothered, and finally because in corpses all the organs are cold and lifeless. If executed criminals were dissected while their bodies were still warm, we should probably see in their hearts the same movements that are observed in the face muscles of those that have been beheaded.

The motive principle of the whole body, and even of its parts cut in pieces, is such that it produces not irregular movements, as some have thought, but very regular ones, in warm-blooded and perfect animals as well as in cold and imperfect ones. No resource therefore remains open to our adversaries but to deny thousands and thousands of facts which every man can easily verify.

If now any one ask me where is this innate force in our bodies, I answer that it very clearly resides in what the ancients called the parenchyma, that is to say, in the very substance of the organs other than the veins, the arteries, the nerves, in a word, that it resides in the organization of the whole body, and that consequently each organ contains within itself forces more or less active according to the need of them.

Let us now go into some detail concerning these springs of the human machine. All the vital, animal, natural, and automatic motions are carried on by their action. Is it not in a purely mechanical way that the body shrinks back when it is struck with terror at the sight of an unforeseen precipice, that the eyelids are lowered at the menace of a blow, as some have remarked, and that the pupil contracts in broad daylight to save the retina, and dilates to see objects in darkness? Is it not by mechanical means that the pores of the skin close in winter so that the cold can not penetrate to the interior of the blood vessels, and that the stomach vomits when it is irritated by poison, by a certain quantity of opium, and by all emetics, etc.? that the heart, the arteries, and the muscles contract in sleep as well as in waking hours, that the lungs serve as bellows continually in exercise . . . that the heart contracts more strongly than any other muscle? . . .

I shall not go into any more detail concerning all these little subordinate forces, well known to all. But there is another more subtle and marvelous force, which animates them all; it is the source of all our feelings, of all our pleasures, of all our passions, and of all our thoughts:

for the brain has its muscles for thinking, as the legs have muscles for walking. I wish to speak of this impetuous principle that Hippocrates calls ἐνορμῶν (soul). This principle exists and has its seat in the brain at the origin of the nerves, by which it exercises its control over all the rest of the body. By this fact is explained all that can be explained, even to the surprising effects of maladies of the imagination. . . .

Look at the portrait of the famous Pope who is, to say the least, the Voltaire of the English. The effort, the energy of his genius are imprinted upon his countenance. It is convulsed. His eyes protrude from their sockets, the eyebrows are raised with the muscles of the forehead. Why? Because the brain is in travail and all the body must share in such a laborious deliverance. If there were not an internal cord which pulled the external ones, whence would come all these phenomena? To admit a soul as explanation of them, is to be reduced to [explaining phenomena by] the operations of the Holy Spirit.

In fact, if what thinks in my brain is not part of this organ and therefore of the whole body, why does my blood boil, and the fever of my mind pass into my veins, when, lying quietly in bed, I am forming the plan of some work or carrying on an abstract calculation? Put this question to men of imagination, to great poets, to men who are enraptured by the felicitous expression of sentiment, and transported by an exquisite fancy or by the charms of nature, of truth, or of virtue! By their enthusiasm, by what they will tell you they have experienced, you will judge the cause by its effects; by that harmony which Borelli, a mere anatomist, understood better than all the Leibnizians, you will comprehend the material unity of man. In short, if the nerve-tension which causes pain occasions also the fever by which the distracted mind loses its will-power, and if, conversely, the mind too much excited, disturbs the body (and kindles that inner fire which killed Bayle while he was still so young); if an agitation rouses my desire and my ardent wish for what, a moment ago, I cared nothing about, and if in their turn certain brain impressions excite the same longing and the same desires, then why should we regard as double what is manifestly one being? In vain you fall back on the power of the will, since for one order that the will gives, it bows a hundred times to the yoke. And what wonder that in health the body obeys, since a torrent of blood and of animal spirits forces its obedience, and since the will has as ministers an invisible legion of fluids swifter than lightning and ever ready to do its bidding!

But as the power of the will is exercised by means of the nerves, it is likewise limited by them. . . .

Does the result of jaundice surprise you? Do you not know that the color of bodies depends on the color of the glasses through which we look at them, and that whatever is the color of the humors, such is the color of objects, at least for us, vain playthings of a thousand illusions? But remove this color from the aqueous humor of the eye, let the bile flow through its natural filter, then the soul, having new eyes, will no longer see yellow. Again, is it not thus, by removing cataract, or by injecting the Eustachian canal, that sight is restored to the blind, or hearing to the deaf? How many people, who were perhaps only clever charlatans, passed for miracle workers in the dark ages! Beautiful the soul, and powerful the will which cannot act save by permission of the bodily conditions, and whose tastes change with age and fever! Should we, then, be astonished that philosophers have always had in mind the health of the body, to preserve the health of the soul, that Pythagoras gave rules for the diet as carefully as Plato forbade wine? The regime suited to the body is always the one with which sane physicians think they must begin, when it is a question of forming the mind, and of instructing it in the knowledge of truth and virtue; but these are vain words in the disorder of illness, and in the tumult of the senses. Without the precepts of hygiene, Epictetus, Socrates, Plato, and the rest preach in vain: all ethics is fruitless for one who lacks his share of temperance; it is the source of all virtues, as intemperance is the source of all vices.

Is more needed (for why lose myself in discussion of the passions which are all explained by the term, ἐνορμῶν, of Hippocrates) to prove that man is but an animal, or a collection of springs which wind each other up, without our being able to tell at what point in this human circle, nature has begun? If these springs differ among themselves, these differences consist only in their position and in their degrees of strength, and never in their nature; wherefore the soul is but a principle of motion or a material and sensible part of the brain, which can be regarded, without fear of error, as the mainspring of the whole machine, having a visible influence on all the parts. The soul seems even to have been made for the brain, so that all the other parts of the system are but a kind of emanation from the brain. This will appear from certain observations, made on different embryos, which I shall now enumerate.

This oscillation, which is natural or suited to our machine, and with which each fiber and even each fibrous element, so to speak, seems to be endowed, like that of a pendulum, cannot keep up forever. It must be renewed, as it loses strength, invigorated when it is tired, and weakened when it is disturbed by excess of strength and vigor. In this alone, true medicine consists.

The body is but a watch, whose watchmaker is the new chyle. Nature's first care, when the chyle enters the blood, is to excite in it a kind of fever which the chemists, who dream only of retorts, must have taken for fermentation. This fever produces a greater filtration of spirits, which mechanically animate the muscles and the heart, as if they had been sent there by order of the will.

These then are the causes or the forces of life which thus sustain for a hundred years that perpetual movement of the solids and the liquids which is as necessary to the first as to the second. But who can say whether the solids contribute more than the fluids to this movement or vice versa? All that we know is that the action of the former would soon cease without the help of the latter, that is, without the help of the fluids which by their onset rouse and maintain the elasticity of the blood vessels on which their own circulation depends. From this it follows that after death the natural resilience of each substance is still more or less strong according to the remnants of life which it outlives, being the last to perish. So true is it that this force of the animal parts can be preserved and strengthened by that of the circulation, but that it does not depend on the strength of the circulation, since, as we have seen, it can dispense with even the integrity of each member or organ.

I am aware that this opinion has not been relished by all scholars, and that Stahl especially had much scorn for it. This great chemist has wished to persuade us that the soul is the sole cause of all our movements. But this is to speak as a fanatic and not as a philosopher.

To destroy the hypothesis of Stahl, we need not make so great an effort as I find that others have done before me. We need only glance at a violinist. What flexibility, what lightness in his fingers! The movements are so quick, that it seems almost as if there were no succession. But I pray, or rather I challenge, the followers of Stahl who understand so perfectly all that our soul can do, to tell me how it could possibly execute so many motions so quickly, motions, moreover, which take place so far from the soul, and in so many different places. That is to suppose that a flute player could play brilliant cadences on an infinite number of holes that he could not know, and on which he could not even put his finger!

But let us say with M. Hecquet that all men may not go to Corinth. Why should not Stahl have been even more favored by nature as a man than as a chemist and a practitioner? Happy mortal, he must have received a soul different from that of the rest of mankind—a sovereign soul, which, not content with having some control over the voluntary muscles, easily held the reins of all the movements of the body, and could suspend them, calm them, or excite them, at its pleasure! With so despotic a mistress, in whose hands were, in a sense, the beating of the heart, and the laws of circulation, there could certainly be no fever, no pain, no weariness . . . ! The soul wills, and the springs play, contract or relax. But how did the springs of Stahl's machine get out of order so soon? He who has in himself so great a doctor, should be immortal.

Moreover, Stahl is not the only one who has rejected the principle of the vibration of organic bodies. Greater minds have not used the principle when they wished to explain the action of the heart . . . etc. One need only read the "Institutions of Medicine" by Boerhaave to see what laborious and enticing systems this great man was obliged to invent, by the labor of his mighty genius, through failure to admit that there is so wonderful a force in all bodies.

Willis and Perrault, minds of a more feeble stamp, but careful observers of nature (whereas nature was known to the famous Leyden professor only through others and second hand, so to speak), seem to have preferred to suppose a soul generally extended over the whole body, instead of the principle which we are describing. But according to this hypothesis (which was the hypothesis of Vergil and of all Epicureans, an hypothesis which the history of the polyp might seem at first sight to favor) the movements which go on after the death of the subject in which they inhere are due to a remnant of soul still maintained by the parts that contract, though, from the moment of death, these are not excited by the blood and the spirits. Whence it may be seen that these writers, whose solid works easily eclipse all philosophic fables, are deceived only in the manner of those who have endowed matter with the faculty of thinking, I mean to say, by having expressed themselves badly in obscure and meaningless terms. In truth, what is this remnant of a soul, if not the "moving force" of the Leibnizians (badly rendered by such an expression), which however Perrault in particular has really foreseen. See his "Treatise on the Mechanism of Animals."

Now that it is clearly proved against the Cartesians, the followers of Stahl, the Malebranchists, and the theologians who little deserve to be mentioned here, that matter is self-moved, not only when organized, as in a whole heart, for example, but even when this organization has been destroyed, human curiosity would like to discover how a body, by the fact that it is originally endowed with the breath of life, finds itself adorned in consequence with the faculty of feeling, and thus with that of thought. And, heavens, what efforts have not been made by certain philosophers to manage to prove this! and what nonsense on this subject I have had the patience to read!

All that experience teaches us is that while movement persists, however slight it may be, in one or more fibers, we need only stimulate them to reexcite and animate this movement almost extinguished. This has been shown in the host of experiments with which I have undertaken to crush the systems. It is therefore certain that motion and feeling excite each other in turn, both in a whole body and in the same body when its structure is destroyed, to say nothing of certain plants which seem to exhibit the same phenomena of the union of feeling and motion.

But furthermore, how many excellent philosophers have shown that thought is but a faculty of feeling, and that the reasonable soul is but the feeling soul engaged in contemplating its ideas and in reasoning! This would be proved by the fact alone that when feeling is stifled, thought also is checked, for instance in apoplexy, in lethargy, in catalepsis, etc. For it is ridiculous to suggest that, during these stupors, the soul keeps on thinking, even though it does not remember the ideas that it has had.

As to the development of feeling and motion, it is absurd to waste time seeking for its mechanism. The nature of motion is as unknown to us as that of matter. How can we discover how it is produced unless, like the author of "The History of the Soul," we resuscitate the old and unintelligible doctrine of substantial forms? I am then quite as content not to know how inert and simple matter becomes active and highly organized, as not to be able to look at the sun without red glasses; and I am as little disquieted concerning the other incomprehensible wonders of nature, the production of feeling and of thought in a being which earlier appeared to our limited eyes as a mere clod of clay.

Grant only that organized matter is endowed with a principle of motion, which alone differentiates it from the inorganic (and can one deny this in the face of the most incontestable observation?) and that among animals, as I have sufficiently proved, everything depends upon the diversity of this organization: these admissions suffice for guessing the riddle of substances and of man. It [thus] appears that there is but one [type of organization] in the universe, and that man is the most perfect [example]. He is to the ape, and to the most intelligent animals, as the planetary pendulum of Huyghens is to a watch of Julien Leroy. More instruments, more wheels, and more springs were necessary to mark the movements of the planets than to mark or strike the hours; and Vaucanson, who needed more skill for making his flute player than for making his duck, would have needed still more to make a talking man, a mechanism no longer to be regarded as impossible, especially in the hands of another Prometheus. In like fashion, it was necessary that nature should use more elaborate art in making and sustaining a machine which for a whole century could mark all motions of the heart and of the mind; for though one does not tell time by the pulse, it is at least the barometer of the warmth and the vivacity by which one may estimate the nature of the soul. I am right! The human body is a watch, a large watch constructed with such skill and ingenuity, that if the wheel which marks the seconds happens to stop, the minute wheel turns and keeps on going its round, and in the same way the quarter-hour wheel, and all the others go on running when the first wheels have stopped because rusty or, for any reason, out of order. Is it not for a similar reason that the stoppage of a few blood vessels is not enough to destroy or suspend the strength of the movement which is in the heart as in the mainspring of the machine; since, on the contrary, the fluids whose volume is diminished, having a shorter road to travel, cover the ground more quickly, borne on as by a fresh current which the energy of the heart increases in proportion to the resistance it encounters at the ends of the blood vessels? And is not this the reason why the loss of sight (caused by the compression of the optic nerve and by its ceasing to convey the images of objects) no more hinders hearing, than the loss of hearing (caused by obstruction of the functions of the auditory nerve) implies the loss of sight? In the same way, finally, does not one man hear (except immediately after his attack) without being able to say that he hears, while another who hears nothing, but whose lingual nerves are uninjured in the brain, mechanically tells of all the dreams which pass through his mind? These phenomena do not surprise enlightened physicians at all. They know what to think about man's nature, and (more accurately to express myself in passing) of two physicians, the better one and the one who deserves more confidence is always, in my opinion, the one who is more versed in the physique or mechanism of the human body, and who, leaving aside the soul and all the anxieties which this chimera gives to fools and to ignorant men, is seriously occupied only in pure naturalism.

Therefore let the pretended M. Charp deride philosophers who have regarded animals as machines. How different is my view! I believe that Descartes would be a man in every way worthy of respect, if, born in a century that he had not been obliged to enlighten, he had known the value of experiment and observation, and the danger of cutting loose from them. But it is none the less just for me to make an authentic reparation to this great man for all the insignificant philosophers—poor jesters, and poor imitators of Locke—who instead of laughing impudently at Descartes, might better realize that without him the field of philosophy, like the field of science without Newton, might perhaps be still uncultivated.

This celebrated philosopher, it is true, was much deceived, and no one denies that. But at any rate he understood animal nature, he was the first to prove completely that animals are pure machines. And after a discovery of this importance demanding so much sagacity, how can we without ingratitude fail to pardon all his errors!

In my eyes, they are all atoned for by that great confession. For after all, although he extols the distinctness of the two substances, this is plainly but a trick of skill, a ruse of style, to make theologians swallow a poison, hidden in the shade of an analogy which strikes everybody else and which they alone fail to notice. For it is this, this strong analogy, which forces all scholars and wise judges to confess that these proud and vain beings, more distinguished by their pride than by the name of men however much they may wish to exalt themselves, are at bottom only animals and machines which, though upright, go on all fours. They all have this marvelous instinct, which is developed by education into mind, and which always has its seat in the brain, (or for want of that when it is lacking or hardened, in the medulla oblongata) and never in the cerebellum; for I have often seen the cerebellum injured, and other observers have found it hardened, when the soul has not ceased to fulfil its functions.

To be a machine, to feel, to think, to know how to distinguish good from bad, as well as blue from yellow, in a word, to be born with an intelligence and a sure moral instinct, and to be but an animal, are therefore characters which are no more contradictory, than to be an ape or a parrot and to be able to give oneself pleasure. . . . I believe that thought is so little incompatible with organized matter, that it seems to be one of its properties on a par with electricity, the faculty of motion, impenetrability, extension, etc.

Do you ask for further observations? Here are some which are incontestable and which all prove that man resembles animals perfectly, in his origin as well as in all the points in which we have thought it essential to make the comparison. . . .

Let us observe man both in and out of his shell, let us examine young embryos of four, six, eight or fifteen days with a microscope; after that time our eyes are sufficient. What do we see? The head alone; a little round egg with two black points which mark the eyes. Before that, everything is formless, and one sees only a medullary pulp, which is the brain, in which are formed first the roots of the nerves, that is, the principle of feeling, and the heart, which already within this substance has the power of beating of itself; it is the *punctum saliens* of Malpighi, which perhaps already owes a part of its excitability to the influence of the nerves. Then little by little, one sees the head lengthen from the neck, which, in dilating, forms first the thorax inside which the heart has already sunk, there to become stationary; below that is the abdomen which is divided by a partition (the diaphragm). One of these enlargements of the body forms the arms, the hands, the fingers, the nails, and the hair; the other forms the thighs, the legs, the feet, etc., which differ only in their observed situation, and which constitute the support and the balancing pole of the body. The whole process is a strange sort of growth, like that of plants. On the tops of our heads is hair in place of which the plants have leaves and flowers; everywhere is shown the same luxury of nature, and finally the directing principle of plants is placed where we have our soul, that other quintessence of man.

Such is the uniformity of nature, which we are beginning to realize; and the analogy of the animal with the vegetable kingdom, of man with plant. Perhaps there even are animal plants, which in vegetating, either fight as polyps do, or perform other functions characteristics of animals. . . .

We are veritable moles in the field of nature; we achieve little more than the mole's journey and it is our pride which prescribes limits to the limitless. We are in the position of a watch that should say (a writer of fables would make the watch a hero in a silly tale): "I was never made by that fool of a workman, I who divide time, who mark so exactly the course of the sun, who repeat aloud the hours which I mark! No! that is impossible!" In the same way, we disdain, ungrateful wretches that we are, this common mother of all kingdoms, as the chemists say. We imagine, or rather we infer, a cause superior to that to which we owe all, and which truly has wrought all things in an inconceivable fashion. No; matter contains nothing base, except to the vulgar eyes which do not recognize her in her most splendid works; and nature is no stupid workman. She creates millions of men, with a facility and a pleasure more intense than the effort of a watchmaker in making the most complicated watch. Her power shines forth equally in creating the lowliest insect and in creating the most highly developed man; the animal kingdom costs her no more than the vegetable, and the most splendid genius no more than a blade of wheat. Let us then judge by what we see of that which is hidden from the curiosity of our eyes and of our investigations, and let us not imagine anything beyond. Let us observe the ape, the beaver, the elephant, etc., in their operations. If it is clear that these activities cannot be performed without intelligence, why refuse intelligence to these animals? And if you grant them a soul, you are lost, you fanatics! You will in vain say that you assert nothing about the nature of the animal soul and that you deny its immortality. Who does not see that this is a gratuitous assertion; who does not see that the soul of an animal must be either mortal or immortal, whichever ours [is], and that it must therefore undergo the same fate as ours, whatever that may be, and that thus [in admitting that animals have souls], you fall into Scylla in the effort to avoid Charybdis?

Break the chain of your prejudices, arm yourselves with the torch of experience, and you will render to nature the honor she deserves, instead of inferring anything to her disadvantage, from the ignorance in which she has left you. Only open wide your eyes, only disregard what you can not understand, and you will see that the ploughman whose intelligence and ideas extend no further than the bounds of his furrow, does not differ essentially from the greatest genius—a truth which the dissection of Descartes' and of Newton's brains would have proved; you will be persuaded that the imbecile and the fool are animals with human faces, as the intelligent ape is a little man in another shape; in short, you will learn that since everything depends absolutely on difference of organization, a well-constructed animal which has studied astronomy, can predict an eclipse, as it can predict recovery or death when it has used its genius and its clearness of vision, for a time, in the school of Hippocrates and at the bedside of the sick. By this line of observations and truths, we come to connect the admirable power of thought with matter, without being able to see the links, because the subject of this attribute is essentially unknown to us.

Let us not say that every machine or every animal perishes altogether or assumes another form after death, for we know absolutely nothing about the subject. On the other hand, to assert that an immortal machine is a chimera or a logical fiction, is to reason as absurdly as caterpillars would reason if, seeing the cast-off skins of their fellow caterpillars, they should bitterly deplore the fate of their species, which to them would seem to come to nothing. The soul of these insects (for each animal has his own) is too limited to comprehend the metamorphoses of nature. Never one of the most skilful among them could have imagined that it was destined to become a butterfly. It is the same with us. What more do we know of our destiny than of our origin? Let us then submit to an invincible ignorance on which our happiness depends.

He who so thinks will be wise, just, tranquil about his fate, and therefore happy. He will await death without either fear or desire, and will cherish life (hardly understanding how disgust can corrupt a heart in this place of many delights); he will be filled with reverence, gratitude, affection, and tenderness for nature, in proportion to his feeling of the benefits he has received from nature; he will be happy, in short, in feeling nature, and in being present at the enchanting spectacle of the universe, and he will surely never destroy nature either in himself or in others. More that that! Full of humanity, this man will love human character even in his enemies. Judge how he will treat others. He will pity the wicked without hating them; in his eyes, they will be but mis-made men. But in pardoning the faults of the structure of mind and body, he will none the less admire the beauties and the virtues of both. Those whom nature shall have favored will seem to him to deserve more respect than those whom she has treated in stepmotherly fashion. Thus, as we have seen, natural gifts, the source of all acquirements, gain from the lips and heart of the materialist, the homage which every other thinker unjustly refuses them. In short, the materialist, convinced, in spite of the protests of his vanity, that he is but a machine or an animal, will not maltreat his kind, for he will know too well the nature of those actions, whose humanity is always in proportion to the degree of the analogy proved above [between human beings and animals]; and following the natural law given to all animals, he will not wish to do to others what he would not wish them to do to him.

Let us then conclude boldly that man is a machine, and that in the whole universe there is but a single substance differently modified. This is no hypothesis set forth by dint of a number of postulates and assumptions; it is not the work of prejudice, nor even of my reason alone; I should have disdained a guide which I think to be so untrustworthy, had not my senses, bearing a torch, so to speak, induced me to follow reason by lighting the way themselves. Experience has thus spoken to me in behalf of reason; and in this way I have combined the two.

But it must have been noticed that I have not allowed myself even the most vigorous and immediately deduced reasoning, except as a result of a multitude of observations which no scholar will contest; and furthermore, I recognize only scholars as judges of the conclusions which I draw from the observations; and I hereby challenge every prejudiced man who is neither anatomist, nor acquainted with the only philosophy which can here be considered, that of the human body. Against so strong and solid an oak, what could the weak reeds of theology, of metaphysics, and of the schools, avail—childish arms, like our parlor foils, that may well afford the pleasure of fencing, but can never wound an adversary. Need I say that I refer to the empty and trivial notions, to the pitiable and trite arguments that will be urged (as long as the shadow of prejudice or of superstition remains on earth) for the supposed incompatibility of two substances which meet and move each other unceasingly? Such is my system, or rather the truth, unless I am much deceived. It is short and simple. Dispute it now who will.

THE NATURAL HISTORY OF THE SOUL

All philosophers who have examined attentively the nature of matter, considered in itself, independently of all forms which constitute bodies, have discovered in this substance, diverse properties proceeding from an absolutely unknown essence. Such are: (1) the capacity of taking on different forms, which are produced in matter itself, by which matter can acquire moving force and the faculty of feeling; (2) actual extension, which these philosophers have rightly recognized as an attribute, but not as the essence, of matter.

However, there have been some, among others Descartes, who have insisted on reducing the essence of matter to simple extension, and on limiting all the properties of matter to those of extension; but this opinion has been rejected by all other modern philosophers . . . so that the power of acquiring moving force, and the faculty of feeling as well as that of extension, have been from all time considered as essential properties of matter.

All the diverse properties that are observed in this unknown principle demonstrate a being in which these same properties exist, a being which must therefore exist through itself. But we cannot conceive, or rather it seems impossible, that a being which exists through itself should be able neither to create nor to annihilate itself. It is evident that only the forms to which its essential properties make it susceptible can be destroyed and reproduced in turn. Thus, does experience force us to confess that nothing can come from nothing.

All philosophers who have not known the light of faith, have thought that this substantial principle of bodies has existed and will exist forever, and that the elements of matter have an indestructible solidity which forbids the fear that the world is going to fall to pieces. The majority of Christian philosophers also recognize that the substantial principle of bodies exists necessarily through itself, and that the power of beginning or ending does not accord with its nature. One finds that this view is upheld by an author of the last century who taught theology in Paris.

Although we have no idea of the essence of matter, we cannot refuse to admit the existence of the properties which our senses discover in it.

I open my eyes, and I see around me only matter, or the extended. Extension is then a property which always belongs to all matter, which can belong to matter alone, and which therefore is inseparable from the substance of matter.

This property presupposes three dimensions in the substance of bodies, length, width, and depth. Truly, if we consult our knowledge, which is gained entirely from the senses, we cannot conceive of matter, or the substance of bodies, without having the idea of a being which is at the same time long, broad, and deep; because the idea of these three dimensions is necessarily bound up with our idea of every magnitude or quantity.

Those philosophers who have meditated most concerning matter do not understand by the extension of this substance, a solid extension composed of distinct parts, capable of resistance. Nothing is united, nothing is divided in this extension; for there must be a force which separates to divide, and another force to unite the divided parts. But in the opinion of these physical philosophers matter has no actually active force, because every force can come only from movement, or from some impulse or tendency toward movement, and they recognize in matter, stripped of all form by abstraction, only a potential moving force.

This theory is hard to conceive, but given its principles, it is rigorously true in its consequences. It is one of those algebraic truths which is more readily believed than conceived by the mind.

The extension of matter is then but a metaphysical extension, which according to the idea of these very philosophers, presents nothing to affect our senses. They rightly think that only solid extension can make an impression on our senses. It thus seems to us that extension is an attribute which constitutes part of the metaphysical form, but we are far from thinking that extension constitutes its essence.

However, before Descartes, some of the ancients made the essence of matter consist in solid extension. But this opinion, of which all the Cartesians have made much, has at all times been victoriously combated by clear reasons, which we will set forth later, for order demands that we first examine to what the properties of extension can be reduced.

The ancients, persuaded that there is no body without a moving force, regarded the substance of bodies as composed of two primitive attributes. It was held that, through one of these attributes, this substance has the capacity for moving and, through the other, the capacity for being moved. As a matter of fact, it is impossible not to conceive these two attributes in every moving body, namely, the thing which moves, and the same thing which is moved.

It has just been said that formerly the name, matter, was given to the substance of bodies, insofar as it is susceptible of being moved. When capable of moving this same matter was known by the name of "active principle." . . . But these two attributes seem to depend so essentially on each other that Cicero, in order better to state this essential and primitive union of matter with its moving principle, says that each is found in the other. This expresses very well the idea of the ancients.

From this it is clear that modern writers have given us but an inexact idea of matter in attempting (through a confusion ill understood) to give this name to the substance of bodies. For, once more, matter, or the passive principle of the substance of bodies, constitutes only one part of this substance. Thus it is not surprising that these modern thinkers have not discovered in matter moving force and the faculty of feeling.

It should now be evident at the first glance, it seems to me, that if there is an active principle it must have, in the unknown essence of matter, another source than extension. This proves that simple extension fails to give an adequate idea of the complete essence or metaphysical form of the substance of bodies, and that this failure is due solely to the fact that extension excludes the idea of any activity in matter. Therefore, if we demonstrate this moving principle, if we show that matter, far from being as indifferent as it is supposed to be, to movement and to rest, ought to be regarded as an active, as well as a passive substance, what resource can be left to those who have made its essence consist in extension?

The two principles of which we have just spoken, extension and moving force, are then but potentialities of the substance of bodies; for in the same way in which this substance is susceptible of movement, without actually being moved, it also has always, even when it is not moving itself, the faculty of spontaneous motion.

The ancients have rightly noticed that this moving force acts in the substance of bodies only when the substance is manifested in certain forms; they have also observed that the different motions which it produces are all subject to these different forms or regulated by them. That is why the forms, through which the substance of bodies can not only move, but also move in different ways, were called material forms.

Once these early masters had cast their eyes on all the phenomena of nature, they discovered in the substance of bodies, the power of self-movement. In fact, this substance either moves itself, or when it is in motion, the motion is communicated to it by another substance. But can anything be seen in this substance, save the substance itself in action; and if sometimes it seems to receive a motion that it has not, does it receive that motion from any cause other than this same kind of substance, whose parts act the one upon the other?

If, then, one infers another agent, I ask what agent, and I demand proofs of its existence. But since no one has the least idea of such an agent, it is not even a logical entity. Therefore it is clear that the ancients must have easily recognized an intrinsic force of motion within the substance of bodies, since in fact it is impossible to prove or conceive any other substance acting upon it.

Descartes, a genius made to blaze new paths and to go astray in them, supposed with some other philosophers that God is the only efficient cause of motion, and that every instant He communicates motion to all bodies. But this opinion is but a hypothesis which he tried to adjust to the light of faith; and in so doing he was no longer attempting to speak as a philosopher or to philosphers. Above all he was not addressing those who can be convinced only by the force of evidence.

The Christian Scholastics of the last centuries have felt the full force of this reflection; for this reason they have wisely limited themselves to purely philosophic knowledge concerning the motion of matter, although they might have shown that God Himself said that He had "imprinted an active principle in the elements of matter" (Gen. i; Is. lxvi).

One might here make up a long list of authorities, and take from the most celebrated professors the substance of the doctrine of all the rest; but it is clear enough, without a medley of citations, that matter contains this moving force which animates it, and which is the immediate cause of all the laws of motion.

We have spoken of two essential attributes of matter, upon which depend the greater number of its properties, namely extension and moving force. We have now but to prove a third attribute: I mean the faculty of feeling which the philosophers of all centuries have found in this same substance. I say all philosophers, although I am not ignorant of all the efforts which the Cartesians have made, in vain, to rob matter of this faculty. But in order to avoid insurmountable difficulties, they have flung themselves into a labyrinth from which they have thought to escape by this absurd system "that animals are pure machines."

An opinion so absurd has never gained admittance among philosophers, except as the play of wit or as a philosophical pastime. For this reason we shall not stop to refute it. Experience gives us no less proof of the faculty of feeling in animals than of feeling in men. . . .

There comes up another difficulty which more nearly concerns our vanity: namely, the impossibility of our conceiving this property as a dependence or attribute of matter. Let it not be forgotten that this substance reveals to us only ineffable characters. Do we understand better how extension is derived from its essence, how it can be moved by a primitive force whose action is exerted without contact, and a thousand other miracles so hidden from the gaze of the most penetrating eyes, that (to paraphrase the idea of an illustrious modern writer) they reveal only the curtain which conceals them?

But might not one suppose as some have supposed, that the feeling which is observed in animated bodies, might belong to a being distinct from the matter of these bodies, to a substance of a different nature united to them? Does the light of reason allow us in good faith to admit such conjectures? We know in bodies only matter, and we observe the faculty of feeling only in bodies: on what foundation then can we erect an ideal being, disowned by all our knowledge?

However, we must admit, with the same frankness, that we are ignorant whether matter has in itself the faculty of feeling, or only the power of acquiring it by those modifications or forms to which matter is susceptible; for it is true that this faculty of feeling appears only in organic bodies.

This is then another new faculty which might exist only potentially in matter, like all the others which have been mentioned; and this was the hypothesis of the ancients, whose philosophy, full of insight and penetration, deserves to be raised above the ruins of the philosophy of the moderns. It is in vain that the latter disdain the sources too remote from them. Ancient philosophy will always hold its own among those who are worthy to judge it, because it forms (at least in relation to the subject of which I am treating) a system that is solid and well articulated like the body, whereas all these scattered members of modern philosophy form no system.

ON THE FIRST GROUND OF THE
DISTINCTION OF REGIONS IN
SPACE *and* WHAT IS
ORIENTATION IN THINKING?

Immanuel Kant

ON THE FIRST GROUND OF THE
DISTINCTION OF REGIONS
IN SPACE

For the positions of the parts of space in relation to one another pre-suppose the region towards which they are ordered in such relation; and this region, in ultimate analysis, consists not in the relation of one thing in space to another (which is properly the concept of position) but in the relation of the system of these positions to the absolute world-space. In anything extended the position of parts relatively to one another can be adequately determined from consideration of the thing itself; but the region towards which this ordering of the parts is directed involves

The first selection, "On the First Ground of the Distinction of Regions in Space," is extracted from *Kant's Inaugural Dissertation and Early Writings on Space*, translated by John Handyside (London: Open Court Publishing Co., 1929), pp. 19–29. Reprinted with the permission of the Open Court Publishing Company and its editor, Eugene Freeman. The second selection, "What Is Orientation in Thinking?" is excerpted from Immanuel Kant's *Critique of Practical Reason and Other Writings in Moral Philosophy* (Chicago: University of Chicago Press, 1949), pp. 294–95. Reprinted with the permission of the translator, Lewis W. Beck.

reference to the space outside the thing; not, indeed, to points in this wider space—for this would be nothing else but the position of the parts of the thing in an outer relation—but to universal space as a unity of which every extension must be regarded as a part.

As the explanation of these concepts is first to be found in what follows, it is not surprising if the reader as yet finds them very unintelligible; and I therefore limit myself to this one further remark, that my aim in this treatise is to investigate whether there is not to be found in the intuitive judgments of extension, such as are contained in geometry, an evident proof *that absolute space has a reality of its own, independent of the existence of all matter, and indeed as the first ground of the possibility of the compositeness of matter.*

Everybody knows how futile have been the endeavours of the philosophers, by means of the most abstract propositions of metaphysics, to settle this point once for all; and I know of no attempt, save one, to carry this out *a posteriori* as it were, that is, by means of other undeniable propositions which, though themselves lying outside the realm of metaphysics, can afford through their application in the concrete a criterion of their correctness. The one attempt, to which I have referred, was made by the celebrated Euler, the elder, in 1748, as recorded in the *History of the Royal Berlin Academy of Sciences* for that year. But so far from fully achieving his purpose, he only brings to view the difficulty of assigning to the most general laws of motion a determinate meaning, should we assume no other concept of space than that obtained by abstraction from the relation of actual things. The no less notable difficulties which remain in the application of the aforesaid laws, when we endeavour to represent them in the concrete according to the concept of absolute space, are left unconsidered. The proof which I here seek should supply, not to the mechanists (as Herr Euler intended), but to the geometers themselves, a convincing ground for asserting the actuality of their absolute space, and should do so with the evidence to which they are accustomed. With this purpose in view, I make the following preparatory observations.

In physical space, on account of its three dimensions, we can conceive three planes which intersect one another at right angles. Since through the senses we know what is outside us only insofar as it stands in relation to ourselves, it is not surprising that we find in the relation of these intersecting planes to our body the first ground from which to derive the concept of regions in space.[1] The plane to which the length of our body stands perpendicular is called, in reference to us, horizontal; it gives rise to the distinction of the regions we indicate by *above* and *below*. Two other planes, also intersecting at right angles, can stand perpendicular to this horizontal plane, in such manner that the length of the human body is conceived as lying in the line of their intersection. One of these vertical planes divides the body into two outwardly similar parts and supplies the ground for the distinction between *right* and *left;* the other, which is perpendicular to it, makes it possible for us to have the concept of *before* and *behind*. In a written page, for instance, we have first to note the difference between front and back and to distinguish the top from the bottom of the writing; only then can we proceed to determine the position of the characters from right to left or conversely. Here the parts arranged upon the surface have always the same position relatively to one another, and the parts taken as a whole present always the same outlines howsoever we may turn the sheet. But in our representation of the sheet the distinction of regions is so important, and is so closely bound up with the impression which the visible object makes, that the very same writing becomes unrecognisable when seen in such a way that everything which formerly was from left to right is reversed and is viewed from right to left.

Even our judgments about the cosmic regions are subordinated to the concept we have of regions in general, insofar as they are determined in relation to the sides of the body. All other relations that we may recognise, in heaven and on earth, independently of this fundamental conception, are only positions of objects relatively to one another. However well I know the order of the cardinal points, I can determine regions according to that order only insofar as I know towards which hand this order proceeds; and the most complete chart of the heavens, however perfectly I might carry the plan in my mind, would not teach me, from a known region, North say, on which side to look for sunrise, unless, in addition to the positions of the stars in relation to one another, this region were also determined through the position of the plan relatively to my hands. Similarly, our geographical knowledge, and even our commonest knowledge of the position of places, would be of no aid to us if we could not, by reference to the sides of our bodies, assign to regions the things so ordered and the whole system of mutually relative positions.

It is even the case that a very notable characteristic of natural organisms, which at times may even give occasion for the distinction of species, consists in the definite direction in which the arrangement of their parts is turned, a feature through which two creatures can be distinguished although they entirely agree both in size and proportion, and even in the position of their parts relatively to one another. The hairs on the crown of every man's head are turned from left to right. The hop-plant always twines round its pole from left to right; beans, however, take the opposite course. Almost all snails, only some three species excepted, have their spiral turning from left to right, that is, if we proceed from above downwards, from the apex to the mouth. Since in the case of the natural existences just cited the cause of the twist or spiral lies in their very germs, this definite character remains constant in creatures of the same species without any relation to the hemisphere in which they may be found, or to the direction of the daily motion of the sun and the moon, which for us runs from left to right but for our antipodes in the opposite direction. On the other hand, when a certain revolution can be ascribed to the path of these heavenly bodies—as Mariotte[2] professes to have observed in the case of the winds, which from new to full moon tend to work round the whole compass from left to right—this motion must in the other hemisphere go from right to left, as indeed Don Ulloa considers to have been established by his observations in the South Seas.

Since the different feeling of right and left side is of such necessity to the judgment of regions, Nature has directly connected it with the mechanical arrangement of the human body, whereby one side, the right, has an indubitable advantage in dexterity and perhaps also in strength. If, therefore, we set aside individual exceptions which, like cases of squinting, cannot disturb the generality of the rule according to the natural order, all the peoples of the earth are right-handed. In mounting on horseback or striding over a ditch, the body is more easily moved from right to left than vice versa. Everywhere men write with the right hand; with it they do everything for which skill and strength are demanded. But if some investigators, e.g., Borelli and Bonnet, are to be believed, while the right hand seems to have the advantage over the left in mobility, the left has the advantage over the right in sensibility. Borelli likewise assigns to the left eye, and Bonnet to the left ear, the possession of a greater sensibility than the corresponding organ on the right side. And thus the two sides of the human body, in spite of their great outer similarity, are sufficiently distinguished by a well-marked feeling, even if we leave out of account the differing positions of the inner parts and the noticeable beat of the heart, which at every contraction strikes with its apex in oblique motion against the left side of the breast.

What, therefore, we desire to show is that the complete ground of determination of the shape of a body rests not merely upon the position of its parts relatively to one another, but further on a relation to the universal space which geometers postulate—a relation, however, which is such that it cannot itself be immediately perceived. What we do perceive are those differences between bodies which depend exclusively upon the ground which this relation affords. If two figures drawn upon a plane are equal and similar, they can be superimposed. But with physical extension and also with lines and surfaces that do not lie in one plane, the case is often quite different. They can be perfectly equal and similar, yet so different in themselves that the boundaries of the one cannot be at the same time the boundaries of the other. A screw which winds round its axis from left to right will not go into a threaded cylinder whose worm goes from right to left, although the thickness of the stem and the number of turns in an equal length correspond. Two spherical triangles can be perfectly equal and similar, and yet not allow of superposition. But the commonest and clearest example is to be found in the limbs of the human body, which are symmetrically disposed about its vertical plane. The right hand is similar and equal to the left, and if we look at one of them alone by itself, at the proportions and positions of its parts relatively to one another and at the magnitude of the whole, a complete description of it must also hold for the other in every respect.

When a body is perfectly equal and similar to another, and yet cannot be included within the same boundaries, I entitle it the incongruent counterpart of that other. To show its possibility, take a body which is not composed of two halves symmetrically disposed to a single intersecting surface, say a human hand. From all points of its surface draw perpendiculars to a plane set over against it, and produce them just as far behind the plane as these points lie in front of it; the extremities of the lines so produced, if connected, then compose the surface and shape of a physical body which is the incongruent counterpart of the first; i.e., if the given hand is the right, its counterpart is the left. The image of an object in a mirror rests upon the same principle; for it always appears just as far behind the mirror as the object lies in front of its surface, and so the mirrored image of a right hand is always a left.

If the object itself consists of two incongruent counterparts, as does the human body when divided by a vertical section from front to back, its image is congruent with it, as can easily be seen by allowing it in thought to make a half turn; for the counterpart of the counterpart of an object is necessarily congruent with the object.

The above considerations may suffice for understanding the possibility of spaces which are completely equal and similar and yet incongruent. We now proceed to the philosophical application of these concepts. From the common example of the two hands, it is already clear that the shape of one body can be completely similar to that of another, and the magnitude of their extension exactly the same, while yet there remains an inner difference, namely that the surface which bounds the one cannot possibly bound the other. Since this surface bounds the physical space of the one but cannot serve as boundary to the other, however one may turn and twist it, this difference must be such as rests upon an inner ground. This inner ground cannot, however, depend on any difference in the mode of connection of the parts of the body relatively to one another; for, as can be seen from the examples adduced, in this respect everything may be completely identical in the two cases. Nevertheless, if we conceive the first created thing to be a human hand, it is necessarily either a right or a left, and to produce the one a different act of the creating cause is required from that whereby its counterpart can come into being.

If we, then, adopt the conception held by many modern philosophers, especially in Germany, that space consists only in the outer relations of the parts of matter existing alongside one another, then in the case before us all actual space would be that which this hand occupies. But since, whether it be right or left, there is no difference in the relations of its parts to one another, the hand would in respect of this characteristic be absolutely indeterminate, i.e., it would fit either side of the human body, which is impossible.

Thus it is evident that instead of the determinations of space following from the positions of the parts of matter relatively to one another, these latter follow from the former. It is also clear that in the constitution of bodies differences are to be found which are real differences, and which are grounded solely in their relation to absolute, primary space. For, only through this relation is the relation of bodily things possible. Since absolute space is not an object of an outer sensation, but a fundamental concept which first makes all such sensations possible, it further follows that whatsoever in the outline of a body exclusively concerns its reference to pure space, can be apprehended only through comparison with other bodies.

A reflective reader will accordingly regard as no mere fiction that concept of space which the geometer has thought out and which clear-thinking philosophers have incorporated into the system of natural philosophy. There is, indeed, no lack of difficulties surrounding this concept, if we attempt to comprehend its reality—a reality which is sufficiently intuitable to inner sense—through ideas of reason. This difficulty always arises when we attempt to philosophise on the first data of our knowledge. But it reaches its maximum when, as in this case, the consequences of an assumed concept [that of spatial relations as subsequent to and dependent on the relations of bodies to one another] contradict the most obvious experience.

WHAT IS ORIENTATION IN THINKING?

To orient one's self in the strict sense of the word means to find, from one given direction in the world (one of the four into which we divide the horizon), the others, especially the east. If I see the sun in the sky and know that it is now noon, I know how to find south, west, north, and east. But for this I certainly need the feeling of a distinction in my own person, that between my right and left hand. I call it a feeling, because the two sides in intuition show no externally noticeable difference. Without the capacity to distinguish between motion from left to right and that in the opposite direction in describing a circle, in spite of the absence of any difference in the objects, I would be unable to determine a priori any difference in the position of objects; I would not know whether to put west to the left or right of the south point of the horizon so as to know how to complete the circle from north through east to the south. Thus I orient myself geographically by all the objective data of the sky only by virtue of a subjective ground of distinction; and if someday a miracle occurred whereby the direction of all the stars changed from east to west but preserved the same pattern and position.

on the next starry night no human eye would notice the slightest change, and even the astronomer, if he attended to what he merely saw and not what he at the same time felt, would be inevitably disoriented. But the ability to distinguish by feeling between the right and the left hand, which is implanted by nature and made familiar by frequent use, would come naturally to his help, and if he once viewed the pole star, he not only would notice the change but would orient himself regardless of it.

This geographical concept of the procedure of orientation can be broadened to purely mathematical orientation so as to include orientation in any given space. In the dark I orient myself in a familiar room when I can seize on a single object whose position I remember. Here obviously nothing helps me except the capacity of determining positions by a subjective ground of distinction. For I do not see the objects whose position I should find, and if someone had played a joke on me by putting on the left what was previously on the right while still preserving their relationships to each other, I could not find my way in a room with otherwise indistinguishably equal walls. But I soon orient myself through the mere feeling of a difference between my right and left sides. This happens at night when I walk and make the proper turns in a street which I know but in which I cannot distinguish any houses.

NOTES

1. Kant returned to this subject in 1786 in his treatise, *Was heisst: sich im Denken orientieren?* [See the second selection included here.—Ed.]

2. See Kant's treatise on the theory of the winds, *Werke*, Berlin ed., Bd. I, p. 502.

PART II

THE BODY

OF A PERSON

SOUL AND BODY

John Dewey

Lest the reader trained in a school which holds that there is nothing to be said of the relations of soul and body, except that there is soul and there is body and that is the end of it, should turn away at the outset in disgust from what must seem to him an attempt to solve the insoluble —let me say a word or two to avoid misapprehension. Lotze has somewhere called attention to the fact that the natural tendency of a historical age, priding itself on its historical sense, and working by a historical method, is to surrender the understanding to the imagination, and to demand pictures instead of principles. We are not contented until we can *see* the object matter as a series of definite images. Instead of explanation we want a drama before our eyes. It is because of this tendency, I believe, that it is assumed that there is some difficulty special in kind surrounding the question of the relations of soul and body which makes all attempts to consider the subject necessarily futile. It seems to be assumed on the one hand that nothing can be said about it unless we can see into the bowels of the molecules constituting the brain, and behold from their mutual attractions and repulsions, a sensation and a thought engendered. Or on the other hand, it is assumed that to know anything about the relations of soul and body, we must be able to contemplate the soul, seated as on a throne in the body, thence sending forth her messengers to lay hold of the nerves and cause them to bring her reports of what is going on in the outlying regions of her domain, or to execute her orders among refractory subjects. And if the

This essay is reprinted by permission of G. P. Putnam's Sons from *Philosophy, Psychology, and Social Practice* by John Dewey, edited by Joseph Ratner, pp. 63–86. Copyright © 1963 by G. P. Putnam's Sons. The essay originally appeared in *The Bibliotheca Sacra*, XLIII (April, 1886), 239–63.

only way of knowing anything about their relations were some such imaginative exploit, the question were well called insoluble. But questions, as science and philosophy can well testify, are more often insoluble by reason of some unnecessary and absurd assumption, than from the inherent nature of the case. And so the failure of all attempts on this line is rather, I conceive, testimony to the absurdity of the mode of search, than to the absurdity of the question itself. We have an understanding as well as an imagination; principles may be thought as well as pictures seen; laws exist as well as panoramas. We may well give up the attempt to imagine the neural and psychical processes so as to see a transition from one to another, and confine ourselves to the less picturesque, but more hopeful, task of inquiring what principles shall be employed in order to render intelligible the relations of the physical and psychical, so far as these relations have been actually made known. We have certain facts declared by physiology and psychology. The sole question is: what principles, conceptions, shall we use in order to explain these facts, i.e., in order to render a consistent, intelligible account of them? To say that this cannot be done is simply to say that there are facts in the universe which are utterly irrational, which have no meaning. And the one who has the capacity of discovering by his reason that certain facts are non-rational to his reason, is not the one whom I address.

Therefore, if it is again stated that the object of this paper is to consider the relations of soul and body, I hope it will be understood that the object is not to get into the inside of nature and behold with mortal eyes what is going on there, but the less ambitious one of inquiring what principles must be used in order to give meaning to the facts of the case. How shall the facts of physiological psychology be interpreted?

What are these facts?

First. The nervous system, complex as it is, consists ultimately of fibers and cells. The fibers serve normally to conduct or transfer nervous stimuli either from the organ of sense to some collection of cells, or ganglion, or from this center back to the muscles and glands, or from one such center to another. The cells, on the other hand, receive the stimuli brought to them from the surface, and react upon them in such a way as either to neutralize them from their own supply of force, or so as to set free their own nervous energy. In short, the fibers conduct the nervous energy; the cells produce it and regulate its distribution. This distinction in the mode of work of the two elements exists. But it has been usual to regard this distinction in such a way as to make of it an actual separation of functions. This introduces a dualism into the action of the nervous system at the start. It has been held that the fibers are purely passive and receptive, while cells are active. This leads to this result: the cells alone are regarded as having psychical bearings, so that the brain is held to be the sole organ of the mind. The nerves and the peripheral organs are eliminated. Some even go so far as to hold that in the brain there must be some particular set of cells to which all stimuli must be conducted, and that this alone is the organ of the soul. We must avoid, at the outset, any such error. The truth is that the distinction between fiber and cell is a relative one. Fibers possess an activity of their own as well as the cells, and cells conduct. The fiber is not a string which, pulled at one end, rings a bell at the other, itself remaining the meantime indifferent to the process; it is a series of nervous elements each reacting upon the stimulus of the one before it, as the cell reacts to the whole, and each passing it on to the one after it, as the cell distributes its energy. It is, in effect, a connected series of cells. What makes it behave differently from the cell proper is the fact that its power of resistance is so small, and its stored-up energy relatively so slight. The cell, on the other hand, is something more than an explosive; it is a conductor. As there is no difference, chemically, between the firing of a gunpowder train and the resulting explosion of the magazine, so there is none, physiologically, between the processes of the nerve and cell. The difference of the result in both cases is due partly to the amount of energy at hand to be set free, and still more to the resistance offered. In the cell there are no tracks laid down for the carrying off of the energy introduced. It meets resistance, friction, and accumulates till either the cell energy inhibits that introduced, or reacts upon it so as to increase it, and send it forth through the nerve.[1]

I may seem to have dwelt needlessly upon so simple a point, but it is the foundation of any further approach to a correct theory of psychophysiological relations. The conclusion which it warrants in this respect is all-important. In brief it is this: The psychical is *homogeneously* related to the physiological. Whatever is the relation of the psychical to the neural, it is related in the same manner to all parts of the neural. The brain is no more the organ of mind than the spinal cord, the spinal cord no more than the peripheral endings of the nerve fibers. The brain is undoubtedly most closely and most influentially connected with the life of the soul, but its connection is of the same *kind* as that of every other part of the nervous system. Now this gives us but one alternative: either there is absolutely no connection between the body and the soul at any point whatever, or else the soul is, through the nerves, present to all the body. This means that the psychical is immanent in the physical. To deny this is to go back to the Cartesian position, and make a miracle of the whole matter—to call in some utterly foreign power to make the transition which is actually found. This may cater to our love of pictures, but it is out of the line which we have laid down for ourselves. The nineteenth-century substitute of a double-faced substance is only another excursion into the land of fancy sketches. It makes the imagination the source of an ontology. But it fares even worse than the Cartesian scheme. A double-faced substance not only refuses to be thought, but, if one is in earnest, refuses to be imagined. It is the result of the decrepitude of the imagination as well as of the laziness of thought. Not colors for the imagination to see, but principles for the understanding to think, is the desideratum. That compromise which seemed to think that the problem of the relations of soul and body was simplified if the connection of the two could be reduced to as small a space as possible, and excluded it first from the fiber, then from the spinal cord, then from the basal ganglia, the cerebellum, all of the cerebrum except the cortex, then possibly one point of the cortex—that, too, must be abandoned. The fact is, that the action of the nervous tissue is the same in kind in the cortex and in the peripheral fiber, and hence if any part of the nervous system has any connection with the soul which is not supernatural in character, every part must have, in kind, the same. All, or none, is the disjunction forced upon us. The immanence of the psychical in the physical is, therefore, the foundation of our future inquiry. The nature of the immanence must now be inquired into. That there is unity of function in the cell and fiber is established. What this function is and what conclusion it warrants are the questions now to be asked.

Second. The fundamental nervous activity is a process of adjustment, consisting in a twofold contemporaneous process of stimulation and reaction or inhibition. If we turn to the same physiological authorities whence we learned of the homogeneous nature of the action of fiber and cell, we shall learn what this action is. Nervous tissue, in the first place, wherever found is a highly unstable chemical compound. Any excitation tends to set up such chemical change as will reduce it to relatively simpler and more stable compounds. There is thus set free an amount of energy equivalent to the amount which would be required to lift this lower compound up to its higher state again. The potential energy of the unstable compound has, in short, become kinetic. The first element in nervous action is, therefore, the excitatory or stimulating, which has the setting free of nervous energy for its result. But if this were all, the energy of the nervous system would be soon used up. Every stimulus would set free nervous force, and the result would be that the body would respond to every stimulus, however slight, and the process would end only with the complete exhaustion of the power. We would be physically in the condition of those having the Saint Vitus's dance; mentally, in the state of some of the insane, who, having no reserve power, react violently upon every impression, intellectual or emotional, until they sink into a stupor, out of which they come only to repeat the process. In short, there must be something which gives control, which regulates the reaction, and which also ensures a reserve power. There must be opposed to the exciting activity one which resists, and thereby prevents the whole force at hand, the whole unstable compound, from being used, and which also restores it as it is expended. And so it is found that there is a complementary process. Not only is energy being constantly put forth, but energy is being constantly stored up or rendered latent. Not all the force which comes to a nervous element is employed in breaking down the unstable compounds and thereby losing energy; part—in some cases much the greater part—is used in building up these unstable compounds, thereby forming a reservoir of energy for future use, while the process itself acts as a restraint upon, a control over, the excitatory factor. Every nervous action is, therefore, a reciprocal function of stimulation, excitation, and inhibition; control through repression. Every nervous activity is essentially an adjustment. It is called forth through the stimulus, but the stimulus is not the sole factor; it does not wander at its own sweet will, but is checked and directed by the reacting activity, the inhibiting. This is true, of course, of every process, whether occurring in fiber or in cell; but because of the structural differences between the two, previously spoken of, the former mode of action greatly *predominates* over the other in the fiber; while in the cell the inhibitory activity exceeds at the expense of the stimulating. Since the fibers correspond, in a general way, to the peripheral nerve system and the cells to the central, it may truly enough be said that the stimulating or exciting is the peripheral, and the reacting and controlling is the central or ganglionic.

Looked at from this point of view, *the unitary nervous activity is evidently that known as reflex action*. In that, we have precisely these relations of excitement on the one hand, and adjusting activity on the other, of which we have just been speaking. Our conclusions are as follows: there is a fundamental mode of nervous activity; in this the psychical is immanent. This mode of activity is an adjusting activity; therefore the psychical is immanent in the physical as directing it toward a given end. It is not only immanent, but it is teleologically immanent. This teleological character is seen in the nature of the function itself as just described. The loss of the proper proportion of the stimulating and the inhibiting activity is a token of morbid disorder. It is pathological. If the centers react on feeble stimuli, they squander their force upon the little stimuli, which are constant, by playing upon them; if they react only upon very strong stimuli, the force they contain is never put forth when needed to perform the proper adjustment of the organism. But in normal life we find that exact proportion between the two activities which ensures that the force shall be used when its expenditure is for the good of the organism, and then alone. If we take the simplest case of nervous action, such a one as occurs in a cold-blooded animal deprived of all its nervous apparatus except the spinal cord, it will only render still more distinct the teleological character as objectively manifested. Read the following account of Wundt:

A decapitated frog moves its legs against the pincers with which it is irritated, or it wipes away with its foot the drop of acid applied to the skin. It sometimes tries to get away from a mechanical or electrical stimulation by a jump. If put into an unusual position (e.g., on its back) it often returns to its normal position. The stimulus does not introduce merely a motion in general, which spreads from the irritated part with increasing intensity of the stimulus and growing irritability, but the movement is adapted *to the external impression*. It may be a movement of defence, or one to get rid of the stimulus, or a movement to remove the body from the sphere of irritation, or finally it may aim at restoration of the previous posture. This *purposive adaptation to the stimulus* stands out even more clearly in experiments by Pflüger and Auerbach in which the ordinary conditions of movement are somewhat changed. A frog, for example, whose leg has been cut off on the side on which it is irritated by acid, first makes some fruitless attempts with the amputated stump, and then, pretty regularly, chooses the other leg, which is wont to remain at rest when the animal is unmutilated. If the decapitated frog be fastened by its back, and the inner side of one of its thighs be sprinkled with acid, it tries to get rid of the latter by rubbing the two thighs against each other; but if the moved thigh be separated far from the other, after a few vain attempts it suddenly stretches this one out, and pretty accurately reaches the point which was irritated. Lastly, if one breaks the upper thighs of decapitated frogs and cauterizes, whilst they are stretched on their bellies the lower part of their backs, they correctly touch the cauterized spot with the feet of the broken limb, in spite of the disturbing nature of the treatment. These observations, which may be varied in diverse ways, show that the animal can adapt its movements to its changed conditions.[2]

Of course what is true of this simplest form of nerve action is still more true of the higher forms, until we have a large number of nerve centers acting coordinately with each other, and all subordinated to the execution of a given act recognized as necessary for the preservation or development of the organism. But it is enough for our purpose to take our stand upon this elementary form of reflex action, and thus cut the very standing ground from under the feet of the materialist.

This, then, is our conclusion: the psychical is immanent in the physical; immanent as directing it toward an end, and for the sake of this end selecting some activities, inhibiting others, responding to some, controlling others, and adjusting and coordinating the complex whole, so as, in the simplest and least wasteful way, to reach the chosen end. We find, therefore, that in the simplest form of nervous action there are involved categories transcending the material; principles to which matter, as such, is an entire stranger. Matter *per se* knows no higher category than that of physical causality. Its highest law is that of the necessities of antecedent and consequent. In nervous action we find the category of teleology. The act is not determined by its immediate antecedents, but by the necessary end. We have gone from the sphere of physical to that of final causation, and thereby we recognize that we have gone from the purely physical to the immanence of the psychical in the physical, directing the latter for its own end and purpose.

The materialist, with his reversed logic, which attempts to get the higher from the lower, instead of accounting for the lower on the ground of the higher, utterly misses the nature of the case. To him, the fact of reflex action, the fact of purposive adjustment (if he be far enough advanced in the elements to recognize the fact at all) is evidence of the self-sufficiency of matter. He forthwith makes teleological action an attribute of matter, and intelligent purposiveness a function of the material. He does not recognize that in doing this he is giving up all that characterizes matter as matter, and is, in effect, recognizing the primacy of spirit. If teleology belong to the essence of matter, and purposive regulated action be the nature of the material, then matter and material cease to be what they are commonly regarded as being (*viz.*, matter and material), and become but the hiding places (which are the dwelling places) of spirit and the psychical. The dispute is not, I suppose, about what words we shall use, but what principles. Nor is the question, again, about pictures, but about laws of explanation. If we cease to form a verbal or pictorial conception of matter we shall find that for scientific purposes it means the principle of physical causation; the constant and invariable relations of antecedent and consequent. To attempt to get more into the conception of matter is unscientific in that it is unwarranted; and unscientific in that, if it were accomplished, it would destroy the basis of all physical science and leave it the field for the play of imaginative fancies by whose side the highest flight of the science of the Greek, or of the Middle Ages, will sink into insignificance. The recognition of this one principle of physical causation, the invariableness of succession, is the theoretic basis of all physical science. To attempt to include more is to destroy the principle without reason, and to introduce unbounded confusion. Some foregleams of the depths of absurdity to which we may reach, once started on this course of surrendering principles to words or images, may be seen in the efforts of some German materialists, who, in their laudable efforts to be consistent, have found it necessary to supply the primordial atoms with sensations, and who hold that the laws of the universe are to be deduced from their primitive loves and hates, their desires and strivings. Such is the only consistent position for a materialist. But it is a consistency which looks marvelously like a *reductio ad absurdum.* And it is suicide as well, for it is to give up the very essence of the materialistic position, and to admit that the nature and laws of the material are constituted by the psychical, which is the determining and prior element in the case. To attempt to swallow up the psychical in the material is not only absurd, but it is useless, for the psychical always revenges itself by encroaching upon the material, and when we finally look for some independent speck of matter, there is none there. It has all been spiritualized. Or, if there be one speck there, it must be defined in terms of the conception of matter just laid down. It will be found to be matter because it acts according to the principles of physical causation and not of final causation; because it is determined by its antecedent, not by an end working itself out in it. So that after all there is no choice for the materialist. If he will but once open his eyes to the fact of purposive action he has no alternative. He may attempt to claim this function as an attribute of matter; if he does, as just seen, he dematerializes his matter. He may admit that there is matter whose principle and law is that of psychical causation. He will then recognize that whatever transcends this principle is essentially non-material, and that with the appearance of teleological action upon the scene, we have passed from the realm of the material into that of the psychical immanent in the material. This is rational, and this saves science from becoming the sport of every inflated and ill-balanced imagination.

There is another method of escaping the significance of purposive action, equally futile, but equally attractive to the mind that prefers panoramas to principles. It is, at present, the more fashionable method. In brief, it is to admit that the actions are at present teleological, but that they became such through a long series of accidental experiments (experiments which were not experiments, as they were not trying to reach any end) of which some happened to be advantageous to the organism, and, surviving, give us now the appearance of purpose. This theory attempts to make the teleological an accidental product of the mechanical. It generally hides itself behind imposing scientific terms connected with the theory of biological evolution. It uses its "variations" and "selection," and "survival of the fittest" and "heredity," and thinks that in the end it has got something out of nothing—purpose out of accident. But the argument is suicidal. It only changes the special case into a general law. It gets rid of the primitive purposiveness of, say, a given reflex act, only by importing purposiveness, and thus intelligence, into the very structure of nature. It simply says that nature is such that, by the observance of its own laws as ascertained by science, it gives rise to action for and by ends. Variation, selection, heredity, as *names,* do not, I suppose, accomplish the result. It is that there are embedded in the very constitution of things, forces and principles which as they work themselves out, by their action and reaction, give rise to activity for an end, to purposive action. In short, not only is the structure of the nervous system such that it gives rise to teleological action, but the structure of nature itself is such that it gives rise to this special kind of purposive action. He who has thought to get rid of teleology, and thereby intelligence, in this special case, has done it only by the recognition of teleology, and thereby intelligence, as a universal principle and acting force. Darwinism, far from overthrowing this principle, merely establishes it as a general law of the universe, of the structure of things. Nature is made teleological all the way through.

From this digression, which has, I hope, developed the argument, as well as secured it from possible misconception, I return to the conclusion. The psychical is teleologically immanent in the physical. The simplest nerve action is not so simple as to exclude the adaptive, purposive factor. It is always an adjustment. It is never a mere mechanical result of a stimulus, but always involves selection, inhibition, and response. The stimulus favorable to the well-being of the organism is selected from the immense number playing upon the organism; others, especially those unserviceable, are inhibited, and then the action results according to the needs, that is, the purpose, of the organism itself. If we broaden our view and take in the consentaneous action of the whole organism, the conclusion appears only the more clearly. The various sensory and muscular stimuli, almost infinite in number, are always coordinated and harmoniously combined. The nerves of the cord, the cord itself, the special sense nerves, the cerebellum, the basal ganglia, the cerebral hemispheres, with their infinitude of fibers and cells, act as an adjusted unity for one purpose, and one alone—the welfare of the organism. At times it may seem as if one part were functioning alone, but it is always found (unless the action be pathological) that it is a relative independence. The end of the organism is best gained by allowing a certain amount of originative and self-executed action by the particular part. The apparent independence is but the evidence of the thoroughly teleological character of the whole. It signifies the division of labor in order that the whole task, the development of the organism, may be the more speedily and economically effected. There is no communistic level, but the due gradation and subordination of the various factors in the unity of the whole, as in a well-organized society. There is, in short, the coordination of all the nerve organs, and the further subordination of all to the end of the whole, self-realization.

Such is the conclusion we arrive at, without leaving the purely physiological sphere. But such a conclusion is one-sided and narrow, until expanded to take in all the phenomena. The body, through the nervous system, is not only a *physiological,* but a *psycho*physiological organism. Expressed in its lowest terms, there is *sensation,* as well as adjustment of all the activities to one end. Those who have asserted the spirituality of the soul have often begun to build too high. They have taken as their fortress abstract thought, or the free will. Now these offer, indeed, an impregnable refuge, but, in opening the campaign from there, ground is abandoned which, by all territorial rights, is the eminent domain of the spiritual soul. To return to the former metaphor, we can finally build higher and more firmly, because on a broader foundation, on the basis of sensation. Too often is the claim of the materialist that sensation, at least, can be accounted for by material processes, admitted explicitly or tacitly. It seems to be thought that because the immediate and close connection of sensations with the nerve organs and the brain can be made out, that thereby their material character is established. At bottom, this is the survival of a metaphor, out of date at its very birth. The mischief that the term "impression" has played with psychology can never be measured. One of the greatest claims which physiological psychology has upon us is that it has forever outlawed the term and the conception. The only word which has any place in psychology as expressing the material antecedent of the psychical state, sensation, is *stimulus*. Our semimaterialists, like Mr. Huxley and Mr. Tyndall, always conclude their baldest assertions of the dependence of the mind upon the brain with some such statement as this: The passage from the physics of the brain, from a nervous irritation, from a change of motion and matter, to a fact of consciousness, to a psychical state, to a sensation, is unthinkable, is an inexplicable mystery, a gulf which imagination cannot span; and so on, *ad libitum*. One would think that if they would cease attempting to picture the transition and endeavor to *think* it, the explanation would be so patent as to stare them fairly out of countenance. The "mystery" would explode in its own fatuous vacuity. The unthinkable arises from the use of wrong categories, wrong principles. No better evidence that the physical and psychical are not related as cause and effect, as producer and product, could be adduced than the utter "mysteriousness" hanging with "inexplicable" persistence over all attempts to get one out of the other. When it is recognized that "inexplicability" is not an ultimate fact to be supremely contented with, but a positive condemnation of the method and principles which have led to it, our scientific men will reflect twice before they thrust their uncomprehended physical categories into the psychical realm, thereby begging the whole question, and, themselves being witnesses, landing the whole affair in a mystery which cannot be discriminated from an absurdity. It was recognized some hundreds of years ago that in geometry a *reductio ad absurdum* is a perfect and beautiful demonstration of the untruth of the original hypothesis. Let us hope that the idea of the unity of all thought will finally dawn upon the scientific men who have taken the contract of philosophizing for the English-speaking portion of the nineteenth century, and that they will recognize that what holds in the basis of all scientific reasoning holds also in the rudiments of philosophical.

We will abandon, then, all attempts to picture the confessedly unimaginable, and those endeavors to explain which lead us into the confessedly inexplicable. We will begin with the facts, and inquire what principle they force upon us to explain them; we will not begin with a principle, and, after having in nine-tenths of the paper victoriously "explained" all facts by it, wind up with confessing that it is all inexplicable, and accordingly go on to revel in the unutterable bathos of the "mysterious." If we take the facts, they are simply these: (1) the constant sequence upon a certain nervous process of a psychical state known as a sensation; (2) the entire lack of any connection between the two by way of physical causation, i.e., by way of identity of matter and motion involved. The principle which this leads us to is that the physical antecedent is a stimulus necessary for the production of a sensation; and that it is only a stimulus. The sensation does not come *from* it, although it would never come *without* it. The sensation has its *occasion* from the nervous process; it has its *cause* from within. The physical process awakens the mind, it incites it to action; the mind, thereupon, spontaneously and by its own laws develops from itself a sensation. The specific names given to the various factors involved are of no importance, as long as it is recognized that the principle concerned is that of stimulus and response; response, which, for its existence, depends upon the physical antecedent, but for its content and nature, upon something else. We must recognize that we have got to go beyond the principle of physical causation to the principle of self-developing activity, though an activity which is not infinite or self-produced, but dependent upon an occasioning impulse beyond it. In short, not only is the soul immanent in the body, as teleological, as subordinating and adjusting its various activities to an end, but the body is the stimulus to the soul. It is the condition of the calling forth of its activities. It is the spark which fires the mind to light its own inextinguishable flame. Sensation, and, *a fortiori*, all higher psychical activities, testify to the creative, self-determining power of the mind, with the proviso attached that this power has been called upon to act. There is just the same mystery about it that there is about every fact in the universe, the mystery that there should be such a fact at all. As to principles involved, there is no more mystery than in the explanation of any physical or chemical fact. In ultimate analysis, the spiritual principle is less mysterious, is lucidly transparent, in comparison with the mechanical; for it is only from the former that the latter gets its explanation and the guarantee of its validity.

If we include within our survey the psychophysiological facts as well as the purely physiological phenomena of nerve action, we come to the conclusion that the soul not only directs and focuses the activities of the organism, but that it transforms them into something which they are not. It realizes itself upon the hints, as it were, given by the body. The soul is not only immanent in the body, as constituting its unity and end; it is transcendent to it, as transforming its activities for its own psychical ends. It uses it as material out of which to build its own structure, as food by which to nourish its own life. These two principles, of the immanence and the transcendence of the soul, to which we have been led by the study of the facts, cannot be left in this isolated way. They must be shown in their unity as necessarily involving each other. And again we turn to the facts of psychophysiological life with the assurance that the principle will be involved in them, and that we are not left to the logical manipulations of our conceptions.

They are the facts connected with the execution of definite psychophysiological functions. They may all be included under the phrase "localization of functions," if the phrase be understood in a broad sense to mean the performance of any definite act of psychical bearings by any specific, organized portion of the body. It would include, therefore, the performance of reflex acts by the spinal cord, as well as the supposed location of the "speech center" in the third frontal convolution of the central hemisphere. The ground for this extension of the term is the unity of all nervous action, as well as particular facts to be presently mentioned. The only difference between the regular and constant "localization" of reflex action in the spinal cord, and of speech in one part of the brain, is a difference of degree, not of kind. The difference is between a localization perfectly formed, and a localization in process of forming. Organization of function might be the better term.

If we turn again to our authorities we shall find the facts substantially as follows:

1) In some form or other localization or, to use the better term, organization of psychical function, is all but universal. The body is not a homogeneous mass which is indifferent, equally as a whole and in all its parts, to the soul. On the contrary, neither as a whole, nor in any of its parts, is it neutral to the soul. That it is not as a whole, we have seen when considering the immanence of the soul in the body; that it is not in any of its parts, is simply a detailed application of the same principle. The soul is not only in the body, but it is in it in definite, particular ways. The body as a whole is not only the organ of the soul, but the various structures of the body are differentiated organs, of various capacities and tendencies, of the soul. That is the meaning of the localization of function, or of the fact that certain activities have certain, more or less defined, nervous centers in various portions of the spinal cord and brain.

To give the specific evidence of this localization would be but to repeat the whole of the morphology and physiology of the nervous system. The nervous system itself is but a differentiation of the ecotoderm; the special sense organs are only so many continuations of the brain and spinal cord. If we take the various movements, we find that, in going from the simplest to the most complex, from the mere reflex action to the most consciously purposive movement, nowhere does the will act without a structure already formed for it. Learning the higher movements, like walking, talking, etc., is but the formation of the organized structures of the body. If these be wanting, no matter how completely the end and the proper means of reaching it are present to consciousness, the volition cannot be performed. If we leave the motor and sensory spheres and come to the higher ideal operations, the evidence for the localization of functions is much less complete and forcible. But we need only to recognize the dependence of thought upon sense for its materials, and largely upon language for its form, to be aware that the same principles must, in some degree at least, hold here also. The fact that in thinking we never deal with the ultimate psychical elements, but with symbolic wholes, with processes already integrated, is still more striking psychological evidence of the same fact. Just as it would take hours to perform a simple act like dressing, if the motor functions did not become organized in the bodily structure, if the will were obliged to go into detail of the act, instead of simply setting the whole mechanism into operation to work itself out, so in the intellectual sphere. If the various sensations and ideas remained isolated, if they were not organized into wholes, if they were not changed from material into structure, the mind would require hours to take in the meaning of a single sentence, or to reason out a simple inference. But the fact is that the mind does not deal with ultimate elements; it always has integral wholes which it may grasp and use without endeavoring or needing to resolve them. And that there is some similar physiological grouping and integration, some corresponding organization of function in the brain, all artificial experiments upon animals, and all natural experiments, performed by disease upon man, go to show.

2) But there must be explicitly stated, what has already been suggested; *viz.*, that the degree of this localization, both as to definiteness and completeness, varies very greatly. The lower the function, the more perfectly and narrowly is it localized. The wider its scope, and the greater its consequent necessity, the more complete and spatial, so to speak, its localization. Thus the functions of breathing, digesting, swallowing, etc., which are necessary to life, and which have only indirect psychical bearings, have very definite and thoroughly localized centers: while the higher activities, like walking, talking, reading, and writing, involving more and more activities and of a more complex kind, have less and less definite local centers. In the higher activities there is no perfect mapping out at all, but all sorts of shadings-off and variations. So if we consider the sensory sphere, we find that, while the sense centers may for some of the lower animals be made out pretty certainly, there is no such certainty and agreement in the case of man. And the reason is evident; in the animals, the sensations remain mostly what they are—pure sense-feelings, while in man these sensations have been so related and interpreted that they have become for the most part perceptions, and even higher ideal relations. Consequently we find that *ideas* as such have no localization whatever. *There is not the slightest evidence whatever that any special idea, whether a percept, an image, or a concept, has any definite specific center. There are all kinds of evidence that it has not.* The elaborate calculations of Mr. Bain in his work upon Mind and Body going to show that there are as many fibers and cells in the brain as the mind has separate ideas and associations, is based upon an utterly unfounded *a priori* assumption; *viz.*, that cells in the brain correspond to ideas, and fibers to associations. It cannot be stated too strongly, or insisted upon too often, that there is not the slightest fragment of experimental evidence for the theory. There is much experimental evidence to show that the case cannot possibly

stand thus. This evidence may be summed up in the statement that all
lines of inquiry, morphological, anatomical, and physiological, converge to one result: the psychical function or bearing of the cell is
dependent, not on its own structure, but upon its connections by means
of the fibers. An "idea," however simple it may seem, has not its physical
basis in a cell, but in a group of cells, connected and interconnected by
multitudinous fibers. If the idea be very complex it may possibly have
relations to all the cells in the brain. This may be an extreme statement,
but, beside the statement that any idea may be localized in a given cell,
it is truth itself. Hence we see the entire failure of all attempts definitely
to localize the higher intellectual functions. The evidence does not
warrant the statement that, upon the whole, they have no physical
connection; it does warrant the statement that the relations involved
are so many, so far reaching, and so complex, that any attempt to find a
sharply marked-out center must be forever in vain.

3) The two statements already made, that localization is practically
universal and yet that the higher intellectual powers cannot be definitely
localized at all, do not contradict each other. They find their reconcilia-
tion in the statement that *localization is not original, but acquired.* It
has already been stated that the localization is no quality originally inherent in the cell; but that it depends upon the cell's connections
through its fibers. As Wundt says, "No element executes specific functions, but the form of the latter depends upon the connections and
relations of the cell."[3] And this dependence of localized function upon
connection is the same as to say that given elements of the brain act in a
certain way only because they have been associated in the performance
of the act. The localization is dependent upon use and exercise. Thus
it is that Wundt goes on to state the following principles: "Every
definite function has, under given conditions of connection, a definite
place in the central organ from which it proceeds: that is to say, whose
elements stand in relations fitted for the execution of the function," and
"Every element is the more fitted to the performance of a definite function, the more often it has been occasioned by external conditions to
its performance." Localization of function is, in short, only the physiological way of saying habit. The organization of function is not in-
dwelling in the brain as so much matter: it has been *learned* by the
brain and learned through the tuition and care of the soul. By no
twisting can the phenomena of localization of function be twisted into
the support of materialism. The very fibers and cells cry out against

such treatment. They all assert that the powers they have, they possess, not of their own original and indefeasible right, but by means of the activity, and under the authority of the soul. This accounts for the various degrees of localization found. The acts most necessary for the soul's ends, and therefore oftenest performed, have, through heredity, become definitely and completely organized, and, like reflex actions, go on without consciousness, or, like instinctive actions, involve others which in complexity and far-reaching influence are beyond the immediate consciousness of the moment. But the soul, for its own ends, requires again that its higher activities be not thus mechanized. There must be a constant growth, adjustment to new relations, intellectual and moral, and this requires plasticity, variability. In the higher activities complete organization would mean stagnation, death. Thus it is that the higher we come, both in the range of animal life and in the range of intellectual function, the less the localization. But in each case the evidence all goes to show that the localization is not original, but is acquired because the soul has repeatedly employed the given elements for the performance of a given act. The soul does not write in water, but in the plastic brain and spinal cord. *Litera scripta manet*.[4] By the performance of its acts the soul gains a mechanism by which to perform them again the more readily, economically, and perfectly.

Thus we see how the phenomena of localization of function give us a standpoint whence to view the nature of the immanence and transcendence of the soul. The soul is immanent in the body just so far as it has made the body its organic instrument. The common saying that the "body is the organ of the soul" is literally much truer and more significant that is usually thought or meant. The term "organ" expresses a much more intimate and internal relation than is commonly understood. Organ presupposes function, and soul and body are related indeed as function and organ, activity and instrument. As Aristotle said so long ago, the body is the organ of the soul, as the eye is the organ of seeing. The body is not an external instrument which the soul has happened upon, and consequently uses, as a musician might happen upon a piano. The body is the organ of the soul because by the body the soul expresses and realizes its own nature. It is the outward form and living manifestation of the soul. To quote from one of the most original and deeply spiritual thinkers whom America has yet produced: "It is the outward man, in and through which the inward powers of the soul express their form and character. It is the necessary mode of our existence in the world of sense, without the intervention of which we have no knowledge, either objective or subjective, no existence in nature, either in space or in time. It is not merely an organ to be conceived as distinct from our personal self, but *it is our proper self as existent in space,* in the order and under the laws of nature."[5]

But this is only one-half the tale. The soul is immanent in the body only because, and in so far as, it has realized itself in the body. The body is its organ only because the soul has *made* the body its organ. The immanence is shown by the localization; the transcendence, by the fact that this localization has come about through the soul's own activities. The body as an organ of the soul is the result of the informing, creating activity of the soul itself. In short, the soul is immanent in the body, not by virtue of the body as mere body, but because, being transcendent, it has expressed and manifested its nature in the body.

The soul, accordingly, is not a powerless, impotent something, so transcendent that it cannot be brought into relation with matter. It is a living and acting force which has formed, and is constantly forming, the body as its own mechanism. This assures, on the one hand, that no act or deed of the mind is ever lost, that it finds its registration and record, and that not alone in some supralunary sphere, but down here in the world of matter; and, on the other hand, it forms a mechanism by which the soul can immediately know, can grasp the fragments of its knowledge into one symbolic whole without laboriously gathering them and piecing them together, and by which it can immediately act. It is, as it were, the mind's automaton, ceaselessly and tirelessly executing the demands responding to the needs of the soul. All the phenomena which the materialist parades forth as "proofs"—the unconscious cerebration, the automatic, yet apparently intelligent, action in many states of unconsciousness; the dependence of perception and memory upon the proper condition and integrity of the brain; the accompaniment of brain disease with unconsciousness and insanity; the ratio between mental power and weight and complexity of the brain, etc., are the farthest removed from the evidence of materialism. They are but the conclusive evidence of the thoroughness with which the soul has done its work, has formed its mechanism. They are all evidence that the soul is not hanging helpless in the air, but has made the body its home, and has realized itself so effectually in this body as its mechanism, that this mechanism can now act all but automatically, while disturbance of the mechanism of the organ excludes the execution of the corresponding activity, until the soul by its power form the organ again. The materialist but looks at the body after the soul has done its work in making the body what it is, and cries, "Lo, see what the body can do." Every one of the phenomena mentioned, as well as all which the materialist can mention, concern the formed body, the body in which the soul has already organized its functions. The true cry is, "Lo, see what the soul *has* done. It has tabernacled in the flesh and transformed that flesh into its own manifestation. The body is the bodying forth of the soul."

It was the "master of those who know" that said that the soul was the perfect realization or expression of a natural body, and at the same time, not the product of body, but its very life, its essence, its truth and reality—at once its final and efficient cause. (Aristotle, *De Anima,* ii.I.) And it was the Teacher of all who know, the Light which lighteth every man that cometh into the world, who said: "Except a corn of wheat fall into the ground and die it abideth alone: but if it die it bringeth forth much fruit." And it was the great disciple of the great Teacher who wrote: "That which thou sowest is not quickened except it die; and that which thou sowest, thou sowest not the body that shall be, but bare grain, it may chance of wheat or of some other grain; but God giveth it a body as it has pleased Him, and to every seed his own body. . . . It is sown a natural body, it is raised a spiritual body. There is a natural body and there is a spiritual body."

Christianity has no sympathy with those who have such a superfine fear of materialism that they aetherialize the soul past all contact with the body. It knows that in the body the soul is incarnate; that through the soul the natural body comes to be a spiritual body, as the soul works itself out, and realizes itself in it. The soul does apparently die in the body; it hides itself so effectually that the materialist says there is no soul; but it has died as dies the seed, to quicken and transform the body. It is by no accident or meaningless chance that we read in the Apostles' Creed those sublime words: "I believe in the Resurrection of the Body." Catholic historic Christianity, having such a confession on its lips, has no alliance with the metaphysical dualism of spirit and matter, and no fear of the exactest demonstrations of physiology regarding the closest connections of body and soul. It takes its stand upon the words of St. Paul, to which these demonstrations can only add more weight: "There is a natural body and there is a spiritual body. . . . Howbeit that was not first which is spiritual, but that which is natural; and afterwards that which is spiritual." There is the body, the natural body, first. Spirit indwells within the body, and manifesting itself, realizing its own nature, it makes that body its own organ and servant. It thus makes it the spiritual body. Let it be no surprise that physiological psychology has revealed no new truth concerning the relations of soul and body. It can only confirm and deepen our insight into the truth divined by Aristotle and declared by St. Paul, and with good reason. *Das Wahre war schon längst gefunden.*[6]

NOTES

1. This is not theory, but physiological fact. The experimental data with the conclusions warranted will be found set forth in Wundt, *Mechanik der Nerven, und Grundzüge der physiologischen Psychologie*, I, 240–64.

2. Ibid., II, 404.

3. Ibid., I, 225.

4. "The written word endures."—Ed.

5. President James Marsh, *Remains*, p. 257.

6. "This truth has been established for a long time."—Ed.

THE PHILOSOPHICAL CONCEPT

OF A HUMAN BODY

Douglas C. Long

The argument from analogy for the existence of other minds has been repeatedly attacked on two general counts. Its defenders have long been criticized for attempting to justify the inference that other "bodies" are associated with minds by an appeal merely to one's own case, while more recently the intelligibility of the concept of mind which the formulation of such an inference requires has been seriously challenged. Nothing has been said, however, about difficulties that come to light when the other half of the Cartesian dualism is given careful scrutiny. In this paper I will argue (1) that philosophers have not clearly introduced the concept of a body in terms of which the problem of other minds and its solutions have been traditionally stated; (2) that one can raise fatal objections to attempts to introduce this concept; and (3) that the particular form of the problem of other minds which is stated in terms of the concept is the offspring of confusion and so requires no solution.

I

Perhaps to some it will not be obvious that we have to bring "bodies" into the problem of other minds at all. Ordinarily we talk about the thoughts and feelings of *human beings,* and for this reason it seems natural to view the problem of other minds as an attempt to give "rational justifications" for statements ascribing psychological states to *persons*

Reprinted from *Philosophical Review* (July, 1964), pp. 321–37. The editor wishes to express his appreciation to Douglas Long and the editors of *Philosophical Review* for their permission to reproduce the following pages.

other than oneself. For example, in one of his essays, A. J. Ayer discusses the position that "the only ground that I can have for believing that other people have experiences, and that some of their experiences are of the same character as my own, is that their overt behaviour is similar to mine."[1] The question he is asking himself is whether or not he is justified in believing that some person is or was or will be in a given psychological state.

Unfortunately, beginning the discussion of the existence of other minds at this level appears to beg an important question, since in referring to "others" as persons it is already assumed that it *makes sense* to ascribe psychological states to them. To be sure, the question whether or not such ascriptions are *true* or *false* remains open. But a philosophical skeptic might refuse to agree that we are justified in believing that the behaving bodies we observe are those of human beings or persons. He could try to suggest, for example, that an automaton might behave in all of the ways that people behave, even including the uttering of intelligible sounds in the form of sentences, and yet not be a creature whose movements serve to justify the ascription to it of thoughts and feelings. So it appears that there is a "gap" between the obvious fact that we are surrounded by physical bodies shaped like ourselves and our "claim" that these have minds. He will go on to point out that we certainly cannot say that the bodies themselves are conscious, that they have feelings, for they are only material objects, and one cannot intelligibly ascribe conscious states in a literal sense to such objects. They are not what we may call "fit logical subjects" for such ascriptions. Saying that a given person is conscious or in pain may be either true or false, but even if it is false, it is intelligible. But saying that a certain "body" is conscious or in pain makes no sense; the wrong sort of entity is in the subject position.

This form of objection, however, raises no difficulty not already recognized by the numerous discussions of the problem of other minds which take *bodies* as their subjects of reference rather than persons. In such discussions the proper subject for the ascription of psychological states is taken to be either the mind itself or the partnership formed by the mind with a body. The philosophical problem is then construed as that of justifying the belief that certain bodies are in fact associated with minds. Thus it is initially an open question whether or not there are other entities to which psychological states can be intelligibly ascribed besides ourselves, and no fundamental question about other minds appears to be begged.

But it is easy to be careless in stating this question. Since the word "body" is one we all use in everyday discourse, it is not surprising to find that those who treat the problem of other minds at the level of bodies give little attention to the introduction of this key term. The concept of the human body seems to be perfectly clear; it is obvious that we all do have bodies, and there is no great mystery about their nature, as there is about the nature of minds. Even those who criticize the whole enterprise of trying to give a general justification of the belief in the existence of other minds continue to suppose that the concept of a body which they accept from the tradition is perfectly in order.[2] Yet, without some acceptable verbal or ostensive definition of the concept to examine, we cannot be certain that we have a term which can be properly used in posing a philosophical question about the existence of other people. In the next section I will consider various ways in which the word "body" might be introduced and show that none of them defines a sense in terms of which that question can be posed.

II

Suppose we ask a skeptic about other minds to provide a verbal definition of the word "body" that will permit him to ask his question about other minds. One can think of various phrases he might suggest. For example, he might say that a human body is "the physical aspect of a person." But clearly this will not do for his purpose, since it brings the word "person" into the definition. If the philosophical skeptic does this, he cannot identify something as a human body—that is to say, as the physical aspect *of a person*—and then go on to ask whether or not it is the body *of a person*. That question is no longer open.

This difficulty may seem easily remedied. Can he not define the word "body" in physical terms without mentioning persons in his definition? This seems to be what a number of philosophers have had in mind when they used the term, though they seldom say so explicitly. For instance, C. D. Broad, after announcing at the beginning of his discussion that he will confine his remarks to "human bodies and their perceptible behaviour," neglects to explain to what he is referring when he speaks of "human bodies," but he does say "when we see anything which has the characteristic shape, size, appearance, and movements of a human body, we treat it as if it were animated by a mind like our own."[3] This suggests that he regards a human body as a physical body that is distinguishable from other physical bodies by the fact that it has a particular shape, size, and so on, and that it moves in ways that other material bodies do not. To be really serviceable, of course, a definition of the phrase "human body" would have to specify the required shape, structure, and material of composition (and possibly origin) in enough detail so that one could pick out a class of material bodies each member of which would be an acceptable candidate for the role of "body of a person." Wax dummies, robots, and even monkeys would have to be carefully ruled out by the physical description.

In addition, a further important qualification must be added. The "human bodies" of which philosophers have been speaking are *living* things, not corpses. Were they dead bodies, the question whether or not they had minds then associated with them could be answered in the negative, for a corpse, like a material object, is nonconscious, rather than merely unconscious. Indeed, in this respect a corpse is nothing but a material object.[4] But the question before us is not about the bodies of dead persons. The philosophical skeptic is concerned with living human bodies.

We must keep in mind, however, that his skepticism compels him to view these bodies in a very special light. It is supposed to be an open philosophical question whether or not they are the bodies of living human beings. But why should we accept this supposition? What we see around us are people; we see their bodies too, of course, but these are the bodies of living persons. We have not yet been told how to pick out living human bodies that *may or may not be the bodies of persons.* Unless this is explained, there is no reason to think that the concept of a living human body is not the same as the concept of the living body of a person or of the body of a living person. And if these are the same concept, the question whether or not such a body is that of a person is still not an open one.

In reply to this objection the philosophical skeptic may offer the following, more sophisticated verbal characterization of the word "body." He will explain that the kind of body he is referring to is that which will become a person's corpse when he dies. Since the individual is not supposed to be dead yet, his body is a living body, but the word "body" is intended to refer only to that "part" of the person which will be his corpse. This explanation leaves us as much in the dark as before, however, because it is not clear what it is of the living person that becomes his corpse. If we say it is the *person* himself that becomes his corpse, this is not what the skeptic means by "a body." Yet if we say that it is the living person's body that becomes his corpse, then the skeptic's defining phrase denotes the bodies of persons and, once again, about bodies in this sense the question of their association with persons is not open.

The skeptic may then try to get me to understand from my own case what is meant by the phrase "human body which may or may not be the body of a human being." Let us suppose he instructs me to imagine what would be left of myself if I had no mind, a kind of reversal of the Cartesian device, employed in the *Meditations,* which is designed to spotlight that part of a person which remains after everything physical is subtracted. Following these instructions I first suppose myself to be without conscious experiences. But this leaves an unconscious person, not a body. So something more fundamental must be removed. Yet it must not be so fundamental that only my dead body remains, because we are not taking corpses as the subjects of reference when discussing the problem of other minds. I should subtract something "in between" consciousness and life which would leave only my living human body—that is, *a* living human body. But whenever I try to take away something short of life itself, I am invariably left with a living human being.

Should the skeptical philosopher become frustrated enough in his attempts to give a verbal definition of "a body," he may try to *show* us the kind of body he means and thereby give an ostensive definition of the phrase. Since a person's body is visible and tangible, it would appear to be perfectly easy to indicate Smith's body by pointing to it and explaining, "This is what I am referring to when I say 'this body.' It is about such a 'body' that I am asking whether or not it is currently the body of a living person."

This attempted ostensive definition will not do either, however. We can simply reply that the skeptic has pointed to Smith or laid his hand upon Smith's shoulder, and this is not a successful way to introduce the required concept of a "human body." It is Smith, *a person,* that we see and feel. To be sure, Smith has a body, and we can look at that and describe it. We can note, for instance, that he has a muscular or lean or lithe body. We might even say, "There's a fine body!" But it is nevertheless the body of a person which we are admiring.[5] Therefore, we cannot see and touch Smith's body while he is alive without necessarily seeing and touching Smith himself.

It may be objected at this point that I am begging the skeptic's question about the existence of other people by insisting that he cannot point to Smith's body without pointing to the body of a person. After all, it may be said, the skeptic wants to *ask* whether what he points to is the body of a person or not, so it is unfair to reply to his attempted ostensive definition of the word "body" by saying that he has pointed in the direction of a person. That it is indeed a person he is pointing to has not yet been shown. All he is claiming so far is that it is a body having physical characteristics.

Such an objection misses the point of my reply to the skeptic. To see just why this is so, it is important to understand that when I insist that it is the body of a person to which the skeptic is referring, the skeptic has *not yet asked* his question about other minds. He has not asked it because he has not yet succeeded in introducing the concept of a body he requires, one which will leave the question about the existence of other people open and philosophically interesting. Therefore I cannot be begging his question. What I am doing is saying that I do not understand what he means by "body" if he points at people and asks whether "those bodies" are the bodies of people. When he tries to point out a "body" in the required sense, all he can do is point helplessly to living people; and his verbal definitions either presuppose that we can identify people and hence their bodies or fail to distinguish his concept from that of the body of a living person. Unless there is a concept in terms of which a meaningful question about whether or not there are other people can be stated, there is no such question to be begged.

There are ways of stipulating that one is using a phrase in a special noncommittal sense, and the possibility of doing this may seem to offer a way to introduce the skeptic's concept of a "body." But instead of employing the suspect word "body" for this purpose, it would be safer to say instead that one intends to use the word "figure" or X as a general term ranging over objects and people indiscriminately. If this were done, it would be possible to ask, "Is that X over there a person or not?" when one sees a spot moving on a distant hillside or a figure at the end of the garden. One could ask whether the X sprawled in the street is a dead body or a living person, or whether the figures in the store window are dummies or window decorators. But although one can ask such questions about the presence or absence of people in particular contexts, these are not philosophically interesting questions. We all know perfectly well how to answer them. We get field glasses or look for movement on the hillside; we take a closer look at the figure in the garden or the one in the store window; we try to find the pulse of the figure in the street. In some instances such questions may present practical difficulties, but not theoretical or philosophical ones of the kind the skeptic wants us to imagine. He wants to ask his question about people who are right in front of him and whom he can see clearly. He already knows that they are not corpses or store dummies or robots in human clothing. What he hopes to suggest is that there is a "gap" between the concept of a living body and the concept of the body of a person such that he can identify an X as a living human body and then ask whether it is also the body of a person. But there is no such "gap," for we cannot identify something as a living human body without necessarily identifying the body of some person or other.

This last statement may seem to be open to objection on the grounds that although there are *in fact* no bodies that are both indistinguishable from human bodies and at the same time not the bodies of people, there might be such. Suppose that scientists could produce something in a chemical vat that is indistinguishable from a living human being. This implies that it would have all of the *physical* characteristics required to be a "human body," ignoring for the moment its artificial origin. But now it seems we can ask whether or not it is a fit logical subject for the ascription of psychological states, a question which certainly looks like one the skeptic has been trying to ask about nonartificial "human bodies."

This is not so much a question, however, as a request for a decision concerning a type of case that we have not before encountered. It is being asked whether or not the lack of natural propagation conceptually blocks a creature's being regarded as a human being. If its behavior were sufficiently like that of a human being, we would probably decide that it could be regarded as such and that psychological states could be ascribed to it. That is to say, it would be a human being with a human body. On the other hand, if we thought that its artificial origin made it importantly different from human beings, we might decide that it could not have conscious states. In that case it would not be regarded as a human being. Nor would it be a human body either;

for if the condition of natural propagation were so important to being a person, that condition would have to be included in the description of what is to be counted as a human body. Thus it can be maintained that this case would not provide an example of a human body that turned out not to be the body of a person.

Doubts about such artificial creatures are not doubts that much interest the skeptic in any case. His hopes rest on the success of attempts to pose a philosophical question concerning the existence of other human beings. He would like to have us acknowledge the possibility, for example, that Smith might suddenly evaporate, not merely losing consciousness, but disappearing from the scene as a person, leaving only his nonconscious body before us to carry on, without any change being detectable, even in "his" behavior. This is not the same as saying that he might die and his corpse continue the discussion, for *that* change would be detectable. We are invited to imagine that everything about Smith remains the same *physically*. All that is different is that there is no longer a conscious person standing before us and talking with us. There is just Smith's living body.

The claim that there might be such a change is unintelligible. This is not simply because the change would be undetectable; the skeptic knows this and is not impressed. It is because the distinction between Smith and a nonconscious, living, human body does not make any sense. As we have seen, no such concept of a body can be introduced. Consequently a change from there being Smith to there being merely such a body makes no sense. Where a living human body is, there also is a person—necessarily. The philosopher's alleged concept of a living human body that might be without a mind, and thus fail to be the body of a person, is a confusion. Therefore, the skeptical question about other minds which is raised at the level of bodies is not an intelligible one, and we are thus absolved from any responsibility to give an answer to it.

III

In view of the difficulties we have encountered in trying to make clear to ourselves the concept of a "body" which occurs in discussions of the problem about the existence of other minds, one may well ask why philosophers have thought they were adequately stating a genuine problem in terms of that concept. One reason for this which I have mentioned already and which I will now illustrate is their failure to see any need for a careful introduction of an apparently ordinary, uncomplicated term. Broad, for instance, initiates his discussion of the problem of other minds with the announcement that he will begin "with propositions about which everyone will agree" and then goes on to observe that the "perception of a foreign body of a certain kind, which moves, alters its expression, makes noises, and so on, in certain characteristic ways, is a necessary part of the basis of our belief in the existence and activity of another mind."[6] Without giving a second thought to this concept of a "foreign body" he is led to the view that no matter how intelligently an "external body" appears to behave, it is always sensible to ask whether it has a mind or is merely an automaton.[7] But what sort of "body" is he referring to? If he means simply "that X over there," it may well make sense to ask whether it is a living human being or a mechanical man. This, however, is not the philosophically difficult question Broad was trying to ask. Yet, if he is pointing in the direction of a living person, knowing that it is not a robot or dummy or the like, then there is no question that the person has a mind in the sense of being a fit subject for the ascription of psychological states. Of course, we may not know how much mental capacity or intelligence he has, but that is a question to be asked and answered at the level of persons.

H. H. Price also poses his question about other minds in terms of the curious phrase "foreign body," and he too fails to see any need to give it special and explicit introduction. He does mention in a footnote that he means "a body other than my own," whether human or not, but this explanation is not very helpful.[8] His own body is the body of a person, namely, that of H. H. Price. But he cannot mean by "foreign body" a *person's body* other than his own body, for if the bodies he is talking about are thought of as those of people, the whole question is decided in advance. On the other hand, if he means by "foreign body" merely "physical body" in the sense of that phrase which refers to physical things or objects, we can immediately protest that the source of the sounds "The bus is coming" is no object but a person who said the words "The bus is coming." Price cannot reply to this that we are begging his question, since he has not yet shown that there is any philosophically significant possibility of its not being a person. It might have been a robot or a wax dummy, but we can see without much difficulty that it is not any of those things; and Price has not made it clear in what way it might not be a person.

Once the initial philosophical question about these "foreign bodies" is undercut, Price's further suggestion that the apparently intelligible sounds coming from those "bodies" may be "explained" by saying that they are produced by a mind loses its point. If a person makes intelligible utterances, we say he has a mind, but not by way of explaining or accounting for his ability. It is a way of saying that he has the ability to speak and act intelligently. In contrast, we may explain the "intelligent behavior" of a robot or other machine by discovering a man at the controls. But Price gets his concepts crossed when he tries to explain the intelligent behavior of a "foreign body" by concluding that there is a mind at the "controls." What we observe are people who either control themselves or lose control, people who behave intelligently or stupidly. And although people do have both minds and bodies, we cannot first identify a living human body and then decide that—because it apparently has a mind associated with it—it is the body of a person. Living human bodies are always necessarily the bodies of living human beings.[9] How we are to justify ascriptions to those human beings of particular thoughts and feelings on particular occasions is of course another matter.

The temptation to assume that the concept of a body used in stating the problem of other minds is perfectly in order, while a key factor, is not the only reason for traditional uncritical acceptance of the problem. In fact it is but one aspect of the general tendency on the part of those who write about the subject to think of it steadfastly in terms of two traditional dichotomies. These are the dichotomies of mind *versus* body and direct *versus* indirect perception or knowledge. Discussions about the existence of other minds almost invariably begin with some version of the dogma that we cannot "directly perceive" the minds of others. Then, since only the physical part of a person remains as a possible object of perception, it seems but a small step to the conclusion that all we can observe are the movements of their bodies— or, rather, the movement of "bodies."

Such reasoning is confused by its own terminology, as can be seen in a brief examination of the initial steps of the arguments in question. The phrase "directly perceive" is stock jargon in epistemology and rarely, if ever, is it used with any careful explanation of what it means in a given context. Nevertheless it has always been easy to accept un-critically the dictum that we cannot directly perceive other minds be-cause it sounds obviously true, whatever it means. Perhaps it is meant to deny that we have some special faculty, such as mental telepathy, by which we might have knowledge of other minds without overt communi-cation, or perhaps it calls our attention to the point that we cannot have the feelings of another.[10] Possibly there are other interpretations which are equally true. But what do these interpretations imply for our actual, presumably "indirect" perception of other minds? They merely imply that we do not know of the thoughts and feelings of others by mental telepathy or by having their thoughts and feelings, which is a long way from showing that we "cannot in any sense observe the exis-tence of other people"[11] or that what we really perceive are only mov-ing "bodies" which emit certain familiar sounds that are "evidence" of minds within.

The repetition of phrases which suggest that we are somehow in-volved in a problem about faculties of perception or barriers to our observation thoroughly obscures the main issue concerning justification of our beliefs. It is curious that even writers like Broad and Ayer, who explicitly state that they seek a justification of certain beliefs, speak in terms of "direct" and "indirect" perception and "extraspection,"[12] as though they were interested in what kind of perception we employ while acquiring our knowledge of other minds. The point that they are trying to bring out can be stated more appropriately in the following way. The question "How do you know?" does not make sense when asked of a person who is expressing or reporting his own sensations and thoughts, whereas in many similar cases it does make sense when asked of someone who is reporting the sensations and thoughts of another. In the latter case the informant's knowledge is "indirect" only in the sense that he obtained it through noting the verbal and physical behavior of *the person* about whom he is speaking, together with the context of that behavior. Thus, when the point behind the claim that we do not have "direct knowledge" of other minds is stated more prosaically, it becomes clear that this does not mean that we are "di-rectly aware" only of "bodies" and "noises" issuing from them or that we cannot refer to the actions and utterances of other *people* when dis-cussing the problem of other minds.

But if there is no genuine basis for a general and profound philo-sophical skepticism about the existence of other people, can one explain what it would be like for someone not to believe that there are others, to fail to believe this in a philosophically interesting way? We know someone could mistakenly believe that the world is flat, and we know roughly how this belief would be expressed and how it might be corrected. But could someone in the same way *mistakenly believe* that there were no other people, no other human beings to whom conscious states could be ascribed? If so, how would this lack of belief in other minds be expressed and how might it be corrected? Or, turning the question around, is there such a thing as a general belief in other minds in the sense that one could be of the opinion that there are other persons and have evidence in support of that opinion? Such questions seem easily answered, but, if what I have argued thus far is correct, they should receive answers contrary to traditional thought on the matter. Since this is an important result which is worth elucidating further, in concluding I will add a few remarks concerning the consequences which my arguments have for our so-called "belief" that there are other people.

I V

It is possible to imagine how a genuine solipsist—let us call him Solomon—might express or betray the fact that he was not aware of the existence of other human beings. A genuine solipsist should, of course, not be confused with a philosophical skeptic who knows that there are other people but who wonders how he knows. Solomon is someone who believes that what are in fact other human beings are merely physical objects. He behaves as though he were all alone in the world, paying no heed to people except to shoulder them out of the way or to walk around them, moving through crowds as one might move through a thicket of bushes. One would expect him to show no particular concern about hitting and bumping into people, though he would very likely be somewhat cautious about being too rough with "things" that could hit back. But he gives no sign of comprehending that they have feelings and are capable of suffering.

How he would react to the speech sounds which these "things" emitted is a bit more difficult to imagine. Broad claims that for such an individual "all statements uttered apparently by other human bodies will be in the position of statements uttered by gramophones, with the important difference that the 'records' will not have been made by bodies which are animated by minds. And there would be no reason to attach any weight to these utterances."[13] But we, of course, do understand the words spoken in a recording, since it is delayed, meaningful human discourse, and we would "attach weight" to the words if they were relevant to the situation at hand, as we do with recorded directions. So it is not easy to see why someone who heard others speak words he understood would not pay heed and reply, acknowledging their attempts to communicate with him. He might not wish to associate with them, but it is difficult to imagine how he could fail to notice that they were living creatures whose words and actions showed that they did understand what he said to them and that they understood the words which they uttered. Their behavior would show this in a way that the operation of an inanimate record player could not. On the other hand, if he regarded their talk as we regard the chattering of monkeys, perhaps treating certain sounds they made as helpful signals warning or informing him, rather like the cries of birds or the barking of dogs, it is most implausible that he would be able to speak and to understand what he himself said. Are we to suppose that he has some selective mental block that allows him to understand his own words but which prevents him from finding significant the same words uttered by others? It is difficult to imagine how this could be so.

But however the details of the case of Solomon are filled in, we would say that anyone who regarded others as mere physical mechanisms is somehow blind to the very important and obvious differences between human beings and machines or other objects. Anyone so deaf to the attempts of others to communicate with him, so opaque to their attempts to engage his attention that we would describe him as not believing that there are other people, would either be of very low-grade intelligence or mad.[14] This is not a surprising conclusion, of course, but what is significant is the fact that his stupidity or madness renders him incapable of distinguishing persons from objects, and thus he cannot be said to understand how to use the word "person," even of himself. His malady would be of interest to the psychologist, but not to a philosopher who is looking for a solipsist, since this poor man would not be in a position even to formulate the solipsistic thesis. We can grant that he might be incapable of seeing any relevant difference between what are in fact trees and machines and people and so regard people much as we do material objects. But if he cannot identify as such the people that are in evidence around him, he does not understand the concept of a person, and so it would not be possible for him to say to himself "I am the only *person* there is; all those other things are just objects." He could not even conjecture whether "these bodies are the bodies of living people," since this conjecture would not be comprehensible to him if he failed to understand the concept of a person.

Doubtless it will be objected that this incredibly stupid or mad solipsist is not the one in whom philosophers are interested. They are interested in the variety of solipsist who is able to formulate the solipsistic thesis. He understands what a person is and also knows that he is one, but he is of the opinion that none of the "things" he observes are in fact people. When the case of this solipsist is examined carefully, however, it turns out to be unintelligible. For if he understands what a person is, enough to know that he himself is one and to wonder whether there are others, he should be able to recognize them when he sees them. If he could not do this, he could not be said to understand the concept of a person. It is not enough to say that he could understand what a person is just from his own case, for this failure to recognize others as people shows that he fails to understand the concept to such a degree that we would have no confidence that he comprehended why the concept applied to him.[15]

This argument ties in with my previous remarks about the philosopher's concept of a "body" in the following way. The concept of a body which a mad solipsist would have is not the one which the philosopher requires in order to state the general problem of other minds. It is simply the concept of a body as a physical object, and this does not leave open the possibility that the body is that of a person. In order for that possibility to be left open, the solipsist would have to be in the position of being free to decide on the basis of evidence whether or not the "bodies" he observes are those of people, and this would require in turn that he understand what a person is. But if he understood what a person is, he would be able to identify other human beings as people and the question would not really be open after all.

When the point is put in this way we can see that there are really only two positions that can be taken with respect to persons. Either one believes that there are only material objects in the world and fails, through some defect of mind or training, even to have the concept of a person, or one has that concept and realizes that there are people, one of them being oneself. There is no middle position than can be intelligibly articulated. Our belief that there are other human beings is not a kind of conjecture concerning which we might be in doubt or in need of more evidence and for which we might reasonably be asked for justification.

In this respect the general problem we have been discussing is quite different from those questions about other minds which require us to justify a particular belief or statement about the thoughts and feelings of a certain individual. My belief that Smith has a headache after seeing a long film is only one of many beliefs about him for which justification could be requested and satisfactorily given. About any one of these beliefs it is possible for one to be at times mistaken without thereby manifesting a failure to understand the concepts in question. But if someone doubted there were *people* in the world, he would show, at the very least, his failure to understand the concept of a person.

NOTES

1. A. J. Ayer, "One's Knowledge of Other Minds," in *Philosophical Essays* (London, 1954), p. 192.

2. In particular I have in mind P. F. Strawson's discussion of the problem of other minds in *Individuals* (London, 1959), ch. iii.

3. Broad, *The Mind and Its Place in Nature* (New York, 1951), p. 321.

4. These remarks are meant to reflect our current attitudes toward corpses. Perhaps it is conceivable that our attitudes might change if, for example, bodies of persons who had been pronounced dead by a physician went on "behaving" and "speaking" in otherwise normal fashion. Yet, even if we continued to ascribe psychological states in such a case, it seems likely that we would also continue to ascribe them to the person whose body it is rather than to the corpse.

5. In this sentence the phrase "the body of a person" is itself somewhat ambiguous. It may refer to a person's whole physical structure or to just the trunk exclusive of head and limbs. Compare "His body was too long for the coffin" with "He had long arms and a large head set on a thick body."

6. Broad, *op. cit.*, p. 318.

7. Ibid., pp. 614–15.

8. Price, "Our Evidence for the Existence of Other Minds," *Philosophy*, XIII (1938), 430 n.

9. Strawson has argued in his critique of the idea of a "pure ego" that the concept of a person is, as he terms it, "logically primitive" (*op. cit.*, p. 102).

It is worth noting that the criticisms of the philosophical concept of a "body" given above constitute valuable support for this conclusion, approaching the question as they do from the opposite side of the Cartesian dualism.

10. See Ayer, *The Foundations of Empirical Knowledge* (London, 1951), p. 138, and *Philosophical Essays*, p. 194, for explicit statements of this latter interpretation.

11. Ayer, *Language, Truth and Logic* (New York, 1946), p. 128.

12. This is Broad's term (*op. cit.*, p. 328).

13. Broad, *op. cit.*, pp. 337–38.

14. This is not to say that certain types of madness in which a person completely ignores other people are necessarily examples of a solipsistic view about other minds. How such a person treats others is important, but we also want to know how he regards others and what reasons he gives for behaving toward them as he does. For instance, it is important to know whether he regards them as being capable of having thoughts and feelings, as opposed to his merely being totally unconcerned with their feelings and beliefs. Such information may not be easily obtained from a madman who ignores us or from a solipsist who is unaware of our existence. But if they kept diaries, we could probably have access to them, since undoubtedly they would feel no concern about leaving them lying about.

15. This argument that an individual could not recognize himself as a person unless he could recognize other persons is also given in a brief statement in Bruce Aune, "The Problem of Other Minds," *Philosophical Review*, LXX (1961), 338.

ARE PERSONS BODIES?

B. A. O. Williams

Problems of mind and body arise at two levels. On the one hand, there are general issues concerning the relations between a subject's mental states and his possession of a body, including in particular their relations to his observable behavior. On the other hand, there are questions concerning the relations between a subject's mental states and certain internal states of his organism (in particular, states of the central nervous system) which might in a developed psychophysical science be correlated with the mental states—the term "correlated" here being not intended to beg any questions.

This second range of problems, which we might call problems at the micro-level, particularly concern how such a correlation may most illuminatingly and economically be characterized; and the most notable recent contribution to this area has been the group of views often called the "identity theory" or "central state materialism." It is not, however, with this range of problems that I shall for the most part be concerned in this paper, but rather with the first range of problems, problems at the macro-level. But it is worth noticing in passing one very important area of overlap between the two ranges: if the occurrence of a mental state (e.g., a sensation) is cited as the *explanation* of a piece of observable behavior, the question arises of how such an explanation is related to an explanation in terms of physical mechanisms, and this, at the inner end, constitutes a problem at the micro-level.

Among problems at the macro-level, some of the most general may convenietly be labeled "metaphysical." They include such questions as: What sorts of things do there have to be in the world for there to be mental states? Do there have to be physical bodies (e.g., organisms)? If so, is this because the sort of thing that "has" mental states must itself be a physical thing? It is with this sort of question that the present paper will be concerned.

I start with some remarks on Mr. Strawson's well-known treatment of the subject.[1] It will be recalled that Strawson distinguishes among predicates ascribed to persons, two classes, of M–predicates and P–predicates. These are introduced, under those labels, by his saying: "The first kind of predicate consists of those which are also properly applied to material bodies to which we would not dream of applying predicates ascribing states of consciousness[2]. . . . The second kind consists of all the other predicates we apply to persons."[3] This distinction I am deliberately going to treat in a simplified form, by regarding P–predicates as those "we would not dream" of applying to material bodies, and M–predicates as those we can apply to material bodies. This is a simplification, since Strawson himself recognizes that not all P–predicates ascribe "states of consciousness";[4] but this is a point which he himself is disposed to take pretty lightly, on the grounds that all P–predicates imply the possession of consciousness on the part of that to which they are ascribed. I do not think that anything in my remarks will turn essentially on the adoption of the simplification. In terms of this distinction among predicates we ascribe to ourselves, I take it to be Strawson's view that the concept of a person is the (primitive) concept of a subject to which both these sorts of predicates can be applied.

I shall sustain the fiction for the purposes of discussion that we can roughly individuate predicates in the relevant ways—though this is in fact a fiction which conceals some major difficulties. "Running down hill" presumably does not express the same predicate when used in connection with a river and with a man; but perhaps it does when used in connection with a man and with a dog. Does "digging a hole" express the same predicate when used in connection with a man, a dog, and a mechanical excavator? Does "adding up the accounts" when used in connection with a bank clerk and a computer? Presumably if we could answer these questions, we would be well on the way with many of our problems; but, for the present discussion, I shall not go on about it.

If it is Strawson's view that the concept of a person is that of a subject to which both M– and P–predicates can be ascribed, the first difficulty is whether this means that a person is the sort of thing to which any P–predicate can be ascribed, or the sort of thing to which some P–predicate can be ascribed. If the latter, then the concept is not that of a person, but of (something like) an animal. If the former, then it may perhaps be the concept of a person; but even this is not clear, because of the unclarity attached to such expressions as "can be ascribed," "ascribable," etc. We might have some creatures to which the whole range of P–predicates was *ascribable*—in whatever sense it is in which Strawson thinks that to material bodies they are not ascribable—but of which they were not all true; and those that were not true were those that imparted precisely the characteristic of *being a person*.

But suppose that we say that persons are just picked out as those to which (as well as M–predicates) *any* P–predicate is ascribable. Then material bodies will be those things to which no P–predicate is ascribable. And we shall have to admit a further class of things to which both M–predicates and some P–predicates are ascribable, namely other animals. And this point seems to me to show a difficulty in Strawson's approach which is not merely minor. Strawson's view was, it seems, that the concept of a person was unique in admitting the joint ascription to things that fall under it of the two sorts of predicate, and this seems important to his thesis in terms of the explications he gives of the possibility of such joint ascription, which connect that possibility intimately with the possibilty of self-ascription. There must, it now seems, to be something wrong with this; and if the concept of a person is, with regard to the ascription of the two sorts of predicates, primitive, then it looks as though there will have to be other such primitive concepts, or at least one such.

I suspect that this difficulty is one aspect of a general and odd feature of Strawson's account, namely the noticeably Cartesian materials out of which it is constructed. Neither Strawson nor Descartes shows much disposition to relate *persons* to any classification of living things; but it can scarcely be an insignificant fact that our paradigm (to put it mildly) of a person is a human being, and human beings form a subclass of living things. The neglect of the continuity of our ascriptions of predicates to human beings and to other animals is bound to produce an artificial (and highly Cartesian) dichotomy between persons and everything else.

I pass to a second difficulty which, if it is real, is certainly more fundamental than this. It turns on what is meant by saying that (in the simplified version of the thesis) P–predicates are predicates which "we would not dream of applying to material bodies." I shall take this, in the first instance, to mean something which could also be expressed by saying that it would *make no sense* to apply such predicates to material bodies: that something on these lines is what Strawson actually means seems to me to receive some support from a passage in which he speaks of ". . . an enormous class of predicates (sc. P–predicates) such that the applicability of those predicates or their negations defines a major logical type or category of individuals:"[5] but I shall not pursue the exegetical issue.

There is certainly an unclarity in saying that it does not make sense to ascribe a certain predicate to a certain type of thing. Category doctrines, notoriously, are often expressed in such terms: thus it may be said that it does not make sense to assert or deny greenness of a prime number. But there is something unsatisfactory about such formulations: for they express a doctrine which should surely be about sense, in terms of reference. "That is green" does not itself become a senseless form of words if someone tried to refer to a prime number in uttering the sentence; nor does "the thing he's talking about is green" if it turns out that the thing he is talking about is a prime number. What surely are categorially senseless, if anything is categorially senseless, are sentences such as "the prime number 7 is green." The point is emphasized by the fact that category-senselessness can equally be diagnosed, if at all, in non-referential statements, e.g., "Any number which is prime is green." If these considerations are right, then it seems that what are categorially senseless (if anything) are conjunctions of predicates; and what we should more accurately say is not that "green" cannot sensibly be ascribed to a prime number, but that "green and a prime number" cannot be ascribed to anything, because it does not make sense.

The thesis which, on the present interpretation, Strawson holds is that P–predicates cannot be sensibly ascribed to material bodies. If what I just said is right, then this must admit of a more accurate paraphrase to the effect that there is some class of predicates—material body predicates—such that the conjunction of them and any P–predicate does not make sense and cannot be ascribed to anything. But at least among such predicates must be the M–predicates; and indeed this class might be thought to be coextensive with the class of M–predicates, for while we have supposedly been told something about predicates which can be sensibly ascribed to persons but not to material bodies, we have been told nothing about any predicates which can be sensibly ascribed to material bodies and not to persons—perhaps any predicate ascribable to a material body can be sensibly, if patently falsely, ascribed to a person. But on this second showing, and perhaps even on the first, it begins to look as though P–predicates and M–predicates cannot be sensibly conjoined, and hence cannot be jointly ascribed to anything. So if persons are precisely things which admit of such joint ascription, there cannot be any persons.

To jump to that conclusion from these premises would of course be unjustified. What the premises entail is that there are various predicates or conjunctive sets of predicates, instantiation of which by a thing constitutes that thing a material body; and that the conjunction of any such set with a P–predicate is senseless. The premises do not entail, what the direct inference of the unpalatable conclusion requires, that the conjunction of a P–predicate with any member, or any proper subset, of such sets would be senseless.

Though we do not get to the unpalatable conclusion so directly, we shall see in a minute that we do get to it eventually. First, however, we must notice that there is a total obscurity about how these conjunctive sets of material-body predicates are in general to be characterized. We can in fact produce a dummy to stand in place of each such set: the predicate "being a material body." But if we try to get the hang of them by taking this seriously, we get nowhere. For what is, in the required sense, a material body? It certainly cannot be merely anything to which M–predicates are ascribable: for then the unpalatable conclusion does follow, instantly. It will have, rather, to be a *merely* material body; and that is, it would seem, just something to which M–predicates are ascribable and P–predicates are not, which gets us nowhere at all. So there seems to be no short way (or at least very short way) of characterizing what it is, the conjunctive ascription of which with P–predicates is senseless.

But, it may be said, why look for such a general characterization? We can provide examples enough of the sorts of predicates and conjunctions of predicates which fall into the "material body" list, such as "being a rock," perhaps, or "being a table," or "being made entirely of sodium," or "being many light-years across and at a surface temperature of 6,000°K." But now we have to recall that the requirements of the thesis with the present interpretation are that the conjunctions of these various items and P–predicates are supposed to be *senseless*. It is not the claim of the thesis that these predicates *empirically* exclude P–predicates—obviously enough. Nor is it the claim that they form logically inconsistent, contradictory conjunctions when conjoined with P–predicates: that would be an interesting line to take, but it is different from, and indeed incompatible with, the "category-senselessness" approach: in order to form a *contradictory* conjunction, predicates must surely belong to the same category (cf. the difference between "all prime numbers are green" and "all prime numbers are divisible without remainder by two"). But we are surely going to be hard put to it to find a doctrine of sense by which, of the following pairs of predicates, for example, the first in each case will make a senseless conjunction with P–predicates, while the second makes a sensible conjunction: being made of the same stuff as the Apollo Belvedere, having the same weight as the Apollo Belvedere; being made entirely of sodium, being made of carbon, oxygen, etc.; frequently to be found in slate, frequently to be found in slate quarries; being a waxwork, looking like a waxwork; being a sponge, being a primate. Perhaps the first members of these pairs are not to be allocated to the (merely) material body list; if not, it is unclear why, or what is.

Apart from these considerations, a more particular argument can be advanced which really does seem to lead back to the original unpalatable conclusion. Let there be an object which has just the properties of a human body; which is, if you like, a human body, save that it is not the body of a person. No P–predicates go with it. The possibility of this, it seems to me, cannot be excluded on the thesis under discussion; for it would be excluded, surely, only if the instantiation of all these properties together entailed the instantiation of P–predicates, and this (on the thesis) seems to be excluded. Now this object is surely a material body. But P–predicates cannot be sensibly ascribed to any material body. This means that P–predicates cannot be sensibly conjoined with any set of predicates which sufficiently specify a thing which is a material body. But since the body just mentioned is a material body, the predicates which specify it must be such a set. Hence they cannot be sensibly conjoined with P–predicates. Hence no human being, at least, is a person, since this conjunction is exactly what would be true of him if he were. The argument, moreover, could be repeated with regard to any other body which was supposedly the body of a person. Hence indeed there are no persons.

These difficulties seem to me to make hopeless the version of Strawson's position which represents it as a thesis about sense. Perhaps, however, the phrase "which we would not dream of applying to material bodies" does not mean "which it would make no sense to apply to material bodies." Perhaps it just means that there are certain predicates which we ascribe to ourselves which we would never for a moment think could be truly ascribed to material bodies: such ascriptions would just, as we all know, be false. If this is what is meant, no category style of difference would have been suggested, and the previous objections would not apply. There is, however, a different objection which will apply. For if it is just false of certain material bodies that psychological predicates apply to them, what obstacle can there be to saying that it is just true of others (e.g., ourselves) that such predicates do apply to them? If we do say this, the concept of a person will be in no way primitive. For now we can say, quite simply, that while many material bodies do not, and no doubt cannot, think (etc.), others (very complex ones) can, and a person is such a body. We shall then have reached the third corner of a triangle with Descartes and with Strawson: saying neither that a person is a mind who has a body, nor yet that he is an unanalyzable subject of mind-predicates and body-predicates; but that he is a material body which thinks (etc.).

Why should we not say that persons form a class of material bodies? Certainly not merely on the ground that they have psychological attributes, as we have seen: that seems to rest either on the view that no material bodies have psychological attributes, which at best begs the question, or on the view that merely material bodies do not have psychological attributes, which is vacuously true.

For the rest of this paper, I shall consider four leading objections to the view that persons are material bodies, and say something against them; what I say will not in every case be very full, but will, I hope, be discouraging, if no more, to the objections—though in the case of the last objection, a certain qualification to the view is perhaps required.

Objection 1: We can conceive of disembodied persons. I shall not here attempt to refute this position, and shall not even consider it in full generality with respect to *non*-bodied persons, but consider only a more restricted idea, of strictly *dis*embodied persons, i.e., of persons formerly embodied who have become disembodied. Even this I shall not argue against categorically, but will confine myself to trying to show merely this, that if we admit the possibility of persons previously embodied becoming disembodied, then we are committed to giving a Cartesian or dualistic account of those persons in their embodied state. Anyone who thinks the Cartesian account mistaken will, if I am right, have reason to give up an idea of a transition to a disembodied state; and since anyone who believes in a permanently non-bodied person is presumably something like a Cartesian anyway, only Cartesians or near-Cartesians will be left.

Let us consider, if we can, the state of a person previously embodied but now disembodied. Somebody raises such questions as "what weight has he?" "what height has he?"; having regard to his disembodied state, it seems that there are two rather different things that might be said about such questions, *(a)* that they have no answer, *(b)* that they have an answer, and the answers are o lbs., o ins., etc. I shall take up these two lines in turn.

a) The force of this seems to be that a person is a thing which, though it can, does not have to exemplify determinates under physical determinables. But this has many difficulties. For surely the understanding of what a given sort of thing is closely involves an understanding of under what determinables a thing of that sort exemplifies determinates. Connected with this, we can recall an important remark of Leibniz: that the real is the fully determinate. If we are given a specification of a thing of a certain sort, and are told that it exemplifies no determinates under determinables associated with things of that sort, we can standardly conclude that it is not the specification of any real thing of that sort, but, e.g., of a fictional thing: part of what it is for Lady Macbeth to be a fictional woman is that there are many questions to which, with regard to any real woman, there must be answers (though we may not know what they are), but which have no answers in the case of Lady Macbeth.

Considerations on these admittedly sketchy lines may well give us reason to say that it is impossible for one and the same thing to have a given collection of determinables apply to it at one time and not at another. If so, we shall say that the possibility of disembodiment would show, not just that a person was a sort of thing that *did not necessarily* exemplify physical determinables, but that it was a sort of thing that *necessarily did not* exemplify such determinables. Then even embodied persons would not have physical attributes, but would be nonphysical things associated with a body, i.e., a Cartesian account would apply.

This is admittedly only the sketch of an answer to *(a)*, but I think that very serious difficulties will be found for *(a)* on these lines. Admittedly, there are some determinables which a given sort of thing can, as it were, lose: thus a material body might become totally colorless (at the extreme, by becoming invisible). This possibility may be taken to show that *having a color* is not essential to being a physical body. The case of a person's losing all his physical attributes would seem in any case graver than that, and more significant for one's understanding of what sort of thing a person was; but in any case, it would certainly show that having physical attributes was not essential to being a person. Now this would not lead directly, of course, to what I have called the Cartesian conclusion; for the fact that persons did not essentially have physical attributes would not (contrary to an inference possibly conducted by Locke with regard to primary and secondary qualities) show in itself that they never had them at all. But this is not all that we have to work from: for it seems true that all the current arguments against the Cartesian position (e.g., Strawson's) do involve saying that it is essential that persons have physical attributes. I am not sure that any coherent account can be given of a sort of thing to which it is essential that it display at some time determinates under a wide range of determinables, but not essential that it do this at all times; yet this is required by line *(a)*.

b) cuts cleanly through that sort of difficulty, at least; but it succumbs to a more clearly definable difficulty. Here we must remember the disembodied person's *body*, which evidently may still exist (embalmed, buried, or whatever). This will display physical attributes like any other material body; let us take the particular case of its weight and suppose its weight $= k$ (which of course $\neq$ o). Now at some earlier time t before disembodiment, something which for the moment we might call this body displayed weight; let us suppose that weight $= m$ ($m \neq$ o, and, we may plausibly suppose, $\neq k$). So we have at t something which weighs m; while at t' (after disembodiment) we have a person who weighs o and a body which weighs k. Now something has, between t and t' changed from weighing m to weighing k; and that thing would seem to be the body.

But it looks also as though there were something that had changed between t and t' from weighing m to weighing o; suppose that there is such a thing. If there is, it cannot be the same thing as the thing we considered last, i.e., the body: for the two predicates ". . . changes just between t and t' from weighing m to weighing o" and "changes just between t and t' from weighing m to weighing k $(k \neq$ o)" are incompatible with one another. So this thing, if it exists, must be a different thing: it would seem to be, in fact, the person (it is, after all, the person who ends up at t' weighing o). So now we have two things, one of which in the given time has changed from weighing m to weighing k, the other from weighing m to weighing o.

This entails that there are two different things, each of which at t weighed m. So what are we to say about the weight at t of something which consists just of those two things? It might seem that such a thing would have to weigh $2m$: in which case, a person together with his body must weigh twice as much as his body weighs, which is absurd. Perhaps there is another possibility. Consider, for instance, a car and the materials of which it is made. These are not identical things since the materials, independently identified, can have a different life-story from that of the car. The concept of weight can be applied to each; yet the car and the total of materials of which it consists at a given time do not of course weigh more than the car weighs. So the weight-doubling paradox can be avoided by saying that a person consists of, is made of, his body. But one who believes in disembodiment surely cannot say *that;* for how can a thing which consists at a given time of certain materials come to consist of nothing at all, save by ceasing to exist? If there are any merits to the quasi-Aristotelian model of *consisting of* for the relations of persons and bodies (and I am doubtful of them), it certainly cannot be consistently combined with the possibility of disembodiment.

The assumption that there were two things which had undergone different changes of weight led to two possible conclusions about the embodied person and his weight, neither of them acceptable. So the only thing left is to deny that the two different changes have occured. But certainly the body has undergone the change specified (from weighing m to weighing k). Hence the only way out is to say that the person, who afterwards weighs o, always did weigh o: i.e., that it has always been a weightless (and by variants of the same argument, extensionless etc.) item associated with a body. That is to say, the Cartesian account of embodied persons follows, on line (b) from the possibility of disembodiment.

Objection 2: "Jones" (taken as referring to a person) and "Jones's body" are not interchangeable SALVA VERITATE.[6] Thus, it might be speciously argued, "Jones feels cold" and "Jones's body feels cold" do not have the same truth-conditions. But this is because "feels cold" has two different senses, one of which is naturally suggested by the choice of the one referential expression, the other by the other; if we take the same sense (imagining, for instance, the doctor laying his hand on Jones's body and saying "Jones feels cold") they do have the same truth-conditions. There are of course many and strong conventions which govern the selection of the expressions "Jones" and "Jones's body"; but what has to be demonstrated is that the grotesqueness of many sentences which result from breaching these conventions suffices to show that Jones and Jones's body are not the same thing; and I doubt whether this can be demonstrated. A rather simple argument to the conclusion that they are not the same thing might be attempted on the point that at least "Jones's body" cannot be substituted for "Jones" *in the context "Jones's body."* But this by itself is obviously a facile objection: an exactly parallel argument could be used to show that "Marks and Spencer's" does not refer to the same thing as "the firm of Marks and Spencer's" or "Marks and Spencer's shop."

Again, Aristotelian enthusiasts will point out that, leaving aside immortality, when Jones (or his body) dies, Jones ceases to exist ("he is no more"), while his body does not. There may be something here: but it surely cannot be pressed too hard. For, taken strictly, it should lead to the conclusion that "living person" is a pleonasm and "dead person" a contradiction; nor should it be possible to see a person dead, since when I see what is usually called that, I see something that exists. And if it is said that when I see a dead person I see the dead but existent body which was the body of a sometime person, this rewriting seems merely designed to preserve the thesis from the simpler alternative that in seeing a dead body I see a dead person because that is what it is.

Behind the conventions I have already referred to, there are deep and important concerns reflected in the ways we talk about persons and their bodies. To take one of thousands, it is certainly not exactly the same thing to love a person and to love his or her body. But this does not show that the many and various things which that distinction says may not be said in ways which make it plainer that it does not entail that persons and bodies are two different things. The thesis is, after all, that bodies are the subjects of psychological attributes;

particularly in ascribing such attributes, or in connections which involve them, we do not, and no doubt never will, use the expression "*X*'s
body." But a demonstration is lacking that that comprehensible fact
shows the thesis to be false.

*Objection 3: If persons are material bodies, then all properties of
persons are material properties; but this is false.* This attacks head-on
the issue of bodies having psychological attributes; but it attacks it so
head-on as to be suspect of begging the question. We can ask, what are
"material properties"? If they are just whatever properties material
bodies have, then it painlessly follows from the thesis that psychological
properties are included among material ones. If it is just defined to
exclude psychological predicates, it patently begs the question. What
the objection needs is a plausible independent characterization of material properties which excludes peculiar, e.g., psychological, properties of
persons. But what is this going to be? Descartes had a clear answer
to this question: a material property will be a mode or determination
of the attributes fundamental to physical theory (in his view, extension).
But this condition, while clear, is absurdly too strong if we are also
to say that quite ordinary material bodies have only material properties;
it excludes, for instance, "observed by the physicists" as a property of
material bodies (a point I owe to Sidney Morgenbesser).

There are much deeper issues in this area which involve the relations between psychological states and the physical states which we
must suppose to underlie them—the problems at the micro-level which
I mentioned at the beginning. I cannot discuss these here; but there
is just one point that I should like very briefly to raise, since it has a
close relation to the thesis of this paper. Some psychological concepts
are clearly causal concepts, in the sense that to apply such a concept
to a person implies a claim about the causation of some mental state
or disposition of his, whether this be by features of his environment or
by others of his mental states, dispositions, or experiences. Perception
is one such concept; memory is another; and I think it is plausible to
suppose that the same is true of knowledge in general. Let us take
memory, a case which can scarcely be disputed. If it is agreed that it
is a necessary condition on *A*'s remembering an event *E* that he should
have present knowledge of *E* which is caused by earlier experience of *E*,
the question arises of how we can conceive of such causation's acting.

Armstrong, in his recent book,[7] has rightly said that it is a philosophical proposition that memory involves such causal relations; but

has said further that it will be a contingent fact (one of several contingencies which must obtain if Central State Materialism is actually to be true, and not merely a conceptual possibility) that these causal relations obtain at a physical level, and not in an immaterial substance. This seems to me a rather odd position to take. It is certainly a philosophical question whether there could be an immaterial substance, and another, whether, if there could, we can form any coherent idea of causal relations obtaining in it. If the answers to both these questions were positive, then what Armstrong regards as a contingency would be a contingency. But it seems to me very far from clear that the answers to these questions could be positive; and, in particular, far from clear that the idea of causal relations obtaining in an immaterial substance could be anything but utterly mysterious. If this idea were incurably confused, then it would at least not be a contingency that the causal relations involved in memory were not realized in an immaterial substance; and it might well be wondered whether there were any coherent alternative in fact to the relations' being realized in states of the person's body. If there were not, then of course there would be no contingency left at this point of the materialist program.

If we did think that there was no alternative to the causal relations running through the body, then there would be a further argument for the view that persons are bodies. It does not immediately follow: it might be said that the most that could follow was that persons had to have bodies. But support would surely be lent to the stronger view by the consideration that the very application of central psychological concepts involves something which, when properly understood, is seen to make an indeterminate reference to internal states of the body.

There may be an objection, of a familiar kind, to the idea that an everyday concept such as memory could possibly involve, even indirectly, such a reference to internal physical states. For, it may be said, people have used a concept of memory for centuries, and people use it now, with no conception of internal physical causation in this regard; and often, indeed, in conjunction with views which are inconsistent with such a requirement. This is not an impressive argument. People successfully use, and there is much point in their using, a concept which implies causal relations between a person's states at different times: the manifest signs of such causation guide their use of the concept, and form the basis of such useful distinctions as those between recalling, being reminded, and learning again. But their successful use of such notions does not mean they need have reflected, or reflected effectively, on how the causation might be conceived as acting; and they can have beliefs (and obviously do have beliefs) which depend on their not having reflected effectively on this point. Thus the argument seems to me a poor one; but it may be considerations on the lines of the argument which have led some materialists to overestimate, at this point at least, the amount of contingency in materialism.

Objection 4: The identity of persons is not the same as the identity of bodies. This is the last objection I shall consider, and also, I think, the most forceful one. If persons are a class of bodies, then "same person" must imply "same body," just as, whales being a species of mammal, "same whale" implies "same mammal," and soldiers being a class of men, "same soldier" implies "same man." But to this requirement that bodily identity be a necessary condition of personal identity, there seems to be at least one persuasive counter-example, namely Shoemaker's example of two men whose brains are taken out and replaced in one another's bodies, with (it is supposed) consequent transfer of character- and memory-traits. If judgments of personal identity in such a case went the way of the character- and memory-traits, as it seems they reasonably might, we would have here a divergence from bodily identity; since clearly it would be absurd to suggest that what governs the identity of the *body* is the identity of the brain, i.e., that the body which now contains the brain of Smith must be the same body as the body which earlier contained the brain of Smith—it quite evidently is not.

I am not altogether happy about Shoemaker's case as a clear case of "changing bodies"; for one thing, I remain unclear about the relation between giving that description of the case, and what is to be said about the expectations of the original persons with regard to their own futures. If this were a clear case of changing bodies, then it should be equally clear that Smith should, before the experiment, rationally expect to be happening to *him* subsequently those things which he can expect to happen to what is now Robinson's body, and not those things which he can expect to be happening to what is now his body; but it is far from clear to me that that is what Smith should rationally expect.

However, let us waive that sort of difficulty. The case as it stands has the advantage over many putative counter-examples against the necessity of bodily identity, that it avoids the *reduplication problem:* that is to say, the principle of personal identity which can be elicited from it is not such as to allow of two contemporaneous persons, not identical with each other, each of which precisely satisfies the principle. For it cannot be the case that there be two bodies, each of which contains at the same time precisely Smith's brain. Of course, as Wiggins has discussed in his book,[8] Smith's brain might be split, and it is imaginable that exactly the same character- and memory-traits should go with the implanting of each half, as go with the implanting of the whole. This is fundamentally no different from the possibility attached to a criterion based on the identity of the whole body, that the whole body should, amoeba-like, split: this is a logical possibility to which all material bodies are heir. This possibility does not show, however, that criteria based on the continuity of material things (whether whole bodies or whole brains) are in absolutely no different case with regard to the reduplication problem than are other criteria not so based. For the reduplication problem arises if a supposed criterion of identity allows there to be two distinct items, B and C, each of which satisfies the criterion in just the way that it would if the other did not exist. But this is not so with bodily continuity; what is true of B when it is in the ordinary way continuous with A is just not the same as what is true of it when, together with C, it has been produced from A by fission.

Someone may suggest that we can reproduce this feature with purely "mental" criteria as well. For let R be the relation of "having memory- and character-resemblance to" (suitably strongly interpreted). "Bearing R to A" cannot by itself provide the criterion of identity with A, since it is liable to the reduplication problem. But "uniquely bearing R to A" can; since if B uniquely bears R to A, then something is true of it which is just not true of it if C bears R to A as well. But this dodge, while it establishes a surface similarity between the two cases, does not eliminate a deeper difference. For there is a fairly clear sense in which what is true of B when it uniquely bears R to A is just the same as what is true of it when it non-uniquely bears R to A; the "uniquely," representing as it does merely the conjunction of a negative existential statement to the original statement about B, makes in this sense no real difference to B. Whereas the difference between being straightforwardly continuous with A, and being a fission-product of A, is a genuine difference in the history of B. Being so, it is also an unalterable feature of B, that B came about in the one way or the other. Whereas, if "uniquely bearing R to A" were a criterion of identity, it looks as though one could *bring it about* that B, not previously identical with A, became identical with A—just by suppressing the rival candidate C: and this seems to show clearly the inadequacy of such a criterion.[9]

The avoidance of the reduplication problem is, then, one feature of the Shoemaker case as it stands. If we accept that case, then the principle of identity underlying it should be represented in such a way as to embody the feature that avoids the reduplication problem: very roughly put, it will come out as something like "A and B are the same person if and only if B displays the same memory- and character-traits as A, and does so because the body of B contains the same brain as the body of A."[10] On this principle, persons will not be bodies, since the identity of persons will diverge from the identity of bodies. Correspondingly, the ascription of properties to persons will not be the ascription of properties to bodies: not even the *bodily* properties which are ascribed to persons will be ascribed to bodies. For if the Shoemaker case is possible, it will be possible truly to say of a certain person that he used to have red hair and weigh 200 lbs., but that he now has black hair and weighs 150 lbs.; and it is not true of any body that it used to have the one set of properties and now has the other. Accepting the Shoemaker case will at any rate leave us with a job still to do, namely to make clear how the ascription of bodily properties to persons is not the ascription of anything to bodies, a problem which, in criticizing the (admittedly very strong) version of such a divergence advanced by Strawson, we found to have its difficulties.

I shall not pursue that further here; but will turn lastly to a class of cases which constitute a very natural extension of the Shoemaker case, but, unlike that case, do admit the reduplication problem. These will arise if we consider, not the physical transfer of brains, but the transfer of information between brains. Thus we can imagine the removal of the information from a brain into some storage device (the device, that is, is put into a state information-theoretically equivalent to the total state of the brain), and is then put back into the same or another brain. (Such a process may, perhaps, be forever impossible, but it does not seem to present any purely logical or conceptual difficulty.) One thing at least seems clear about the consequences of this; we shall get this out of the way first. If this were done to one man, information being removed from his brain (for purposes of brain-repair, for instance) and then put back—then, supposing that he recovered all the dispositions, with regard to memory, that he had had before, we should not dream of saying that he did not, at the later stage, really remember. The passage of the information *via* the device would not be counted as the kind of causal route to his later knowledge which is incompatible with that knowledge's being memory. As things are, the sorts of causal route that go outside the body do not count for memory: if a man learns anew of his past experiences by reading what he earlier wrote about them in his diary, then precisely he does not remember his earlier experiences (there is of course the intermediate case of *being reminded*). But the imagined passage of the information *via* the device is obviously not a case which would fall under this ban: the replacement of the information is not, as such, "learning again." So at least we can be clear that passage of information *via* the device is not in itself incompatible with later knowledge's being memory.

It seems also pretty clear that under these circumstances a person could be counted the same if this were done to him, and in the process he were given a new brain (the repairs, let us say, actually required a new part). This shows that the crude principle of identity extracted from the Shoemaker case must indeed be too crude; here we have personal identity without the same brain, though of course we have identity of the rest of the body to hold onto. But now it looks as though the information could be put back, not merely into a new brain, but into a new brain in a new body—"new," that is to say, relative to the body the person originally had, whether it was or was not newly manufactured. And here we have a process which is open to the reduplication problem: for we could of course print off more than one person in accordance with these conditions.

Now I think we *can* give a sense to the statement that all the resultant persons are the same person as the original prototype and indeed—consonant with the transitivity of identity—the same person as each other. This will be in a *type* sense of "same person." If the prototype person was Smith, all the resultants will be, significantly, *Smiths;* and "person," like other type-token words, will have a plural differently applicable under two different principles of counting—a room containing two Smiths and three Robinsons will contain, in the one sense, five, in the other, two, persons.

Under these arrangements, would persons be bodies? A type-person would be something (very roughly) like a class of bodies; and to be confronted with the same type-person would be to be confronted with either the same body of the same type or with different bodies of the same type. However, we have to notice that the question of what set of bodies a type-person would be equivalent to, is one that might have to be made relative to time; both because fresh token-persons might be later printed off, and because (presumably) a given particular body might be changed from exemplifying one type to exemplifying another. However—though I think this needs further investigation—I do not think that this would force on us the conclusion that *token*-persons were not bodies, since remarks about personal identity which were not equivalent to remarks about bodily identity could be adequately represented in terms of bodies belonging to the same or different person-types.

There are many intriguing consequences of this situation. One very important feature of the situation is this. Since we are not supposing that the token-persons, once printed off from the same prototype, have intercommunicating experiences (and it might be very far from clear what it would be to suppose this), they will be divergently affected by different experiences, and will tend to get increasingly dissimilar. Looked at as copies of the prototype, they will become copies which are increasingly blurred or written-over; looked at in their own right, they will become increasingly individual personalities. This might be welcomed. For someone who loved one of these token-persons might well love her not because she was a Mary Smith, but despite the fact that she was a Mary Smith (a weak version of which arises even now with regard to members of families who share very pronounced characteristics). The more they diverged, the more secure hold the lover might feel he had on what particularly he loved.

If someone loved a token-person *just* as a Mary Smith, then it might well be unclear that the token-person was really what he loved. What he loves is *Mary Smith*, and that is to love the type-person. We can see dimly what this would be like. It would be like loving a work of art in some reproducible medium. One might start comparing, as it were, performances of the type; and wanting to be near the person one loved would be like wanting very much to hear some performance, even an indifferent one, of *Figaro*—just as one will go to the scratch provincial performance of *Figaro* rather than hear no *Figaro* at all, so one would see the very run-down Mary Smith who was in the locality, rather than see no Mary Smith at all.

Much of what we call loving a person would begin to crack under this, and reflection on it may encourage us not to undervalue the deeply body-based situation we actually have. While in the present situation of things to love a person is not exactly the same as to love a body, perhaps to say that they are basically the same is more grotesquely misleading than it is a deep metaphysical error; and if it does not sound very high-minded, the alternatives that so briskly grow out of suspending the present situation do not sound too spiritual, either.

NOTES

1. Although Professor Williams' essay takes its point of departure from P. F. Strawson's "Persons," I did not include the latter in this anthology since it is available, although somewhat reworked, in numerous places aside from its appearance in Strawson's *Individuals: An Essay in Descriptive Metaphysics*. The essay "Persons" is reprinted in the following collections: (1) *Minnesota Studies in the Philosophy of Science*, II: *Concepts, Theories, and the Mind-Body Problem*, eds., Herbert Feigl, M. Scriven, and G. Maxwell (Minneapolis: University of Minnesota Press, 1958), 330–53; (2) *The Philosophy of Mind*, ed., V. C. Chappell (New Jersey: Prentice-Hall, 1962), pp. 127–46; (3) *Essays in Philosophical Psychology*, ed., Donald F. Gustafson (New York: Doubleday & Co., 1964), pp. 377–403; (4) *Wittgenstein and the Problem of Other Minds*, ed., Harold Morick (New York: McGraw-Hill Book Co., 1967), pp. 127–53; (5) *An Introduction to Philosophical Inquiry*, ed., Joseph Margolis (New York: Alfred A. Knopf, 1968), pp. 374–91.—Ed.

2. This sentence is grammatically ambiguous. I have taken the expression "material bodies to which we would not dream of applying predicates ascribing states of consciousness" as meaning "material bodies, namely those things to which we would not dream of applying etc."; and taking it in this way is indeed central to my argument. It could, however, mean "those among material bodies to which we would not dream of applying etc."; that is to say, as implying that persons were themselves included among material bodies. This latter interpretation seems scarcely consistent with other features, and the general emphasis, of Strawson's theory; it would make it, in fact, little different from the view I advance. But if this is what he actually meant, then my criticisms should be read as attaching not to Strawson but to a prevalent interpretation of Strawson.

3. *Individuals: An Essay in Descriptive Metaphysics* (London: Methuen & Co. Ltd., 1959), p. 104.

4. Ibid., p. 105.

5. Ibid., p. 99, note.

6. Ie., preserving the truth-value (of the sentence in which the term "Jones" occurs).—Ed.

7. David M. Armstrong, *A Materialist Theory of the Mind* (London: Routledge & Kegan Paul, 1968).

8. David Wiggins, *Identity and Spatio-Temporal Continuity* (Oxford, Blackwell, 1967, p. 52 *seq.*

9. At least this will be so on a tensed interpretation of the negative existential statement implied by "uniquely." It would not be so on an untensed (or an omni-temporal) interpretation; but I think that further difficulties would be found with such an interpretation.

10. A sophisticated version of such a criterion is suggested by Wiggins, *op. cit*, p. 55.

PART III

TOWARD

A PHILOSOPHICAL

ANTHROPOLOGY

A. Philosophy
of Embodiment

LIVED BODY, ENVIRONMENT,
AND EGO

Max Scheler

THE LIVED BODY AND ENVIRONMENT

We have already touched upon the concepts of the *lived body [Leib]* and environment *[Umwelt]* in the analysis of deeds. We sharply distinguished these concepts from the ego and external world and the

The following pages have been translated by Manfred S. Frings from the fifth edition of Max Scheler's *Der Formalismus in der Ethik und die materiale Wertethik* (Bern and Munich: Francke Verlag, 1966), Part II, Chapter VI, sections A, e, and f). Permission to reprint the English translation has been granted by Northwestern University Press through the office of John B. Putnam. Thanks to the combined efforts of Manfred Frings, Francke Verlag, and Northwestern University Press, these sections of Scheler's monumental work were made available for inclusion in this collection. The entire translation of *Der Formalismus* will be published by Northwestern University Press.

TRANSLATOR'S NOTE: The following excerpt is a translation of sections A, e, and f, of Chapter VI of the Second Part of Max Scheler's *Der Formalismus* person and world.* We are now concerned with an explanation of the relation of their corresponding data of givenness to those of the person and world—without claiming to furnish an exhaustive explanation of these data as such.

Firstly, there cannot be any doubt that the *lived body does not* belong to the *sphere of the person and the sphere of acts*. It belongs to the *objective sphere* of any "consciousness of something" and its kind and ways of being. The lived body's phenomenal mode of givenness with its foundations is essentially different from that of the *ego*, its states, and experiences.

In order to obtain a correct cognition of these states of affairs let us begin critically to look into some main types of prevailing opinions in this matter so that we can then pursue a positive investigation of the facts involved.

It is our assertion that *"lived bodiliness"* [*Leiblichkeit*] represents a special non-formal datum of an essential givenness (for pure phenomenological intuition) which, in any factual perception of a lived body, functions as a form of perception (we can also say as a category in the sense of the aforementioned precise characteristic of anything categorical).[1] This implies that its *givenness* is neither reducible to a form

---

in der Ethik und die materiale Wertethik. The manuscripts of these sections were completed by 1913 and first published in 1916. Scheler makes a phenomenological distinction between the *lived body* [*Leib*] and a *thing-body* [*Körper*]. This distinction, important for the entire phenomenological movement, can be traced back to his essay "Die Idole der Selbsterkenntnis," 1911.

The following translated excerpt requires, as do all Scheler's works, patient reading. In this selection Scheler analyzes the respective views of Ernst Mach and Avenarius concerning the body and environment and investigates the leveled relationship between the lived body and the ego. This relationship forms a part of Scheler's phenomenology of the person and of value-being which he discusses in detail prior to these translated sections. Although the following translation can be fully evaluated only if it is seen within the whole context of Max Scheler's *Der Formalismus*, whose fifth edition (1966) consists of 659 pages, it is of particular value and interest to us as an example of Scheler's foresight regarding phenomenological investigation at the beginning of this century, a number of his views differing from those of Husserl.

The asterisks in the text refer to the cross-references of pages 397 to 410 of the fifth edition of *Der Formalismus*, published by the Francke Verlag, Bern and Munich. They may be found on page 596 of that text. All parentheses are Scheler's. All brackets are the translator's and contain some German words of the original.—MANFRED S. FRINGS

of outer and inner perception nor reducible to a coordination of the contents of these, let alone is it reducible to a fact of inductive experience, i.e., the perception of an individual thing. This also implies that, conversely, the lived body must never be understood as a primary givenness on whose foundation only we "come upon" [*Vorgefundenes*] something which is psychophysically indifferent, and which differentiates and sets itself off as something "psychic" or "physical" by different relations between what we "come upon" and the lived body. If the psychic and the physical have been shown to belong to two irreducible perceptual directions (of inner and outer perception) the twofold lived relationship of their series of contents to the datum "lived body" must, nevertheless, lead to two sciences whose properties will clearly reveal themselves to us.

We wish to make a very sharp distinction between two points. This distinction is, unfortunately, not made in our time in scientific terminology: "lived body" and "thing-body" [der *Leib* und der *Körper*]. If we think away the functions of all external senses by which we perceive the external world then all possible perception of our own "thing-body" would be abolished along with the perception of all other different bodies. We could neither touch ourselves and have any access to the forms of our chest, hands, legs, etc., as we can of external bodies, e.g., inanimate ones, nor would we be able to look at ourselves (with or without mirrors); we could neither hear any sounds of our voice or those otherwise produced, nor could we taste anything or smell ourselves, etc. But the phenomenon of our "lived body" would by no means be annihilated in this case. For—no matter how precisely one may focus on this point—we do have of our lived body, along with its possible external consciousness, also an inner consciousness which we lack in regard to inanimate bodies. There have usually been two kinds of interpretations of this inner consciousness of our lived body: (1) one interpretation that identifies it with the sum total or the product of the fusion of so-called *organic sensations* (e.g., sensations of muscles, of changing joints, of pain, or itching); and (2) another interpretation that distinguishes these "sensations" from those of our outer senses, such as sensation of colors and sounds, only in regard to *qualitative* and *local* occurrences. And this, in turn, leads to a terminology in the sciences—a most curious one, indeed, for unsophisticated people's thinking—according to which a painful sensation in the forehead, or an occurrence of "itching," is referred to as a "psychic phenomenon" and, hence, are with woe or sadness, for instance, included in a basic class of phenomena, namely the so-called "psychic phenomena." Of course, for this point of view there is neither a possibility for an irreducible and non-analyzable sphere of consciousness in the sense of a lived body-consciousness, nor is there a phenomenon such as the *lived body* at all. There is for this standpoint, on the other hand, only one's own "body" which we "think into" the sense contents of optical, tactile, etc., outer perceptions in the same manner as we think other "bodies" into other sense contents (e.g., the body of the inkwell standing in front of me into my own optical picture of it). On the other hand, there are only certain components of my psychic stream of consciousness which are coordinated to such sense contents only by an outer observation of their appearance and disappearance which are dependent on changes in this my body and on changing states of certain organs (e.g., my hands, legs, muscles, joints, etc.). In this interpretation the coordination would, of course, result in a *justification* of calling those "sensations," for instance, "sensations of organs," of "muscles," of "joints," etc., whereas, according to their "phenomenal" facticity, there would be nothing contained in them that could betray to me the existence of a muscle, of a stomach, etc. In short, the "lived body" is equated here with a factual, animated body and lived body-consciousness with a mere coordination of either psychic and corporal facticities or of a mere relationship and order of them.

Who would not at first sight see, however—if he is still uninfluenced and can see the visible—that this way of forcefully explaining away a lived body is nothing but a totally empty and irrelevant construction alien to intuitional comprehension?

A first incomprehensible element in this theory is that it ignores the doubtless *fact* that there exists, for example, through the senses of touch and sight, a strict and immediate *unity of identity* between such an *inner consciousness* which everyone has "of" the existence and "hereness" [*Befinden*] of the lived body—firstly of one's own lived body—and the *outer perception* of one's lived body (as the thing-body) [*Leibkörpers*]. It may be true that there is a requirement of *learning* and of a gradual "development" to have one's right hand, whose being, Gestalt, and movement of fingers I possess as elements of my inner lived body-consciousness and which hand may now "ache," as the *same thing* when I touch it with the left hand, and which thing corresponds to my own optical picture of it. By analogy, I have a thing-like identification of where

I feel hungry with that which represents itself as a stomach for the anatomist. Yet, this process of learning always refers only to two factors: (1) the coordination of the *corresponding parts* to "sides" of this one "lived body" (seen from within and from outside) in which coordination the *immediate identity* of the whole lived body-object, given from within and outside, is already *presupposed;* and (2) this process of learning does not pertain to the relationship of immediately given appearances of the same objective thing as such but it refers only to those of *thing-like* significance or the symbolic co-functions for *certain things,* as, for instance, this *thing* "hand," this *thing* "stomach," etc. This is to say that everything is here analogous to the fact that we must relate also the *differences* of depths, in which mere things of sight are given— and, indeed, given in an *original* manner—to the objective proportions of distances of real bodies (including also the body "eye") as a kind of system of signs for such distances (Hering). By no means do we have to "learn" the seeing of depths itself, nor does this seeing come from so-called sensations not yet containing anything like depths and their differences. Hence, we do not have to learn the identity of the same *lived body* given in inner and outer consciousness, here as a *lived body-soul,* there as a *thing-body* as we wish to say! The lived body is, rather, given as a totally uniform phenomenal fact and as a subject of "being here" so, or other than so [*So- und Anders "befindens"*]. This fact is independent and, in the order of givenness, prior to any special so-called "organic sensations" and special kinds of outer perception. Its immediate and total perception *founds* the givenness of a lived body-soul as well as of a thing-body. It is precisely *this* basic phenomenon that is a *lived body* in the strictest sense of the term.

In contrast to this the above-mentioned theory tends to prove that an *identically* intended lived body is only an imagination: that *in practice* there is supposed to be only one class of purely psychic so-called sensations (later termed "organic sensations") as well as a gradually *fixating coordination* of them and their unities and changes [*Wechsel*] to other classes of sensations which are related to a thing-body in no other sense than they are to inanimate physical bodies not belonging to it. In this theory this implies that the *difference* between the two groups of "sensations" lies only in a certain *constancy* in the first group and frequent appearances of "twofold sensations" (e.g., if I touch my body. Such a "twofold sensation" does not exist in seeing my body.[2] In hearing, my voice experiences in the larynx, mouth, etc., are connected with sound qualities), and it also implies that from an immediately given identity of the lived body, making such a constancy and coordination as something senseful only possible, there is supposed to arise a mere constancy of a part of my experiences (something totally "incomprehensible") and a mere "coordination," which is supposed to be nothing more than a mere "fixed" association. Apart from the deficiencies in the bases of this theory the criteria of a separation of sensations related to the "lived body" and to extra-bodily objects are insufficient. For someone sentenced to life imprisonment the walls of a prison are no less "constant" than are his hands he looks at. Yet, it is impossible for him to begin to take them for his lived body. A so-called "twofold sensation" is not at all given in the phenomenon on occasion of touching: it is only by looking at a finger and by touching the palm of the hand with it that we are able to relate two functional processes of *sensing* to the *same* content. But by positing these functional processes the differences between a lived body, its parts, as well as other bodies are already presupposed.

Let us summarize the various erroneous starting points of this customary theory: it is erroneous

a) to consider inner *lived body-consciousness* as only a group of sensations.

b) to consider *lived body sensations* as different by degrees from "organic sensations," and that organic sensations are differentiated only by degrees and contents from "sensations" of sound, color, taste, or smell, rather than by the kind of givenness of the states of a lived body that essentially belongs to them.

c) to believe that the lived thing-body [*Körperleib*] is met with in the same original sense as other bodies.[3]

d) to take *lived body sensations* for "psychic phenomena."

e) to consider inner *lived body-consciousness* as something disordered, but coming to an order only in dependency of the parts of the body to which it is only related in a secondary manner. A converse assertion would equally be wrong.

f) to hold that the contents of inner lived body-consciousness are more deceptive than those of outer consciousness (inner diagnostics).

g) to think that inner lived body-consciousness is originally non-extended and without any spatial-temporal order.

h) to think that there is no essential difference between a volitional disposing of the lived body and of external objects.

i) to hold that the unity of the lived body is only one of associative character. This is erroneous because it is the lived body that makes such associative combinations only possible.

One more word on the first of these errors![4]

The *first* error of this theory consists in the assumption that it is justified to simply equate the inner consciousness of our lived body with the sum total of sensations experienced as localized in specific organs. For, in fact, consciousness of our lived body is always given as a consciousness of a whole and of more or less vague structurization. This is independent of and *prior* to the givenness of any special complex of "organic sensations." The relation, however, of this *lived body*-consciousness and organic sensations is not comparable to a whole and its parts, or to a relation holding between two "terms." It is one between *form* and its *content*. In the same sense as all psychic experiences are only together in an "ego" and conjoined into a unity of a special kind, all organic sensations are necessarily given as "together" in a lived body. In the same sense as the "ego" must accompany all our (psychic) experiences (as Kant pointedly said) so also our lived body must accompany all organic sensations. The lived body is, therefore, the underlying form through which all organic sensations are conjoined and through which they are organic sensations of a *particular* lived body, and not of any other body. For also in cases when special organic sensations are observed or otherwise more set off, as is the case in painful sensations, there are (1) a vague whole of the lived body co-experienced as their "background," and (2) the *whole* of the lived body co-intended in any *organic sensation* as a special kind of sensation. From this it clearly follows that we do not have to "learn" by experience—in the sense of a gradual induction—that we are *no angels,* rather, we are embodied. We "learn" only the orientation in the manifold of our given body as well as the "sense and meanings" of the vicissitudes of its own manifold for the states of limb-units within the unity of the lived body that are likewise given in inner fashion as well as body-organs. However, for any finite consciousness there is an interconnection of essence between *"ego"* and *"lived body."* This interconnection is not of inductive-empirical or associative nature. One has often falsely interpreted otherwise correct observations of infants in this regard. Certainly, an infant is in a state of "wonder" seeing his feet for the first time. He may also kick his feet like strange external bodies, and there may come a time when he has to learn that the optical picture

of the upper corner of his bed does not approach his body like the picture of his foot. But the difference itself of the spheres "lived body"
and "external world" is already *presupposed* here as a given. The child
does not learn how to distinguish these spheres as such; but it is only
the *seen things* belonging to these separate spheres that a child "learns."

THE "LIVED BODY" AND "ENVIRONMENT" ARE NO PRESUPPOSITIONS FOR THE DISTINCTION BETWEEN "PSYCHIC" AND "PHYSICAL"

It was Avenarius in particular among modern scholars, and quite
independently of him ("coming from the idealistic camp," as he said),
it was Ernst Mach who furnished a theory of cognition in which it is
maintained that a distinction between psychic and physical phenomena
is possible only on the basis of a pre-given lived body and environment.
Avenarius asserts that there is a plain "coming upon" [*Vorfinden*] (in
which there is neither an "ego" nor a distinction between act, object,
and content presupposed) and that the content of this plain "coming
upon" represents the datum of a "natural conception of world." But
this datum, he says, does not contain anything more than a lived body
and its environment whose contents possess certain dependencies of
their variations. The dependencies existing between the parts of the
environment are said to represent elementary outlines [*Vorwurf*] of
the sciences of physics, chemistry, etc. The dependencies between
these and the parts and processes of the body are said to form objects
of biology. The objects of psychology are supposed to be the changes
of contents existing between environmental parts and the parts of the
body. They are not to be seen in dependencies of contents. It is further
maintained that there arose a false and "artificial" concept of the
world in that the variational relationship between a content one "comes
upon" (e.g., a "tree") in environment and a lived body (which is then
reduced to a system C, i.e., the brain with its spinal continuation) was
made a special object, first with regard to "fellow men." The object
is then said to have been "introjected" into the lived body of our fellow
men. One proceeded to poetize into this the "perception" or "representation" of said tree and, into these again, new "psychic" forms or
"contents of consciousness," etc. In this fashion, so runs the argument,
there arose the "concept of the soul" and of the "psychic" as well as
the assumption of a special perceptual source for such "fictional" ob-

jects, viz., the concept of *"inner per*ception." Also, the distinction between (psychic) acts and the (physical) objects corresponding to them, was, among other things, seen to have its source in all of this with other different scholars.

The above assertions and, *mutatis mutandis,* those of Mach himself, do not require a serious refutation today. They are already judged by their inevitable consequences: for one is forced here to reduce *all* feeling-states to organic sensations and their (sensuous) character, to reduce the experience of the ego, and even that of the person, to complex derivations of such experiences; one is forced to reduce all pictorial recollections to a reappearing of faint ("shadow-like") elements of environment, and all "thinking" to mere economy and to a most economical use of some pictures and their contents. For a psychology dealing at least with some facts such initial inevitable consequences are not arguable.

We are interested in these (now antiquated) theories here only in regard to the *lived body*. Avenarius' basis is that the "lived body of our fellow men," that the "environment" and all "statements" made by our fellow men, are all in equal fashion "come upon." But he fails to see right from the beginning that he is, in fact, unable to account for a distinction with regard to a "lived body," an "environment," and "statements" implicit in this "primary" material we are supposed to come upon. What is it supposed to be that distinguishes a "lived body" from an "element of environment," e.g., from some inanimate object of an equal sensible content? What is it that distinguishes a "statement" from any combination of sounds or noises? What is it that makes it, after all, a "statement," or even only a mere "phenomenal expression"? How could this explain that a "lived body" is not located like *one* thing-body between other thing-bodies, but that it is given as a "center" of thing-bodies functioning *as* its "environment"? How can it be that in this *given* fact something like "expressions," and even "statements," are no simple changes of thing-bodies determined by changing relationships to other thing-bodies, as is the case with a sound of a piece of steel hitting the ground, but that such expressions and statements are, rather, always present in terms of a twofold symbolic relation?[5] Where could one find all this in the *givenness* of such plain "coming upon"? The alternatives to the answer to these questions are simple: Avenarius' conception of this plain and independent "coming upon" is either no such thing at all, or it must have a *different mode* and *form* for a lived body, for an environment, and for any statement (which all potentially contain the *same* sensible material). What one "comes upon" must by nature, then, also have a different, although intuitive, but nevertheless non-sensible structure corresponding to such a form. Otherwise the above distinctions cannot be accounted for at all. Avenarius obviously makes the mistake of identifying the "lived body" with a thing-body, instead of seeing an interconnection of essence according to which the *same* lived body is capable of a totally different—inner—givenness (e.g., of hunger, of lust, of pain). He also is mistaken in seeing this latter point on the basis of an "introjection," analogous to that of the introjected environmental "tree" "into" a lived body as the "perception" of a tree. Even *if* there is such an "introjection" and if we would on this premise make the assumption of the existence of the "psychic" having the same fictitious structure of a thing-like "relation," such as a "perception," a "representation," or an "ego," if we would make the assumption of a special source of cognizing this "ego" = "inner perception": never could there be "introjected" something like "being hungry," or "tickling" in an analogous fashion. For where could we find an "environmental element" for this, or what would the introjected "character" be like? For there to happen such an "introjection," which cannot at all be found in inanimate objects a unity of a lived body, that is different in essence from such environmental elements, must be presupposed. (No animist[6] would have a stone "perceive" an animal in the same way as an animal perceives a stone.) We consider this "theory of introjection," as far as it does not only refute the well-known and old "theories of projections" of sensations, as a completely groundless theory. On one point, however, we agree with Avenarius, as opposed to his many critics: no matter how the idea of the "ego" has to be understood and no matter how the "ego" of our fellow man is "given": the perception of such a fact as that of the essence "lived bodiliness" has *not* its foundation in the assumption of an "ego" or of any psychic facts we come upon. There is no foundation such that the "ego" must be given to us (our own ego or that of others) as a necessity for cognizing and finding any appearances as those of a "lived body."[7] True, any given lived body of a human being is (for that human being concerned) given as "my" lived body, (for someone else) as "his" lived body: but it is not this relation of the ego that makes a *lived body* as a unity separable from the manifold of other "given" contents. It is on the *basis* of the independence of its givenness that its unity must, in essence, be different from that of inanimate things.[8] This pertains analogously to Mach's theory. Mach considers his *elements of being* [*Seinselemente*] as "sensations" by trying to show that their givenness and their absence are dependent on the being of an "organism." If, for instance, a sphere becomes yellow, not because of sodium light but because someone takes santonine, the element of being "yellow" is psychic. But how do the piles of said elements L (lived body) representing a *lived body* differ from other such elements E (environment) so that also the variations in E with their mutual "dependencies" can differ from the variations in L and their own mutual dependencies? Where is the phenomenal difference between "sensations" that are supposed to be the very elements *as* related to the lived body and such elements *of which* the lived body is supposed to consist? There is no answer to this question to be seen in this theory. Both scholars do not see that there is an essence *lived bodiliness* that is not inductively abstracted from factual lived bodies, and whose possible intuition in presence of an empirical object (e.g., my present lived body or that of some one else, etc.), yields it as one that is different from inanimate objects and as an *essentially* different lived body object. They both equate lived bodiliness with a concrete lived body and the latter with a mere body-thing, i.e. (in our terminology), the lived body as an object of only outer perception. Avenarius' assertion of there not being any differentiation of "outer" and "inner" perception with regard to what we come upon reveals a false polemic in that he reduces all perceptions to the concept of "outer perception"—a polemic directed against the concept of "inner perception." Avenarius tries to show that facts of inner perception consist of the same elements as the "simplest" complexities of outer perception. This reveals the same erroneous, one-sided artificiality with which Berkeley attempted to show that Locke's "sensation" is a mere border-case of a "reflection"—as if it were true that colors and sounds (supposed to be related to an ego and only experienced in this relation) are given in the same fashion as are pain, or muscular tensions, as if outer sense perception were nothing else but a strong representation. Moreover, he tries to do away with any perceptive *direction* of "inner perception" by assuming that these terms refer to a perception of something psychic "in" an objective thing-body and that there is no "blue in one's head" or any pain "in" the (anatomic) arm on occasion of sensing "blue" or "pain." These assumptions resulted in a (later widely accepted) theory implying that all specific phenomena experienced in a lived body, such as pain, tickling, tension, relaxing, and even all actively experienced motoric impulses, as opposed to so-called kinaesthetic passive phenomena, are complexes of "sensations" which also are present as "elements" of outer perception. (Kinaesthetic passive sensations are, in fact, only consequences of tactile sensations in sinews and joints and phenomena of position and form [*Lage- und Formphänomene*]. They can be "interpreted" as "sensations of movements" on the basis of previously experienced impulses of movements). From all of this there also resulted the opinion that there are no non-extensive psychic experiences at all, as we have them in spiritual feelings and especially the experience of the ego which, unquestionably, belongs to experiences of this particular kind. Indeed, Avenarius did not even see that the difference of the direction of "inner" and "outer" perception is not at all relative to that which is (in a spatial sense) "inner" and "outer" for a body-thing [*Leibkörper*]. But there is here, in fact, a difference in the *direction of the acts* essentially conjoined with the special form of its given manifold. This difference of direction and form remains as a residuum, notwithstanding a complete operation of thinking the lived body away. But once this difference of direction and form is uniformly related to a "given" lived body—given, in principle, *without* the differences of direction of perceptual acts—it projects two entirely different "sides" of a lived body so that it becomes evident that it relates to the *same* facticity of a "lived body."[9]

It is equally impossible to conceive the difference between the "psychic" and the "physical" as only a different *relationship* and "order" of the *same contents* and *elements* as both Avenarius and Mach mean to assert. In fact, they always conceive *physical* elements as primary factors of giveness (as elements of *outer* perception, not yet comprehended as something thing-like or even corporeal). Much as Mach endeavours, like Hume, to deduce the thing-category from his "elements of being" as a relatively solid complex of them, his "elements of being"[10] are, in fact, even true and genuine *physical things* (i.e., things of the senses of sight, touch, etc.) having all phenomenological determinations of essence belonging to them (as do Hume's "impressions"). As *sensations,* i.e., as "related to an organism," such "elements" are not pure "contents" of sensations but they already are things of sensations. And it is precisely in this point that we find ourselves dealing with the implicit formal "materialism" of this philosophy. As a qualitative materialism it is as much as any materialism. Moreover, any other form of a *theory of order* which would have to avoid this mistake, would also fail.* It can never happen that an "element" of sorrow or woe "also" occurs as an element of a physical appearance (even if this concept would contain so-called organic sensations). Neither can it occur as a "character" of, say, a landscape. For the mere identical quality of the feeling-state of sorrow—when "I am sad"—and the identical quality of the "character" of a "sorrow landscape" represents no *real* element in either case. If a theory of order would only hold that the "psychic" and the "physical" are *no empirically definable* objective units (i.e., definable *per genus proximum* and *differentia specifica*) then it would contain a correct assumption. For these units, taken in that sense, would then not imply a difference in *essence*. For there is the criterion for such a difference of essence, that, in attempting to define it, we must presuppose it and that we are necessarily trapped in a *circulus in definiendo* while defining it. The above assumption would not compel us to posit *two different modes of perception* and of direction, instead of positing a perception plus two different empirical concepts of objects (as in: "I perceive trees," "I perceive houses," etc.).[11] Yet, it would not follow from such a negatively correct assertion in a "theory of order" that there are no non-formal differences between the psychic, physical, and all lived body-phenomena at all, and that we are concerned with *differences of order* from only a logical and formal viewpoint. For it only follows that different non-formal contents already residing in the essence of psychic and physical objects are essentially connected with both perceptual directions.[12]

It is, therefore, out of the question that *ego-ness itself* and *individual ego-being* are somehow based in genetically and historically explainable processes like that of an "introjection," instead of considering them to be a datum of immediate intuition corresponding to the "materiality" of objects of outer perception void of any hypothetical positing of a specific thing-like "matter." Only the thousand kinds of beliefs and superstitions in a substance-soul may be reduced to analogous processes—but they, too, are dependent upon the *presupposition* of intuitive facts. The essence "ego-ness," however, *constitutes* the essence "psychic" and is, together with the direction of inner perception, an *interconnection of essence* that is still given in both factors in a formless, *pure* intuition itself. The "theory of the projection of sensations," which Avenarius correctly refutes, and the quite similar "doctrine of empathy of feelings" of "values," "characters," or

forces and phenomena of life cannot establish a basis for the phenomena of an "external world" (with or without "unconscious causal inferences" as Schopenhauer and Helmholtz believed). They are as
incorrect as is an "introjection" trying to make comprehensible the assumption of the spheres of the psychic, of the ego, etc. Whenever such
processes occur they presuppose both spheres, their areas, and essential
contents, into which there is projected, feelingly empathized, and
introjected.[13]

Although we emphasized that *lived bodiliness* "can be given" without regard to a psychic ego (we are in agreement with Avenarius in
this point) we must also state that we do not have to *pass through*
any givenness of the *lived body* in order to comprehend *ego-ness* in
every psychic experience—let alone do we have to pass through the
perception of another, alien lived body of a fellow man. Neither is
there a necessitation of passing through the perception of one's own
ego and lived body to comprehend another's ego and his lived body.[14]
Even if we perform the operation of reducing organic sensations of
our lived body to a zero point, the ego and its spiritual feelings remains
"given" (for there are, in fact, moments in our lives when only the
schema of our lived body exists for us without any mediation—almost
without positive contents—moments in which we seem to be lifted
from all "heaviness of the earth" [*Erdenschwere*]. There are also cases
of deeply pathological anaesthesis of bodily sensations and feelings).
There is an essential difference between the modes of how I "am sad,"
i.e., the way sadness is related to the ego and "fills" it, and the mode
of how I "feel *myself*" weak, strong, hungry or appeased, ill or healthy,
or even how I feel "my leg hurt" or "my skin itch." The different characters of the givenness in the phenomenal essence is by no means affected
by the fact that it is often difficult, sometimes even impossible, in a
concrete state of being to distinguish the modes of the feeling-state of
life [*Legensgefühl*] and lived body-sensations from an experienced fact
of an ego-determination and one which is immediately related to the
ego. Although self-deceptions are obviously possible here (esp. regarding affections, which are always admixtures of the psychic, the body,
and outer sensations), again, the different characters of givenness of the
phenomenal essence are by no means affected by this. One could only
come to the conclusion of a "transition" ranging from colors and sounds
to feelings of hunger, or understand facts like "to be hungry" in the
same sense as sensations of the inner body, sensations of colors as

"sensations" of extra-bodily objects, by making a deficient separation between, on the one hand, inner bodily sensations of touch (which possess the quality of contents of touch) as manifest in joints or sinews which still belong to the exterior spheres of senses, and, on the other hand, bodily sensations and bodily feeling-states, and nerve-impulses proper, as we find them in pain, tickling, and the feeling and impulses of hunger. But, in fact, the experienced *states* of the lived body are absolutely distinguishable from contents and qualities of functions of the outer senses, and these (e.g., colors and sounds), in turn, are distinguishable from their "sensation" and its main types (e.g., seeing or hearing). Although the same content of touching may serve as the same basis for phenomenal body-determinations, such as smoothness, softness, hardness, which are phenomena that are implicit when we say that something feels "soft," "hard," "rough," "smooth" as it can also be the basis for experiences that are more than sensuous states—this is *totally impossible* with respect to pain, tickling, or being hungry. These can never be "given" as determinations of inanimate bodies, but, at best, as experienced effects on a lived body. There are also no "elements" of them which could make them "given" as such determinations.

True, what is always, and by evident necessity, given in an act of the nature of *inner perception* is only the essence and individuality of the ego and "any" of its *experiences* and *determinations*. In every factual comprehension of these and with regard to their special contents the following proposition holds: All contents in the sphere of inner intuition [*innere Anschauung*] become *in all degrees of clarity and distinction* also contents of real perception, but only in so far as their being or non-being, their being so or other than so, posits some *variations* of a *lived body*. This I describe thusly: All *inner perception acts itself out* [*vollzieht sich*] *in terms of an "inner meaning,"* by virtue of which all contents of possible inner perception that do *not* posit a variation of the lived body, remain in the sphere of the "subconscious,"[15] and by virtue of which it is not the inwardly perceived itself, but it is the form of givenness of "appearances" that sets in factual perceiving and which also partakes in the forms of the manifold that are essential for facts of a phenomenal *lived body*. Hence, also, a factual perception of the ego and a perception of the sphere of "pure" psychic facts is *no* immediate perception, yielding such facts, but it is one that is *mediated* through a *sensible lived body*. Factual perception of the ego and of psychic facts is, for this reason, subject to deception as factual perception is by outer "sensibility."[16] In both cases "sensibility" neither "creates" nor "produces" anything at all. It only suppresses or selects in accordance with the significance of psychic experiences (or possible contents of outer perception) for a lived body and its immanent, entelechial direction [*Zielrichtung*] of its activity.

Only from this it becomes clear why the pure non-extended *interwovenness* [das pure *Ineinander*] of experiences of the ego obtains in factual perception a *sequential* character [*Nacheinander*seins] and the character of *extensionality* [*Aussereinander*seins] which must already be attributed to a phenomenal lived body (but, therefore, without any trace of temporality and spatiality); and it becomes also clear from this how psychic experiences must separate into "present," "past," and "future" ones.

First of all, there is no other characteristic feature which distinguishes in essence all phenomena of the *lived body* from psychic phenomena more sharply than *extension* and *non-extension*. Moreover, both types of phenomena have a "position" which is "different in kind" in relation to an ego. These respective differences of the relation to the ego have, in turn, their subdivisions. For instance, pain is clearly extended: It "spreads" "across the back," or changes its area of localization. "Hunger" is something that occurs in the areas of the stomach and chest. Even "fatigue," although it has no specific area of localization as does tickling or "tiredness in the legs," is still "spread throughout" the extended whole of a lived body. Such characteristics are completely non-sensical with regard to "sorrow," "woe," "serenity," etc. Nevertheless, such lived body-phenomena are by no means "in space," neither in an objective space (e.g., in an arm as an anatomic, objective form-unity), nor are they in a phenomenal space. They share, rather, "non-spatiality" with everything belonging to the purely psychic.

Lived body-phenomena are, however, not only of an extended nature. They also reveal the character of *extensionality* and within this manifold form, in turn, a being-*side-by-side* [*Nebeneinander*] and a *sequential* character. There is also "change" [*Wechsel*] within these forms of manifolds. Neither the being-side-by-side nor the sequential character are factors in space and time, i.e., in *one* space and *one* time—let alone are they measurable relations. There is, here, however, something like a "more" or "less" of this being-side-by-side and the sequential character and then the "side-by-side" and sequence of, e.g., from pain to tickling. But there are no spatial and temporal lines that would connect these phenomena. There is also no fixed situation in space and time. Pain may "change" into tickling in the same area. But, in such a case it is senseless to say that a specific bodily area "changed itself" from a painful one toward a ticklish one. Pain spreads "out" and, although this or that limb may ache (e.g., in the case of gout), there is no trace to be found here "of pain moving from one to another area." This particular manifold has, then, to be distinguished from *extra* lived body-phenomena.

This manifold is no less to be distinguished from the non-extended "interwovenness in the ego" pertaining to (purely) *psychic* facts. It would be senseless to assert that a thought, a spiritual feeling, or an expectation are "asunder," "sequential," or "side-by-side." The fact that one attributes a sequential character to them more often than a being-side-by-side character is only a consequence of identifying the types of their *givenness* with the *content* in them through which they come to the fore in our inner senses. It is not the "purely" psychic phenomena, out of which there is taken every state of a lived body that is the condition for their factual perception, rather, it is solely their *appearing in this and that content* of a plurality of acts of the type and form of the "inner intuition" that brings about a "sequential character" of thoughts, spiritual feelings, or expectations. Yet, an act A of inner perception may possess more fullness in its content than an act B. But this difference of *fullness* is not one of a "sequential" manifold. True, a third act C of inner intuition may even *encompass* the fullness of A and B in its content. In this case the fullness of A and B ($=F$ and F_1) may appear in a "sequential" manifold within the fullness of act C (F_2)—but this is because F and F_1 were coordinated to *states of the lived body which are factually sequential*. This sequential manifold of F and F_1, within the act C is only a partial content of the *content* of its own fullness, whereas F and F_1 do not possess any existence as separate units of fullness. Thus, the inner field of viewing one's own ego (or another's ego) may *wax* and *wane*—but without there being a sequential manifold in the contents in this field. It is, therefore, not that which appears there, but it is the mode *how* it appears that reveals a "sequential" character. Let us avail ourselves of a model. If one moves a light along a dark wall (the light source unknown) the various areas on the wall are successively illuminated; nevertheless, there is no sequential manifold of the parts of the wall but only a sequence of their illumination. He who does not know the mechanism involved is led to believe that there are sequential parts of the wall. Since it is the factually sequential manifold of lived body-states that illuminate non-extended interwoven determinations of the ego for inner perception according to specific laws of direction, it may seem that these determinations are *in themselves* sequential, whereas they are coordinated to only different, successively appearing lived body-states and at the same time conditioned by them.

In this sense all that we experience (and also all that which appears from a given lived body as past) is experienced as *together and interwoven* in the ego. We can neither say that that which appears as "past" is lasting throughout objective time but not perceived now (or that a psychic disposition of it lasts), nor can we say that it does *not* last and is annihilated and what lasts is only a physiological disposition to bring it back to life (Epiphenomenalism of the psychic). Both of these opposing theories suffer from the *same* πρῶτον ψεῦδος [primary mistake] to conceive the ego and its determinations and their manifolds as originally *sequential,* instead of seeing that we are concerned with a different positive manifold, viz., that of non-extended *interwovenness* whose elements are coordinated only as appearing elements of inner perception to the sequential nature of lived body-states on the part of a being endowed with a lived body. There is no use for such theories precisely because any psychic experience determines the *totality* of the ego *differently.* The ego itself, however, neither belonging to a sequential character, nor to *pure extensionality* does not last, nor does it cease to be (i.e., to be or cease to be in a successive point of time, if it *were* existing in a preceding point of time).

EGO AND LIVED BODY (ASSOCIATION OR DISSOCIATION)

On the basis of the connection of essence with a lived body (inner and outer) intuition separates into differences of act-qualities (sense-*perception, remembering, expecting*) which are, however, contained in the uniform character of intuition as such. To these act-qualities there correspond the spheres of objects that we can willfully manipulate [*Sachspären*]. These spheres possess the being-*present* (*hic* and *nunc* sphere), a past, and a future-sphere, which do not belong to objective time. It is a synthetic proposition to say that "perception," in the sense of an act-quality in which something is given at once in terms of a *lived body* and *senses, can only give something "present,"* i.e., the contents of inner and outer *sense*-perception. Only someone who wishes to define perception by way of the concepts of *sense* and *sensation*, and who ignores thereby the special quality implicit in the act, can deny this proposition.[17]

If we consider inner and outer intuitions with their absolute differences of their direction and their form—differences which are not relative to a lived body—as performed independently from any givenness of a lived body they would yield the inner and outer world of the person as it exists independently of these directions. It is only the (necessary) interposition of a *lived body* and its "sensibility," (varying among different living organizations) as well as its "movement," which is "free" in regard to laws of causality of inanimate nature, that determines the *dissociation* and *selection* of these units of intuition according to specific laws. All investigations of various dependencies must be guided, therefore, by the proposition that it is not only outer intuition but inner intuition as well that is connected to "sensibility," to the structure of movements and the drives of a lived body in their factual execution. There is no less mediation by sensibility in an inner perception than there is in outer intuition.[18] It executes itself by an "inner meaning."

The special function of the sensibility of a lived body (i.e., the functions of seeing, hearing, etc., possessing their own *proper* laws independently of peripheral and central organs) is, in principle, *identical* for both inner and outer intuition, no matter how one must differentiate between psychic and physiological "functions." Functional laws of senses remain independent of the structure, order, and irritability, etc., of sense-*organs* and their corresponding "sensations." They are also antecedent to the structural character of the laws of the latter. The inner world, too, receives the structure of the vivification of its givenness by the twofold selection of psychic being and life. This selection takes place by sensuous functions and on the basis of the significance of psychic being as the factor of irritation with respect to a lived body and its organic sensations. In precisely analogous manner the same uniform and *identical structure* of tendencies of the lived body serves as the foundation for its functional structures of movement and the drive-structure of its soul.[19] But the nature of laws inherent in this structure is as independent of kinetic organs and their corresponding systems of kinetic impulses as the functional sensibility is independent of the sense organs and their corresponding sensations. Finally, within the entire sphere of the lived body and of life there exists a relation of laws between the structure of tendencies of movement and the functional structure of sensibility, namely, in the sense that the latter remains *dependent* upon the former. This is because of the fact that only such sensible functions (and, therefore, especially their corresponding sense-organs and sensuous capacities) come to develop which, for objects situated within the entelechial direction of kinetic body tendencies, can serve as a fitting means of conveyance for possible intuition as such.

Concerning the question of the determination of the relationship between the manifold units of the ego and the lived body there are among the many detailed answers two principal ones—if we set aside the metaphysical theory of two substances: Firstly, the uniform inner interwovenness of the ego is *dissociated* by the lived body in terms of what is found as a given individual experience of inner perception. Secondly, basic psychic facts, originally differentiated, are *associated* by the lived body into the complex union of the "ego."

According to the latter view the ego represents a conglomeration of objects [*Sachen*] and processes, being distinctly connected to some special excitations of the lived body. All psychic units are said to depend on all the types of connections of these excitations in the unity of a lived body (theory of association).

According to the former opinion the *ego* is a *unity* of a manifold of *pure interwovenness*. It represents something whose *fullness only* can wax or wane insofar as it is conceived as purely by itself and with a reduction of the lived body. The units of the observable *experiences*, however, are said to be *consequences of dissociation* of the unity of the ego occurring for and through a lived body only by an expression in the body and by the utilization of purely psychic contents as enclosed in the ego-manifold. The lived body, then, does not "assemble" but splits up and *divides* this manifold into different parts, viz., the *empirical experiences*.

The understanding of this view is, above all, dependent upon learning to see that purely *psychic facts* possess a special form of a manifold, viz., that of the *interwovenness in the ego*. This unity disappears both in intuition if one thinks of the "ego" as somehow opposed to psychic experiences, "opposed" in the sense of an unchangeable object lasting in time, and by which object such experiences pass—and if one considers it as this stream *itself* (a "stream of events"). In the first case mentioned this ego becomes something totally empty and "simple" *without* a manifold. It petrifies, as it were, to an X of a substance to whom one can attribute similar unknown "psychic dispositions." One can say in this case that "past" experiences have no being, but that they had effects on the "ego" (=soul) and that they left traces of "psychic dispositions." These are then supposed to be excitable in the "soul" by certain irritations. But in contrast to this view the following holds: "Past" experiences do not at all have to cease to exist and cease to have effects. They *exist* in the ego and "*in*" the ego. Any removal of any of its experiences would, in principle, let a present total experience *vary* in certain degrees. They are just not inwardly perceived since a bodily excitation is necessary for this *perception* in a similar fashion as a bodily excitation was necessary when they were experienced in the past. These past experiences are, however, encompassed by a pure inner intuition and they are purely psychically effective in their totality. They also "would be" given in "present" experiences of the ego—*if* it were not for the inner meaning, essentially connected with a lived body, to separate them with regard to the perception of their being and effectiveness by specific laws. If one recognizes the errors in a theory of a substance-soul and if one does not see at the same time this interwovenness of a genuine manifold *in* the ego, one posits the interwovenness as something *asunder* right from the beginning. This "in the ego" will then get out of sight and one is led to identify a *respective* momentary content of inner perception with the psychic in general. "Past experiences" will not exist then; neither do their "psychic dispositions," and the nature of the psychic appears only as a mere *present*-appearance disconnected (psychically) from an antecedent present-experience, which is supposed to form an interconnective whole by an existing body-*thing* in objective time and its inherent physiological causality (epiphenomenalism). In this view there are only "physiological dispositions." No doubt, the very assumption of there being something psychic at all which extends beyond a present and concrete moment becomes here philosophically absurd. No doubt, that the fact of remembering becomes, in this view, incomprehensible.[20]

Such conclusions result from not seeing that a psychic manifold—as well as types of its inherent combinations—represents a genuine *interwovenness in the ego*. It is a genuine being of experiences "in" the ego and not outside of it. Now, if one would ask the question: how, then, "are" past experiences? I answer: *They "are" in my ego* which "*becomes*" *different* in all experiences—without "changing" as a thing would change. They are, therefore, not located in a mystic area of the past, resembling lifeless shadows knocking sometimes at the door of my present to taste the blood of my life. Nevertheless, it would be equally wrong to assert that they, as experiences, do *not* exist, and that they only exist as "dispositions" of a soul or of a body. Something psychically un-experienced (even subconsciously un-experienced) would be a purely transcendent assumption, a purely removable symbol for which there is no impletion in intuition. A past experience "in" the ego is still given as *effective* and also in inner intuition insofar as each variation of one of these experiences varies a respective *total content* of this intuition in a special direction. Past experiences "speak to me" from all directions of the spheres of my life; they "motivate" all my oncoming experiences in one uniformly experienced efficiency. Yet, their special, articulated, and positive content is not present in inner, sensibly conditioned perception—which is restricted to a lived body and to something "present," as is the case with any type of sensible perception. This holds, as we know, analogously for the outer perception in as much as here, too, there is nothing present in an articulated fashion which co-determines, as a part of the "unity of situation" in the "environment"[21] of a lived body, each experienced content. Hence, epiphenomenalism takes the "physiology of the inner sense" for psychology. For the assertion that my past ego-experiences *are* not, and do not exist, is as nonsensical as the assertion that the sun of my natural world-view [=*natural stand-point*] does not exist because I did not see it a moment ago.

The main point is, then, to bring to one's intuition both the purely psychic manifold and the interwovenness of the ego in its peculiar character, viz., this very interwoven non-extended structure that can both wax and wane in its fullness in such a manner that the phenomenon of "waxing" is a nontemporal becoming. Furthermore, the task is given before us to elaborate, above all, on a phenomenology of "having one-self" in order to see this phenomenon.

There are states in our existence which our language calls "ingathered-ness" [*Sammlung*]. By this is meant a concentrated being-in-oneself, or "to live deeply in oneself." In such a state our total psychic life, including our past, is *one* and effective as *one*. These states occur very rarely in our lives—e.g., they may occur before making a grave decision or when we are compelled to take a crucial action. Everything is somehow "present" and "effective" in such a moment and no "particulars" of our past are remembered. We are not empty, but inwardly *replete* and fully *imbued* and truly "with ourselves." Effective experiences speak to us from all ends of our lives and at the same time a thousand "calls" reach us both from the past and from out of our future. We are "looking over" our *whole* ego in its total manifold, experiencing it as a totum entering into *one* act, one deed, one action, one work. Yet, we neither come "upon" any singular past experience here, nor do we direct our attention to anything particular of or to "our ego." But we "live" in the experience in its totality in a peculiarly concentrated manner. He who knows about this phenomenon also knows about the unmistakable character of the *givenness of lived body* connected with the phenomenon at this moment. One's own lived bodiliness is given here as "belonging" to this concentrated totality that may exercise "power" and sway over it. Our lived bodiliness is given here as "only present," as a moment enclosed as a part in our given "enduring" existence. The respective contents of this bodiliness appear to "float by" this enduring existence, as it were. There are also states of an opposite nature: a totally *converse* phenomenal relationship between the ego and lived body-givenness. We "live in our body," as it were, (e.g., in increasing fatigue, tiredness, high indolence, in losing oneself in empty pleasures, diversions, etc.). The niveau of our experienced existence peculiarly *vacillates* between the total interwovenness of the ego with its contents and the body-ego with its character of extensionality. We are then living near the edge of our lived body and its extensionality and the sequential characters of its states. It is precisely here where everything is now *empty* where everything was "full" before, this "emptiness" still being given to us. We are living here also "*in* a moment" to the same extent as we are living in a lived body, and to the same extent as it is *this* lived body that now occupies the "place of the ego." To live in a lived body does not mean to possess it objectively. This is out of the question. It means: "to be in it" through one's inner experience, or to "ween" [*wähnen*] in it. In the latter case it becomes quite clear that the purely psychic begins to obtain the character of "floating away" although it still remains given and present. Thinking and feeling, etc., appear only as a "small movement" "passing through" one's head and body. Although the lived body in the case concerned is given in its presence (and in its states) it is not "our own" and subject to our sway, neither is it given only momentarily. Rather, the lived body is, or appears to be, the ego itself. The lived body is a *solid, enduring, and continuous X* filling out objective time. The psychic floats by it as something "transient."

It is these two poles of the phenomenal characters of an *immediate givenness-to-oneself* that are the intuitive basis of materialistic (and epiphenomenal) and rational *theories* (asserting psychically autonomous causality). These theories neither have this basis from observations and subsequent theories drawn from them, nor do they have this basis from any arbitrary methodological "objectives." These particular *kinds of experiences* antecede any observation and theory. Depending on the kinds of experiences in question, very different classes of facts may result for *possible* observations.

There is a *plurality of such niveaux* or of such *different levels* throughout the *depth*-ranges of our ego-experiences which are subject to a precise determination.[22] Each of these levels possesses its special *basic type of connection* of the manifold appearing on it, i.e., of things and events, which connection serves for an explanatory psychology as their basis in terms of symbols. The most peripheral level is the connection of "tactile association," a deeper one is that in which the connection rests on "similarity," a yet deeper level is that of genuine "assimilation." This is followed by ample levels of different forms of attention (instinctive, volitional, passive, active, sensible, and spiritual attention). These again are followed by directions of attitudes which are the foundation for directions of interests.[23] The most central level is the uniformly waxing and waning efficiency of the purely psychic ego *itself* in its manifold.

These niveaux themselves and their changes represent at the same time the levels of *relative existence* [*Daseinsrelativität*] of objects of inner intuition and inwardly experienced efficiency in the sense that these objects are relative to a human being's ego-totality. But the vacillations [*Wechsel*] of these levels are not subject to any psychic causality: These changes only follow the acts of a person, "free" from all psychic causality, and they follow only the nature of a person's self-effected being [*Selbststellung*].

In a *final* analysis psychic causality is, therefore, always ego-causality, i.e., an experienced efficiency of a uniform ego. It is an *individual* causality, one in which the "same causes and effects" never occur. Hence, any change in the ego is dependent upon all experiences of the ego having taken place up to this change. We can call this *purely psychic causality* the *causality of motivation*. It forms the foundation of the humanities. *Objective psychology* [*verstehende Psychologie*] must investigate this area from all angles. This psychology does not "explain" but seeks to "understand" *all* processes of individual and typically psychic units in terms of their individually typical contents. It does *not* set aside *individuality* and "types" of respective total egos, rather *it is these that it sticks to,* making them special objects from which it derives an "understanding."

Although this objective psychology seeks to determine all *purely* psychic being and happenings, no single *concrete* psychic event, as it is given in inner observation, is strictly speaking determined by this psychology. For this determination also requires knowledge of the psychophysiological mechanism of the *inner meaning* according to which total egos, purely unfolding by themselves in a comprehensible fashion, are parted and *dissociated* by their relationship to a bodily organization. It is only by explicitly *setting aside* the being and efficacy of the always individual ego-totalities that we can investigate into these laws according to principles of reproduction, assimilation, association, determination, etc. This problematic *alone* is the object of psychology as a science, i.e., of a "physiology of inner meanings." There are for every "level," however, noninductive principles of explanation. "Psychology" in the latter sense does not bring to "understanding," but it only "explains." It establishes psychophysiological causal laws of objectively factual, elementary processes that are as "non-understandable" as are the facts contained in the laws of falling bodies.

A clear determination of concrete psychic happenings results, then, only from the *superposition* of concrete causality of motivation and understandability with these psychophysiological laws. This is analogous to the fact that for the outer perception any concrete object and its properties requires a physical and physiological explanation at the same time.[24]

Not seeing this complex state of affairs and assuming that there is a physiology of inner meanings alone—which has its a priori non-formal presuppositions in the principles of association—is a result of the same deception that led to the assumption of the world-view of classical mechanics, believed to have been an absolute picture of real nature. This deception has two implicit factors: first, one of not seeing that objects of *both* associative psychology *and* classical mechanics are *relative* to an *embodied being* with its tendencies of utilizing its psychic experiences (i.e., the contents of its outer intuition) in terms of body-tendencies; second, one of not seeing the principles of positing technical purposes (for psychology the educational, political, medical purposes), through which only *those* elements are selected from the given of inner and outer intuition that are in a direct dependency of possible body irritations and which are, therefore, also determinable by way of possible outside effects on a lived body (or technically controllable by body movements in outward direction). But within a *pure* psychic causality there is neither "prediction" nor any calculation possible. Here, any cause has an effect only *once*. Although the formal a priori proposition—same causes, same effects—is true, it is not "valid" in our context because there are just no "same causes"! The absence of some causes make any "controlling" impossible. "Modern" man, athirst to "control," wanted not only to recognize as real what is controllable in outer reality but he wanted to recognize as real also what is controllable in psychic life. He was inclined to recognize only the associative-mechanical side of the soul as a true soul and, hence, his eyes became blind to its non-mechanical side. He came to think that the soul is a "bundle of associations" of derivated sensations because, owing to his educationally technological attitude, he was only *interested* in what is dependent on a body and in what is both calculable and changeable by means of outside effects. But, in fact, neither is a physical mechanism able absolutely to determine a concrete natural event, because of there always being available multitudes of other thinkable mechanisms that equally well explain such natural events, nor is any concrete psychical event absolutely determinable by an associative mechanism which in its appearance functions only by the inner meaning.

NOTES

1. See Part I, section 2, "Formalism and Apriorism" A.
2. Except if one wants to see a twofold sensation in the sensations of the tension and position of ocular muscles of opened eyes which are at rest.

3. This presupposition makes an argument of Th. Lipps plausible. It is directed against an original three-dimensional type of seeing: he argues that any comprehension of distance presupposes the perception of two distant bodies but the eye itself is not perceived, hence . . .

4. It is not my intention here to clarify completely this difficult problematic of the givenness of the lived body. I will treat this point in detail in a projected phenomenological investigation of basic concepts of the science of biology. In the above I am only concerned to demonstrate the limits of the systematic place of the givenness of the lived body within the interconnections of the givenness of the ego and a thing-body.

5. This pertains both to an expressed experience and to the object potentially meant in the expression. In statements [*Aussagen*] an object is always co-intended.

6. It is obvious that animism to which Avenarius is referring presupposes the formation of the idea of an "ego" and a "soul" as opposed to anything dead.

7. This is the case with Lipps's and Ettlinger's viewpoint.

8. Also another assumption underlying Avenarius' critique of a pure experience which implies that the system *C* aims at a maximum of "preservation" in all of its utilizations of irritations and, hence, at utilizing everything on the basis of "the smallest use of force" already contains the *presupposition* of "non-mechanical" factors involved. No matter how justified also in our view this presupposition may be, there is no justification for it in his theory of cognition which holds that a lived body is met in the same manner as is a thing. Even if one would *try* the impossible, viz., to deduce logical principles from a principle of an economy in thinking—which would, in turn, imply a demonstration of their validity as the "conditions of the preservation of a lived body" (including even his "system *C*")—one has to connect with a lived body a *teleological* principle determining its *unity*—a tendency toward self-preservation with the least means possible. But then one cannot *also* be a mechanist in the science of biology.

9. The following may be added concerning Avenarius' assertion that one implicitly thinks of a perception of the "interior" of something corporeal on occasion of an "inner" perception: There is, strictly speaking, no "interior" and "exterior" in the spatiality of outer perception. There is only *extensionality*, but no genuine "interwovenness" [*Ineinander*]. It follows only from the peculiar way of lived embodying [*Verleiblichung*] even inanimate things, so characteristic of the natural standpoint, that we can, for instance, say that a ball is "in" a box, and even that a box is "in" space. For both cases presuppose that we first *add* here the spacial form of the ball to the box in intuition and then subtract its form (as belonging to the ball) from the "box." The evident a priori proposition of the impenetrability of a "body" is the reason why it "seems" that there is an "in" here. Hence the *converse* of Avenarius' position holds true. Any *interwovenness* is an analogy to the way elements can be with one another in the manifold of inner perception. This "analogy" holds even when we say: my heart is "in" my lived body-thing [*Leibkörper*].

10. E. Mach: *Die Analyse der Empfindungen,* Jena, 1903, esp. sections 7 and 8.

11. If there were a property X that physical objects could have, and psychic objects could not have, one could only maintain then that there is a perception of physical objects on the one hand, and a perception of psychic objects on the other—like a perception of tables and chairs; but one could not maintain that there are two different perceptual directions like those of inner and outer perception.

12. In the same manner as E. Husserl's "noema" and "noesis" are, in their qualitative nature, mutually interdependent.

13. The ancient theory of projection as well as the theory of introjection (which is its pure opposite) make the same basic error of not distinguishing between psychic, physical, and lived-body phenomena as the basically essential differences of phenomena and their respective types of perception that belong to them.

14. See the Appendix of my book *Zur Phänomenologie und Theorie der Sympathiegefühle,* Halle 1913.*

15. We have already discussed this concept on p. 391 [of the *fifth* edition of *Der Formalismus*].

16. Overlooking that factually psychic self-perception is mediated through a lived body and sensibility resulted in the difficulties of understanding the the cognition of the alter-psychic. I have shown this in my book on Sympathy mentioned above on page 133 (Appendix).*

17. For elaborations on this point reference is made to my essay on "Self-Deception," *loc. cit.,* and to my book, *Zur Phänomenologie und Theorie der Sympathiegefühle,* Halle, 1913.

18. A detailed proof of these points will be given in a projected study. I make mention of this here only to complement the whole of the subject-matter.

19. "Tendency" is here a qualitatively identical element of drives and vital [= lived] movement.

20. Already the very assumption of a past psychic life is fully unfounded on this premise. For it is clear that I can set aside all past psychic life—if only all physiological dispositions of former effects of irritation remain—without there being the slightest change in the content of my present-experience.

21. Concerning the concept "environment" [*Umgebung*], see Part I, section III, pp. 153 ff. [of the fifth edition of *Der Formalismus*].

22. A more precise determination of them has to be postponed to my projected studies.

23. The concepts of "interest" and "attitude" have been delineated in Part I, section III [of the fifth edition of *Der Formalismus*].

24. See Part I, section II, pp. 157 f. [of the fifth edition of *Der Formalismus*]. The term "physical" is, of course, not used here for physics alone but for the totality of the sciences of inanimate being. "Physiological," however, is used for the totality of the sciences of life in general.

METAPHYSICAL JOURNAL *and*

A METAPHYSICAL DIARY

Gabriel Marcel

METAPHYSICAL JOURNAL

May 7th, 1914

The problem of the relations of the soul and the body is only really raised when thought becomes conscious of itself. Only we must note that for thought that is fully conscious of itself, that problem, by the very fact of assuming all its acuteness, ends up by losing all meaning; at least this happens inasmuch as the mind, which is constructed, as I have said, by overcoming exteriority, far from being capable of maintaining objectively determinable relations with exteriority, in some way absorbs exteriority into itself. This goes to show that a philosophy of mind should be careful to distinguish between the pseudo-problem that I have just disposed of (it collapses as soon as we grasp that the mind could not be in relation with anything else) and the quite different problem that concerns the relations of the body with the soul—the latter being defined as the material of spiritual action. Yet we must recognise that this distinction scarcely seems to bring us any nearer our solution: for

The following pages from *Metaphysical Journal* were translated from the French, *Journal Métaphysique* (Paris: Librairie Gallimard, 1927) by Bernard Wall and published by Henry Regnery Co., Chicago, 1952. Permission to reprint pages 124–27, 132, 188–90, 242–87, 315–16, 332–39 was granted by Henry Regnery Co. Permission to reprint pages 14–18 of Gabriel Marcel's "A Metaphysical Diary" was granted by A. & C. Black Ltd., London, the publishers of *Being and Having*, first issued in the Fontana Library, 1965, by Collins Press. First published in 1949.

either the soul implies consciousness, and we are up against the insoluble problem of the soul; or it does not imply consciousness, and the "insoluble" problem arises in a zone intermediary between the two zones that I have just distinguished. So my elucidation still seems to be very insufficient.

What helps to obscure the problem is, I feel, the fact that the notion of body is *not at all univocal*. We really need to take into account the way in which the notion of body varies correlatively with the notion of the soul. The definition of the body as a mechanical complexus is one of the mind's modes of realisation. Of course this does not mean that the mind begets the body (even ideally); for the mind is only constituted as knowing when it thinks the known as a datum anterior to the act of knowing. But, for all that, the mode of representation of the relations of the soul and the body which depends on the way in which the body itself is thought, also depends indirectly on that very movement by which the mind is realised in knowledge. In other words (if we only envisage the body), the notion that the mind can form of the relations of the soul and body must be in function of the movement by which the notion of body is constructed. Now this construction of the body is shown to be bound up in an extraordinarily close way with the construction of the external world itself. Can we say, then, that there is a construction of the soul in the sense in which there is a construction of the body (the notion of the relations of the soul and the body would result immediately from bringing these two constructions together)? It seems to me that as soon as we have clearly distinguished the soul and the mind we are obliged to answer this question negatively. It is certainly not possible to define a movement in which the notion of the soul is elaborated in a way parallel to the movement by which the notion of body is defined—and on this point Kantian criticism should be regarded as entirely valid (indeed Kant perhaps did not draw all the conclusions from this that he might have done).

We have to set out from the principle, I think, that, whether we consider it as desiring or as perceiving, the soul is not thinkable, if not definable, outside all relations with the external world.

May 8th, 1914

Clearly we are here in full confusion. Only one point seems plain to me; it is, as I have already pointed out, that our conception, our representation of the relations of the body and the soul depends closely on the conception we form of the nature of the body. The parallelist representation, for instance, is in function of the mechanicist conception of the body; which means that parallelism does not remain true at successive stages of the evolution of the notion of body.

In other words there is no ground for positing dogmatically the possibility of a unique relation which would remain valid for modes of representation of the body (or of the soul) that are in themselves absolutely distinct; such a relation is itself function of the modes of representation. Parallelism is only valid from the standpoint of a mechanical representation of the body, and it implies, I think, a representation of the nature of the soul which cannot be regarded as *absolute*.

I insist for the moment on these very general and very indeterminate propositions. We can see immediately the problem they force us to raise: are these multiple representations of the relation of the soul and of the body contingent in relation to a reality to which they "approximate" ever more closely? It is clear that this presupposes another question, namely, what is the reality of the body? (I still leave aside the question of the soul.) If the body has a substantial reality, that amounts to saying that one (and one only) representation of the body exists—a representation which coincides with its object and of which the other representations are only images, inexact transpositions. This real representation would necessarily imply a mode of figuration, also real, of the union of the soul and the body (the figuration being also converted into object). Thus the problem of the reality of the body is shown to be the central problem and upon its solution everything else depends. It is important to state this problem in terms that are as explicit as possible, and I will formulate it thus: under what conditions is it possible to define a reality of the body in relation to which any other representation of the body must be said to function as appearance? When thus stated the problem solves itself. The conditions under which a reality can be defined as such for us can only be of a rational, intelligible order.

Thus the monist theory of the relation of the soul and the body can only have an absolute value if the representation of the body on which it is based can be regarded as real. Here it must be noted that the theory is not univocal; it can either think the body as identical with the soul (on condition that it defines the body as non-extended), or it can think the body as being the extended aspect of one and the same reality which is also soul inasmuch as it perceives itself as non-extended. One of these interpretations can be preferred to the other only if we accept an ontological value superior to the notion of the body.

But if it is true that such an ontological value can never be absolute (in the sense that the transition from the intelligible to the real is always and everywhere critical) it seems to me that we must conclude that no metaphysical judgment bearing on the relations of the soul and the body is valid. This amounts to saying that we cannot even think a real and fixed formula, that of this relation, to which we can "approximate" ever closer idefinitely. I admit that this seems to be in contradiction to experience; it seems, indeed, to amount to saying that the relation of the soul to the body is not objectively determinable; whereas the existence of numerous psychophysical constants appears to militate in favour of the opposite thesis. Only it is clear that all that I have said so far is entirely applicable to the soul. If the soul is conceived as a substantial unity, as a dynamic centre, it is only too clear that what I could call the parallelistic index is not properly applicable to the relation thought between the soul and the body. Are we able to deny outright that the soul is such a unity or such a centre? In the measure in which it passes beyond pure phenomenalism, voluntarism does not seem to be in a position to dispense entirely with that notion. Thus on the plane on which the soul is so conceived, parallelism is shown to be unthinkable. But what metaphysical value can be accorded to psychophysical constants? Can we really say that they show a fundamental and definite connection in a univocal way?

May 14th, 1916

I realised today in an impressive though confused way that the reality of bodies is and only can be a reality of interposition; bodies are mutually interposed or interpose themselves. The function of the body is at one and the same time to bind together and to separate. But *what* does it bind? *What* does it separate? There is a complete mystery here; the data of common sense and of scientific knowledge are clearly insufficient. All that I can see is this: What binds together (or what separates) ought to be in some way homogeneous in relation to what is bound. Hence thought cannot conceive the body, for instance, as binding together the psychic and the spatial. It only binds thought to the world of space inasmuch as thought is *position* (this is extremely obscure), or again inasmuch as the external world escapes from space— which is not clear either. We must go further. If the body binds the spatial in the sense that it is itself spatial, it can only bind the psychic to the psychic inasmuch as it it psychical, inasmuch as it is *charged with meaning*, and itself *is meaning*. . . .

March 13th, 1919

Had an interesting conversation yesterday with P. Admitting in principle the possibility of a "mind" (define) utilising the repertory or tabulation of someone living (mine for instance), I suggested the idea that that "mind" might be sufficiently "suggestible" to be plunged once again by us, through our will for communication, into the world of signs from which death (?) withdrew it, so that it would make an effort—entirely illusory in its very principle—to recall what we asked of it, and would seek, in our collection or aggregate of "notes" for the means of satisfying us. . . . I admit that this hypothesis is extremely bold. But at least it partially accounts for the facts. If it is true we can understand why we needed to lend *ourselves*, that is to say to lend our body, to the "mind"; if we put up a resistance, communication (the word is improper because we are really dealing with a partial substitution) would become impossible.

I would like to take this up more methodically, because it may well be that the hypothesis raises other difficulties that are insurmountable. In the first place, under what conditions would *evocation* in the strict sense be possible? To evoke a being, have we really to *invoke* it? Unquestionably it seems as if some beings are evoked when we are in no way thinking about them. But it must be admitted that this is bound up with questions that are in practice insoluble: we do not know how a body "in a trance" or "in the process of going into a trance" can appear to a "mind" that is animated by the will to communicate. The body needs in some way to be given to it (it makes itself felt). How? The problem would doubtless seem absurd to almost everybody, but my tendency to think that the body must have a sort of psychic reality, and that without it life would be inconceivable, is not of recent growth. Yet even in my eyes this statement is very vague. What I mean is that the body should be capable of being apprehended as psychical, as a psychic unity, with an apprehension that cannot be compared to a mode of perception. This would doubtless be an incipient action and susceptible of being thwarted or even totally "inhibited" by the subject himself.

As I have already pointed out we should never speak here of communication, but only of substitution or possession. I can only communicate with someone else through signs or symbols. Now no exchange of signs is possible between this "mind" and me, since this "mind" is only expressed through me and thanks to what it borrows from me (so that I naturally keep asking myself whether all that occurs does not "come" from me). But how does the "mind" preserve its power of selection? How does it manage to make use of the instrument I loan to it? Must we not suppose that when it becomes incarnate it recovers a—very partial—faculty of "re-memoration" that it was incapable of possessing "beforehand" (has this adverb a meaning?). In a word I would say that it only becomes once more capable of making use of the instrument when it is furnished with it, at which time it becomes a complete living being. The "mind" is there, it is where my body is, just as I am, and a precarious sort of psychical symbiosis is established between it and me. This allows us to understand the mistakes that are being detected, as well as the "mind's" incapacity to give information regarding its new surrounding. The surroundings cease to be its own as soon as it becomes incarnate and it only keeps, doubtless, a confused recollection of them. Moreover, it could only inform us about them by communicating with us; now *it is us* or at least forms with us a whole which for the moment cannot be decomposed.

This hypothesis is the only one that corresponds to my experience. I have certainly had the feeling that beings were making use—very unequally good use—of the instrument I lent them. We can see why a struggle should repeatedly occur between the medium who is insufficiently in a trance, who reacts—and the "mind" to which the medium does not lend himself without reserve. I would like to call this the struggle for the instrument.

I will make no further insistence on such reflections as these. Though they are very interesting they do not yet permit of a philosophical elucidation that is entirely satisfying.

And once again I resume with what I have already said about the object. The more I think it as object the less I need to appear to myself as consubstantial with it. As object it appears to me to be in communication with me. But in that measure I too become an object, or more exactly another receiving and transmitting station.

October 23rd, 1920

. . . Supposing we could conceive a world, a beyond, in which the relations of consciousness to consciousness were reduced to processes of partial identification and participation, that world would be the kingdom of the unverifiable. In last analysis even the distinction between beings would be abolished like the distinction between experiences; and the very notion of truth would lose its content. Thus if a beyond in this sense exists, we must either presume that communications by way of messages are still possible in it, or else that the beings who people it depend on "mediums" to whom they must needs have recourse so as to actualise themselves and that they only become self-conscious in the measure in which they make use of this kind of "mediation." Is this second alternative thinkable? In practice it merges with the anti-spiritist's hypothesis. Thus, contrary to appearances, it seems indeed as if a real survival of consciousness is only conceivable if in the beyond communications by means of messages are still possible; in a word *if death does not involve disincarnation*.

But can it not be maintained that death, i.e., the destruction of the instrument which allows us to send and to receive messages, involves the pure and simple negation of a life that is only maintained thanks to that interchange of messages? To see whether this is really so we must re-examine with the greatest care the idea of the message itself. What is the relation between myself and the instrument that I make use of— i.e., my body? Obviously I do not restrict myself to *making use of* my body. There is a sense in which I *am* my body, whatever that may mean. Note that communication by signs or symbols can only be effected on the basis of sensation and that sensation can in no way be compared with a message. Beings who did not feel one another, that is to say, did not grasp one another as affected, could not communicate in that way. And in consequence if death is not an absolute cessation it cannot be the pure and simple suppression of feeling itself; it can only mean a transformation in the *way* of feeling. If we admit this positive reality of death it becomes perfectly obvious that *death* can be compared to someone of whom we have ceased to know anything, someone who can give us no information about himself.

For an inquiry such as the one I am tackling here, it is essential to disentangle the exact meaning of the ambiguous formula: "I am my body." It can be seen straight away that *my* body is only *mine* inasmuch as, however confusedly, it is felt. The radical abolition of coenesthesia, supposing it were possible, would mean the destruction of my body insofar as it is mine. If I am my body this is insofar as I am a being that feels. It seems to me that we can be even more exact and say that I am my body in the measure in which my attention is brought to bear on my body *first of all*, that is to say before my attention can be fixed on any other object whatsoever. Thus the body would benefit from what I may be allowed to call an absolute priority.

I only *am* my body more absolutely than I am anything else because to be anything else whatsoever I need first of all to make use of my body (here we come back to the idea of the body being *interposed*).

From this standpoint the problem of death becomes clearer. Is it *absolute distraction* or does some mode of paying attention to the real still remain possible after the destruction of what I call my body? Yet does not this attention in question imply a centre—a point of application —in a word, a body?

I am jotting down the chance thoughts that occur to me. Perhaps at some given moment a way will open up. Is it not only inasmuch as it is not an idea, inasmuch as it is not thought as object that my body can function as instrument for me? My incapacity to carry out a habitual movement if I concentrate my attention on it would seem to bear out this remark.

All that we have so far gathered—and even that is not certain— could be formulated as follows: I am my body (in the sense in which I *am* my ideas or my work) only in the measure in which I do not treat my body as an instrument. There seems to be room for a double relation between my body and myself, granting that the term relation fits here. But then a singular problem arises. If I can only exercise my attention through the medium of my body, it follows that my body is in some way unthinkable for me; for in last analysis the attention which is concentrated on my body presupposes it. Supposing it be maintained that what is true for my body is not true for the body of others. But it is obvious that I can treat myself as *him*, as someone else, and inversely.

The argument would thus amount to proving that my body is unthinkable, and that when I imagine I am thinking its destruction I am really thinking of the destruction of something else which is not my body, something that I substitute for my body. To posit the absolute priority of the body is to say that the mediation of the body is necessary for paying attention to anything whatever, hence for knowing it itself. But under such conditions how could the nature of this mediating function come within the grasp of attention and so be known?

Hence it follows that as soon as we posit the absolute priority of the body we make it unknowable, by withdrawing it from the world of objects. I return once more to this cardinal point. At bottom only three hypotheses are possible:

1) Either we deny the absolute priority of the body which amounts to saying that the attention can be exercised on any object without mediation.

2) Or else this priority is recognised, but then either (*a*) we admit that each time the attention is exercised something enters into play which cannot be conceived as object and which, in consequence, is not identical with what I habitually call my body; or (*b*) we posit that in principle this X and my body must be identical.

The first hypothesis, I think, must be immediately rejected as being incompatible with the structure of our universe. The alternative that I have just pointed out, stands.

October 24th, 1920

I am not at all sure about the soundness of the observations I made yesterday. This is the point I thought I had reached: if *I am my body* only means "my body is an object of actual interest for me" we have nothing that can confer on my body a real priority in relation to other objects. This is not so if "my body" is regarded as the necessary condition for an object to become a datum for my attention. But in that case the attention which is brought to bear on my body presupposes the exercise of this mediating element which itself falls outside the realm of the knowable. Only by an arbitrary step of the mind as in (*b*) can I identify the body-as-object with the body-as-mediator.

But what are we to think of the idea of a primary instrument of the attention (whether or not it coincides with what I habitually call my body)? From what I pointed out yesterday it emerges that no idea of a mediating principle by which the attention can be exercised is possible for me. But is that which can in no way be an object for me by that very fact incapable of being an object for anyone? Can we not conceive a type of organic structure and optics of the intellect that are different from ours so that from their standpoint the problem would collapse?

We must first of all delve deeper into the nature of the instrumental relation. Fundamentally it seems to me that every instrument is a means of extending or of strengthening a "power" that we possess. This is just as true as regards a spade as regards a microphone. To say that these powers themselves are instruments would be merely playing with words; for we would need to determine what these powers themselves really prolong. There must always be some community of nature between the instrument and the instrumentalist. But if I look on my body as my instrument am I not yielding to a sort of unconscious illusion by which I give back to the soul the very powers which are merely prolonged by the mechanical dispositions to which I have reduced my body? It must be noted, moreover, that if I deny that the body is entirely thinkable, I am contesting that it can be treated as an instrument, since an instrument is essentially that of which an idea is possible, indeed that which is only possible through this idea of it.

Under such conditions the initial question changes its appearance. When I insisted on the necessity of a mediation for the attention to be concentrated on any object, had I not the impression that I was speaking of an instrument? And on the other hand when I said that, strictly speaking, I could not form an idea of that mediation, was I not implicitly denying that it was an instrument? I appear to be involved in a whole network of contradictions. All this should be taken up in detail.

If I think of my body as instrument I thereby attribute to the soul, whose tool it is, the potentialities which are actualised by means of this instrument. Nor is that all. I furthermore convert the soul into a body and in that way become involved in regression without end. To suppose on the other hand that I can become anything whatever, that is to say, that I can identify myself with anything whatever, by the minimum act of attention implied by an elementary sensation without the intervention of *any mediation whatsoever,* is to undermine the very foundations of spiritual life and pulverise the mind into purely successive acts. But I can no longer conceive this mediation as being of an instrumental order. I will therefore call it "sympathetic mediation." Is the idea of such mediation possible for an intelligence that is different from ours? Once again we need to make a roundabout approach. Instrumental mediation and sympathetic mediation seem to be bound up together and even unthinkable apart. But what exactly does their bond imply?

All that I can say from the standpoint which I have so far attained is that telepathy, for example, is doubtless only a particular case of a general mode of mediation which is alone capable of making instrumental mediation possible. But obviously we will not get an inch nearer the solution of the problem I have stated by interposing an unknown occult body between spiritual activity and the visible body. Moreover, the expression "spiritual activity" does not satisfy me. Things must be considered on a higher level. To say that the attention cannot be exercised directly on an object is to refuse to regard the attention as an independent reality. Could we not say that attention is always attention to self and inversely that there is only self where there is attention? Besides it is quite clear that to pay attention to something is always to pay attention to oneself as a feeling being. Yet we need to grasp that this *self* still *falls short* of all objectivity. Here we come back to the criticism that I made earlier of formalistic doctrine of the ego (as object that has nothing objective about it, that is neither a *what* nor a *who*).

I am unable to appear to myself otherwise than as an attentive activity bound up with a certain *"this"* on which it is exercised and without which it would not be itself. But have I not said that no idea of this *"this"* is possible? Whereas must it not at every moment be a given *such*, that is to say, must it not be determined? (I would not like to insist here on the problem regarding time that we will come up against soon enough). The *this* of which I am speaking is not an object, but the absolute condition for any object whatever to be given to me as datum. I wonder whether I would be betraying the thought I am trying to "bring to birth" at this moment if I said that there is no attention save where there is at the same time a certain fundamental way of feeling that cannot in any way be converted into an object, that is in no way reduced to the Kantian *I think* (since this is not a universal form) and without which the personality is annihilated. To sum up, this fundamental sensation is confounded with attention to self (the self being no more than absolute immediacy treated as mediation).

But we must grasp clearly that this *Urgefühl* can in no way be felt, precisely because it is fundamental. For it could only be so in function of other sensations—but by that very fact it would lose its priority. But is it not conceivable that for other beings placed on another plane, this fundamental quality can on the contrary be felt? . . .

When I re-read the bulk of the foregoing reflections I think I can see a "hole" in my argument. Can I not be reproached for having taken as a sort of self-evident postulate that this fundamental quality cannot be identified with my body? Whereas I am really unable to identify the object and the condition of objectivisation.

Nor are we at the end of our difficulties. If my body is not to be identified with this mediating quality, how does it happen that my body appears to me as being *more* than an object amongst other objects? I think the answer is that for sympathetic mediation to take place, there must also be instrumental mediation. Hence, for there to be a medium there must also be a knowable instrument—i.e., a body.

The kind of antinomy involved in all this is essentially bound up with the very nature of personal life, because were all instrumental mediation lacking, we would be in the realm of pure diversity, of that which cannot be grasped.

October 27th, 1920
Several points to examine. To begin with, are the beings that make up what I have called my spiritual surrounding or aura conscious? Look into the meaning of this question.

This morning during the elementary explanations that I was giving to my pupils on the relations of the soul and the body, the problem of the instrument occurred to me again with renewed force. I am obliged to compare my brain with a keyboard on which an unlimited number of combinations can be carried out. Yet it would be absurd to say that it is no more than that. I must *be* the instrument. What are we to understand by that, if not that the instrument is given to me as datum in sensation? But what is immediately given to me falls short as it were of the instrumental relationship. Now if to perceive or to imagine anything whatever this instrumental action has to be exercised, then this immediate datum *cannot* become object, it must instead be the condition of all objectivisation.

I think that now I can see the meaning and bearing of the foregoing inquiries. We are concerned essentially with determining the metaphysical conditions of personal existence. As regards this, my remarks of the 23rd are of capital importance. A world of spirit in which the identification of beings were no longer possible, would be in itself contradiction.[1] It is essential for personalities to be able to identify one another. Without that they cease to exist for themselves. Hence, between them, messages or instrumental mediations must be possible, and this excludes disincarnation in the strict sense. Yet the idea of instrumental mediation seems itself to involve contradictions, since the being is and is not its instrument, which goes to show that here we have a relative category and nothing more.

Now to ask oneself what are the conditions of personal life inevitably involves adopting both an ontological and a phenomenological standpoint. But it is first and foremost the phenomenological standpoint that I am adopting here. A being will never be able to appear to itself as a personality unless it appears as bound up with a body which it can regard as endowed with an absolute priority as regards all other objects, yet which it cannot therefore treat merely as instrument. The obscurity that surrounds the idea of "relation to an organism" is thus involved in the very idea of absolute instrument. Now what am I to say from the purely metaphysical point of view regarding the conditions under which personal life is able to be realised? If the phenomenal unity of the person is bound up with the existence of a body, the real unity of the person only seems possible if we suppose an immediate that is not self-mediatisable, which I will call sensation or fundamental experience. It is obviously impossible to deduce the phenomenological conditions from the ontogical conditions, since an object cannot be explained by speaking of something which by definition cannot be an object for us. To what extent should we emphasize the words: *"for us"*? This is the vital question. But we must clearly grasp that this immediate can only be apprehended as object where it is not at the same time the condition of objectivisation, that is to say, by beings whose power of apperception it does not mediatise. Yet I admit that this still seems to me rather obscure.

Perhaps there is something here analogous to what happens in the instance of any sensation. According to all appearances a colour in itself is a determined immediate which appears to me as object in virtue of the (unobjectifiable) power of mediation which allows me to apprehend anything whatever. But to other minds, even this power itself would appear as a quality, just as the "fundamental distillation" of the flower is presented to me as a colour or a perfume. In this sense the metaphysical conditions of the possibility of the body would lie *in another world*.

Hence "materialisation" in the technical sense of the word appears to be theoretically possible, but the objective conditions on which it depends are of necessity indeterminable for us, just as are the conditions that govern the apparition of organised bodies. Why are we irresistibly inclined to believe that the personality depends on conditions that can be determined objectively? Is it not because objectivity as such excludes limits (space, time, causality: *unlimited*)?

I may be asked whether I am really doing anything more than resurrecting the idea of spiritual substance. But for me veritable substance consists in the object conceived as relation between diverse predicates. Now the *this* of which I have spoken (the non-mediatisable immediate) is nothing of the kind and can only function as object in a spiritual context that is foreign to our world.

I am perfectly willing to admit that this metaphysical argument gives me a feeling of uneasiness. Am I not running the risk of confounding what is thought and what is felt? Even if I admit that beings belonging to a world different from mine see me otherwise than as I see myself, does their sight permit them to explore my thought? Am I not becoming a victim of materialistic paralogisms?

Perhaps we must admit that to experience a sensation is really to become in some manner the thing sensed, and that a sort of temporary coalescence is established between beings situated on different planes of reality, and in consequence belonging to distinct worlds?

October 28th, 1920

From this standpoint what becomes of the general problem of sensation? I leave aside the epistemological question, that of knowing how sensation can be interpreted objectively. My concern is to examine whether sensation itself can be regarded as a message. It seems to me that the question is of the same order as that regarding the instrumental value of the body. Every message supposes a sensation. Sensation can no more be treated as a message than the body can be treated *simply* as an instrument.

That is, it would be meaningless to suppose that at the outset a certain quality is transcribed into movement—is transmitted, and then retranscribed. To feel is not to communicate, since all communication supposes a mode of feeling. But then if this initial act of feeling is really immediate, how comes it to look as if it were conditioned by mediations? And furthermore, how avoid comparing blindness to the interruption of a current or of a circuit? Sensation appears as though bound up with the normal functioning of an instrument.

Inasmuch as the body is an absolute instrument (or appears to be such) it must needs appear to be interposed between us and objects, and we are therefore convinced that it mediatises our apprehension of the objects; whereas in the only sense that is metaphysically valid, treating the body in this way involves a contradiction. Examine the consequences of this as regards sensation.

From the point of view of the mechanical world which is the world in which we act, the world in relation to which the body functions as instrument, sensation is bound inevitably to seem *emitted* and *transmitted*. Only, as I have long realised, this interposition is in some way illusory. Hence there is a sense in which sensation differs radically from any conceivable message. But from this new point of view sensation ceases to be defined in function of an object. To feel is not to receive but to participate in an immediate way. But personal life involves the impossibility of dissociating this immediate participation from the inevitable appearance of mediation and of communication. Hence the metaphysically unintelligible element in sensation.

We need to inquire whether these remarks throw a new light on volition and action. To act, it seems to me, is to emit a certain quantity of force, it is first and foremost to *exteriorise*. Such a definition is bound up with the instrumentalist view and involves the same contradictions. But it has its roots in the very nature of personal life. Hence its element of inevitability. If we went deeper into this we would get back to the idea of will as relaxation that I tried to extricate some time ago.

Possible transition to the theory of the *thou*. From the instrumentalist standpoint, other consciousnesses are bound to appear to be sources of information. Other consciousnesses are confounded—yet are not confounded—with their bodies. Show here how the *him* can become a *thou*. By a real association without which the spiritual aura or surrounding could not be made real. Could not this association comprehend *even* things? Thus we would find the basis for psychometry; and the possibility of this association would depend on the double nature of sensation.

November 6th, 1920
I *am* my body; but I *am* also my habitual surrounding. This is demonstrated by the laceration, the division with myself that accompanies exile from my home (this is an order of experience that Proust has expressed incomparably). Am I my body in a more essential way than I am my habitual surrounding? If this question is answered in the negative, then death can only be a supreme exile, not an annihilation.

This way of stating the problem may at first sight seem childish. But that, I think, is mistaken. We must take in their strictest interpretation words such as *belong to* (a town, a house, etc.): and the word *laceration*. It is as though *adhesions* are broken.

Can all this be defined more exactly? I can see clearly that the value of the copula (in I *am* my body) is uncertain. It has not the value here that it has in the judgment of predication (cf. my notes of January 23rd, 1919).

November 8th, 1920
There is a close relationship between *I am my body* and *I am my past*, for my body has registered all my former experiences. Of course here a distinction is obligatory.

November 9th, 1920
When I say that I am my body I mean that no relation of thing to thing (or even of being to being) can here be considered. I am not the master or the proprietor of the content of my body, etc. It follows that as soon as I treat my body as a thing, I exile myself in infinite degree: the negative justification of materialism; we end up with the following formula: "My body is (an object), I am nothing." The idealists can seek a refuge by saying that I am at least the act that posits the objective reality of my body. But is this more than a piece of sleight of hand? I am afraid not. Between any such idealism and materialism the difference is, so to speak, evanescent. Everything happens as though materialism were true—and the privilege of the act of feeling which is at the root of the affirmation *I am my body*, and is its necessary foundation, is left aside. I am only my body in virtue of mysterious reasons which account for my continually feeling my body and because this feeling conditions for me all other feeling. But am I this feeling itself? This feeling seems bound up with real fluctuations that scarcely seem to me to be capable of bearing on anything save on the body's potential action, its instrumental value at a given moment. But if this is so my body is only felt inasmuch as it is me-as-acting: feeling is a function of acting. But in that case would not *I am my body* signify: "I am a determined power of acting which apprehends itself as instrument, and at the same time grasps itself as alternately inhibited and favoured in its exercise by external conditions"? An "energetic" interpretation of the body. Unfortunately nothing could be more ambiguous. For what

is this power of acting? Nothing in this notion or pseudo-notion accounts for the real unity implied in feeling (unity sometimes compromised and as often restored). And if we decide to say that I am a being to whom this power "belongs," all the difficulties reappear.

Thus I believe that the formula can only be given a negative meaning: i.e., *it is not true to say* that I am not my body, that my body is exterior to a certain central reality of myself, for no truth regarding the relation binding this pseudo-reality with my body is possible.

November 18th, 1920

There is no problem of the relations between the soul and the body. I cannot confront myself with my body (as I must do when I think an object), and ask what it is in relation to me. If it is thought my body ceases to be mine.

In short I wonder whether, whereas a body is in itself an object, the body of *someone* does not become—for me who am trying to think it—my own body, and straightway therefore ceases to be thought.

Fundamentally what does to think "someone else" mean? It means to set recollections and images in motion round a particular centre; but this may take the form of a rudimentary sketch, or it may, on the contrary, be a concrete evocation which extends beyond available information, and arouses an original flow of recollection and of the imagination: I set myself in a particular current and recollections begin to flow. This is only possible regarding beings that I have known. The more real my experience has been, the less the dissociation between soul and body is possible. What I have been given as datum is neither one nor the other (the importance of the evocation of a gesture, of an inflection in the voice, etc.). Whereas as soon as I am dealing not with the undivided experience of a *thou*, but with a total collection of information that I have gathered, I tend to think as a dualist.

December 3rd, 1920

. . . Long ago I realised that every existent must appear to me as prolonging my body in some direction or other—*my* body inasmuch as it is *mine*, that is to say, inasmuch as it is nonobjective. In this sense my body is at one and the same time the prototype of an existant and in a still deeper sense a landmark for existants. The world *exists* in the measure in which I have relations with it which are of the same type as my relations with my own body—that is to say inasmuch as I am *incarnate*. I have already noted that it is incarnation that makes the dialectical standpoint possible. Dialectics which were not based on an experience which is not completely mediatisable would not even be dialectics. This brings me back to my reflections of last October. The non-instrumental mediation that I tried to define as being the condition of any sort of objectivity would thus be the secret spring of the existential judgment.

December 9th, 1920
I am inclined to think that there can only be a body where there is the act of feeling, and for there to be this feeling the distinction between the *here* and *there* needs to cease to be rigid. The distinction is only valid on the instrumental plane. Now the body-as-instrument supposes a metaphysical body (the real kernel of the doubtless mythical notion of the "fluid body"). Am I in process of discovering the ontological foundations of invocation? This must be looked into very carefully. (Because this particular road might in the end lead me to fetishism.)

These days I am very preoccupied with the phenomena of vision through solids yet I cannot manage to state the problem in satisfactory terms. I am convinced that the idea of sensation is still the key.

I must admit that what I can see at present is rather vague. In front of me I have a gummed-up letter. Normally I can only get to know its contents if I go through certain movements. In that case the "sensation" is clearly in function of a determined instrumental activity. And even the idea of the *closed book* has reference to steps that it is possible for me to take. In a word, the order in accord with which objects are set out for us is relative to the activity of the body-as-instrument, but as soon as I cease to treat my body as an instrument the correlative order of objects is likewise transformed.

As example I take the clairvoyant who from a distance describes to me what is happening in my flat. Inasmuch as his vision is ordered in relation to his instrumental activity, it does not really differ from mine and it is subject to the same limitations. But here our task is on another plane and we need to understand how a *re-grouping* of the real is possible. We usually suppose that this re-grouping implies an objective change. To see what is happening in some particular place we imagine that we must go there, that is to say that we must put our instruments or registering apparatus *within reach*. In this way many occultists suppose that I have at my disposal a second body that I can send to represent me, a sort of messenger who makes the trip on my behalf and brings me the relevant information. But this seems to me absurd; and there is no reason why we should envisage such a hypothesis if we set out by recognising the relativity of the instrumental point of view.

At this point it would be worth while to re-examine Mill's definition so as to see what exactly it means. To say that matter is a permanent possibility of sensation is surely to suppose that it is a possibility of actions made by the body to which determined sensations normally correspond. The "phenomenist" theory of knowledge is entirely dependent on the idea of this connection.

But this definition is obviously unsatisfactory. We cannot admit that existence should be defined as a mere possibility; moreover, the clairvoyant's vision seems bound up with the fact that there is a margin between existence and possibility—a margin that is deliberately ignored in rational foresight. Thus a re-grouping, which implies no change in the disposition of the "elements," must somehow be possible. The clairvoyant has no need to act in order to see—on the contrary his vision is in function of his passivity just as much as my normal perception is in function of my activity. But on the other hand, unless I am mistaken, the structure of an acting being of necessity implies at least the ideal possibility of this kind of vision. Under what conditions can it occur? I can now see clearly that the future is the more apparent to a being the less that being is prisoner of his own activity and of his own value as instrument. The world of time is no less completely disposed in relation to my instrumental activity than the world of space.

September 29th, 1922

As I have often said, the object is that which is thought as not taking me into account (even idealists recognise that everything occurs as *though* the realists were right). But the word *me* here does not mean my body; it is my desire (there is a fundamental agreement between scientific knowledge and an ethical system which is essentially stoical). Yet I can constrain things to take me into account in the measure in which I function as physical agent. My body is the indispensable mediator by which I can act on things, because it itself is homogeneous in relation to things. Yet the body itself takes *me* into account (e.g., an erotic image immediately entails a physical modification); in this measure it is not objective in the sense defined above. In this sense I depend on its interposition; it is in the measure that I depend on it that things depend on me; in a word a real potentiality is bound up with a "non-knowing"; my knowledge is function of something which is its very negation.

May 24th, 1923

. . . It is in relation to me as conscious of my body, that is to say as grasping it at one and the same time as object (body) and as non-object (my body), that all existence is defined. In a word, to state the existence of a being or of a thing would be to say: This being is of the same nature as my body and belongs to the same world; only this homogeneity doubtless bears less on the (objective) essence than on the intimacy that the word *my, my body*, involves. In this way we could explain that which in existence is incapable of definition—since the fact for my body of being my body is not something of which I can genuinely have an idea, it is not something that I can conceptualise. In the fact of *my body* there is something which transcends what can be called its materiality, something which cannot be reduced to any of its objective qualities. And the world only exists for me inasmuch as I think it (this expresses it badly), inasmuch as I apprehend it as bound up with me by the thread which also binds me to my body.

To this must be linked the fact that the world only exists inasmuch as I can act on it: for there is only action inasmuch as I am my body, inasmuch as I cease to think my body. The nonobjectivity of *my body* becomes clear to our mind as soon as we remember that it is of the essence of the object as such that it does not take me into account. In the measure in which it does not take me into account my body seems to me not to be my body.

This summary is very important. It should throw some light on the problem I stated yesterday. But I will only reach my goal by roundabout ways.

At this immediate moment I am wondering whether we cannot throw light on the nature of belief by setting out from this theory of existence. Is not belief always the act by which I skip over one of the continuous series which bind up my immediate experience to a particular fact, and treat this fact as if it were given to me in the same way as my own body is given to me? It must of course be emphasised that my body is not an object of belief: all belief is based on the model of that which is not, in itself, a belief. But in that case might it not be said that all belief comes to bear on facts of a material order? No, because I can conceive infinite prolongations of the central act, unlimited possibilities of vision, etc. There is no need to underline how much this conclusion strengthens what I would like to call my "sensualistic" metaphysics. For obviously the connection between existence and sensation is as close as it could be. Is the connection with the theory of the *thou* equally easy to grasp? As I see things at present, it is. We must set out from the *him*, from the *that*. *That* is that of which I speak to someone else, i.e., that from which I turn away, in a word that which I treat as not taking into account the act by which I think it (and here I am speaking of a concrete, detailed, and present thought). Briefly, I put my emphasis on objectivity and not on existence, if we understand existence in the sense explained above. To treat a being as not taking us into account is in some way to disinterest ourselves from this being (even if we concentrate our attention on it); it is to adopt an attitude which is fundamentally opposed to the attitude implied by love. This needs defining. If I treat a being as not taking me into account, to what extent does that mean that I do not take him or it into account? The answer to this question seems to me very plain: it is that I do not treat him as a *me*, as possessing the faculty of depending on himself and taking himself into account, the faculty which is at the very root of existence. . . .

APPENDIX
(FROM "EXISTENCE AND OBJECTIVITY")

. . . Inasmuch as I look on myself as carrying on communications with objects or, if you like, with *things* that are distinct from me, it is perfectly natural that my body should appear to me as interposed between those things and me, or, to be more exact, that it should be presented to me as pre-eminently the instrument of which I make use both for receiving and sending messages (which may, moreover, easily be reduced to simple signs. In a world constituted by or at least marked out by stations in communication with one another, *my* body like other bodies functions as an apparatus for signalling). But when set up as an absolute this very simple and seductive interpretation gives rise to difficulties that are insurmountable.

In the first place the idea of interposition is very obscure in itself. A thing can be interposed between two things or, more exactly, a term can be slipped in between two terms. But is this logical schema applicable here? When I say that my body is interposed between me and things, I am only expressing a pseudo-idea. Because what I call *me* cannot be identified with a thing or with a term. Of course it is possible to say that my body is interposed between a body *A* which affects it and a body *R* on which it reacts. But in that case what happens to *me*, to the subject? The subject seems to *withdraw into an indeterminate sphere from which it contemplates*—without existing for itself—*the anonymous play of the universal mechanism*.

Yet if I adopt the purely instrumentalist way of representing what I call my body, I run into even worse difficulties. Note in the first place that the expression "I make use of my body" allows for a very wide margin between itself and the rich and confused experience that it claims to translate. In the consciousness that I have of my body and of my relations with my body, there is something that this affirmation fails to *render*. Hence the protest we can scarcely repress: "I do not *make use of* my body, I *am* my body." In other words, there is something in me that denies the implication that is to be found in the purely instrumentalist notion of the body that my body is external to myself. And, as I see it, materialism constitutes an effort—though an unfortunate effort—to organise this protest and transform it into a positive doctrine. In this respect there is an instructive connection between materialism and sensualism. Both translate one and the same defence-reaction of thought—and all idealists are bound to recognise that this is absolutely legitimate.

It would not be enough merely to note the uneasiness with which the mind entertains the formulae of instrumentalism. The real question is whether this uneasiness can be justified rationally. An analysis closely resembling the analysis to which we have already submitted the idea of "message" will enable us to answer this question.

When I make use of any kind of tool, in reality I do no more than prolong and specialise a way of behaving that already belongs to my body (whether to my limbs or to my senses). This is just as obvious when applied to a spade or a hammer as to a telescope or microscope. Not only is the instrument *relative* to my body—between the instrument and my body there is a deep community of nature. But given these conditions can I treat the body itself as an instrument? As soon as we get to grips with the meaning of this question we discover that we are obliged to imagine a *physical soul* furnished with powers and faculties; and the mechanical terms, to which my body seems reduced, are really only prolongations or transpositions of these powers or faculties. But how avoid distrusting such a hybrid notion as this?

Either we are condemned to follow the ladder endlessly from physical instrument to physical instrument.

Or else we stop arbitrarily in the series of regressions and maintain that an instrument can be utilised (but how?) by a principle (?) which has a nature quite different from itself. This amounts to saying that an instrument may possibly be an instrument of nothing.

Hence there is at least an indirect justification for the repugnance I feel about looking on my body as "something that I make use of." I feel confusedly that it is still my body that makes use of my body and that I am involved in a dead end.

I believe that what I should like to call *instrumental mediation* can only conceivably take place within a world of objects and between bodies of which none are regarded as *my body*, that is to say, as affected by this special index which in part removes it from the order of that about which we can hold discourse either with someone else or with ourselves.

Thus, in the measure in which I speak of my body as an instrument, I treat it as an object, that is to say as *not-mine*. I adopt the position of a *third person* regarding it and any definition I am able to make of it is bound up with the *ideal disincarnation* to which I have previously had recourse, and with the act by which I delegated to a sort of fictitious *double* the "power" of utilising this instrument. Inasmuch as I act I identify myself with this double which in this way regains the reality of which I dispossessed it when I detached myself from it. It follows that we re-create the unity that had been broken up by analysis when it substituted for this unity the duality of instrumentalist and instrument.

Thus the role of reflection—whether this be exercised on *feeling* or on *acting*—consists not in cutting to pieces and dismembering but, on the contrary, in re-establishing in all its continuity that living tissue which imprudent analysis tore asunder.

I will doubtless be blamed for substituting the unintelligible terms of a problem for a solution which, though perhaps imperfect, is at least clear. But at this point, as in the case of existence, our procedure must consist in asking whether thought here is not guilty of a dialectical abuse, that of positing a problem where there is not and cannot be anything problematical. What I mean is this: inasmuch as I consider my body either in its relations with other bodies or in its own structure, I am confronted with something which is essentially an occasion for a problem, and hence an object of possible knowledge, by very reason of the *detachment from myself* to which I have proceeded so as to isolate and define this totality of terms. To the extent to which my body lends itself to such treatment it is certainly converted to an object. But in submitting it to this treatment I cease to look on it as *my body*, I deprive it of that absolute priority in virtue of which *my body* is posited as the centre in relation to which my experience and my universe are ordered. Thus my body only becomes an occasion for a problem under conditions such that the very problem that we intended to state loses all meaning. This problem consists in asking how my body is bound up with the X whose body it is: it is only by a sort of mental sympathy, by identifying myself with the personality of others, that I can (or think I can) state it in universal terms. In reality this problem only has meaning for *me* (a *me* that I can expand and contract at will). But on the other hand it is precisely as regards me—and as regards my body—that this problem cannot be stated without involving a contradiction.

This point is particularly delicate and I consider it is necessary to emphasise it. So as to demonstrate its contradictory character let us consider the above formula: how is *my body* bound up (= what relation unites it to the X *of which* it is the body)? But the relation expressed by the genitive *of which* is itself formally negated by the words *my body*. To say *my body* is to refuse to attribute it *to this or that person*. At first sight this may seem outrageously paradoxical. Instead of saying my body, could I not name myself, point out the *person* to whom the body belongs? But what I am maintaining is that by this operation, which is presented logically as the substitution of one term for an equivalent term, I effect a transition from a given order into an order that is irreducibly different. When I think *my body* (and not that of another person to whom I give my name) I am in a situation which it becomes impossible to account for as soon as I substitute for it the idea of a relation between terms that are hypothetically dissociated. For if I effect this substitution I place myself in conditions that are strictly incompatible with the initial state which it was my business to explain.

So as to give a more complete elucidation of the meaning of this paradox I propose to throw a beam of light all around it so as to make clearer its importance.

When I treat my body as a term which is in a certain relation to *that* of which it is the body, I misrepresent the conditions which permit the definition of a term in general. For only that which can be apprehended thanks to an act of attentive discrimination is susceptible of functioning as terms for the mind. Now this only applies to *my body* if my thought, so to speak, retires away from it to a distance and considers it as an object among other objects. But if I proceed in this way, I am operating as though I had forgotten that this body is *mine*. I disincarnate myself in idea—to use the expression already employed earlier. If on the other hand I reintegrate myself with my body, my body ceases to appear to me as a possible term or object of discourse. But to think *my body* is manifestly to throw light on this re-establishment of possession and *reincarnation;* it means that I knowingly re-establish the state of non-division that had been broken up by rudimentary reflection.

Furthermore we need, doubtless, to generalise the result we reached when we criticised the instrumentalist interpretation of the body. Whatever be the relation I pretend to establish between myself and my body, I will end up in error or, more exactly, I will in fact be speaking of something other than what I think I am speaking about; for if I mentally retrieve all that is implied by the expression "my body" this ceases to be a term external to a further term, X, which is myself.

But what about the instance of a passer-by who is given to me as datum under the aspect of a particular organic body of which objective knowledge is possible? I cannot avoid supposing that this person, P, has a psychological nature and constitutes a particular mental system in process of development in time. Between this mental system and this physical system how can there not be a relation, X, whatever this X may be? How, in brief, if I reason by analogy, can I avoid concluding that I too must appear to other people as a particular physical system bound up with a special mental system, and that the relation that exists in the first instance must also exist in the instance of myself? At first sight such reasoning cannot fail to appear decisive.

Yet for all that it may possibly be an illusion. What am I really trying to say when I maintain that I cannot avoid attributing to P a particular mental system? I cannot insist too much that this system is not an object of possible experience in the sense in which a portion π of P's body is. Strictly speaking there is nothing there that can be an object for me. All that can happen is the production of certain material conditions that will allow me to "sympathise" with P and embrace his "interior becoming." But to this extent, however fallaciously and partially, I am identifying myself with P. Hence in relation to P's mental system I cease to occupy the *external* position that I still maintain regarding his body. And it is only an illusion if I imagine things to be otherwise. Hence:

Either this mental system is discovered to me, and that means that I have for an instant become P, that P's body has ideally become my body,

Or else P's body continues to be "that other body," an object situated in space and in a given manner in relation to "my own body"; but in that case P's mental system remains entirely closed to me and inaccessible.

Doubtless in practice we imagine things otherwise. We construct a certain idea of P's mental system which remains "in us" (that is to say we treat it as a piece of our psychological life); but as this idea is not P and in no way coincides with P's mental reality, we are unable, without absurdity, to question ourselves on the relation that unites it with P's body. The problem of the relations between P's soul and body thus only arises if *I take my stand*, so to speak, in an intermediary region, a sort of between worlds, which for thought should only be a point of passage —to take one's stand there is contradictory. As soon as I have attained P's mental reality (supposing that this is possible, as I for my own part believe), and have become identified with it, there can be *no longer* any question of raising this problem, and—furthermore—this problem could not be raised *before* I made the mental journey which led from myself to P.

This analysis would need to be filled out as follows: I am not satisfied with forming a mere idea (a kind of mental effigy) of *others*. By a sort of recoil I end up by executing an analogous operation on myself and establish an account of myself like the one to which I tend to reduce P. This animated account or sketch I call my soul, my spiritual reality; it tends to be converted into a personality; and it is regarding the relations of this mythical personality with my body (which is detached from me in the sense pointed out earlier) that—as a pseudo-philosopher—I embark on the vain enterprise of thinking.

These considerations lead us to make a general and very important distinction between data that are susceptible of forming the occasion for a problem—that is, objective data—and data *on which the mind must be based* so as to state any problem whatsoever. It is impossible to treat the latter data as problematic without involving oneself in the worst of contradictions. Sensation (= the fact of feeling, of participating in a universe which creates me by affecting me), and the intellectually indefectible bond that unites me with what I call my body, are data of this second kind. And it is easy to see that in all likelihood these data are confounded together at the heart of existence as we *recognised* (as distinct from identified) it at the beginning of this essay.

What is commonly—but improperly—called the union of soul and body must be considered to be a metaphysical form of *hicceity*. Like hicceity this union is indivisible and reflection can obtain no hold upon it. Of course this is not to say that it is *unknowable,* for that would amount to supposing that it conceals a mechanism with a secret operation that escapes us.

Yet here again it is difficult to deny that we seem to be not only going against the data of common sense but also against the age-long results of philosophical analysis.

I have the idea of a movement that is to be performed; I then carry out this movement. How deny that there must be a relation, X, between the idea and the movement? But in reality we are being taken in by words. What I call the idea of raising my arm is only the abstract schematisation of a particular posture that I cannot really think or represent to myself, but only adopt, i.e., mentally reproduce. But once I have placed myself in this situation, am I able to continue to consider the act of raising my arm from the outside; can I still treat it as an object? Doubtless yes. But the hybrid character of this position is obvious. Inasmuch as I identify myself with the man who "thinks of raising his arm" this arm must appear to me as mine. Otherwise it is meaningless to declare that one and the same person *has the idea of lifting his arm* and *really lifts it.* Thus the whole question is reduced to: "How am I going to raise my arm?" But unless this question is stated in purely physical and objective terms, it ceases to be a problem. For there is only a problem when a particular content is detached from the context that unites it with the *I*. Now here, on the contrary, I needed to re-establish that contact. Thus no physical science is possible regarding the transition which leads from the idea to the act, or rather, regarding what—by a vicious though doubtless inevitable transposition—we think we can represent to ourselves as a communication between spheres that are distinct.

A METAPHYSICAL DIARY

Notes for a Paper to the Philosophical Society

Undated, written in 1927 or 1928[2]

When I affirm that something exists, I always mean that I consider this something as connected with my body, as able to be put in contact with it, however indirect this contact may be. But note must be taken that the priority I thus ascribe to my body depends on the fact that my body is given to me in a way that is not exclusively objective, i.e., on the fact that it is *my* body. This character, at once mysterious and intimate, of the bond between me and my body (I purposely avoid the word *relation*) does in fact colour all existential judgments.

What it comes to is this. We cannot really separate:

1. Existence;
2. Consciousness of self as existing;
3. Consciousness of self as bound to a body, as incarnate.

From this several important conclusions would seem to follow:

(1) In the first place, the existential point of view about reality cannot, it seems, be other than that of an incarnate personality. Insofar as we can imagine a pure understanding, there is, for such an understanding, no possibility of considering things as existent or nonexistent.

(2) On the one hand, the problem of the existence of the external world is now changed and perhaps even loses its meaning; I cannot in fact without contradiction think of my body as nonexistent, since it is in connection with it (insofar as it is *my* body) that every existing thing

is defined and placed. On the other hand, we ought to ask whether there are valid reasons for giving my body a privileged metaphysical status in comparison with other things.

(3) If this is so, it is permissible to ask whether the union of the soul and body is, in essence, really different from the union between the soul and other existing things. In other words, does not a certain experience of the self, as tied up with the universe, underlie all affirmation of existence?

(4) Inquire whether such an interpretation of the existential leads towards subjectivism.

(5) Show how idealism tends inevitably to eliminate all existential considerations in view of the fundamental unintelligibility of existence. Idealism *versus* metaphysics. Values detached from existence: too real to exist.

Existential and personalist interests closely linked. The problem of the immortality of the soul is the pivot of metaphysic.

Every existent is thought of as an obstacle by which we take our bearings—as something we could collide with in certain circumstances —resistant, impenetrable. We *think* of this impenetrability, no doubt, but we think of it as not completely thinkable. Just as my body is thought of insofar as it is *a* body, but my thought collides with the fact that it is *my* body.

To say that something exists is not only to say that it belongs to the same system as my body (that it is bound to it by certain connections which reason can define), it is also to say that it is in some way united to me as my body is.

Incarnation—the central "given" of metaphysic. Incarnation is the situation of a being who appears to himself to be, as it were, *bound* to a body. This "given" is opaque to itself: opposition to the *cogito*. Of this body, I can neither say that it is I, nor that it is not I, nor that it is *for* me (object). The opposition of subject and object is found to be transcended from the start. Inversely, if I start from the opposition, treating it as fundamental, I shall find no trick of logical sleight of hand which lets me get back to the original experience, which will inevitably be either eluded or (which comes to the same thing) refused. We are not to object that this experience shows a contingent character: in point of fact, all metaphysical enquiry requires a starting-point of this kind. It can only start from a situation which is mirrored but cannot be understood.

Inquire if incarnation is a fact; it does not seem so to me, it is the "given" starting from which a fact is possible (which is not true of the *cogito*).

A fundamental predicament which cannot be in a strict sense mastered or analysed. It is exactly this impossibility which is being stated when I declare, confusedly, that I *am* my body; i.e., I cannot quite treat myself as a term distinct from my body, a term which would be in a definable connection with it. As I have said elsewhere, the moment I treat my body as an object of scientific knowledge, I banish myself to infinity.

This is the reason why I cannot think of *my death*, but only of the standstill of *that* machine (*illam*, not *hanc*). It would perhaps be more accurate to say that I cannot anticipate my death, that is, I cannot ask myself what will become of *me* when the machine is no longer working.

February 29th, 1929

Have detected, perhaps, an important fallacy involved in the idea (cf. my previous notes on incarnation) that opacity must be bound up with otherness. But surely the contrary is really the case. Surely opacity really arises from the fact that the "I" interposes between the self and the other, and intervenes as a third party?

The obscurity of the external world is a function of my own obscurity to myself; the world has no intrinsic obscurity. Should we say that it comes to the same thing in the end? We must ask up to what point this interior opacity is a result; is it not very largely the consequence of an act? and is not this act simply sin?

My ideas are hardest for me to grasp where they are most completely *my* ideas; that is, where they are impenetrable to me. The problem I am setting myself is to find out whether this applies to the whole of reality. Is not reality impenetrable to me just in proportion as I am involved in it?

Of course all this is horribly difficult to think out clearly. In a different terminology (that of the *Journal Métaphysique*) I could easily say that insofar as my body is an absolute mediator, I so far cease to have communication with it (in the sense that I have communication with any objective sector of the Real). Let us say again that my body is not and cannot be given to me. For everything "given" attracts to itself a process of indefinite objectification, and that is what I understand by the word "penetrable." The impenetrability, then, of my body belongs to it in virtue of its quality of absolute mediator. But it is obvious that my body, in that sense, is myself; for I cannot distinguish myself from it unless I am willing to reduce it to an object, i.e., unless I cease to treat it as an absolute mediator.

We must, therefore, break away once and for all from the metaphors which depict consciousness as a luminous circle round which there is nothing, to its own eyes, but darkness. On the contrary, the shadow is at the centre.

When I try to make clear to myself the nature of my bond with my body, it appears to me chiefly as something of which I have the use (as one has the use of a piano, a saw, or a razor); but all these uses are extensions of the initial use, which is simply the use of the body. I have real priority to my body when it is a question of active use, but none whatever when it is a question of knowledge. The use is only possible on the basis of a certain felt community. But the community is indivisible; I cannot validly say "I and my body." The difficulty arises from the fact that I think of my relation with my body on the analogy of my relation with my instruments—whereas in fact the latter presupposes the former. . . .

NOTES

1. Unless this world were a unique consciousness.
2. This paper was never delivered.

THE BODY

Jean-Paul Sartre

The problem of the body and its relations with consciousness is often obscured by the fact that while the body is from the start posited as a certain *thing* having its own laws and capable of being defined from outside, consciousness is then reached by the type of inner intuition which is peculiar to it. Actually if after grasping "my" consciousness in its absolute interiority and by a series of reflective acts, I then seek to unite it with a certain living object composed of a nervous system, a brain, glands, digestive, respiratory, and circulatory organs whose very matter is capable of being analyzed chemically into atoms of hydrogen, carbon, nitrogen, phosphorus, etc., then I am going to encounter insurmountable difficulties. But these difficulties all stem from the fact that I try to unite my consciousness not with *my* body but with the body *of others*. In fact the body which I have just described is not *my* body such as it is *for me*. I have never seen and never shall see my brain nor my endocrine glands. But because I who am a man have seen the cadavers of men dissected, because I have read articles on physiology, I conclude that my body is constituted exactly like all those which have been shown to me on the dissection table or of which I have seen colored drawings in books. Of course the physicians who have taken care of me, the surgeons who have operated on me, have been able to have direct experience with the body which I myself do not know. I do not

The following pages are extracted from Jean-Paul Sartre's *Being and Nothingness: An Essay on Phenomenological Ontology* (New York: Philosophical Library, 1956), pp. 303–7, 309–10, 318–30, 357–59. These pages are translated from the French, *L'être et le néant* (Paris: Librairie Gallimard, 1943), by Hazel E. Barnes. Reprinted with the permission of Literary Masterworks, Inc., New York, and the translator.

disagree with them, I do not claim that I lack a brain, a heart, or a stomach. But it is most important to choose the *order* of our bits of knowledge. So far as the physicians have had any experience with my body, it was with my body *in the midst of the world* and as it is for others. My body as it is *for me* does not appear to me in the midst of the world. Of course during the radioscopy I was able to see the picture of my vertebrae on a screen, but I was *outside* in the midst of the world. I was apprehending a wholly constituted object as a *this* among other *thises,* and it was only by a reasoning process that I referred it back to being *mine;* it was much more my *property* than my *being.*

It is true that I see and touch my legs and my hands. Moreover nothing prevents me from imagining an arrangement of the sense organs such that a living being could see one of his eyes while the eye which was seen was directing its glance upon the world. But it is to be noted that in this case again I am the *Other* in relation to my eye. I apprehend it as a sense organ constituted in the world in a particular way, but I cannot "see the seeing"; that is, I cannot apprehend it in the process of revealing an aspect of the world to me. Either it is a thing among other things, or else it is that by which things are revealed to me. But it cannot be both at the same time. Similarly I *see* my hand touching objects, but do not *know* it in its act of touching them. This is the fundamental reason why that famous "sensation of effort" of Maine de Biran does not really exist. For my hand reveals to me the resistance of objects, their hardness or softness, but not *itself*. Thus I see my hand only in the way that I see this inkwell. I unfold a distance between it and me, and this distance comes to integrate itself in the distances which I establish among all the objects of the world. When a doctor takes my wounded leg and looks at it while I, raised up on my bed, watch him do it, there is no essential difference between the visual perception which I have of the doctor's body and that which I have of my own leg. Better yet, they are distinguished only as different structures of a single global perception; there is no essential difference between the doctor's perception of *my* leg and my own present perception of it. Of course when I touch my leg with my finger, I realize that my leg is touched. But this phenomenon of double sensation is not essential: cold, a shot of morphine, can make it disappear. This shows that we are dealing with two essentially different orders of reality. To touch and to be touched, to feel that one is touching and to feel that one is touched

—these are two species of phenomena which it is useless to try to reunite by the term "double sensation." In fact they are radically distinct, and they exist on two incommunicable levels. Moreover when I touch my leg or when I see it, I surpass it toward my own possibilities. It is, for example, in order to pull on my trousers or to change a dressing on my wound. Of course I can at the same time arrange my leg in such a way that I can more conveniently "work" on it. But this does not change the fact that I transcend it toward the pure possibility of "curing myself" and that consequently I am present to it without its *being me* and without my *being it*. What I cause to exist here is the *thing* "leg"; it is not the leg as the *possibility which I am* of walking, running, or of playing football.

Thus to the extent that my body indicates my possibilities in the world, seeing my body or touching it is to transform these possibilities of mine into dead-possibilities. This metamorphosis must necessarily involve a complete *thisness* with regard to the body as a living possibility of running, of dancing, etc. Of course, the discovery of my body as an object is indeed a revelation of its being. But the being which is thus revealed to me is its *being-for-others*. That this confusion may lead to absurdities can be clearly seen in connection with the famous problem of "inverted vision." We know the question posed by the physiologists: "How can we set upright the objects which are painted upside down on our retina?" We know as well the answer of the philosophers: "There is no problem. An object is upright or inverted in relation to the rest of the universe. To perceive the whole universe inverted means nothing, for it would have to be inverted in relation to something." But what particularly interests us is the origin of this false problem. It is the fact that people have wanted to link *my* consciousness of objects to the body of the *Other*. Here are the candle, the crystalline lens, the inverted image on the screen of the retina. But to be exact, the retina enters here into a physical system; it is a *screen* and only that; the crystalline lens is a *lens* and only a lens; both are homogeneous in their being with the candle which completes the system. Therefore we have deliberately chosen the physical point of view—i.e., the point of view of the outside, of exteriority—in order to study the problem of vision; we have considered a dead eye in the midst of the visible world in order to account for the visibility of this world. Consequently, how can we be surprised later when consciousness, which is absolute interiority, refuses to allow itself to be bound to this object? The relations which I establish

between the Other's body and the external object are *really* existing
relations, but they have for their being the being of the for-others;
they suppose a center of intra-mundane flow in which knowledge is a
magic property of space, "action at a distance." From the start they are
placed in the perspective of the Other-as-object.

If then we wish to reflect on the nature of the body, it is necessary to
establish an order of our reflections which conforms to the order of
being: we cannot continue to confuse the ontological levels, and we
must in succession examine the body first as being-for-itself and then as
being-for-others. And in order to avoid such absurdities as "inverted
vision," we must keep constantly in mind the idea that since these two
aspects of the body are on different and incommunicable levels of
being, they cannot be reduced to one another. Being-for-itself must
be wholly body and it must be wholly consciousness; it cannot be
united with a body. Similarly being-for-others is wholly body; there
are no "psychic phenomena" there to be united with the body. There is
nothing *behind* the body. But the body is wholly "psychic." We must
now proceed to study these two modes of being which we find for
the body.

THE BODY AS BEING-FOR-ITSELF: FACTICITY

It appears at first glance that the preceding observations are opposed
to the givens of the Cartesian *cogito*. "The soul is easier to know than the
body," said Descartes. Thereby he intended to make a radical distinction
between the facts of thought, which are accessible to reflection, and the
facts of the body, the knowledge of which must be guaranteed by
divine Providence. It appears at first that reflection reveals to us only
pure facts of consciousness. Of course on this level we encounter
phenomena which appear to include within themselves some connection with the body; "physical" pain, the uncomfortable, pleasure,
etc. But these phenomena are no less *pure facts of consciousness*. There
is a tendency therefore to make *signs* out of them, affections of consciousness *occasioned* by the body, without realizing that one has
thereby irremediably driven the body out of consciousness and that
no bond will ever be able to reunite this body, which is already a
body-for-others, with the consciousness which, it is claimed, makes the
body manifest.

Furthermore we ought not to take this as our point of departure but rather our primary relation to the in-itself: our being-in-the-world. We know that there is not a for-itself on the one hand and a world on the other as two closed entities for which we must subsequently seek some explanation as to how they communicate. The for-itself is a relation to the world. The for-itself, by denying that it is being, makes there be a world, and by surpassing this negation toward its own possibilities it reveals the *"thises"* as instrumental-things.

But when we say that the for-itself is-in-the-world, that consciousness is consciousness *of* the world, we must be careful to remember that the world exists confronting consciousness as an indefinite multiplicity of reciprocal relations which consciousness surveys without perspective and contemplates without a point of view. *For me* this glass is to the left of the decanter and a little behind it; *for Pierre,* it is to the right and a little in front. It is not even conceivable that a consciousness could survey the world in such a way that the glass should be *simultaneously* given to it at the right and at the left of the decanter, in front of it and behind it. This is by no means the consequence of a strict application of the principle of identity but because this fusion of right and left, of before and behind, would result in the total disappearance of *"thises"* at the heart of a primitive indistinction. Similarly if the table leg hides the designs in the rug from my sight, this is not the result of some finitude and some imperfection in my visual organs, but it is because a rug which would not be hidden by the table, a rug which would not be either under it or above it or to one side of it, would not have any relation of any kind with the table and would no longer belong to the "world" in which *there is* the table. The in-itself which is made manifest in the form of the *this* would return to its indifferent self-identity. Even space as a purely external relation would disappear. The constitution of space as a multiplicity of reciprocal relations can be effected only from the abstract point of view of science; it cannot be lived, it cannot even be represented. The triangle which I trace on the blackboard so as to help me in abstract reasoning is necessarily to the right of the circle tangent to one of its sides, necessarily to the extent that it *is* on the blackboard. And my effort is to surpass the concrete characteristics of the figure traced in chalk by not including its relation to me in my calculations any more than the thickness of the lines or the imperfection of the drawing.

Thus by the mere fact that *there is* a world, this world cannot exist without a univocal orientation in relation to me. Idealism has rightly insisted on the fact that relation makes the world. But since idealism took its position on the ground of Newtonian science, it conceived this relation as a relation of reciprocity. Thus it attained only abstract concepts of pure exteriority, of action and reaction, etc., and due to this very fact it missed the world and succeeded only in making explicit the limiting concept of absolute objectivity. This concept in short amounted to that of a *"desert world"* or of "a world without men"; that is, to a contradiction, since it is through human reality that there is a world. Thus the concept of objectivity, which aimed at replacing the in-itself of dogmatic truth by a pure relation of reciprocal agreement between representations, is self-destructive if pushed to the limit. . . .

This absolutely necessary and totally unjustifiable order of the things of the world, this order which is myself in so far as I am neither the foundation of my being nor the foundation of a *particular* being— this order is the body as it is on the level of the for-itself. In this sense we could define the body as *the contingent form which is assumed by the necessity of my contingency.* The body is nothing other than the for-itself; it is not an in-itself *in* the for-itself, for in that case it would solidify everything. But it is the fact that the for-itself is not its own foundation, and this fact is expressed by the necessity of existing as an engaged, contingent being among other contingent beings. As such the body is not distinct from the *situation* of the for-itself since for the for-itself, to exist and to be situated are one and the same; on the other hand the body is identified with the whole world inasmuch as the world is the total situation of the for-itself and the measure of its existence.

But a situation is not a pure contingent given. Quite the contrary, it is revealed only to the extent that the for-itself surpasses it toward itself. Consequently the body-for-itself is never a given which I can know. It is there everywhere as the surpassed; it exists only in so far as I escape it by nihilating myself. The body is what I nihilate. It is the in-itself which is surpassed by the nihilating for-itself and which reapprehends the for-itself in this very surpassing. It is the fact that I am my own motivation without being my own foundation, the fact that I am nothing without having to be what I am and yet in so far as I have to be what I am, I am without having to be. In one sense therefore the body is a necessary characteristic of the for-itself; it is not true that the body is the product of an arbitrary decision on the part of a demiurge nor that the union of soul and body is the contingent bringing together of two substances radically distinct. On the contrary, the very nature of the for-itself demands that it be body; that is, that its nihilating escape from being should be made in the form of an engagement in the world. Yet in another sense the body manifests my contingency; we can even say that it is *only* this contingency. The Cartesian rationalists were right in being struck with this characteristic; in fact it represents the individualization of my engagement in the world. And Plato was not wrong either in taking the body as *that which individualizes the soul*. Yet it would be in vain to suppose that the soul can detach itself from this individualization by separating itself from the body at death or by pure thought, for the soul *is* the body inasmuch as the for-itself *is* its own individualization. . . .

A sense is not given *before* sensible objects. For is it not capable indeed of appearing as an object to the Other? Neither is it given *after* sensible objects; for in that case it would be necessary to suppose a world of incommunicable images, simple copies of reality the mechanism of whose appearance was inconceivable. The senses are contemporaneous with objects; they are things "in person" as they are revealed to us in perspective. They represent simply an objective rule of this revelation. Thus sight does not *produce* visual *sensations;* neither is it affected by light rays. It is the collection of all visible objects in so far as their objective and reciprocal relations all refer to certain chosen sizes—submitted to all at once—as measures, and to a certain center of perspective. From this point of view the senses must in no way be identified with subjectivity. In fact all variations which can be registered in a perceptive field are *objective* variations. In particular, the fact that one can cut off vision by "closing the eyelids" is an *external* fact which does not refer to the subjectivity of the apperception. The eyelid, in fact, is merely one object perceived among other objects, an object which hides other objects from me as the result of its objective relation with them. *No longer to see* the objects in my room because I have closed my eyes is *to see* the curtain of my eyelids. In the same way if I put my gloves on the tablecloth, then *no longer to see* a particular design in the cloth is precisely *to see the gloves*. Similarly the *accidents* which affect a sense belong to the province of objects. "I see yellow" because I have jaundice or because I am wearing yellow glasses. In each case the reason for the phenomenon is not found in a subjective modification of the sense nor even in an organic change but in an objective relation between objects in the world; in each case I see "through" something, and the *truth* of my vision is objective. Finally if in one way or another the center of visual reference is destroyed (since destruction can come only from the development of the world according to its own laws—i.e., expressing in a certain way my facticity), visible objects are not by the same stroke annihilated. They continue to exist *for me*, but they exist without any center of reference, as *a visible totality* without the appearance of any particular *this;* that is, they exist in the absolute reciprocity of their relations. Thus it is the upsurge of the for-itself in the world which by the same strokes causes the world to exist as the totality of things and causes senses to exist as the objective mode in which the qualities of things are presented. What is fundamental is my relation to the world, and this relation at once defines the world and the senses according to the point of view which is adopted. Blindness, Daltonism, myopia originally represent *the way in which there is* a world for me; that is, they define my visual sense in so far as this is the facticity of my upsurge. This is why I can know and objectively define my senses but only *emptily,* in terms of the world; all that is necessary is that my rational and universalizing thought should prolong in the abstract the indications which things give to myself about *my* sense and that it *reconstitute* the sense in terms of these signs as the historian reconstitutes an historical personality according to the evidence indicating it. But in this case I have reconstructed the world on the ground of pure rationality by abstracting myself from the world through thought. I survey the world without attaching myself to it; I place myself in an attitude of absolute objectivity, and each sense becomes one object among objects, a center of *relative* reference and one which itself supposes coordinates. But thereby I establish in thought the absolute equivalence of all centers of reference. I destroy the world's quality of being a world—without my even being aware of it. Thus the world by perpetually indicating the senses which I am and by inviting me to reconstitute it impels me to eliminate the personal equation which I am by reinstating in the world the center of mundane reference in relation to which the world is arranged. But by the same stroke I escape—through abstract thought—from the senses which I am; that is, I cut my bonds with the world. I place myself in a state of simple surveying, and the world disappears in the absolute equivalence of its infinite possible relations. The senses indeed are our being-in-the-world in so far as we have to be it in the form of being-in-the-midst-of-the-world.

These observations can be generalized; they can be applied *in toto* to *my body* inasmuch as it is the total center of reference which things indicate. In particular our body is not only what has long been called "the seat of the five senses"; it is also the instrument and the end of our actions. It is impossible to distinguish "sensation" from "action" even if we use the terms of classical psychology: this is what we had in mind when we made the observation that reality is presented to us neither as a *thing* nor as an *instrument* but as an instrumental-thing. This is why for our study of the body as a center of action we shall be able to take as a guiding thread the reasoning which has served us to reveal the true nature of the senses.

As soon as we formulate the problem of action, we risk falling into a confusion with grave consequences. When I take this pen and plunge it into the inkwell I am acting. But if I look at Pierre who at that same instant is drawing up a chair to the table, I establish also that he is acting. Thus there is here a very distinct risk of committing the mistake which we denounced *a propos* of the senses; that is, of interpreting *my* action as it *is-for-me* in terms of the Other's action. This is because the only action of which I can *know* at the same time that it is taking place is the action of Pierre. I see his gesture and at the same time I determine his goal: he is drawing a chair up to the table *in order to* be able to sit down near the table and to write the letter which he told me he wished to write. Thus I can apprehend all the intermediate positions of the chair and of the body which moves it as instrumental organizations; they are ways to arrive at one pursued end. The Other's body appears to me here as one instrument in the midst of other instruments, not only as a tool to make tools but also as a *tool to manage tools,* in a word as a tool-machine. If I interpret the role of *my* body in relation to *my* action, in the light of the knowledge I have gained of the Other's body, I shall then consider myself as disposing of a certain instrument which I can dispose of at my whim and which in turn will dispose of other instruments all functioning toward a certain end which I pursue.

Thus we are brought back to the classical distinction between the soul and the body; the soul utilizes the tool which is the body. The parallel with the theory of sensation is perfect. We have seen indeed that the latter started from the knowledge of the Other's senses and that subsequently it endowed me with senses exactly similar to the sensible organs which I perceived in the Other. We have seen also the difficulty which such a theory immediately encountered: this is because I then perceive the world and particularly the Other's sense organs through my own sense, a distorting organ, a refracting environment which can give me no information on its own affections. Thus the consequences of the theory ruin the objectivity of the very principle which has served to establish them. The theory of action, since it has an analogous structure, encounters analogous difficulties. In fact if I start with the Other's body, I apprehend it as an instrument and in so far as I myself make use of it as an instrument. I can *utilize it* in order to arrive at ends which I could not attain alone; I *command* its acts through orders or supplications; I can also provoke its act by my own acts. At the same time I must take precautions with respect to a tool which is particularly delicate and dangerous to handle. In relation to it I stand in the complex attitude of the worker with respect to his tool-machine when simultaneously he directs its movements and avoids being caught by it. Once again in order to utilize the Other's body to my best interests I need an instrument which is my own body just as in order to perceive the Other's sense organs I need other sense organs which are my own. Therefore if I conceive of my body in the image of the Other's body, it is an instrument in the world which I must handle delicately and which is like a key to the handling of other tools. But my relations with this privileged instrument can themselves be only technical, and I need an instrument in order to handle this instrument—which refers us to infinity. Thus if I conceive of my sense organs as like those of the Other, they require a sense organ in order to perceive them; and if I apprehend my body as an instrument like the Other's body, it demands an instrument to manage it; and if we refuse to conceive of this appeal to infinity, then we must of necessity admit that paradox of a physical instrument *handled* by a soul, which, as we know, causes us to fall into inextricable aporias.

Let us see whether we can attempt here as with the problem of sensations to restore to the body its nature-for-us. Objects are revealed to us at the heart of a complex of instrumentality in which they occupy a determined *place*. This place is not defined by pure spatial coordinates but in relation to axes of practical reference. "The glass *is on the coffee table*"; this means that we must be careful not to upset the glass if we move the table. The package of tobacco *is on* the mantelpiece; this means that we must clear a distance of three yards if we want to go from the pipe to the tobacco while avoiding certain obstacles—end tables, footstools, etc.—which are placed between the mantel piece and the table. In this sense perception is in no way to be distinguished from the practical organization of existents into a *world*. Each instrument refers to other instruments, to those which are its *keys* and to those for which it is the *key*. But these references could not be grasped by a purely contemplative consciousness. For such a consciousness the hammer would not refer to the nails but would be *alongside* them; furthermore the expression "alongside" loses all meaning if it does not outline a path which goes from the hammer to the nail and which *must* be cleared. The space which is originally revealed to me is a hodological space; it is furrowed with paths and highways; it is instrumental and it is the *location* of tools. Thus the world from the moment of the upsurge of my For-itself is revealed as the indication of acts to be performed; these acts refer to other acts, and those to others, and so on. It is to be noted however that if from this point of view perception and action are indistinguishable, action is nevertheless presented as a future efficacy which surpasses and transcends the pure and simple perceived. Since the perceived is that to which my For-itself is presence, it is revealed to me as co-presence; it is immediate contact, present adherence, it brushes lightly over me. But as such it is offered without my being able *at present* to grasp it. The thing perceived is full of promises; it touches me lightly in passing, and each of the properties which it promises to reveal to me, each surrender silently consented to, each meaningful reference to other objects engages the future.

Thus I am *in the presence* of things which are only promises beyond an ineffable *presence* which I cannot possess and which is the pure "being-there" of things; that is, the "mine," my facticity, my body. The cup is there on the saucer; it is presently given to me with its bottom side which *is there*, which everything indicates but which I do not see. And if I wish to see the bottom side—i.e., to make it explicit, to make it "appear-on-the-bottom-of-the-cup"—it is necessary for me to grasp the cup by the handle and turn it upside down. The bottom of the cup is at the end of my projects, and it amounts to the same thing whether I say that the other structures of the cup indicate it as an indispensable element of the cup or that they indicate it to me as the action which *will* best *appropriate* the cup for me with its meaning. Thus the world as the correlate of the possibilities which I *am* appears from the moment of my upsurge as the enormous skeletal outline of all my possible actions. Perception is naturally surpassed toward action; better yet, it can be revealed only in and through projects of action. The world is revealed as an "always future hollow," for we are always future to ourselves.[1]

Yet it must be noted that this future of the world which is thus revealed to us is strictly objective. The instrumental-things indicate other instruments or objective ways of making use of them: the nail is "to be pounded in" this way or that, the hammer is "to be held by the handle," the cup is "to be picked up by its handle," etc. All these properties of things are immediately revealed, and the Latin gerundives perfectly translate them. Of course they are correlates of non-thetic projects which we are, but they are revealed only as structures of the world: potentialities, absences, instrumentalities. Thus the world appears to me as objectively articulated; it never refers to a creative subjectivity but to an infinity of instrumental complexes.

Nevertheless while each instrument refers to another instrument and this to another, all end up by indicating an instrument which stands as the *key* for all. This center of reference is necessary, for otherwise all the instrumentalities would become equivalent and the world would vanish due to the total undifferentiation of gerundives. Carthage is "*delenda*" for the Romans but "*servanda*" for the Carthaginians. Without relation to its centers Carthage is no longer anything; it falls into the indifference of the in-itself, for the two gerundives annihilate each other. Nevertheless we must of necessity see that the *key* is never *given* to me but only indicated by a sort of gap.[2] What I objectively apprehend in action is a world of instruments which encroach on one another, and each of them as it is apprehended in the very act by which I adapt myself to it and surpass it, refers to another instrument which must enable me to utilize this one. In this sense the nail refers to the hammer and the hammer refers to the hand and the arm which utilizes it. But it is only to the extent that I cause the nails to be pounded in by the Other that the hand and the arm become in turn instruments which I utilize and which I surpass toward their potentiality. In this case the Other's hand refers me to the instrument which will allow me to utilize this hand (to threats-promises-salary, etc.) The first term is present everywhere but it is only *indicated*. I do not apprehend *my* hand in the act of writing but only the pen which is writing; this means that I use my pen in order to form letters but not *my hand* in order to hold the pen. I am not in relation to my hand in the same utilizing attitude as I am in relation to the pen; I *am* my hand. That is, my hand is the arresting of references and their ultimate end. The hand is only the utilization of the pen. In this sense the hand is at once the unknowable and non-utilizable term which the last instrument of the series indicates ("book to be read—characters to be formed on the paper—pen") and at the same time the orientation of the entire series (the printed book itself refers back to the hand). But I can apprehend it—at least in so far as it is acting—only as the perpetual, evanescent reference of the whole series. Thus in a duel with swords or with quarterstaffs, it is the quarterstaff which I watch with my eyes and which I handle. In the act of writing it is the point of the pen which I look at in synthetic combination with the line or the square marked on the sheet of paper. But my hand has vanished; it is lost in the complex system of instrumentality in order that this system may exist. It is simply the meaning and the orientation of the system.

Thus, it seems, we find ourselves before a double and contradictory necessity: since every instrument is utilizable and even apprehensible only by means of another instrument, the universe is an indefinite, objective reference from tool to tool. In this sense the structure of the world implies that we can insert ourselves into the field of instrumentality only by being ourselves an instrument, that we can not *act* without *being acted on*. Yet on the other hand, an instrumental complex can be revealed only by the determination of a cardinal meaning of this complex, and this determination is itself practical and active—to pound a nail, to sow seed. In this case the very existence of the complex immediately refers to a center. Thus this center is at once a tool objectively defined by the instrumental field which refers to it and at the same time the tool which we cannot *utilize* since we should thus be referred to infinity. We do not use this instrument, for we *are* it. It is given to us in no other way than by the instrumental order of the world, by hodological space, by the univocal or reciprocal relations of machines, but it cannot be *given* to my action. I do not have to adapt myself to it nor to adapt another tool to it, but it is my very adaptation to tools, the adaptation which I am.

This is why if we reject the analogical reconstruction of my body according to the body of the Other, there remain two ways of apprehending the body: First, it is *known* and objectively defined in terms of the world but *emptily;* for this view it is enough that rationalizing thought reconstitute the instrument which I am from the standpoint of the indications which are given by the instruments which I utilize. In this case, however, the fundamental tool becomes a relative center of reference which itself supposes other tools to utilize it. By the same stroke the instrumentality of the world disappears, for in order to be revealed it needs a reference to an absolute center of instrumentality; the world of action becomes the world *acted upon* of classical science; consciousness surveys a universe of exteriority and can no longer in any way *enter into the world.* Secondly the body is *given concretely* and fully as the very arrangement of things in so far as the For-itself surpasses it towards a new arrangement. In this case the body is present in every action although invisible, for the act reveals the hammer and the nails, the brake and the change of speed, not the foot which brakes or the hand which hammers. The body is *lived* and not *known.* This explains why the famous "sensation of effort" by which Maine de Biran attempted to reply to Hume's challenge is a psychological myth. We never have any sensation of our effort, but neither do we have peripheral sensations from the muscles, bones, tendons, or skin, which have been suggested to replace the sensation of effort. We perceive the *resistance* of things. What I perceive when I want to lift this glass to my mouth is not my effort but the *heaviness* of the glass—that is, its resistance to entering into an instrumental complex which I have made appear in the world.

Bachelard rightly reproaches phenomenology for not sufficiently taking into account what he calls the "coefficient of adversity" in objects.[3] The accusation is just and applies to Heidegger's transcendence as well as to Husserl's intentionality. But we must understand that the instrumentality is primary: it is in relation to an original instrumental complex that things reveal their resistance and their adversity. The bolt is revealed as too big to be screwed into the nut; the pedestal too fragile to support the weight which I want to hold up, the stone too heavy to be lifted up to the top of the wall, etc. Other objects will appear as threatening to an instrumental complex already established— the storm and the hail threatening to the harvest, the phyloxera to the vine, the fire to the house. Thus step by step and across the instrumental complexes already established, their threat will extend to the center of reference which all these instruments indicate, and in turn it will indicate this center through them. In this sense every *means* is simultaneously favorable and adverse but within the limits of the fundamental project realized by the upsurge of the For-itself in the world. Thus my body is indicated originally by instrumental complexes and secondarily by destructive devices. I *live* my body in danger as regards menacing machines as for manageable instruments. My body is every-where: the bomb which destroys *my* house also damages my body in so far as the house was already an indication of my body. This is why my body always extends across the tool which it utilizes: it is at the end of the cane on which I lean and against the earth; it is at the end of the telescope which shows me the stars; it is on the chair, in the whole house; for it is my adaptation to these tools.

Thus at the end of this account sensation and action are rejoined and become one. We have given up the idea of *first* endowing ourselves with a body in order to study *second* the way in which we apprehend or modify the world through the body. Instead we have laid down as the foundation of the revelation of the body as such our original relation to the world—that is, our very upsurge into the midst of being. Far from the body being first *for us* and revealing things to us, it is the instrumental-things which in their original appearance indicate our body to us. The body is not a screen between things and ourselves; it manifests only the individuality and the contingency of our original relation to instrumental-things. In this sense we defined the senses and the sense organs in general as our being-in-the-world in so far as we have to be it in the form of being-in-the-midst-of-the-world. Similarly we can define *action* as our being-in-the-world in so far as we have to be it in the form of being-an-instrument-in-the-midst-of-the-world. But if I am in the midst of the world, this is because I have caused the world to-be-there by transcending being toward myself. And if I am an instru-ment in the world, this is because I have caused instruments in general to-be-there by the projection of myself toward my possibles. It is only *in a world* that there can be a body, and a primary relation is in-dispensable in order that this world may exist. In one sense the body is what I immediately am. In another sense I am separated from it by the infinite density of the world; it is given to me by a reflux of the world toward my facticity, and the condition of this reflux of the world toward my facticity is a perpetual surpassing.

We are now able to define our body's *nature-for-us*. The preceding observations have allowed us to conclude that the body is perpetually the *surpassed*. The body as a sensible center of reference is *that beyond which* I am in so far as I am immediately present to the glass or to the table or to the distant tree which I perceive. Perception, in fact, can be accomplished only at the very place where the object is perceived and *without distance*. But at the same time it unfolds the distances, and that in relation to which the perceived object indicates its distance as an absolute property of its being is the body. Similarly as an instrumental center of instrumental complexes the body can be only the *surpassed;* it is that which I surpass toward a new combination of complexes and which I shall perpetually have to surpass whatever may be the instrumental combination at which I arrive; for every combination from the moment that my surpassing fixes it in its being indicates the body as the center of reference for its own fixed immobility. Thus the body, since it is surpassed, is the Past. It is the immediate presence to the For-itself of "sensible" things in so far as this presence indicates a center of reference and is *already surpassed* either toward the appearance of a new *this* or toward a new combination of instrumental-things. In each project of the For-itself, in each perception the body is there; it is the immediate Past in so far as it still touches on the Present which flees it. This means that it is at once *a point of view* and *a point of departure*—a point of view, a point of departure which I *am* and which at the same time I surpass toward what I have to be.

This point of view which is perpetually surpassed and which is perpetually reborn at the heart of the surpassing, this point of departure which I do not cease to leave and which is myself remaining behind me—this is the necessity of my contingency. It is doubly necessary. First it is necessary because it is the continual reapprehension of the For-itself by the In-itself and the ontological fact that the For-itself can be only as the being which is not its own foundation. To have a body is to be the foundation of one's own nothingness and not to be the foundation of one's being; I *am* my body to the extent that I *am; I am not* my body to the extent that I am not what I am. It is by my nihilation that I escape it. But I do not thereby make an object of it, for what *I am* is what I perpetually escape. The body is necessary again as the obstacle to be surpassed in order to be in the world; that is, the obstacle which I am to myself. In this sense it is not different from the absolute order of the world, this order which I cause to arrive in being by surpassing it toward a being-to-come, toward being-beyond-being. We can clearly grasp the unity of these two necessities: being-for-itself is to surpass the world and to cause there to be a world by surpassing it. But to surpass the world is not to survey it but to be engaged in it in order to emerge from it; it is necessary always that a *particular* perspective of surpassing be effected. In this sense *finitude* is the necessary condition of the original project of the For-itself. The necessary condition for me to be what I am not and to not-be what I am—beyond a world which I cause to come into being—this condition is that at the heart of the infinite pursuit which I am there should be perpetually an inapprehensible given. This given which I am without having to be it—except in the mode of non-being—this I can neither grasp nor know, for it is everywhere recovered and surpassed, utilized for my assumed projects. On the other hand everything indicates it to me, every transcendent outlines it in a sort of hollow by its very transcendence without my ever being able to turn back on that which it indicates since I *am* the being indicated. In particular we must not understand the indicated-given as a pure center of reference of a static order of instrumental-things. On the contrary their dynamic order, whether it depends on my action or not, refers to it according to rules, and thereby the center of reference is defined in its change as in its identity. The case could not be otherwise since it is by denying that I am being that I make the world come into being and since it is from the standpoint of my past—i.e., in projecting myself beyond my own being—that I can deny that I am this or that particular being. From this point of view the body—i.e., this inapprehensible given—is a necessary condition of my action. In fact if the ends which I pursue could be attained by a purely arbitrary wish, if it were sufficient to hope in order to obtain, and if definite rules did not determine the use of instruments, I could never distinguish within me desire from will, nor dream from act, nor the possible from the real. No project of myself would be possible since it would be enough to conceive of it in order to realize it. Consequently my being-for-myself would be annihilated in the indistinction of present and future. A phenomenology of action would in fact show that the act supposes a break in continuity between the simple conception and the realization—that is, between a universal and abstract thought such as "A carburetor must *not be clogged*" and a technical and concrete thought directed upon *this* particular carburetor as it appears to me with its absolute dimensions and its absolute position. The condition of this technical thought, which is not distinguished from the act which it directs, is my finitude, my contingency, finally my facticity.

Now, to be exact, I am *in fact* in so far as I have a past, and this immediate past refers to the primary in-itself on the nihilation of which I arise through *birth*. Thus the body as facticity is the past as it refers

originally to a *birth;* that is, to the primary nihilation which causes me
to arise from the In-itself which I am in fact without having to be it.
Birth, the past, contingency, the necessity of a point of view, the factual
condition for all possible action on the world—such is the *body,* such it
is for *me.* It is therefore in no way a contingent addition to my soul; on
the contrary it is a permanent structure of my being and the permanent
condition of possibility for my consciousness as consciousness *of* the
world and as a transcendent project toward my future. From this point
of view we must recognize both that it is altogether contingent and
absurd that I am a cripple, the son of a civil servant or of a laborer,
irritable and lazy, and that it is nevertheless *necessary* that I be *that* or
something else, French or German or English, etc., a proletarian or
bourgeois or aristocrat, etc., weak and sickly or vigorous, irritable or of
amiable disposition—precisely because I cannot *survey* the world without the world disappearing. *My birth* as it conditions the way in which
objects are revealed to me (objects of luxury or of basic necessity are
more or less *accessible,* certain social realities appear to me as *forbidden,*
there are barriers and obstacles in my hodological space); *my race* as it
is indicated by the Other's attitude with regard to me (these attitudes
are revealed as scornful or admiring, as trusting or distrusting); *my
class* as it is disclosed by the revelation of the social community to
which I belong inasmuch as the places which I frequent refer to it; my
nationality; my *physiological structure* as instruments imply it by the
very way in which they are revealed as resistant or docile and by their
very coefficient of *adversity;* my *character;* my *past,* as everything which
I have experienced is indicated as my point of view on the world by the
world itself: all this in so far as I surpass it in the synthetic unity of my
being-in-the-world is *my body* as the necessary condition of the existence of a world and as the contingent realization of this condition.

Now at last we can grasp clearly the definition which we gave earlier
of the body in its being-for-us: the body is the contingent form which is
taken up by the necessity of my contingency. We can never apprehend
this contingency as such in so far as our body is *for us;* for we are a
choice, and for us, to be is to choose ourselves. Even this disability from
which I suffer I have assumed by the very fact that I live; I surpass it
toward my own projects, I make of it the necessary obstacle for my
being, and I cannot be crippled without choosing myself as crippled.
This means that I choose the way in which I constitute my disability
(as "unbearable," "humiliating," "to be hidden," "to be revealed to

all," "an object of pride," "the justification for my failures," etc.). But this inapprehensible body is precisely the necessity that *there be a choice,* that I do not exist *all at once.* In this sense my finitude is the condition of my freedom, for there is no freedom without choice; and in the same way that the body conditions consciousness as pure consciousness of the world, it renders consciousness possible even in its very freedom.

It remains for us to arrive at a conception of what the body is *for me*; for precisely because the body is inapprehensible, it does not belong to the objects in the world—i.e., to those objects which I know and which I utilize. Yet on the other hand since I can be nothing without being the consciousness of what I am, the body must necessarily be in some way given to my consciousness. In one sense, to be sure, the body is what is indicated by all the instruments which I grasp, and I apprehend the body without knowing it in the very indications which I perceive on the instruments. But if we limit ourselves to this observation, we shall not be able to distinguish, for example, between the body and the telescope through which the astronomer looks at the planets. In fact if we define the body as a contingent point of view on the world, we must recognize that the notion of a point of view supposes a double relation: a relation with the things *on which the body is* a point of view and a relation with the observer *for whom the body is* a point of view. When we are dealing with the body-as-a-point-of-view, this second relation is radically different from the first; it is not truly distinct when we are dealing with a point of view in the world (spectacles, a look-out point, a magnifying glass, etc.) which is an objective instrument distinct from the body. A traveler contemplating the landscape *from a* belvedere sees the belvedere as well as the landscape; he sees the trees between the columns of the belvedere, the roof of the belvedere hides the sky from him, etc. Nevertheless the "distance" between him and the belvedere is by definition less great than that between his eyes and the panorama. The *point of view* can approach the body to the point of almost being dissolved in it, as we see, for example in the case of glasses, pince-nez, monocles, etc., which become, so to speak, a supplementary sense organ. At its extreme limit—if we conceive of an absolute point of view—the distance between it and the one for whom it is a point of view is annihilated. This means that it would become impossible to withdraw in order to "give oneself plenty of room" and to constitute a new point of view on the point of view. It is precisely this fact, as we have seen, which characterizes the body. It is the instrument which I cannot use in the way I use any other instrument, the point of view on which I can no longer take a point of view. This is why on the top of that hill which I call a "good viewpoint," I take a point of view at the very instant when I look at the valley, and this *point of view on the point of view* is my body. But I cannot take a point of view on my body without a reference to infinity. Therefore the body can not be *for me* transcendent and known; the spontaneous, unreflective consciousness is no longer the consciousness *of the* body. It would be best to say, using "exist" as a transitive verb—that consciousness *exists its body*. Thus the relation between the body-as-point-of-view and things is an *objective* relation, and the relation of consciousness to the body is an *existential* relation. What do we mean by an existential relation?

First of all, it is evident that consciousness can exist in its body only as consciousness. Therefore *my* body is a conscious structure of my consciousness. But precisely because the body is the point of view on which there cannot be a point of view, there is on the level of the unreflective consciousness no consciousness *of* the body. The body belongs then to the structures of the non-thetic self-consciousness. Yet can we identify it purely and simply with this non-thetic consciousness? That is not possible either, for non-thetic consciousness is self-consciousness as the free project toward a possibility which is its own; that is, in so far as it is the foundation of its own nothingness. Non-positional consciousness is consciousness (of the) body as being that which it surmounts and nihilates by making itself consciousness—i.e., as being something which consciousness is without having to be it and *which it passes over* in order to be what it has to be. In short, consciousness (of) the body is lateral and retrospective; the body is the *neglected*, the *"passed by in silence."* And yet the body is what this consciousness *is;* it is not even anything except body. The rest is nothingness and silence. . . .

We have not with these observations exhausted the description of the appearances of my body. It remains to describe what we shall call an *aberrant* type of appearance. In actuality I can see my hands, touch my back, smell the odor of my sweat. In this case my hand, for example, appears to me as one object among other objects. It is no longer *indicated* by the environment as a center of reference. It is organized with the environment, and like it indicates my body as a center of reference.

It forms a part of the world. In the same way my hand is no longer the instrument which I can not handle along with other instruments; on the contrary, it forms a part of the utensils which I discover in the midst of the world; I can *utilize* it by means of my other hand—for example, when I hold an almond or walnut in my left fist and then pound it with my right hand. My hand is then integrated with the infinite system of utensils-utilized. There is nothing in this new type of appearance which should disturb us or make us retract the preceding statements. Nevertheless this type of appearance must be mentioned. It can be easily explained on condition that we put it *in its proper place* in the order of the appearances of the body; that is, on condition that we examine it last and as a "curiosity" of our constitution. This appearance of my hand means simply that in certain well-defined cases we can adopt with regard to our own body the Other's point of view or, if you like, that our own body can appear to us as the body of the Other. Scholars who have made this appearance serve as a basis for a general theory of the body have radically reversed the terms of the problem and have shown themselves up as understanding nothing about the question. We must realize that this possibility of *seeing* our body is a pure factual given, absolutely contingent. It can be deduced neither from the necessity on the part of the for-itself "to have" a body nor from the factual structures of the body-for-others. One could easily conceive of bodies which could not take any view on themselves; it even appears that this is the case for certain insects which, although provided with a differentiated nervous system and with sense organs, cannot employ this system and these organs to know each other. We are dealing therefore with a particularity of structure which we must mention without attempting to deduce it. To have hands, to have hands which can touch each other—these are two facts which are on the same plane of contingency and which as such fall in the province of either pure anatomical description or metaphysics. We cannot take them for the foundation of a study of corporeality.

We must note in addition that this appearance of the body does not give us the body as it acts and perceives but only as it is acted on and perceived. In short, as we remarked at the beginning of this chapter, it would be possible to conceive of a system of visual organs such that it would allow one eye to see the other. But the seen eye would be seen as a thing, not as a being of reference. Similarly the hand which I grasp with my other hand is not apprehended as a hand which is grasping but as an apprehensible object. Thus the nature of *our body for us* entirely escapes us to the extent that we can take upon it the Other's point of view. Moreover it must be noted that even if the arrangement of sense organs allows us to see the body as it appears to the Other, this appearance of the body as an instrumental-thing is very late in the child; it is in any case later than the consciousness (of) the body proper and of the world as a complex of instrumentality; it is later than the perception of the body of the Other. The child has known for a long time how to grasp, to draw toward himself, to push away, and to hold on to something before he first learns to pick up his hand and to look at it. Frequent observation has shown that the child of two months does not see his hand as *his* hand. He looks at it, and if it is outside his visual field, he turns his head and seeks his hand with his eyes as if it did not depend on him to bring the hand back within his sight. It is by a series of psychological operations and of syntheses of identification and recognition that the child will succeed in establishing tables of reference between the body-existed and the body-seen. Again it is necessary that the child begin the learning process with the Other's body. Thus the perception of my body is placed chronologically after the perception of the body of the Other.

Considered at its proper place and time and in its original contingency, this appearance of the body does not seem to be capable of giving rise to new problems. The body is the instrument which I am. It is my facticity of being "in-the-midst-of-the-world" in so far as I surpass this facticity toward my being-in-the-world. It is, of course, radically impossible for me to take a global point of view in this facticity, for then I should cease to be it. But why is it so astonishing that certain structures of my body, without ceasing to be a center of reference for the objects of the world, are ordered from a radically different point of view as compared with other objects in such a way that along with the objects they point to one of my sense organs as a partial center of reference raising itself as a figure on the body-as-ground? That my eye should see itself is by nature impossible. But why is it astonishing that my hand touches my eyes? If this seems surprising to us, it is because we have apprehended the necessity for the for-itself to arise as a concrete point of view on the world as if it were an ideal obligation strictly reducible to knowable relations between objects and to simple rules for the development of my achieved knowledge. But instead we ought to see here the necessity of a concrete and contingent existence in the midst of the world.

NOTES

1. *"Creux toujours futur."* There is a suggestion here of a mold to be filled but, of course, with no idea of a determined future. [Tr.]
2. *Indiquée en creux*; literally, "indicated in a hollow (or mold)." [Tr.]
3. Bachelard, *L'Eau et les Rêves*, 1942. Editions José Corti.

THE SPATIALITY OF THE
LIVED BODY AND MOTILITY

Maurice Merleau-Ponty

Let us first of all describe the spatiality of my own body. If my arm is resting on the table I should never think of saying that it is *beside* the ash-tray in the way in which the ash-tray is beside the telephone. The outline of my body is a frontier which ordinary spatial relations do not cross. This is because its parts are interrelated in a peculiar way: they are not spread out side by side, but enveloped in each other. For example, my hand is not a collection of points. In cases of allocheiria,[1] in which the subject feels in his right hand stimuli applied to his left hand, it is impossible to suppose that each of the stimulations changes its spatial value on its own account.[2] The various points on the left hand are transferred to the right as relevant to a total organ, a hand without parts which has been suddenly displaced. Hence they form a system and the space of my hand is not a mosaic of spatial values. Similarly my whole body for me is not an assemblage of organs juxtaposed in space. I am in undivided possession of it and I know where each of my limbs is through a *body image* in which all are included. But the notion of body image is ambiguous, as are all notions which make their appearance at turning points in scientific advance. They can be fully developed only through a reform of methods. At first, therefore, they are used only in a sense which falls

These pages are excerpted from Maurice Merleau-Ponty's *Phenomenology of Perception* (New York: Humanities Press, Inc., 1962), pp. 98–115, 136–147, with the permission of the publishers of the English translation. The translator is Colin Smith. For the original text see *Phénoménologie de la perception* (Paris: Librairie Gallimard, 1945), pp. 114–134, 158–172.

short of their full sense, and it is their immanent development which
bursts the bounds of methods hitherto used. "Body image" was at
first understood to mean a *compendium* of our bodily experience,
capable of giving a commentary and meaning to the internal impressions and the impression of possessing a body at any moment. It was
supposed to register for me the positional changes of the parts of my
body for each movement of one of them, the position of each local
stimulus in the body as a whole, an account of the movements performed at every instant during a complex gesture, in short a continual
translation into visual language of the kinaesthetic and articular
impressions of the moment. When the term body image was first used,
it was thought that nothing more was being introduced than a con-
venient name for a great many associations of images, and it was
intended merely to convey the fact that these associations were firmly
established and constantly ready to come into play. The body image
was supposed gradually to arise in the course of childhood in proportion as the tactile, kinaesthetic, and articular contents were associated
among themselves or with visual contents, and more easily evoked
them.[3] Its physiological representation could then be no more than a
focus of images in the classical sense. Yet in the use made of it by
psychologists, it is clear that the body image does not fit into this
associationist definition. For example, in order that the body image
may elucidate allocheiria, it is not enough that each sensation of the
left hand should take its place among generic images of all parts of
the body acting in association to form around it, as it were, a superimposed *outline* of the body; these associations must be constantly
subject to a single law, the spatiality of the body must work downwards
from the whole to the parts, the left hand and its position must be
implied in a comprehensive bodily *purpose* and it must originate in
that purpose, so that it may at one stroke not only be superimposed or
brought down onto the right hand, but actually become the right
hand. When we try[4] to elucidate the phenomenon of the phantom
limb by relating it to the body image of the subject, we add to the
accepted explanations, in terms of cerebral tracks and recurrent sensations, only if the body image, instead of being the residue of habitual
cenesthesis, becomes the law of its constitution. If a need was felt
to introduce this new word, it was in order to make it clear that the
spatial and temporal unity, the intersensory or the sensorimotor unity
of the body is, so to speak, *de jure,* that it is not confined to contents

actually and fortuitously associated in the course of our experience, that it is in some way anterior to them and makes their association possible. We are therefore feeling our way towards a second definition of the body image: it is no longer seen as the straightforward result of associations established during experience, but a total awareness of my posture in the intersensory world, a "form" in the sense used by Gestalt psychology.[5] But already this second definition too is superseded by the analyses of the psychologists. It is inadequate to say that my body is a form, that is to say a phenomenon in which the totality takes precedence over the parts. How is such a phenomenon possible? Because a form, comparable to the mosaic of a physicochemical body or to that of "cenesthesis," is a new type of existence. The fact that the paralyzed limb of the anosognosic no longer counts in the subject's body image, is accounted for by the body image's being neither the mere copy nor even the global awareness of the existing parts of the body, and by its active integration of these latter only in proportion to their value to the organism's projects. Psychologists often say that the body image is *dynamic*.[6] Brought down to a precise sense, this term means that my body appears to me as an attitude directed towards a certain existing or possible task. And indeed its spatiality is not, like that of external objects or like that of "spatial sensations," a *spatiality of position*, but a *spatiality of situation*. If I stand in front of my desk and lean on it with both hands, only my hands are stressed and the whole of my body trails behind them like the tail of a comet. It is not that I am unaware of the whereabouts of my shoulders or back, but these are simply swallowed up in the position of my hands, and my whole posture can be read so to speak in the pressure they exert on the table. If I stand holding my pipe in my closed hand, the position of my hand is not determined discursively by the angle which it makes with my forearm, and my forearm with my upper arm, and my upper arm with my trunk, and my trunk with the ground. I know indubitably where my pipe is, and thereby I know where my hand and my body are, as primitive man in the desert is always able to take his bearings immediately without having to cast his mind back, and add up distances covered and deviations made since setting off. The word "here" applied to my body does not refer to a determinate position in relation to other positions or to external coordinates, but the laying down of the first coordinates, the anchoring of the active body in an object, the situation of the body in face of its tasks. Bodily space can be distinguished from external space and envelop its parts instead of spreading them out, because it is the darkness needed in the theatre to show up the performance, the background of somnolence or reserve of vague power against which the gesture and its aim[7] stand out, the zone of not being *in front of which* precise beings, figures, and points can come to light. In the last analysis, if my body can be a "form" and if there can be, in front of it, important figures against indifferent backgrounds, this occurs in virtue of its being polarized by its tasks, of its *existence towards* them, of its collecting together of itself in its pursuit of its aims; the body image is finally a way of stating that my body is in the world.[8] As far as spatiality is concerned, and this alone interests us at the moment, one's own body is the third term, always tacitly understood, in the figure-background structure, and every figure stands out against the double horizon of external and bodily space. One must therefore reject as an abstraction any analysis of bodily space which takes account only of figures and points, since these can neither be conceived nor be without horizons.

It will perhaps be replied that the figure-background structure or the point-horizon structure themselves presuppose the notion of objective space; that in order to experience a display of dexterity as a figure *against* the massive background of the body, the hand and the rest of the body must be linked by this relationship of objective spatiality, so that the figure-background structure becomes once again one of the contingent contents of the universal form of space. But what meaning could the word "against" have for a subject not placed by his body face to face with the world? It implies the distinction of a top and a bottom, or an "orientated space."[9] When I say that an object is *on* a table, I always mentally put myself either in the table or in the object, and I apply to them a category which theoretically fits the relationship of my body to external objects. Stripped of this anthropological association, the word *on* is indistinguishable from the word "under" or the word "beside." Even if the universal form of space is that without which there would be for us no bodily space, it is not that by which there is one. Even if the form is not the *setting in which,* but the *means whereby* the content is posited, it is not the sufficient means of this act of positing as far as bodily space is concerned, and to this extent the bodily content remains, in relation to it, something opaque, fortuitous, and unintelligible. The only solution along this road would be to recognize that the body's spatiality has no meaning of its own to distinguish it from objective spatiality which would do away with the content as a phenomenon and hence with the problem of its relation to form. But can we pretend to discover no distinctive meaning in the words "on," "under," "beside," or in the dimensions of orientated space? Even if analysis discovers in all these relationships the universal relation of externality, the self-evidence of top and bottom, right and left, for the person who has his being in space, prevents us from treating all these distinctions as nonsense, and suggests to us that we should look beneath the explicit meaning of definitions for the latent meaning of experiences. The relationships between the two spaces would therefore be as follows: as soon as I try to posit bodily space or bring out its meaning I find nothing in it but intelligible space. But at the same time this intelligible space is not extracted from orientated space, it is merely its explicit expression, and when separated from that root has no meaning whatsoever. The truth is that homogeneous space can convey the meaning of orientated space only because it is from the latter that it has received that meaning. In so far as the content can be really subsumed under the form and can appear as the content *of* that form, it is because the form is accessible only through the content. Bodily space can really become a fragment of objective space only if within its individuality as bodily space it contains the dialectical ferment to transform it into universal space. This is what we have tried to express by saying that the point-horizon structure is the foundation of space. The horizon or background would not extend beyond the figures or round about it, unless they partook of the same kind of being as it, and unless they could be converted into points by a transference of the gaze. But the point-horizon structure can teach me what a point is only in virtue of the maintenance of a hither zone of corporeality from which to be seen, and round about it indeterminate horizons which are the counterpart of this spectacle. The multiplicity of points or "heres" can in the nature of things be constituted only by a chain of experiences in which on each occasion one and no more of them is presented as an object, and which is itself built up in the heart of this space. And finally, far from my body's being for me no more than a fragment of space, there would be no space at all for me if I had no body.

If bodily space and external space form a practical system, the first being the background against which the object as the goal of our action may stand out or the void in front of which it may *come to light*, it is clearly in action that the spatiality of our body is brought into being, and an analysis of one's own movement should enable us to arrive at a better understanding of it. By considering the body in movement, we can see better how it inhabits space (and, moreover, time) because movement is not limited to submitting passively to space and time, it actively assumes them, it takes them up in their basic significance which is obscured in the commonplaceness of established situations. We should like to analyze closely an example of morbid motility which clearly shows the fundamental relations between the body and space.

A patient[10] whom traditional psychiatry would class among cases of psychic blindness is unable to perform "abstract" movements with his eyes shut; movements, that is, which are not relevant to any actual situation, such as moving arms and legs to order, or bending and straightening a finger. Nor can he describe the position of his body or even his head, or the passive movements of his limbs. Finally, when his head, arm, or leg is touched, he cannot identify the point on his body; he cannot distinguish two points of contact on his skin even as much as three inches apart; and he cannot recognize the size or shape of objects placed against his body. He manages the abstract movements only if he is allowed to watch the limb required to perform them, or to go through preparatory movements involving the whole body. The localization of stimuli, and recognition of objects by touch also become possible with the aid of the preparatory movements. Even when his eyes are closed, the patient performs with extraordinary speed and precision the movements needed in living his life, provided that he is in the habit of performing them: he takes his handkerchief from his pocket and blows his nose, takes a match out of a box and lights a lamp. He is employed in the manufacture of wallets and his production rate is equal to three-quarters of that of a normal workman. He can even,[11] without any preparatory movement, perform these "concrete" movements to order. In the same patient, and also in cerebellar cases, one notices[12] a dissociation of the act of pointing from reactions of taking or grasping: the same subject who is unable to point on order to a part of his body, quickly moves his hand to the point where a mosquito is stinging him. Concrete movements and acts of grasping therefore enjoy a privileged position for which we need to find some explanation.

Let us examine the question more closely. A patient, asked to point to some part of his body, his nose for example, can only manage to do so if he is allowed to take hold of it. If the patient is set the task of interrupting the movement before its completion, or if he is allowed to touch his nose only with a wooden ruler, the action becomes impossible.[13] It must therefore be concluded that "grasping" or "touching," even for the body, is different from "pointing." From the outset the grasping movement is magically at its completion; it can begin only by anticipating its end, since to disallow taking hold is sufficient to inhibit the action. And it has to be admitted that a point on my body can be present to me as one to be taken hold of without being given in this anticipated grasp as a point to be indicated. But how is this possible? If I know where my nose is when it is a question of holding it, how can I not know where it is when it is a matter of pointing to it? It is probably because knowledge of where something is can be understood in a number of ways. Traditional psychology has no concept to cover these varieties of consciousness of place because consciousness of place is always, for such psychology, a positional consciousness, a representation, *Vor-stellung*, because as such it gives us the place as a determination of the objective world and because such a representation either is or is not, but, if it is, yields the object to us quite unambiguously and as an end identifiable through all its appearances. Now here, on the other hand, we have to create the concepts necessary to convey the fact that bodily space may be given to me in an intention to take hold without being given in an intention to know. The patient is conscious of his bodily space as the matrix of his habitual action, but not as an objective setting; his body is at his disposal as a means of ingress into a familiar surrounding, but not as the means of expression of a gratuitous and free spatial thought. When ordered to perform a concrete movement, he first of all repeats the order in a questioning tone of voice, then his body assumes the general position required for the task; finally he goes through the movement. It is noticeable that the whole body is involved in it, and that the patient never cuts it down, as a normal subject would, to the strict minimum. To the military salute are added the other external marks of respect. To the right hand pantomine of combing the hair is added, with the left, that of holding a mirror; when the right hand pretends to knock in a nail, the left pretends to hold the nail. The explanation is that the order is taken quite seriously and that the patient manages to perform these concrete movements on order only provided that he places himself mentally in the actual situation to which they correspond. The normal subject, on giving, to order, a military salute, sees in it no more than an experimental situation, and therefore restricts the movement to its most important elements and does not throw himself into it.[14] He is using his body as a means to play acting; he finds it entertaining to pretend to be a soldier; he escapes from reality in the role of the soldier[15] just as the actor slips his real body into the "great phantom"[16] of the character to be played. The normal man and the actor do not mistake imaginary situations for reality, but extricate their real bodies from the living situation to make them breathe, speak and, if need be, weep in the realm of imagination. This is what our patient is no longer able to do. In the course of living, he says "I experience the movements as being a result of the situation, of the sequence of events themselves; myself and my movements are, so to speak, merely a link in the whole process and I am scarcely aware of any voluntary initiative. . . . It all happens independently of me." In the same way, in order to make a movement to order he places himself "in the affective situation as a whole, and it is from this that the movement flows, as in real life."[17] If his performance is interrupted and he has the experimental situation recalled to him, all his dexterity disappears. Once more kinetic initiative becomes impossible, the patient must first of all "find" his arm, "find," by the preparatory movements, the gesture called for, and the gesture itself loses the melodic character which it presents in ordinary life, and becomes manifestly a collection of partial movements strung laboriously together. I can therefore take my place, through the medium of my body as the potential source of a certain number of familiar actions, in my environment conceived as a set of *manipulanda* and without, moreover, envisaging my body or my surrounding as objects in the Kantian sense, that is, as systems of qualities linked by some intelligible law, as transparent entities, free from any attachment to a specific place or time, and ready to be named or at least pointed out. There is my arm seen as sustaining familiar acts, my body as giving rise to determinate action having a field or scope known to me in advance, there are my surroundings as a collection of possible points upon which this bodily action may operate—and there is, furthermore, my arm as a mechanism of muscles and bones, as a contrivance for bending and stretching, as an articulated object, the world as a pure spectacle into which I am not absorbed, but which I contemplate and point out. As far as bodily space is concerned, it is clear that there is a knowledge of place which is reducible to a sort of coexistence with that place, and which is not simply nothing, even though it cannot be conveyed in the form of a description or even pointed out without a word being spoken. A patient of the kind discussed above, when stung by a mosquito, does not need to look for the place where he has been stung. He finds it straight away, because for him there is no question of locating it in relation to axes of coordinates in objective space, but of reaching with his phenomenal hand a certain painful spot on his phenomenal body, and because between the hand as a scratching potentiality and the place stung as a spot to be scratched a directly experienced relationship is presented in the natural system of one's own body. The whole operation takes place in the domain of the phenomenal; it does not run through the objective world, and only the spectator, who lends his objective representation of the living body to the acting subject, can believe that the sting is perceived, that the hand moves in objective space, and consequently find it odd that the same subject should fail in experiments requiring him to point things out. Similarly the subject, when put in front of his scissors, needle, and familiar tasks, does not need to look for his hands or his fingers, because they are not objects to be discovered in objective space: bones, muscles, and nerves, but potentialities already mobilized by the perception of scissors or needle, the central end of those "intentional threads" which link him to the objects given. It is never our objective body that we move, but our phenomenal body, and there is no mystery in that, since our body, as the potentiality of this or that part of the world, surges towards objects to be grasped and perceives them.[18] In the same way the patient has no need to look for a theatre of action and a space in which to deploy these concrete movements: the space is given to him in the form of the world at this moment; it is the piece of leather "to be cut up," it is the lining "to be sewn." The bench, scissors, pieces of leather offer themselves to the subject as poles of action; through their combined values they delimit a certain situation, an open situation moreover, which calls for a certain mode of resolution, a certain kind of work. The body is no more than an element in the system of the subject and his world, and the task to be performed elicits the necessary movements from him by a sort of remote attraction, as the phenomenal forces at work in my visual field elicit from me, without any calculation on my part, the motor reactions which establish the most effective balance between them, or as the conventions of our social group, or our set of listeners, immediately elicit from us the words, attitudes, and tone which are fitting. Not that we are trying to conceal our thoughts or to please others, but because we are literally what others think of us and what our world is. In the concrete movement the patient has a positing awareness neither of the stimulus nor of his reaction: quite simply he is his body and his body is the potentiality of a certain world.

What, on the other hand, happens in experiments in which the patient fails? If a part of his body is touched and he is asked to locate the point of contact, he first of all sets his whole body in motion and thus narrows down the problem of location, then he comes still nearer by moving the limb in question, and the process is completed in the form of quiverings of the skin in the neighbourhood of the point touched.[19] If the subject's arm is extended horizontally, he cannot describe its position until he has performed a set of pendular movements which convey to him the arm position in relation to the trunk, that of the forearm to the rest of the arm, and that of the trunk in relation to the vertical. In the case of passive movement, the subject feels that there is movement but cannot say of what kind and in what direction. Here again he resorts to active movements. The patient concludes that he is lying down from the pressure of the mattress on his back, or that he is standing from the pressure of the ground on his feet.[20] If the two points of a compass are placed on his hand, he can distinguish them only if he is allowed to rotate his hand, and bring first one and then the other point into contact with his skin. If letters or figures are traced out on his hand, he identifies them only provided that he can himself move his hand, and it is not the movement of the point on his hand which he perceives, but conversely the movement of his hand in relation to the point. This is proved by tracing on his left hand normal letters, which are never recognized, then the mirrored image of the same letters, which is immediately understood. The mere touching of a paper rectangle or oval gives rise to no recognition, whereas the subject recognizes the figures if he is allowed to make exploratory movements to "spell out" the shapes, to spot their "characteristics" and to identify the object on this basis.[21] How are we to coordinate this set of facts and how are we to discover by means of it what function, found in the normal person, is absent in the patient? There can be no question of simply transferring from the normal person what the deficient one lacks and is trying to recover. Illness, like childhood and "primitive" mentality, is a complete form of existence and the procedures which it employs to replace normal functions which have been destroyed are equally pathological phenomena. It is impossible to deduce the normal from the pathological, deficiencies from substitute functions, through merely changing the sign. We must take substitutions as substitutions, as allusions to some fundamental function that they are striving to make good, and the direct image of which they fail to furnish. The genuine inductive method is not a "differential method"; it consists in correctly reading phenomena, in grasping their meaning, that is, in treating them as modalities and variations of the subject's total being. We observe that when the patient is questioned about the position of his limbs or of a tactile stimulus, he tries, by means of preparatory movements, to make his body into an object of present perception. Asked about the shape of an object in contact with his body, he tries to trace it out himself by following the outline of the object. Nothing would be more misleading than to suppose the normal person adopting similar procedures, differing merely in being shortened by constant use. The kind of patient under consideration sets out in search of these explicit perceptions only in order to provide a substitute for a certain mutual presence of body and object which is a datum of normal experience and which we still have to reconstitute. It is true that even in the normal person the perception of the body and of objects in contact with the body is vague when there is no movement.[22] The fact remains that the normal person can, in the absence of any movements, always distinguish a stimulus applied to his head from one applied to his body. Are we to suppose that[23] excitations felt as coming either from outside or from one's own body have brought into play, in that person, "kinaesthetic residua" which take the place of actual movements? But then how could data supplied by the sense of touch arouse "kinaesthetic residua" of a determinate kind unless they carried within themselves some characteristic which enables them to do so, unless they themselves, in other words, had some well-defined or obscure spatial significance?[24] At least we can say that the normal subject can immediately "come to grips" with his body.[25] He enjoys the use of his body not only in so far as it is involved in a concrete setting, he is in a situation not only in relation to the tasks imposed by a particular job, he is not open merely to real situations; for, over and above all this, his body is correlated with pure stimuli devoid of any practical bearing; he is open to those verbal and imaginary situations which he can choose for himself or which may be suggested to him in the course of an experiment. His body, when touched, is not presented to him as a geometrical figure in which each stimulus occupies an explicit position, and Schneider's disease lies precisely in his need, in order to find out where he is being touched, to convert the bodily area touched into the form of a figure. But each stimulus applied to the body of the normal person arouses a kind of "potential movement," rather than an actual one; the part of the body in question sheds its anonymity, is revealed, by the presence of a particular tension, as a certain power of action within the framework of the anatomical apparatus. In the case of the normal subject, the body is available not only in real situations into which it is drawn. It can turn aside from the world, apply its activity to stimuli which affect its sensory surfaces, lend itself to experimentation, and generally speaking take its place in the realm of the potential. It is because of its confinement within the actual that an unsound sense of touch calls for special movements designed to localize stimuli, and for the same reason the patient substitutes, for tactile recognition and perception, a laborious decoding of stimuli and deduction of objects. For a key, for instance, to appear as such in my tactile experience, a kind of fulness of touch is required, a tactile field in which local impressions may be coordinated into a shape just as notes are mere stepping-stones in a melody; and that very viscosity of tactile data which makes the body dependent upon actual situations reduces the object to a collection of successive "characteristics," perception to an abstract account, recognition to a rational synthesis or a plausible conjecture, and strips the object of its carnal presence and facticity. Whereas in the normal person every event related to movement or sense of touch causes consciousness to put up a host of intentions which run from the body as the centre of potential action either towards the body itself or towards the object, in the case of the patient, on the other hand, the tactile impression remains opaque and sealed up. It may well draw the grasping hand towards itself, but does not stand in front of the hand in the manner of a thing which can be pointed out. The normal person *reckons with* the possible, which thus, without shifting from its position as a possibility, acquires a sort of actuality. In the patient's case, however, the field of actuality is limited to what is met with in the shape of a real contact or is related to these data by some explicit process of deduction.

The analysis of "abstract movement" in patients throws into relief this possession of space, this spatial existence which is the primary condition of all living perception. If the patient is ordered to shut his eyes and then perform an abstract movement, a set of preparatory operations is called for in order to enable him to "find" the operative limb, the direction or pace of the movement, and finally the plane in which it is to be executed. If, for instance, he is ordered to move his arm, with no detail as to how, he is first of all perplexed. Then he moves his whole body and after a time his movements are confined to the arm, which the subject eventually "finds." If it is a question of "raising his arm" the patient must also "find" his head (which symbolizes "up" for him) by means of a set of pendulum movements which are continued throughout the action and which serve to establish the objective. If the subject is asked to trace a square or a circle in the air, he first "finds" his arm, then lifts it in front of him as a normal subject would do to find a wall in the dark, and finally he makes a few rough movements in a straight line or describing various curves, and if one of these happens to be circular he promptly completes the circle. Moreover he can find the requisite movement only in a certain plane which is not quite perpendicular to the ground, and apart from this special plane he cannot begin to trace the figures.[26] Clearly the patient finds in his body only an amorphous mass into which actual movement alone introduces divisions and links. In looking to his body to perform the movement for him he is like a speaker who cannot utter a word without following a text written beforehand. The patient himself neither seeks nor finds his movement, but moves his body about until the movement comes. The order given is not meaningless to him, since he recognizes the inadequacy of his first attempts, and also since, if a fortuitous gesture produces the required movement, he is aware of it and can immediately turn his piece of good fortune to account. But if the order has an *intellectual significance* for him and not a *motor* one, it does not communicate anything to him as a mobile subject; he may well find in the shape of a movement performed an illustration of the order given, but he can never convert the thought of a movement into actual movement. What he lacks is neither motility nor thought, and we are brought to the recognition of something between movement as a third-person process and thought as a representation of movement—something which is an anticipation of, or arrival at, the objective and is ensured by the body itself as a motor power, a "motor project" (*Bewegungsentwurf*), a "motor intentionality" in the absence of which the order remains a dead letter. The patient either conceives the ideal formula for the movement, or else he launches his body into blind attempts to perform it, whereas for the normal person every movement is, indissolubly, movement and consciousness of movement. This can be expressed by saying that for the normal person every movement has a *background*, and that the movement and its background are "moments of a unique totality."[27] The background to the movement is not a representation associated or linked externally with the movement itself, but is immanent in the movement inspiring and sustaining it at every moment. The plunge into action is, from the subject's point of view, an original way of relating himself to the object, and is on the same footing as perception. Light is thus thrown upon the distinction between abstract and concrete movement: the background to concrete movement is the world as given, whereas the background to abstract movement is built up. When I motion my friend to come nearer, my intention is not a thought prepared within me and I do not perceive the signal in my body. I beckon across the world, I beckon over there, where my friend is; the distance between us, his consent or refusal are immediately read in my gesture; there is not a perception followed by a movement, for both form a system which varies as a whole. If, for example, noticing that there is no response to my move, I vary my gesture, we have here, not two distinct acts of consciousness. What happens is that I see my partner's unwillingness, and my gesture of impatience emerges from this situation without any intervening thought.[28] If I then execute "the same" movement, but without having any present or even imaginary partner in mind, and treat it as "a set of movements in themselves";[29] if, that is, I perform a "flexion" of the forearm in relation to the upper arm, with "supination" of the arm and "flexion" of the fingers, my body, which a moment ago was the vehicle of the movement, now becomes its end; its motor project is no longer directed towards someone in the world, but towards my fore and upper arm, and my fingers; and it is directed towards them, furthermore, in so far as they are capable of breaking with their involvement in the given world and giving shape round about me to an imaginary situation, or even in so far as, independently of any fictitious partner, I look with curiosity upon this strange signifying contrivance and set it to work for my amusement.[30] The abstract movement carves out within that plenum of the world in which concrete movement took place a zone of reflection and subjectivity; it superimposes upon physical space a potential or human space. Concrete movement is therefore centripetal whereas abstract movement is centrifugal. The former occurs in the realm of being or of the actual, the latter on the other hand in that of the possible or the nonexistent; the first adheres to a given background, the second throws out its own background. The normal function which makes abstract movement possible is one of "projection" whereby the subject of movement keeps in front of him an area of free space in which what does not naturally exist may take on a semblance of existence. One knows of patients with powers less seriously affected than Schneider's who perceive forms, distances, and objects in themselves, but who are unable either to trace in objects the directions which are useful from the point of view of action, or to arrange them according to some given principle, or generally to assign to the spatial scene delimitations in human terms which make it the field of our action. For instance, patients faced with a dead end in a labyrinth have difficulty in finding "the opposite direction." If a ruler is laid between them and the doctor they cannot, on order, distribute the objects between "their side" and "the doctor's side." They are very inaccurate in pointing out, on another person's arm, the point corresponding to the one stimulated on their own. Knowing that the month is March and the day a Monday, they will have difficulty in saying what the previous month and day were, though they may well know by heart the days and months in their correct order. They are incapable of comparing the number of units contained in two sets of sticks placed in front of them: they may count the same stick twice over, or else include in one set of sticks some which belong to the other.[31] The reason is that all these operations require the same ability to mark out boundaries and directions in the given world, to establish lines of force, to keep perspectives in view, in a word, to organize the given world in accordance with the projects of the present moment, to build into the geographical setting a behavioural one, a system of meanings outwardly expressive of the subject's internal activity. For these patients the world exists only as one ready-made or congealed, whereas for the normal person his projects polarize the world, bringing magically to view a host of signs which guide action, as notices in a museum guide the visitor. This function of "projection" or "summoning" (in the sense in which the medium summons an absent person and causes him to appear) is also what makes abstract movement possible: for, in order to be in possession of my body independently of any urgent task to be performed; in order to enjoy the use of it as the mood takes me, in order to describe in the air a movement formulated only verbally or in terms of moral requirements, I must reserve the natural relationship in which the body stands to its environment, and a human productive power must reveal itself through the density of being.

It is in these terms that the disorder discernible in the movements in question may be described. But it may be thought that this description (and this criticism has often been made of psychoanalysis)[32] presents to us only the significance or essence of the disease and not its cause. Science, it may be objected, waits upon explanation, which means looking beneath phenomena for the circumstances upon which they depend, in accordance with the tried methods of induction. Here, for example, we know that the motor disorders of Schneider are related to far-reaching disorders of sight, which in turn arise from the occipital injury which lies at the root of his condition. Schneider does not recognize any object by merely looking at it.[33] His visual data are almost-amorphous patches.[34] As for objects not in sight, he is unable to form any visual image of them.[35] It is known, on the other hand, that "abstract" movements become possible for the subject provided that he keeps his eyes fixed on the limb which is to perform them.[36] Thus the remnant of volitional motility is aided by what remains of visual knowledge. The famous methods of Mill might allow us to conclude here that abstract movements and *Zeigen* are dependent on the power of visual representation, whereas concrete movements, which are preserved by the patient as are those imitative movements, whereby he compensates for his paucity of visual data, arise from the kinaesthetic or tactile sense, which incidentally was remarkably exploited by Schneider. It would appear, then, that the distinction between concrete and abstract movement, like that between *Greifen* and *Zeigen,* is reducible to the traditional distinction between tactile and visual, and the function of projection or evocation, which we brought to light above, to perception and visual representation.[37]

In reality, an inductive analysis carried out according to Mill's methods is fruitless. For the disturbances of abstract movement and *Zeigen* are encountered not only in cases of psychological blindness, but also in cerebellar patients and in many other disorders.[38] There is no justification for picking out as crucial just one of these concordances and using it to "explain" the act of pointing out. In face of the ambiguity of facts one must abandon the mere statistical noting-down of coincidences, and try to "understand" the relation which they reveal. In cerebellar cases it is observed that visual as distinct from auditory stimuli produce only imperfect motor reactions, and yet there is with them no reason to presume any primary disturbance of the visual function. It is not because the latter is deficient that designatory movements become impossible, but, on the contrary, because the attitude of Zeigen is impossible that the visual stimuli arouse only partial reactions. We must admit that the sound, of itself, prompts rather a grasping movement, and visual perception the act of pointing. "The sound always leads us towards its content, its significance for us; in visual presentation, on the other hand, we can much more easily 'disregard' the content and we are drawn much more definitely towards the part of space where the object is to be found."[39] A meaning then is definable less in terms of the indescribable quality of its "mental contents" than in terms of a certain manner of presenting its object, of its epistemological structure having its quality as concrete realization and, in the language of Kant, exhibition. The doctor who brings to bear upon the patient "visual" or "auditory stimuli" believes that he is testing "visual" or "auditory sensibility" and drawing up an inventory of sensible qualities which make up consciousness (in empiricist language) or of the material at the disposal of cognition (in intellectualist language). The doctor and the psychologist borrow the concepts of "sight" and "hearing" from common sense which considers them univocal, because our body includes as a matter of fact sets of visual and auditory apparatus which are anatomically distinct and to which isolatable contents of consciousness are supposed to correspond according to a general postulate of "constancy" which expresses our natural ignorance of ourselves. But, when taken up and systematically applied by science these confused concepts hinder research and finally necessitate a general revision of these naïve categories. In fact, what the measuring of thresholds tests is functions prior to any specific identification of sensible qualities and to the elaboration of knowledge; it is the way in which the subject causes his surroundings to exist for him, either as a pole of activity and the terminus of an act of seizure or expulsion, or else as a spectacle and theme of knowledge. The motor disturbances of cerebellar cases and those of psychological blindness can be coordinated only if we identify the basis of movement and vision not as a collection of sensible qualities but as a certain way of giving form or structure to our environment. We are led back by the use of this very inductive method to "metaphysical" questions which positivism would wish to avoid. Induction succeeds only provided that it is not restricted to noting things as present or absent, with concomitant variations, and that it conceives and comprehends facts as subsumed under ideas not contained in them. It is not a matter of choosing between a description of the disorder which furnishes the meaning and an explanation which provides the cause. There are, moreover, no explanations without comprehension. . . .

The study of a pathological case, then, has enabled us to glimpse a new mode of analysis—existential analysis—which goes beyond the traditional alternatives of empiricism and rationalism, of explanation and introspection. If consciousness were a collection of mental facts each disturbance should be elective. If it were a "representative function," a pure power of signification, it could be or not be (and with it everything else), but it could not cease to be having once been, or become sick, that is, deteriorate. If, in short, it is a projective activity, which leaves objects all around it, like traces of its own acts, but which nevertheless uses them as springboards from which to leap towards other spontaneous acts, then it becomes understandable that any "content" deficiency should have its repercussions on the main body of experience and open the door to its disintegration, that any pathological degeneration should affect the whole of consciousness— and that nevertheless the derangement should on each occasion attack a certain "side" of consciousness, that in each case certain symptoms should dominate the clinical picture of the disease, and, in short, that consciousness should be vulnerable and able to receive the illness into itself. In attacking the "visual sphere," illness is not limited to destroying certain contents of consciousness, "visual representations" or sight literally speaking; it affects sight in the figurative sense, of which the former is no more than the model or symbol—the power of "surveying" (*überschauen*) simultaneous multiplicities,[40] a certain way of positing the object or being aware. However, as this type of consciousness is only the sublimation of sensory vision, as it is schematized constantly within the dimensions of the visual field, albeit endowing them with a new meaning, it will be realized that this general function has its psychological roots. Consciousness freely develops its visual data beyond their own specific significance; it uses them for the expression of its spontaneous acts, as semantic evolution clearly shows in loading the terms "intuition," "self-evidence," and "natural light" with increasingly rich meaning. But conversely, not one of these terms, in the final sense which history has given them, is understandable without reference to the structures of visual perception. Hence one cannot say that man sees because he is Mind, nor indeed that he is Mind because he sees: to see as a man sees and to be Mind are synonymous. In so far as consciousness is consciousness of something only by allowing its furrow to trail behind it, and in so far as, in order to conceive an object one must rely on a previously constructed "world of thought," there is always some degree of depersonalization at the heart of consciousness. Hence the principle of an intervention from outside: consciousness may be ailing, the world of its thoughts may collapse into fragments—or rather, as the "contents" dissociated by the illness did not appear in the role of parts in normal consciousness and served only as stepping-stones to significances which outstrip them, consciousness can be seen trying to hold up its superstructures when their foundations have given way, aping its everyday processes, but without being able to come by any intuitive realization, and without being able to conceal the particular deficiency which robs them of their complete significance. It is in the same way theoretically understandable that mental illness may, in its turn, be linked with some bodily accident; consciousness projects itself into a physical world and has a body, as it projects itself into a cultural world and has its habits: because it cannot be consciousness without playing upon significances given either in the absolute past of nature or in its own personal past, and because any form of lived experience tends towards a certain generality whether that of our habits or that of our "bodily function."

These elucidations enable us clearly to understand motility as basic intentionality. Consciousness is in the first place not a matter of "I think that" but of "I can."[41] Schneider's motor trouble cannot, any more than his visual deficiency, be reduced to any failure of the general function of representation. Sight and movement are specific ways of entering into relationship with objects and if, through all these experiences, some unique function finds its expression, it is the momentum of existence, which does not cancel out the radical diversity of contents, because it links them to each other, not by placing them all under the control of an "I think," but by guiding them towards the intersensory unity of a "world." Movement is not thought-about movement, and bodily space is not space thought of or represented. "Each voluntary movement takes place in a setting, against a background which is determined by the movement itself. . . . We perform our movements in a space which is not 'empty' or unrelated to them, but which on the contrary, bears a highly determinate relation to them: movement and background are in fact, only artificaly separated stages of a unique totality."[42] In the action of the hand which is raised towards an object is contained a reference to the object, not as an object represented, but as that highly specific thing towards which we project ourselves, near which we are, in anticipation, and which we haunt. Consciousness is being towards the thing through the intermediary of the body. A movement is learned when the body has understood it, that is, when it has incorporated it into its "world," and to move one's body is to aim at things through it; it is to allow oneself to respond to their call, which is made upon it independently of any representation. Motility, then, is not, as it were, a handmaid of consciousness, transporting the body to that point in space of which we have formed a representation beforehand. In order that we may be able to move our body towards an object, the object must first exist for it, our body must not belong to the realm of the "in-itself." Objects no longer exist for the arm of the apraxic, and this is what causes it to remain immobile. Cases of pure apraxia in which the perception of space remains unaffected, in which even the "intellectual notion of the gesture to be made" does not appear to be obscured, and yet in which the patient cannot copy a triangle,[43] cases of constructive apraxia, in which the subject shows no gnosic disturbance except as regards the localization of stimuli on his body, and yet is incapable of copying a cross, a *v*, or an *o*,[44] all prove that the body has its world and that objects or space may be present to our knowledge but not to our body.

We must therefore avoid saying that our body is *in* space, or *in* time. It *inhabits* space and time. If my hand traces a complicated path through the air, I do not need, in order to know its final position, to add together all movements made in the same direction and subtract those made in the opposite direction. "Every identifiable change reaches consciousness already loaded with its relations to what has preceded it, as on a taximeter the distance is given already converted into shillings and pence."[45] At every moment, previous attitudes and movements provide an ever ready standard of measurement. It is not a question of a visual or motor "memory" of the starting position of the hand: cerebral lesions may leave visual memory intact while destroying awareness of movement. As for the "motor memory," it is clear that it could hardly establish the present position of the hand, unless the perception which gave rise to it had not, stored up in it, an absolute awareness of "here," for without this we should be thrown back from memory to memory and never have a present perception. Just as it is necessarily "here," the body necessarily exists "now"; it can never become "past," and if we cannot retain in health the living memory of sickness, or, in adult life that of our body as a child, these "gaps in memory". merely express the temporal structure of our body. At each successive instant of a movement, the preceding instant is not lost sight of. It is, as it were, dovetailed into the present, and present perception generally speaking consists in drawing together, on the basis of one's present position, the succession of previous positions, which envelop each other. But the impending position is also covered by the present, and through it all those which will occur throughout the movement. Each instant of the movement embraces its whole span, and particularly the first which, being the active initiative, institutes the link between a here and a yonder, a now and a future which the remainder of the instants will merely develop. In so far as I have a body through which I act in the world, space and time are not, for me, a collection of adjacent points nor are they a limitless number of relations synthesized by my consciousness, and into which it draws my body. I am not in space and time, nor do I conceive space and time; I belong to them, my body combines with them and includes them. The scope of this inclusion is the measure of that of my existence; but in any case it can never be all-embracing. The space and time which I inhabit are always in their different ways indeterminate horizons which contain other points of view. The synthesis of both time and space is a task that always has to be performed afresh. Our bodily experience of movement is not a particular case of knowledge; it provides us with a way of access to the world and the object, with a "praktognosia,"[46] which has to be recognized as original and perhaps as primary. My body has its world, or understands its world, without having to make use of my "symbolic" or "objectifying function." Certain patients can imitate the doctor's movements and move their right hand to their right ear and their left to their nose, so long as they stand beside the doctor and follow his movements through a mirror, but not if they face him. Head explained the patient's failure in terms of the inadequacy of his "formulation": according to him the imitation of the action is dependent upon a verbal translation. In fact, the formulation may be correct although the imitation is unsuccessful, or again the imitation may be successful without any formulation. Writers on the subject[47] then introduce, if not exactly verbal symbolism, at least a general symbolic function, an ability to "transpose," in which imitation, like perception or objective thought, is merely a particular case. But it is obvious that this general function does not explain adapted action. For patients are capable, not only of formulating the action to be performed, but of picturing it to themselves. They are quite aware of what they have to do, and yet, instead of moving the right hand to the right ear and the left hand to the nose, they touch one ear with both hands, or else their nose and one eye, or one ear and one eye.[48] What has become impossible is the application and adaptation to their own body of the objective particularity of the action. In other words, the right and left hand, the eye and ear are still presented to them as absolute locations, and not inserted into any system of correlations which links them up with the corresponding parts of the doctor's body, and which makes them usable for imitation, even when the doctor is face-to-face with the patient. In order to imitate the actions of someone facing me, it is not necessary that I should know expressly that "the hand which appears on the right side of my visual field is for my partner the left one." Now it is precisely the victim of disturbances who has recourse to these explanations. In normal imitation, the subject's left hand is immediately identified with his partner's, his action immediately models itself on the other's, and the subject projects himself or loses his separate reality in the other, becomes identified with him, and the change of coordinates is pre-eminently embodied in this existential process. This is because the normal subject has his body not only as a system of present positions, but besides, and thereby, as an open system of an infinite number of equivalent positions directed to other ends. What we have called the body image is precisely this system of equivalents, this immediately given invariant whereby the different motor tasks are instantaneously transferable. It follows that it is not only an experience of my body, but an experience of my body in the world, and that this is what gives a motor meaning to verbal orders. The function destroyed in apraxic disturbances is therefore a motor one. "It is not the symbolic or sense-giving function in general which is affected in cases of this kind: it is a much more primary function, in its nature motor, in other words, the capacity for motor differentiation within the dynamic body image."[49] The space in which normal imitation operates is not, as opposed to concrete space with its absolute locations, an "objective space" or a "representative space" based on an act of thought. It is already built into my bodily structure, and is its inseparable correlative. "Already motility, in its pure state, possesses the basic power of giving a meaning (*Sinngebung*)."[50] Even if subsequently, thought and the perception of space are freed from motility and spatial being, for us to be able to conceive space, it is in the first place necessary that we should have been thrust into it by our body, and that it should have provided us with the first model of those transpositions, equivalents, and identifications which make space into an objective system and allow our experience to be one of objects, opening out an "in itself." "Motility is the primary sphere in which initially the meaning of all significances (*der Sinn aller Signifikationen*) is engendered in the domain of represented space."[51]

The acquiring of a habit as a rearrangement and renewal of the body image presents great difficulties to traditional philosophies, which are always inclined to conceive synthesis as intellectual synthesis. It is quite true that what brings together, in habit, component actions, reactions, and "stimuli" is not some external process of association.[52] Any mechanistic theory runs up against the fact that the learning process is systematic: the subject does not weld together individual movements and individual stimuli but acquires the power to respond with a certain type of solution to situations of a certain general form. The situations may differ widely from case to case, and the response movements may be entrusted sometimes to one operative organ, sometimes to another, both situations and responses in the various cases having in common not so much a partial identity of elements as a shared significance. Must we then see the origin of habit in an act of understanding which organizes the elements only to withdraw subsequently?[53] For example, is it not the case that forming the habit of dancing is discovering, by analysis, the formula of the movement in question, and then reconstructing it on the basis of the ideal outline by the use of previously acquired movements, those of walking and running? But before the formula of the new dance can incorporate certain elements of general motility, it must first have had, as it were, the stamp of movement set upon it. As

has often been said, it is the body which "catches" (kapiert) and
"comprehends" movement. The acquiring of a habit is indeed the grasping of a significance, but it is the motor grasping of a motor significance.
Now what precisely does this mean? A woman may, without any calculation, keep a safe distance between the feather in her hat and
things which might break it off. She feels where the feather is just as
we feel where our hand is.[54] If I am in the habit of driving a car, I
enter a narrow opening and see that I can "get through" without comparing the width of the opening with that of the wings, just as I go
through a doorway without checking the width of the doorway against
that of my body.[55] The hat and the car have ceased to be objects
with a size and volume which is established by comparison with other
objects. They have become potentialities of volume, the demand for a
certain amount of free space. In the same way the iron gate to the
metro platform, and the road, have become restrictive potentialities
and immediately appear passable or impassable for my body with
its adjuncts. The blind man's stick has ceased to be an object for
him, and is no longer perceived for itself; its point has become an area
of sensitivity, extending the scope and active radius of touch, and
providing a parallel to sight. In the exploration of things, the length
of the stick does not enter expressly as a middle term: the blind man
is rather aware of it through the position of objects than of the position
of objects through it. The position of things is immediately given
through the extent of the reach which carries him to it, which comprises the arm's own reach the stick's range of action. If I want to get
used to a stick, I try it by touching a few things with it, and eventually
I have it "well in hand," I can see what things are "within reach" or out
of reach of my stick. There is no question here of any quick estimate
or any comparison between the objective length of the stick and the
objective distance away of the goal to be reached. The points in space
do not stand out as objective positions in relation to the objective position occupied by our body; they mark, in our vicinity, the varying range
of our aims and our gestures. To get used to a hat, a car, or a stick is to
be transplanted into them, or conversely, to incorporate them into the
bulk of our own body. Habit expresses our power of dilating our being
in the world or changing our existence by appropriating fresh instruments.[56] It is possible to know how to type without being able to say
where the letters which make the words are to be found on the banks

of keys. To know how to type is not, then, to know the place of each letter among the keys, nor even to have acquired a conditioned reflex for each one, which is set in motion by the letter as it comes before our eye. If habit is neither a form of knowledge nor an involuntary action, what then is it? It is knowledge in the hands, which is forthcoming only when bodily effort is made, and cannot be formulated in detachment from that effort. The subject knows where the letters are on the typewriter as we know where one of our limbs is, through a knowledge bred of familiarity which does not give us a position in objective space. The movement of her fingers is not presented to the typist as a path through space which can be described, but merely as a certain adjustment of motility, physiognomically distinguishable from any other. The question is often framed as if the perception of a letter written on paper aroused the representation of the same letter which in turn aroused the representation of the movement needed to strike it on the machine. But this is mythological language. When I run my eyes over the text set before me, there do not occur perceptions which stir up representations, but patterns are formed as I look, and these are endowed with a typical or familiar physiognomy. When I sit at my typewriter, a motor space opens up beneath my hands, in which I am about to "play" what I have read. The reading of the word is a modulation of visible space, the performance of the movement is a modulation of manual space, and the whole question is how a certain physiognomy of "visual" patterns can evoke a certain type of motor response, how each "visual" structure eventually provides itself with its mobile essence without there being any need to spell the word or specify the movement in detail in order to translate one into the other. But this power of habit is no different from the general one which we exercise over our body: if I am ordered to touch my ear or my knee, I move my hand to my ear or my knee by the shortest route, without having to think of the initial position of my hand, or that of my ear, or the path between them. We said earlier that it is the body which "understands" in the acquisition of a habit. This way of putting it will appear absurd, if understanding is subsuming a sense-datum under an idea, and if the body is an object. But the phenomenon of habit is just what prompts us to revise our notion of "understand" and our notion of the body. To understand is to experience the harmony between what we aim at and what is given, between the intention and the performance—and the body is our anchorage in a world. When I put my hand to my knee, I experience at every stage of the movement the fulfilment of an intention which was not directed at my knee as an idea or even as an object, but as a present and real part of my living body, that is, finally, as a stage in my perpetual movement towards a world. When the typist performs the necessary movements on the typewriter, these movements are governed by an intention, but the intention does not posit the keys as objective locations. It is literally true that the subject who learns to type incorporates the key-bank space into his bodily space.

The example of instrumentalists shows even better how habit has its abode neither in thought nor in the objective body, but in the body as mediator of a world. It is known[57] that an experienced organist is capable of playing an organ which he does not know, which has more or fewer manuals, and stops differently arranged, compared with those on the instrument he is used to playing. He needs only an hour's practice to be ready to perform his programme. Such a short preparation rules out the supposition that new conditioned reflexes have here been substituted for the existing sets, except where both form a system and the change is all-embracing, which takes us away from the mechanistic theory, since in that case the reactions are mediated by a comprehensive grasp of the instrument. Are we to maintain that the organist analyses the organ, that he conjures up and retains a representation of the stops, pedals, and manuals and their relation to each other in space? But during the short rehearsal preceding the concert, he does not act like a person about to draw up a plan. He sits on the seat, works the pedals, pulls out the stops, gets the measure of the instrument with his body, incorporates within himself the relevant directions and dimensions, settles into the organ as one settles into a house. He does not learn objective spatial positions for each stop and pedal, nor does he commit them to "memory." During the rehearsal, as during the performance, the stops, pedals, and manuals are given to him as nothing more than possibilities of achieving certain emotional or musical values, and their positions are simply the places through which this value appears in the world. Between the musical essence of the piece as it is shown in the score and the notes which actually sound round the organ, so direct a relation is established that the organist's body and his instrument are merely the medium of this relationship. Henceforth the music exists by itself and through it all the rest exists.[58] There is here no place for any "memory" of the position of the stops, and it is not in objective space that the organist in fact is playing. In reality his movements during rehearsal are consecratory gestures: they draw affective vectors, discover emotional sources, and create a space of expressiveness as the movements of the augur delimit the *templum*.

The whole problem of habit here is one of knowing how the musical significance of an action can be concentrated in a certain place to the extent that, in giving himself entirely to the music, the organist reaches for precisely those stops and pedals which are to bring it into being. Now the body is essentially an expressive space. If I want to take hold of an object, already, at a point of space about which I have been quite unmindful, this power of grasping constituted by my hand moves upwards towards the thing. I move my legs not as things in space two and a half feet from my head, but as a power of locomotion which extends my motor intention downwards. The main areas of my body are devoted to actions, and participate in their value, and asking why common sense makes the head the seat of thought raises the same problem as asking how the organist distributes, through "organ space," musical significances. But our body is not merely one expressive space among the rest, for that is simply the constituted body. It is the origin of the rest, expressive movement itself, that which causes them to begin to exist as things, under our hands and eyes. Although our body does not impose definite instincts upon us from birth, as it does upon animals, it does at least give to our life the form of generality, and develops our personal acts into stable dispositional tendencies. In this sense our nature is not long-established custom, since custom presupposes the form of passivity derived from nature. The body is our general medium for having a world. Sometimes it is restricted to the actions necessary for the conservation of life, and accordingly it posits around us a biological world; at other times, elaborating upon these primary actions and moving from their literal to a figurative meaning, it manifests through them a core of new significance: this is true of motor habits such as dancing. Sometimes, finally, the meaning aimed at cannot be achieved by the body's natural means; it must then build itself an instrument, and it projects thereby around itself a cultural world. At all levels it performs the same function which is to endow the instantaneous expressions of spontaneity with "a little renewable action and independent existence."[59] Habit is merely a form of this fundamental power. We say that the body has understood, and habit acquired when it has absorbed a new meaning, and assimilated a fresh core of significance.

To sum up, what we have discovered through the study of motility, is a new meaning of the word "meaning." The great strength of intellectualist psychology and idealist philosophy comes from their having no difficulty in showing that perception and thought have an intrinsic significance and cannot be explained in terms of the external association of fortuitously agglomerated contents. The *Cogito* was the coming to self-awareness of this inner core. But all meaning was *ipso facto* conceived as an act of thought, as the work of a pure *I*, and although rationalism easily refuted empiricism, it was itself unable to account for the variety of experience, for the element of senselessness in it, for the contingency of contents. Bodily experience forces us to acknowledge an imposition of meaning which is not the work of a universal constituting consciousness, a meaning which clings to certain contents. My body is that meaningful core which behaves like a general function, and which nevertheless exists, and is susceptible to disease. In it we learn to know that union of essence and existence which we shall find again in perception generally, and which we shall then have to describe more fully.

NOTES

1. A disorder of sensation in which sensations are referred to the wrong part of the body (Translator's note). Cf., for example, Head, *On disturbances of sensation with especial reference to the pain of visceral disease.*

2. Ibid. We have discussed the notion of the local signal in *La Structure du Comportement*, pp. 102 ff.

3. Cf., for example, Head, *Sensory disturbances from cerebral lesion*, p. 189; Pick, *Störungen der Orientierung am eigenen Körper;* and even Schilder, *Das Körperschema*, although Schilder admits that "such a complex is not the sum of its parts but a new whole in relation to them."

4. As for example Lhermitte, *L'Image de notre corps.*

5. Konrad, *Das Körperschema, eine kritische Studie und der Versuch einer Revision*, pp. 365 and 367. Bürger-Prinz and Kaila define the body image

as "knowledge of one's own body as the collective expression both of the mutual relations of its limbs and of its parts." Ibid., p. 365.

6. Cf., for example, Konrad, *op. cit.*

7. Grünbaum, *Aphasie und Motorik*, p. 395.

8. We have already seen that the phantom limb, which is a modality of the body image, is understood in terms of the general movement of being-in-the-world.

9. Cf. Becker, *Beiträge zur phänomenologischen Begründung der Geometrie und ihrer physikalischen Anwendungen.*

10. Gelb and Goldstein, *Über den Einfluss des vollständigen Verlustes des optischen Vorstellungsvermögens auf das taktile Erkennen.—Psychologische Analysen hirnpathologischer Fälle,* Chap. II, pp. 157–250.

11. Goldstein, *Über die Abhängigkeit der Bewegungen von optischen Vorgängen.* This second work makes use of observations made on the same patient, Schneider, two years after those collected in the work just referred to.

12. Goldstein, *Zeigen und Greifen,* pp. 453–66.

13. Ibid. This is a cerebellar case.

14. Goldstein, *Über die Abhängigkeit,* p. 175.

15. J. P. Sartre, *L'Imaginaire,* p. 243.

16. Diderot, *Paradoxe sur le Comédien.*

17. Goldstein, *Über die Abhängigkeit,* pp. 175 and 176.

18. It is not a question of how the soul acts on the objective body, since it is not on the latter that it acts, but on the phenomenal body. So the question has to be reframed, and we must ask why there are two views of me and of my body: my body for me and my body for others, and how these two systems can exist together. It is indeed not enough to say that the objective body belongs to the realm of "for others," and my phenomenal body to that of "for me," and we cannot refuse to pose the problem of their relations, since the "for me" and the "for others" coexist in one and the same world, as is proved by my perception of an other who immediately brings me back to the condition of an object for him.

19. Goldstein, *Über den Einfluss . . .,* pp. 167–206.

20. Ibid., pp. 206–13.

21. For example, the subject runs his fingers over an angle several times: "My fingers," he says, "move straight along, then stop, and then move off again in another direction; it is an angle, it must be a right angle."—"Two, three, four angles, the sides are each two centimetres long, so they are equal, all the angles are right angles. . . . It's a die." Ibid., p. 195. Cf. pp. 187–206.

22. Goldstein, *Über den Einfluss . . .,* pp. 206–13.

23. As Goldstein does, ibid., pp. 167–206.

24. Cf. supra the general discussion of the "association of ideas."

25. A patient named Schneider says he needs *Anhaltspunkte.*

26. Goldstein, *Über den Einfluss . . .,* pp. 213–22.

27. Goldstein, *Über die Abhängigkeit,* p. 161; "Bewegung und Hintergrund bestimmen sich wechselseitig, sind eigentlich nur zwei herausgegriffene Momente eines einheitlichen Ganzes."

28. Goldstein, *Über die Abhängigkeit*, . . ., p. 161.

29. Ibid.

30. Goldstein (ibid., pp. 160 ff.) merely says that the background of abstract movement is the body, and this is true in that the body during abstract movement is no longer merely the vehicle, but becomes the aim of the movement. Nevertheless, by changing function, it also changes its existential modality and passes from the actual to the possible.

31. Van Woerkom, *Sur la notion de l'espace (le sens géométrique)*, pp. 113–19.

32. Cf., for example, H. Le Savoureux, "Un philosophe en face de la Psychanalyse," *Nouvelle Revue Française*, February 1939. "For Freud the mere fact of having related symptoms to each other through plausible logical links is a sufficient confirmation that a psychoanalytical interpretation, which means a psychological one, is soundly based. The adoption of logical coherency as the criterion for accepting an interpretation brings Freudian proof much nearer to metaphysical deduction than to scientific explanation. . . . In the medical treatment of mental disease, psychological probability is regarded as practically worthless in the investigation of causes" (p. 318).

33. He succeeds only by being allowed "imitative movements" (*nachfahrende Bewegungen*) of the head, hands, or fingers which sketch in the imperfect outline of the object. Gelb and Goldstein, *Zur Psychologie des optischen Wahrnehmungs-und Erkennungsvorganges, Psychologische Analysen hirnpathologischer Fälle*, Chap. I, pp. 20–24.

34. "The patient's visual data lack any specific and characteristic structure. His impressions, unlike those of a normal person's, have no firm configuration; they have not, for instance, the typical look of a 'square,' a 'triangle,' a 'straight line,' or a 'curve.' Before him he sees only patches in which his sight allows him to pick out only salient characteristics, such as height and breadth and their relation to each other" (ibid., p. 77). A gardener sweeping a path fifty yards away is "a long streak with something moving backwards and forwards towards the top of it" (p. 108). In the street the patient distinguishes men from vehicles by the fact that "men are all the same; long and thin—vehicles are wide, unmistakably so, and much thicker" (ibid.).

35. Ibid., p. 116.

36. Gelb and Goldstein, *Über den Einfluss* . . ., pp. 213–22.

37. It was in this sense that Gelb and Goldstein interpreted Schneider's case in the first works which they devoted to him (*Zur Psychologie* . . . and *Über den Einfluss*). It will be seen how subsequently (*Über die Abhängigkeit* and particularly *Zeigen und Greifen* and the works published under their editorship by Benary, Hocheimer, and Steinfeld) they broadened their diagnosis. The progress of their analysis is a particularly clear example of the progress of psychology.

38. *Zeigen und Greifen*, p. 456.

39. Ibid., pp. 458–59.

40. Cf. *La Structure du Comportement*, pp. 91 ff.

41. This term is the usual one in Husserl's unpublished writings.

42. Goldstein, *Über die Abhängigkeit*, p. 163.

43. Lhermitte, G. Lévy, and Kyriako, *Les Perturbations de la représentation spatiale chez les apraxiques*, p. 597.

44. Lhermitte and Trelles, *Sur l'apraxie constructive, les troubles de la pensée spatiale et de la somatognosie dans l'apraxie*, p. 428. Cf. Lhermitte, de Massary, and Kyriako, *Le Rôle de la pensée spatiale dans l'apraxie*.

45. Head and Holmes, *Sensory disturbances from cerebral lesions*, p. 187.

46. Grünbaum, *Aphasie und Motorik*.

47. Goldstein, Van Woerkom, Boumann, and Grünbaum.

48. Grünbaum, *op. cit.*, pp. 386–92.

49. Grünbaum, *op. cit.*, pp. 397–98.

50. Ibid., p. 394.

51. Ibid., p. 396.

52. See, on this point, *La Structure du Comportement*, pp. 125 ff.

53. As Bergson, for example, thinks when he defines habit as "the fossilized residue of a spiritual activity."

54. Head, *Sensory disturbances from cerebral lesions*, p. 188.

55. Grünbaum, *Aphasie und Motorik*, p. 395.

56. It thus elucidates the nature of the body image. When we say that it presents us immediately with our bodily position, we do not mean, after the manner of empiricists, that it consists of a mosaic of "extensive sensations." It is a system which is open on to the world, and correlative with it.

57. Cf. Chevalier, *L'Habitude*, pp. 202 ff.

58. "As though the musicians were not nearly so much playing the little phrase as performing the rites on which it insisted before it would consent to appear." (Proust, *Swann's Way*, II, trans. C. K. Scott Moncrieff, Chatto & Windus, p. 180.) "Its cries were so sudden that the violinist must snatch up his bow and race to catch them as they came" (ibid., p. 186).

59. Valéry, *Introduction à la Méthode de Léonard de Vinci, Variété*, p. 177.

B. The Lived-Body

ANTHROPODOLOGY:[1]

MAN A-FOOT

Richard M. Griffith

1 Cor. 12 ". . . For the body is not one member but many
. . . And if they were one member, where were the body?
. . . If the foot should say, Because I am not the hand, I
am not of the body . . ."

In what low estate the foot is held! I adorn my fingers with diamonds
and rubies and imprison my toes in leather. The foot, we are told,
just makes possible the upright posture,[2] the noble posture of man,
which orients head and mind toward heaven, which frees the clever

This article is reprinted from *Conditio Humana*, a *Festchrift* for Erwin W.
Straus in celebration of his 75th birthday, published by Springer-Verlag,
Berlin-Heidelberg-New York,1966, pp. 84–101. The editor wishes to express
his appreciation to Mrs. Richard M. Griffith and Springer-Verlag for permission to reproduce this article in its entirety.

hand. Indentured to serve the heavy labor of stance and carriage for the Cinderella-sisters of eye, mouth and hand, what does the foot receive in recompense? Abuse. The burden of body and shoe rewards with puffing and pain; corns, broken arches and ingrown nails. Yet let us see what we can do without more readily, the foot or the hand. Here is the footless man:

Slide showing detail from PIETER BREUGHEL THE ELDER: *The Fight Between Carnival and Lent*. A cripple pulls herself through the dirt, sliding along on a plate-like sled, her useless legs bent up against the back. Each hand grasps artificial "feet" whose stick-legs give her the traction to pull. Her back is severely arched, head thrown back, her mouth opened in the effort and her agony. She is unkempt. Pictorially, she is "degraded"— as she literally is, i.e., "de-stepped."

And here is one with no hands:

Slide of a teen-aged girl, the empty arms of her shirt turned inside. She sits upright on a couch, writing on a pad with pencil held by toes. Not deprived of dignity, she finds ways to groom herself.

Such an indispensable thing treated so "shod-dily." Each step it is pressed against the dirt and grovels in the dust from which we rose. The foot needs a champion. Would that I could fill the shoe. This paper is a humble tribute to the lowly foot. But if the psychologist will turn his gaze downward from the genitalia and majestic things, with a sight open to revelation, the world will be opened to him; the human condition, no less, is what he will see, as never seen before.

Man is at one with his body, his psychology inseparable from the structure of his several parts and the harmony which is between them. The body is at once what man *has* and what he *is*. The Cartesian chasm is not bridged by that simple sentence; no, not bridged over but closed, by the earthquake of it. For man *is* a synthesis: he is not spirit, mind and matter glued together, but a synthesis of these things so tragically ripped apart. Study of the mind must be extended from mind to man; psychology must seek its true base in an anthropology.

The parts have a doubly directed relationship to the whole. Together they constitute the whole; yet, the intent of the whole in some way permeates—thus, constitutes—each. Each part plays out its part in the overall, each unit diversely bespeaks that unity. Because of the reflection of the unity in the parts which the whole comprises, we could, if detective enough, perceive in each all the others. The foot "sub-stantiates" man; upright, man is a-foot.

In our task, and joy, of placing the foot, at long last, on a pedestal, we will also elevate man; if the foot is accorded its rightful respect, we need not neglect the hand. We set out, then, to see man in his foot-ness. Even in our lowliest part shall we find ourself.

BONE AND MUSCLE

Let us treat lightly of muscle, bone and tendon. The cartoon shows the professor lecturing the young medical students on the anatomy of the foot; the caption reads, "I realize that those of you who are planning to go into psychiatry may find this dull." The intent of my paper, as you will realize from what has gone before, is to turn the humor of that cartoon into irony. The Head Doctor should know the foot; the student of the mind should begin as Professor of the Foot. But we cannot afford much time on the anatomy of the foot, it's a course I've not completed; we would launch *Anthropodology,* not podology as such; and the one way in which the foot has been lauded, I'm tempted to say in that alone, is as specialized physical structure admirably evolved for the job it has to do.

Ponder a bit on transportation. Bones, of course, support weight by remaining rigid under pressure. Before bones developed, the organism had of necessity to reside in water, in a medium with minimal mechanical stresses; it would flatten out like a jellyfish on land. Emerging onto marsh land a fin-like foot could first push it along, as with the turtle, on its stomach. This was all right for the half-swim-half-walk through slime and mud; to move on higher ground it had to lift itself to walk—locomotion became transportation, it had to *carry itself.*[3] To escape the friction the organism literally had to lift itself. Walking is a lifting and a thrusting. Gravity gives bones their burden—it is what man stands up to; the counter thrust of the gritty and cohesive surface of dry earth permits the push in walking (instead of impeding, friction now propels). Man has always aspired to further freedom, he would like to fly; and he also despises crawling, that's for snakes and worms. Walking is the crossing of a ground which wears on one, comes in humps and is solid. The nature of the earth resulted in these ways of locomotion, these transportations. To add another was the fabled invention of wheel.[4]

Thus—though no one can speak first-foot for such an evolutionary account—we arrive at the foot, the part which pushes upward to sustain weight and laterally to impart motion. It is "stuck" against the ground and "sticks" there; while the body moves, it remains "stationary," then hurries to catch up and go before to relieve the other foot. There is another way to go from one place to another and that is to swing through trees. Some say that if he had not passed through such a stage of transportation man would never have reached his upright stance. It may not be wholly true but near enough to say that in the tree four feet became four hands. The torso became wider than thick, in brachiation arms were pulled to the sides; in order to grasp the tree limb, one toe became contrapositioned to the others, split from them as the thumb is from the fingers. (Leave this four-handed creature in the tree a moment while I insert a brief commercial for one of my theses: How much the foot of the dog, the rooster, duck, cow, elephant and the waterbug could tell us of the body above which it supports and moves, and the way it goes about it; the animal *is* his foot.) Returning to earth, the *upper* hand further developed its grasping function on such things as baseball bats and brooms, but it could never have done it if the *bottom* hand had not subserved it.

Look now at the sole of the foot of the ape and of man. (Slide) The feet to the left not only still have thumbs of a sort and toes almost as long as fingers, but they have another characteristic—they are flat, as flat as the palm of the hand. The persistent upright posture would be impossible for them to maintain. The body above them tilts forward— indeed, most comfortably leans on its arms—the knee is bowed and buckled. These vestigial hands are still more pad or paw than human foot; heel-to-toe gait is not possible for them. That depends on a structural miracle—the metatarsal arch.

> Slide of the metatarsal arches with their graduated degrees of arc, then another depicting the stresses and strains to which they are adapted.

How is that for architecture?

Man has two slim ankles, but in a sense he has four feet. His weight is supported not on two points but on four, the heels and the balls of the feet. In standing, the center of weight falls between these four points. In walking, the heel and ball reduce the rise and fall gait of a man on stilts to a level, more steady progression. The heel catches the weight which is transferred gradually to the ball, which, in a final flip to the tip of the toes as the companion heel takes over, propels the body forward. In running, the ball of the foot accepts the total burden and the spring of calf muscle adds significantly to the motion of knee and hip.

With that we are finished with the anatomy of statics and dynamics with evolutionary comments. However long we went on, we could never more than start. What appeals to us at the moment is not what man *was* but rather what he *is*. In Anthropodology we study man afoot; heuristically, as man, a foot.

FOOT TO EARTH: HUMILITY AND TRANSCENDENTAL DIGNITY

Let's get down to earth (in our task to un-earth the foot) by starting with my relation to the earth. Whatever else the foot is, it occupies the unique position between me and the ground. Hence, we begin there with what is underneath us, then turning upward, we will consider the relation of foot to body. Between the two sections we will insert some observations on the phenomenon of the shoe.

The ground is not only what I take my stand on (the underground of me) but the background against which as human I may be perceived the most sharply. I am earth: from dust becometh, to dust returneth. But only *against* the earth, in opposition to it, do I exist as human. I must maintain my separation from the earth. When I would withdraw, radically remove myself, dissolve myself from embarrassment, I would like to "sink down through the floor."

Adam in Hebrew means "earth." The word "human" comes from the Latin *humanus*, literally, "a creature of the earth," man plus *humus*, the ground. Yet language and myth tell us that man is a little more lordly than this. God breathed the spirit into Adam. In Greek mythology there were creatures of nothing but the earth, the autochthons. But Hercules, son of Zeus and woman, subdued Antaeus, son of Gaea, Mother Earth, by lifting him off the ground, the only source of his strength. Let us never forget, however noble we may be, that we, as did Hercules, get our strength from the ground. Lifted off the ground I lose my leverage, no longer have a purchase, and am as helpless as a terrapin waving his legs on his back. The boxer hits with his feet, his blow being, as it were, a transposed kick.

Though we rely upon the ground we are different from it. The very word "exist" is from the Latin *existere,* meaning to stand forth, to arise, to set out, to stand out—from the ground, the underground.

My direct experience is not that I am of the ground (only on reflection do we conclude that all things come from it), rather my experience is of opposition to the earth. My triumphant ancestor whose picture I have seen striking his chest and breaking forth with an exultant whoop celebrates not a minor victory unessential to the race; it appears to me that he has just assumed the upright posture and thereby vanquished the earth. As phylogenetic re-enactment of this drama, the face of the infant lights up when he stands up even though he is not yet old enough to know what he has done. I have little comprehension of gravity, those invisible lines of force emanating from the center of a globe which is flat; weight, the weight which I know, is opposition to the earth. Everything sinks back to the earth. That I rise and stand above the ground defines me, is the immanent truth of my existence. Every morning I rise and I lie down with the night—until I arise no more (dust unto dust). I am very much aware of what it costs to raise my parts off the ground. I lift heavy bodies off the ground and they drop back to it. I fall, slip—we say, "lose my feet" (as with the demented man we say he has "lost his mind," or in anger he "lost his head")— and *land* on the ground (the land), break my bones upon it. Weight, with its central importance to all my experiencing, is the fundamental experience of separation from the earth, the most direct and domineering aspect of my relation, I-to-Earth.

But the earth will not stay underfoot. It infringes on me, it would invade and dominate me. I wash my feet, shine my shoes (if I am well-groomed, they are the shiniest part of all), smooth scuffed leather, bind stubbed toes, favor stone bruises. Between me and the ground is an area of damage and repair. To keep the earth in its place requires eternal vigilance. I have roofs and hats to keep the sun and rain off my topside; my bottom boundary has problems of its own. At the end of the day's journey in parched lands, the traveler washes the earth from off his feet. In this ritual he does not so much remove filth but rather acts to maintain his own integrity and sovereignty, his identity over and against the encroaching earth and its sovereignty. "Rise and shine!" the sergeant calls out, unaware of the universal force of his command.

In reporting the Last Supper, St. John tells of Jesus' washing the feet of the disciples. Neither Matthew, Mark nor Luke mentions the enaction; St. John on his part does not recall the sacrament of bread and wine, so important to the other three evangelists and so sacred to the Christian Church.

He riseth from supper, and laid aside his garments;
and took a towel and girded himself.

After that he poureth water into a basin, and began to wash the disciples'
feet, and to wipe them with the towel wherewith he was girded. [John 13]

For St. John the lesson from this Last Supper was in the words:

If I then, your Lord and Master, have washed your feet; ye also ought to
wash one another's feet.

The lesson is of humility (the word "humility" also comes from *humus*,
the soil); and such an interpretation is good, indeed. However, in the
context of the Last Supper and from the viewpoint of the unfolding
theme of the earth and I, let us venture another significance. Peter
said unto Him,

Lord, dost thou wash my feet? . . . Thou shalt never wash my feet.

Jesus answered him,

If I wash thee not, thou hast no part with me.

Could this not be a second "baptism"? Knowing of Judas' betrayal,
Jesus said,

Ye are not all clean. . . . I speak not of you all: . . . He that eateth bread
with me hath lifted up his heel against me.

Thus, though He *humbled* Himself equally before Judas, He did not
cleanse him. What better rite of sanctification could there be than to
wash off the dust of the earth? In this act Jesus purified the disciples,
symbolically separating them from this earth as much as possible since
they were still of this earth, unclean and burdened with its cares.

Departing a place we wash off the dust and leave it behind. During
his journey on the earth, the feet of Jesus had more than any other
part suffered its earthiness. They were more of this earth. In the last
days they were bathed with tears and anointed with precious oil. We
are unclean and heavy. Our ethical and religious practices and thoughts
may be translated into these terms of lifting myself above the lowly
earth.

My foot is a border partaking of the double character of me and of
the earth, a neutral zone separating me from the ground. Look once
more at the legless man. (Slide of Breughel: *The Cripples*) The foot-

less, crippled beggars painted by Breughel are pathetic and disturbing chiefly because they have nothing between them and the earth. Without the foot do they qualify as human? We can see why the warrior's vulnerability is in his Achilles tendon; but more: my Achilles tendon is my Achilles tendon—not just as warrior but as man. The foxtails pinned about their clothing, for long a mysterious detail of the painting, has recently been recognized as the warning sign the leper was forced to wear. But were only lepers crippled? Breughel here employed the sign of leprosy to portray in horrid fashion the ostracizing stigma of the de-humanizing loss of the feet.[5]

Breughel's man is a lump of clay; he is a great foot man.

> Slide of *The Peasant Dance* . . . faces dull and feet heavy clopping . . . followed by a slide of his *Landscape with the Fall of Icarus* in which Icarus can be found if one searches, as he falls asprawl into the sea off to the right, and the hero is the peasant, plowing in the foreground.

The second picture gives the place in his thought of the noble man of Greek mythology. Icarus put on wings, but he soared too high, too near the sun, and the wax melted; he fell into the sea. Neither could the tower of Babel quite reach the sky. But the two stories show man as dreaming to rise higher above the earth than he is able. When Breughel portrays Icarus in the Breughel scheme of things, he is nothing but an upended, ungainly pair of legs disappearing into the sea, small and lost, appropriately, in the over-idealized, white landscape. In the foreground of the picture is reality. The peasant, dominating the scene, plows the ground, foot planted in the upturned earth. *His* dreams and *his* follies are earthy, don't soar very high.

Dirt on the foot is necessary evil to be avoided as much as possible by walking around mud puddles and out of the dust onto the grass; but still earth will transgress the boundary. But suppose I fall and catch myself with my hands; I look at them with loathing, shake them, wipe them, wash them. Further, suppose that I fall "flat on my face," as we say. I struggle up with "mud in my eye," my face suffering the ultimate indignity. I'm a hilarious sight. That fellow leaning against the post there brays like an ass. He can't explain why; he doesn't think it is funny, it doesn't get funny by his thinking, it *is* funny. But for this to be comic he "knows" far more than he knows. He knows that man is upright, struggles with the earth, and of his pretense to be too far from it removed. It's a funnier scene yet if I have top hat on my head. The more dignity that I put on (particularly if it's "airs"), the more "stilted" that I am, the more comic is my fall.

But, of course, however uprightly majestic I may be, I stand upon the earth. In order to stand I need something solid and substantial to support me. (How rich is every word: "substance" is derived from the Latin *substare*, to "exist," literally, "to stand near or beneath"; my essence is to *stand*.) To stand I need to be certain of the ground on which I stand. When the earth shakes my very being is quaked. I am anchored, I have a pivot point. This point of foot-to-ground defines my personal here-ness, my place. (The word "place" traces back to *planta*, the sole of the foot.) This place belongs to me and to no one else. Many people inhabit this country, this village, but this point of my foot is uniquely mine, my place and mine alone. It is my stand-point, my foothold, my position; from it I sustain my viewpoint and belief. On it I am lonely and individualistic. If I have no standpoint I am giddy.[6]

My footsteps are my marks, my stamps. As signs of where I've been I leave these prints. How distinctive they are may be proven by trying to walk in the footprints of another. In soft snow I step where he has stepped before. But it doesn't work. I am awkward, nothing is right or natural. My gait is not his.

I walk with support on many faces of the earth: the hard slick ice, the cold soft snow, slushy mud, squashy filth, broken glass, the green lawn, hot sand, piercing nails, hot dust. And there are the fearful precipice and sucking quicksand. These are poetic images I am evoking, barefoot images. It is not often we return to the pristine earth. Except on temporary vacations we desire the dullness of the man made, level surface. The history of civilization is the history of the flat surface.[7] As we depersonalize our feet with shoes, we neutralize the earth with road and floor. On a path free of tree roots to stumble on and mud to sink in, out thoughts may leave the foot and engage less routine matters. The route becomes routine.

Walkways and floors are idealized earth, planes free of perturbations. Cobblestones, concrete, Greek marble, Japanese rice mats, oriental carpets, vinyl tile, polished white ash, the varnished maple of ballroom, basketball floor and bowling lane are human solutions like the jug and arrowhead. With each of these we go beyond utility to elegance and artistry, each permits esthetic elaboration as with mosaic tile and intricate oriental pattern. The nomad pitches his tent and spreads his rug; how different from the monotonous sand on which it lies! Kings never set foot to the bare ground, only walk on carpets—penitents prefer coals, small boys, plowed ground. We are aloof from the earth and sandwich a humanized layer of insulation between us and the earth.

THE SHOE

To keep my foot out of the dirt, to guard it, and thus to release the mind, I put on shoe. We are not satisfied with the body the way it is, wanting to improve on nature. The shoe is much more intimate to me than is clothing which hangs on me and, as a sort of screen, conceals my nakedness. With the shoe I improve on the way I'm made. In some sense all tools do this. The club extends the arm and hits a harder blow; all tools bridge between me and the world. But the shoe is peculiar as a tool, becoming much more a part of me than do those instruments which I grasp and turn loose of easily. Comparable complements to the body came much later—with eyeglasses, false teeth and hearing aid. In a giant stride of evolution we have jumped ahead some millenia and returned to leather hoof. With the shoe I need not test each place I put my foot, but can lift my eyes from my path and proceed oblivious of the process.

Any discussion of the shoe could fatally lead us to the untold variety of shoes which have been devised, not only for ends but as objects in themselves. We must embellish things for sight as much as for job; if it weren't for looks my shoe wouldn't pinch the way it does. We will not make a scholarly historical survey, nor take a trip around the world (for we still have a lot of ground of a different kind to cover). Moccasin, flip-flop, Dutch wooden sabot, the funny shoes the jester wore with toe turned up in the spiral—sharp pointed ones, broad ones, cowboy boots with spur—we're already exhausted and we've done no more than look.

To show what might be done with each of the many types of shoes, we should attempt an analysis—an Anthropodological analysis— accounting from our new vantage point for the senseless high heel which our women wear, the spiked heels which "distribute the weight of the body incorrectly, and also impede locomotion." In the safety sign the lady has just been unceremoniously on the floor be-seated;

"A heel was the cause of her downfall," the message reads, "wear safe sensible shoes."

My shoe, being on foot between me and the ground, should reveal aspects of my relation to body and to earth. Someone has said that the woman in our culture is fitted with high heels because of the jealous husband who would like her to stay home. In a more accepted explanation we speak of increased height, the illusion of slenderness and more shapely calves. No one claims they are much use in the mud (that's their "point"). The striving for height with the flame headdresses of Southeastern Asia, the Gothic hat, and so on indefinitely, is to accentuate the upright posture; however, the high heel tells us more specifically of woman's place in our culture. They are the pedestals upon which we place her. (Someplace in this paper we should dwell on the word "pedestal" and its import and the whole family of that root, such as "pedestrian.") In practical matters we need our feet planted firmly on the ground. I see the sound and respected banker standing in the doorway of his office, firmly rooted, feet apart, unshakable, a column of integrity and worldliness. His wife ("supported" by him) tips trippingly by on her toes. She is elevated above the heavy world of his toil. As we prize most dearly useless things, to de-utilize her helps place her in the realm of the beautiful.

This pedestal for the woman makes drunkenness in her so abhorrent. High heels not only are an im*pedi*ment to the intoxicated lady, swaying down the street, ankles flopping in and out, her carriage rather chancy; they remind us of the peak from which she has fallen and testify to the seriousness of her offense, her falling from "grace."

What better evidence could one offer than the high heel that the wearer is not a tiller of the soil? Gentlewomen in the cultures with which we are acquainted are removed from contact with the earth. The binding of feet of the Chinese girl should not be criticized because it interferes with her walking—that is its aim; not to prevent her from running away, however, but to make of her a queen. The gentlewoman holds her teacup daintily, minimizing contact even with this beautiful thing so remote from "earthenware," a painted, fragile piece of china. The spoon, the knife and the fork are the stilts and spiked heels for the hand. Spotless white gloves shield her to her elbows and further attest her purity from dirt. Of course, we have returned to the theme of our not wishing to be *soiled*.

It is a poor man who has no shoe. It should be shined and kept snugly tied for it reflects my *station* and my *status*. If my shoes are down at the heels, I am "down at the heels." And what does the expression mean? Again the best demonstration would be for you to put your body through it: try walking down at the heels (for that is how the shoes get worn that way). It's a heavy gait, there's no spring of optimism, and no one who is "going places" would ever use it. Don't lend money to such a man. If the shoe fits, wear it, let's go on to . . .

FOOT AND BODY

If anyone asks why I have relied so much on quotations from the Bible, I won't try to answer beyond saying that the Bible is rich with allusions to the foot, as to other bodily parts. It is, you may remember, more ancient than Descartes.

In a dream there was an image (DAN. 2):

> Thou, O King, sawest, and behold a great image. This great image, whose brightness *was* excellent, stood before thee; and the form thereof was terrible.
> This image's head *was* of fine gold, his breast and his arms of silver, his belly and his thighs of brass,
> His legs of iron, his feet part of iron and part of clay.

This is man: gold, silver at the top, brass, iron . . . and then clay. On the color chart showing the infusion of the spirit through the body, the intense concentration in the eye, lips, face, breast and hand shades off to a pale neutrality in the foot. My foot has less me-ness about it than any other part of the muscular body. It is a stick separating me from the earth and a spoke transporting me. The foot takes on the properties of the ground and, architecturally speaking, is like the foundation of a building, sunken and similar in composition and appearance to the bedrock upon which it stands.

This servile foot is an awkward country cousin, sitting in the corner until called. But he may take the center of the stage. We say of the teen-ager—who is at the stage of discovering his body—that he is "all feet." Under embarrassment and on the dance floor, the ego invades areas with which it doesn't usually bother. The foot takes on me-ness and, searching for a pocket, hides behind the other. The foot is re-claimed—"re-owned."

A dead animal lies in the road on which I walk; to study it more closely, I turn it over with my toe. It doesn't "touch me" much that way. Keep disgusting things from my hands and my lips for those are close to my core. A common man, I may be allowed to touch my lips to the tip of the King's shoes—my most intimate part to his least noble.

The psychological remoteness and niggardly investment of the foot permit accounting for psychosexual perversions. The shoe fetish and the foot fetish are perversions of *distance*. If the male cannot invade and inhabit the female, he can at least covet her most extended and distant part. With this approach we may see why the foot and the shoe fetish are restricted only to males.

Two lovers have quarreled. They lie in bed beside each other, pride and hurt between them. They cannot speak nor touch. How can the void be overcome? As though by accident one reaches out a toe and touches a toe of the other. What follows is symbolic of the first courtship from stranger to lover, from distance to intimacy—from the first contact of shoe under café table to nudeness in bed together.

The foot has potential aplenty. If it did not have to work so hard it, too, could be clever and handy. The infant in the crib waves arms and legs alike in strange contrast to the silent feet and vocal arms of the adult. With my feet I may thresh grain, tramp the grapes for wine, pack the soil, pump an organ, lift water, pedal my bike, push the clutch of my car—tasks which I perform essentially through modifications of walking. But the true range of potentialities inherent in the foot before its bondage may be realized in the person who has no arms. Though still strong enough to transport the body (something the arms cannot do well) the foot performs the most intricate and delicate operations. Persons without hands have learned to feed themselves, write, type and thread a needle to sew. The powers of Houdini, his secret weapons, we are told, were his skilled and educated feet.

THE NON-WORKING FOOT

Relieved of the duty to convey the foot may do other things, in its leisure develop many hobbies. In the Halloween game children bite on apples floating in a tub of water without touching them, playing at doing something with the mouth more easily done with the hands; thus do the feet play at soccer.

Play and freedom go together. The shoe symbolizes all confinement. In the privacy of her home the woman quickly shucks off girdle and shoe. Sometimes on the dance floor, sometimes after some drink, sometimes after unexpected news, the shoe is kicked off in glorious abandon. For many a country boy the summer vacation and barefoot days correspond. The foot is free to play. My foot shares in the freedom of the seashore. I stretch my toes, draw patterns in the sand, and am naked. The seductive lady lies back on the couch (reclining from the upright; one leans toward evil but never toward right), crosses one leg over the other and points her shoe-less toes. Representing as it does the giving up of strictures, the naked foot of the female may incite an erotic response.

The plodding foot may be thought a most uninteresting fellow. But he reveals that he is something more than clod. The lady carries the image of her lover locketed in the warm embrace of her bosom; in her wrath she crushes the locket, grinding it under her heel. In the foot scene of the Last Supper Jesus said of Judas: "He . . . hath lifted up his heel against me." Through the years the newsreel picture has persisted of Hitler stamping his foot in an odd sort of exultant hop outside the railroad car in conquered France; it was an exclamation point for all he had done and for what he was as a person. The high-kneeing drum majorette and the goose-stepping soldier remind us that marching is something more than walking by the numbers. Harmony is to be in step together. The foot is the organ for rhythm.

Body members engaged in labor cannot be expressive; expression is an art of leisure. A chewing dog has only his tail left to wag. As serf performing my intercourse with the earth, the foot is not at liberty to join the orchestra of members concerned with play of expression. But if we watch and catch it, it speaks too. The human spirit pervades the body as though it were porous. Shakespeare says:

> There's language in her eye, her cheek, her lip,
> Nay, her foot speaks; her wanton spirits look out
> At every joint and motive of her body.[8]

And Sartre writes:

> I can separate a bent branch from a tree but never an upraised arm or a

clinched fist from a man. The *man* raises his arm, the *man* clinches his fist, the *man* is the indissoluble unit and the absolute source of his movements. Furthermore, he is an enchanter of signs; they cling to his hair, shine in his eyes, dance between his lips, perch on his fingertips. He speaks with his whole body; . . . when he talks he speaks . . . when he runs he speaks. . . .[9]

The foot, the foot to whom I direct your attention, is human and participates to the fullness of the human world. In the foot we can discover the human condition. We think of the lowly foot as base; we should remember that it is also basic.

FURTHER ANTHROPODOLOGICAL ANALYSES: CLOWN AND TAP DANCER

As a test of our new discipline, as an example of the understanding which may follow on incorporating the human foot into psychology, I will contrast two artistic exaggerations of the human condition, both of which entertain us, being what we are: the clown and the tap dancer. Both touch much that is deep within us. And we can't say what.

One aspect of the clown is his large shoe. Whereas the upright human stands erect by a miracle, giving the appearance of a cone balanced on its tip with the heavier portion at the top, the clown when seen in the light of Anthropodology is a cone on its base; his small hat, sloping shoulders, oversized breeches and monstrous shoes seat him solidly on the ground. (How comical that this cone on its base still falls over!) Everything about him is pulled downward and is heavy. The clown works best in mud and dust. The foot, the foot above—or below—all, spells his nature.

In the film, *The Gold Rush,* possibly his greatest, Charlie Chaplin is reduced to eating one of his famous shoes. What respect he pays it. He eats with over-styled gestures, winding the shoelace-spaghetti around his fork, mincing the last morsel from each nail-bone. This scene would not have been as funny had he eaten his hat, we can be sure of that, for the hidden motif throughout the film, the chord for all his tunes, is the foot. The Alaskan climate requires that he replace the shoe he's eaten. He wraps his foot with layer upon layer of burlap, making it more cumbersome than before. This is the film in which he gave his inspired bread dance, the dance which may contain the purest image of the clown. He sinks forks into two dinner rolls shaped like submarines. These fork-legs and bun-feet frolic in a way which he could not, for Charlie cannot dance. At one point the camera shows the forks terminating underneath his chin (as though he had stuck his head through the canvas at a carnival with only feet painted beneath). We see Charlie Chaplin as he is, a pathetic face above two monstrously out-sized feet. Toward the end of the film, with the suddenness and the contradiction which marks the humorous, he kicks his gross sack-foot against his backside from the knee. It is as though the foot acted flippantly on its own as an abrupt denial of heaviness and inarticulation; it brings the audience into the fun as though the foot had turned to us and winked.

In different ways dances essentially express the unity and the poetry of the human body in and for itself. Folk dancers romp, chorus girls kick, ballet dancers dress in airy gauze as angels, reducing contact with the earth to the tiniest of points. The tap dance belongs solely to the foot. The tap dancer is before us, full-bodied, with his dress accentuating man *as* dressed—vest, top hat, boutonniere, and spats—as Fashion beyond the fig leaf. His cane, this limb on which lean the lame, is slender, short and jauntily carried (rather than carrying)— all show and no support (he above all needs none). He's all dress and show. The tap dancer is an inverted Taj Mahal. He does not deny his nature, he makes sport of it. The heavy-topped cone which should fall capers on the earth. It is easy to drum with the idle fingers, but the feet of the tap dancer at once hold him up and play with the idea. When he makes to fall he can't (in contrast to the clown who couldn't fall but does). He taunts the floor. He has music in his feet. Each little note with all its human richness is driven one by one into the lifeless floor. The music stops, the rapid tap continues, as though to say it can make its own. That the tap dancer requires a sharp-resounding surface for his art may be thought because of the sound, but there are other meanings: he practices best on man-made, non-earth *floor;* the more stylized, slick and polished it is the better "suited" (as his clothes) for his artistic purposes. The spirits of his feet cast off their bars. We are carried away by the show before our eyes and envision little elf men springing out his toes and wheeling off across the stage. He who understands the tapping feet understands weight and play and much to do with time and music.

What a pair they make on the human stage—the Clown and the Tap Dancer. And what shows we make of ourselves, trying to play them both.[10]

TO STICK A TOE IN METAPHYSICS:
ON FOOT AND TIME

When I talk of time don't think that I will be skating on thin ice, a surface which doubly may not hold me and one on which I may slip. There are connections between foot and time—let Anthropodology find them. If the foot be human that is bound to be so; the question is whether the place of the foot is privileged, as in the other analyses we've given, and whether time may be illuminated by study of the foot. Mysterious time presents more than a worthy challenge to our new discipline, though one not crucial to it. Can we place a foot on time and hold it down? We don't know how high we can jump until we reach the point we can't.

Be-coming is a coming, a motion into place. The foot is both agent for *stability* (my stand-point, hence my identity, my *being*), and for *motility* (my action-deed, hence my identity, my *becoming*). (Not to pass the word "deed" by without noting: the original sense of "to do" was "to put," "to place.") I am a creature of place—both "here" and oriented to the "there." Motion-to is inherent in the there. Through motion, place is placed in *space*.

In transiting from place to place I pick up space-and-time, hitch-hikers. Start to move and they appear from nowhere, I could not travel without them. Space and time co-sprout from motion. Space and time, so different, are in some way the same, at least in source—Anthropodology would say so. There are con-structive constructs. Another way to view it: from *my* motion from place to place—*via the simple footstep*—from motion, I fractionate space as stable timeless-ness, and time as moving spacelessness; then forget in my high-flown intellect that it is *body*, me, who is walking. How could we put a foot on such things as these? How *far* it is is how long it takes to get there; how *long* it's been is how far I've come to get here.

To make these things mean anything to *me*, I must come back to the body, to *footstep* (picking myself up from the ground, for I just now tried to fly). The mile is a thousand (mille) steps. The rhythm of poetry is in feet and in meters. I walk toward a goal, I walk back and forth around the conference table, I pace the floor in the lobby; thus do I pass through time. I sit in my armchair gazing into (not *at*) the dancing flames of the fire. I sit on a bench watching tug boats and dead and derelict trees on the lazy Ohio. Thus does time pass me by. This last is a type of timeless time, a passive time of suspension; something happens and I am called back to myself. But meanwhile, I have been doing *something;* I've been watching. Watching is a kind of walking, a walking with the eyes. (And it is gratifying to note that the eye doesn't swing but goes in nystagmic jumps.)

Time is never experienced directly, purely, by itself alone. Time flows, we say, flows as a ceaseless river. This thought-time is as a snake to our eyes.[11] My footstep introduces time and contains its paradoxes: (1) time moves forward, just as my step (a sidewise step is not progression); (2) discontinuous, my step imparts continuous motion (the step is the quantum of motion, yet the wave-form is visible, too; in it being and becoming co-reside). When the toddler first toddles he raises unknown sorts of metaphysical problems. The sharp staccato of the tap dancer reminds me that I am not equipped to handle the continuous flow of time but must chop it into pieces. However stately I may move, my gait is ever punctiform.[12] I proceed by step and step. I cannot grasp time and hold it except through its articulations: years, moons, weeks, ticks—by steps.

Time is the inner sound of footsteps.

With such a burst of clarity I end this psalm to the foot. We have tiptoed softly to witness many scenes; barefooted, have picked and stumbled our way through some etymologies and metaphysics when we should have best had shoes, no doubt stubbing our toes as we went.

Things synthesized cannot be separated by breaking pieces apart. Man is body; man is foot; foot is man. In the lowest do we find the highest. Verily, the foot is a marvelous thing. The base, it is indispensably basic.

I began with some words from First Corinthians, trailing off a sentence,

> And if the foot should say, Because I am not the hand, I am not of the body . . .,

to insert my paper . . .
which First Corinthians should also conclude:

> And if the foot should say, Because I am not the hand, I am not of the upon these we bestow more abundant honor. . . . And (if) . . . one member

is honored, all members rejoice with it . . . God hath tempered the body together . . . That there be no schism in the body. . . .

HANDNOTES

1. A new specialty properly inaugurated with a psalm to the foot (a pedestrian psalm, in prose), written in barefoot style, without the discipline-shoe of science. Let it further be understood before we start: we are not interested in playing footsy with any anti-podes. For its historical importance let it be recorded that the paper was first read (we ask the reader to visualize a few of the slides) before the Lexington Torch Club, April 16, 1964.

2. This paper is only a note, only a "handnote," to Dr. Erwin W. Straus's "The Upright Posture." It is reported that in conversation with the eminent Swiss psychiatrist, Dr. Ludwig Binswanger, Dr. Straus was told that his approach, centered in the lived-body, is rather mundane and, transcendentally speaking, not very lofty. Dr. Straus acknowledged the qualification with pleasure; offered in friendship, it was a tribute, through its aptness, to his life's work. For his call and contract has been to lay bodily foundations. What could be more fundamental than the foot? And more mundane?

3. Since nothing could carry itself, that's manifestly an absurd idea, we see why the foot is excluded from me, and what is "me" seems to extend from the crotch to the head. Witness: ask anyone where his bottom is.

4. And, of course, the mounting of the chair onto the wheel rescues those crippled in the legs from their Breughel misery.

5. More generally, we shrink from the dismembered and disfigured, a spontaneous reaction we have difficulty counteracting.

6. To have nothing solid to stand on is the source of giddiness and nausea. Impudently, I would say: Sartre's nausea comes when his transcendental ego peers down at the earth (his sinuous tree roots), as though from stilts on high; Kierkegaard's dizziness, from gazing too long at the sky. In either case when giddy the impulse is to sink back "down to all fours."

7. Human ingenuity has fallen short before the dangerous change in level—the curbstone and the stair. Ramps are inclined to be slick and are awkward to stand on. The inventor of the wheel has yet to solve the problem of elevating the level, or leveling elevation. Steps cut in the side of the mountain documents the desire of my foot for a level "hold."

8. *Troilus and Cressida*, Act IV, Scene 5.

9. Sartre, Jean-Paul: *Essays in Aesthetics,* pp. 82–83, transposed. New York: Citadel, 1963.

10. Both clown and tap dancer are masculine. As usual when the human

situation is portrayed, the actor is a male. We still see men as man. The word "woman" came late, oddly, with her admission into the race, the generic. In the ethereal movement of the ballet, the dancers tend toward sexlessness (as of angels).

11. His horrid way of progression is the curse on the snake—his slithering, sliding, silently mysterious, *step-less* motion: ". . . upon thy belly shalt thou go. . . ." Before this did the "most cunning" serpent walk on legs? If so, what happened to them? No, we can imagine that he, too, was upright (in some way he even had to be *above* man), as a matter of fact, balanced on the tip of his tail, gently, seductively swaying as he stood, springing from point to point as he went. Only thus could we imagine his suasion to have been as great as it was, and only from such a height could his curse have so cut him down.

12. If a paper on the foot should stand on its own two feet it should have two endings, as it were. Therefore, and to make the point that the foot is the point of points, I tender, in a contrapuntal movement, a fortunate quotation, grabbing the reader by the collar if he be impatient, offering thereby an alternate ending and a second stand-point to my paper:

"Picasso says," Balso broke in, "Picasso says there are no feet in nature . . . And, thanks for showing me around. I have to leave."

But before he was able to get away, the guide caught him by the collar. "Just a minute, please. . . . Please explain your interpretation of the Spanish master's dictum."

"Well, the point is . . ." Balso began. But before he could finish the guide started again. "If you are willing to acknowledge the existence of points," he said, "then the statement that there are no feet in nature puts you in an untenable position. It depends for its very meaning on the fact that there are no points. Picasso, by making this assertion, has placed himself on the side of monism in the eternal wrangle between the advocates of the Singular and those of the Plural. As James puts it, 'Does reality exist distributively or collectively—in the shape of *eaches, everys, anys, eithers,* or only in the shape of an *all* or *whole?*' If reality is singular then there are no feet in nature, if plural, a great many. If the world is one (everything part of the same thing—called by Picasso nature) then nothing either begins or ends. Only when things take the shapes of *eaches, everys, anys, eithers* (have ends) do they have feet. Feet are attached to ends, by definition. Moreover, if everything is one, and has neither ends nor beginnings, then everything is a circle. A circle has neither a beginning nor an end. A circle has no feet. If we believe that nature is a circle, then we must also believe that there are no feet in nature.

"Do not pooh-pooh this idea as mystical. Bergson has . . ."

"Cézanne said, 'Everything tends toward the globular.'" With this announcement Balso made another desperate attempt to escape.

"Cézanne?" the guide said, keeping a firm hold on Balso's collar. "Cézanne is right. The sage of Aix is . . ."

With a violent twist, Balso tore loose and fled.

(West, Nathanael: *The Dream Life of Balso Snell,* pp. 113–14. New York: Avon, 1965.)

MAN AND HIS BODY

Herbert Plügge

THE PHYSICAL BODY AS PHENOMENON

For more than half a century now several physicians and their students have been attempting to liberate themselves from the yoke of the natural science conception of the body which derives from Descartes. This revolt is by no means ended. The task has been defined as delimiting the concept of the *physical body* from that of the *live bodily,* or to investigate the involvement of the bodily as physical in the bodily as lived and conversely of the bodily as lived in the bodily as physical, in all its modifications, in all its possible structures, all its paradoxes and lawful regularities.[1] From the side of medicine A. Prinz Auersperg, F. J. J. Buytendijk, V. E. von Gebsattel, V. von Weizsäcker and his followers, E. Straus, J. Zutt, and others (not to mention psychoanalytically oriented researchers) have made outstanding contributions, with ever new approaches, toward clarifying this problem sphere. It is impossible within the framework of this study to undertake even a rough survey of all these efforts.

Consequently we will restrict ourselves to indicating one important point which—as it seems to us—is important for understanding our own effort to clarify the phenomenon of live bodily spatiality.

The excerpted pages are taken from Herbert Plügge's *Der Mensch und sein Leib* (Tübingen: Max Niemeyer Verlag, 1967), pp. 34–42 and 57–68. The translation into English was made available by Erling Eng, Ph.D., Unit Psychologist, Veterans Administration Hospital, Lexington, Kentucky. The editor would like to thank the cooperative efforts of Herbert Plügge, Erling Eng, and Max Niemeyer Verlag which made the appearance of these pages possible.

This is the unavoidable critique of the concept of science. Here we are guided—merely for the sake of brevity—by the most recent works of phenomenologically oriented research aimed at working out an anthropology.

According to them the physical body—as classical physiologists and biologists see it—is a morphologically determined and regulated substrate, in which the stimulus outcome in the reflex arc is described as the effect of a physically defined stimulus. But even where the stimulus outcome is recognized as a finally determined reaction, the stimulus is defined not in its *significance* but in its physical characteristics. The consequence is to isolate the organism from everything it meets with in the world.

On the other hand, everything that is *bodily live* is, as something never completed but ever newly arising, to be understood as a phenomenon crucially determined by the given situation and its meaning, changing from one to another form, personal and yet belonging to the world. The extreme instance of the physical body is "l'homme machine" described by Descartes and La Mettrie. But all that is *bodily live* actualizes itself, through continuous self-transformation, within the situation.

For a long time it had remained unperceived that classical physiology was thus dealing with already elaborated facts (*phénomènes travaillées*),[2] and that its thinking is operational thinking (*pensée opératoire*),[3] a manipulation with "fitted" objectality, whose actual primary character is never considered in its procedures.

In this way physiological processes and their regulations are detached from their live bodily ground, from their roots in a world we in-habit. The phenomena become manipulable objects.

The live bodiness of man, which can never be anything but *my* live bodiness (always in the sense too of a subjectivity embracing the other), is incomprehensible if one separates the physical body from things in the world. The other is not merely the partner of consciousness in a conversation which can be started or stopped at will. The *bodily live arises* in situations in which an egoic live body indissolubly united with *my* world and with the other are born in ever new engagements and to ever new forms. All things take their rise in the live body (*la génèse de toutes choses*),[4] since, phenomenologically viewed, perception is the indispensable presupposition for every emergence of all the things in the world.

How little this is something merely thought or abstract, we may see from an analysis of the act of touch. All active touching occurs in a "formal circle" [*Gestaltkreis*], in which, step by step through the groping movement of the finger, the object erects itself in similarly stepwise clarifications of knowing. The tactile *movements* and the individually successive phases of *perceiving* are entirely and reciprocally intertwined. Perceiving calls for proleptically oriented tactile *movement*, which in turn finds its analeptic fulfillment in an encounter at the "right" moment.

Here a separation of motor and sensory spheres is impossible. If it were insisted on, one would end up not with original facts, but with arti-facts (*phénomènes travaillées*)—arrangements in which the original phenomenon has already been denatured, in order to deal with it according to the rule of natural scientific thought and manipulation. Motor and sensory spheres are related to each other in terms of continuing convergence and divergence, of mutual guidance and interpretation. Now the earlier quotation becomes more comprehensible: "All things take their rise in the live body." My world of objects requires my live bodiness to arise, just as my live bodiness is called into existence only in encounter with things of the world I inhabit.

My live body, through which I am rooted in the world, and through which alone the mundane is able to arise for me, is present

> when between the seeing and the seen, between touching and touched, between one eye and the other a kind of exchange occurs, when the spark of the feeling-feelable is kindled, when this fire is lit which never stops burning until some accident of the body destroys what no accident could ever have sufficed to produce.[5]

All these comments are but to emphasize that in the human sphere no line of separation can be drawn between the bodily live and world, between perceiving and acting. Instead we see a continual movement in which the bodily live and mundane alike participate, generating one another.

But we see also a "to-and-fro," a commingling, and a reciprocal occultation insoluble rationally. Thus there arise, under circumstances —and not only in terms of rationality—the necessarily contradictory, the reciprocal confusions, the emergence of dubious conditions, stemming simply from the permeability of the bodily live, its silent mediation, its continual transformation, conditioned too on the other hand by the resistiveness of the bodily as physical as resistiveness of "nature." The result is that *ambiguïté*[6] which not only characterizes but actually constitutes the bodily human and live.

In the half-century-long investigation of those structures in which the bodily live and the mundane can meet, mix, mingle, mutually develop, and thereby become one, the physical body—to put it simply —has come off badly. There was quite enough to be done, as we have said, to establish the character of phenomenal live bodiness, to see this as *the* reality. It should not be forgotten that attempts to enthrone the phenomenal live body were possible only with difficulty, with detours punctuated by defeats and necessary stages of deliberation. This effort forced the phenomenologically oriented anthropologist[7] to take a stance over against the concept of the *bodily as physical* as an elaborated phenomenon, i.e., *reduced* by natural science. In fact it became impossible, if one began from the phenomenon of healthy live bodiness, to do otherwise than deny the character of phenomenon to the physical body. It turned into the substrate of an abstraction reduced to the morphological as well as physiological, to a "weakened image" [*image appauvrie*].

Only the physician continually at grips with the pathology of the live human body was able to discover the existence of the *bodily as physical,* not merely as an abstraction but also as phenomenon. This is a discovery that could scarcely have come from psychologist or philosopher.

What our hypothesis, namely that the bodily as physical also exists phenomenally within the frame of the bodily live, can contribute to the question of the spatiality of the prereflectively and reflectively lived body we now propose to examine. It will be found that we have touched on many points already, while others will be added.

> This reality of the spatially-thinglike physical body is already implicit in the *paresthesias* depicted earlier. We not only experience our unfeeling leg as dead, we also treat it as a lifeless or in any event virtually lifeless thing. The paresthetic limb shows—often merely vaguely, often more strongly defined—many characteristics of objective thinglikeness, such as an importunate heaviness, burden, weight, with the quality of a substance that feels essentially strange, wooden, like plaster of paris, in any event as largely space-filling and hence not altogether as a part of ourselves.

But we noted above that even in the case of the paresthesias the quality of thingness is not univocally experienced. That character of a certain spatiality which forces itself on us here shows almost always, it is true, the properties of something strange, removed from our live bodiness; but at the same time a kind of countermovement occurs in us: what estranges itself is felt and treated as a part of us, more than ever, as our very own; it kindles our care, our concern, a real maternal solicitude.

So that if it be undeniable that thinglike and quasi-geometrical spatial features appear in these cases, yet these blend in one and the same event with the reflective experiencing of a live bodiness assignable to the phenomenal sphere. That estrangement, localizability, and emergence of "mass" *simultaneously* and spontaneously mediates our marked ownership of this thing approaching lifelessness, this—as paradox, or as example of that ambiguity constitutive for the bodily live—is also to be found elsewhere.

We need only apply the term "paresthesia" to all evidences of a presence, a pressure, feeling of fullness, weight or burden, even to a pain localizable *inside* our body, to discover the same state of affairs: the within, otherwise so unvocal and weightless, discloses itself in a language communicating at one and the same time an experience of estrangement as well as one of intensified ownership.

Out of the mute live bodiness continually merging into action something spatial, thinglike becomes evident, from one instance to another more or less clear, more or less delimitable; yet it never becomes thing *entirely*, it never becomes *completely* lifeless.

It is similar, and yet by not inconsiderable nuances dissimilar, to the case of a mortally ill person consumed with suffering. Across the appearance presented by such a patient lies a peculiar stillness, often in fact an apparent lifelessness. His skin shows folds, is dull, and lacks luster. Play of gesture and expression, all live bodily orientation outward have become sparse, often even extinguished. These patients question less and less; the intentional character of all healthy live bodiness is on the wane. Just as they withdraw from their own living and live human body, they withdraw too from their world. Just as their world, their earlier ways, have become pointless and uninteresting, so has their live bodiness suffered a similar change. They abandon their live bodiness, as we sought to describe in an earlier work,[8] gradually moving *inward*. In the truest sense of the word they withdraw. With this not merely does their world fade but their live bodiness becomes husk. Voice and echo become softer and softer. As the sick person prepares to

surrender his world he surrenders in the same process the pluripotentiality of his live bodiness. The irrelevancy of the world is identical with the
irrelevancy of the bodily live. But that is to say that live bodiness in this
process increasingly assumes the quality of the *bodily as physical*. The
transformation into the bodily as physical always means discomfort and
malaise. The character of husk, which our live bodiness here increasingly assumes, shows itself in its onerousness, bringing heaviness,
burden, weight. We have compared this emergence of the bodily as
physical within our live bodiness to the shabbiness of an old wornout
suit which no longer fits: the suit is no longer really "lived in." It droops
in folds, wrinkled, devoid of any actual connection with us, as if hung
on a clothes tree. Thus the negligence and indifference of dying patients
to their exterior becomes explicable. What no longer belongs to me,
what is no longer continually and repeatedly embodied, no longer
requires care.[9]

What we are here calling physical body denotes the alteration of
the bodily live toward the thinglike and objectal, whose characteristics
are heaviness and extension, the nearly measurable and separable. The
non-vocality of the bodily as live, its solution in action, the muteness
of the flesh in its role of a transcendence (of intentionality) undergoes,
through invasion of the quasi lifeless-spatial (space *modo geometrico*),
loss of pluripotentiality, of the possibility of self-transformation, and
thus of actualizing itself in ever changing forms.

Accordingly the shift toward the material appears identical with
the transformation of the bodily as live into something to be borne,
dragged along, an onus and onerousness.

Undoubtedly this aperçu is serviceable as starting-point, as a means
of insight into the possibility of the spatial character of our live body.
But even this aperçu is too naïve. Its naïveté lies in its too broad
exclusion of the material element from healthy live bodiness. Absolute
truths of this sort simply do not fit precisely with all that is involved in
live bodiness. Any such confident assertion does insufficient justice to
the many-sidedness of live bodiness.

We said that transformation of the (objectively understood) non-
spatiality of the bodily live in the direction of what is thinglike and
objectal with properties of spatiality as defined by natural science, the
disappearance of absolute non-vocality in favor of a vocal, nagging, in
any event self-announced physical bodiness is invariably a sign of
pathological transformation. Certainly cases of paresthesias, gangrenes,

the special features of consuming illness, etc., speak for this hypothesis. Also the entire sphere of subjective symptoms of internal illnesses can be fitted into the Procrustes' bed of this hypothesis.

We have always adopted as a guideline this contraposition of an action schema of the bodily live to that of a spatial schema of pathological "thickening."

Yet now, in view of experiences with persons with phantom limbs, we have taken thought. Th. Hasenjäger and O. Pötzl,[10] Georg Christian,[11] Chr. Wunderlich,[12] and ourselves[13] have described experiences of perceptive phantom limb bearers, the gist of which is that although they had no doubt of the live bodily reality of their phantom limb they nevertheless sensed the "shell-like," "empty," and "formal" as comprising the difference from the healthy limb.

In addition the "dilemma" in which we placed our phantom limb subjects in experiments described earlier is, as Wunderlich rightly emphasizes, not simply a dichotomy of rational processing and experienced reality, but is "prefigured in reflective experience."[14]

To us it appears that within the reflective experience of a healthy limb, no matter how silent and weightless it may be in action, there is yet, indetectably hidden, a certain "heft." Else it would be impossible for the spontaneous experience of it to change with loss of material substance (in the case of amputation). The reflective experiencing of the "discrepancy," the "void," the "shell-likeness" of the phantom limb would otherwise be impossible. In the basic experiencing of the bodily as live there evidently inheres, extremely covert but demonstrable, an experience of materiality. It is that to which we refer when we speak of the *phenomenon of the bodily as physical*. In the instance of the phantom it becomes apparent as belonging to the phenomenon of the bodily as live. The phenomenon of the bodily as physical referred to here is, we must infer, a *feature* of phenomenal live bodiness generally. To be sure it is hidden deeply within the reflective experiencing of our own limbs. Yet in the case of the phantom it becomes manifest as lacking, as expression of deficient materiality. The phantom limb reveals the presence of moments of heaviness as indispensable as normally they remain entirely obscure; morbid process by contrast shows "thickening" of this customarily hidden "heft" to a reflectively experienced spatial thing.

Thus our live bodiness is not simply and solely comprehensible as an *event* of mediation between *I* and my world, but contains at the same time the experience of a heaviness. For we are not merely that which is spiritual, but also a "lump of earth."[15]

HUMAN LIVE BODINESS AND PHYSICAL BODINESS AS MUTUALLY DELIMITING

If a sick or injured person has an arm, leg, or portion of an extremity removed, then immediately or soon after the operation, a phantom limb develops. This has been known ever since Ambroise Paré,[16] and since then has never ceased to amaze neurologists, neurophysiologists, and psychologists. Depending on the scientific position, the kind and degree of the writer's scientific or unscientific bias, reference has been made to illusion, to bodily hallucination (*hallucination corporelle*, for example, in Lhermitte,[17] Hécain and Ajuriaguerra[18]), or to physiologically explicable effects of the neural periphery of the stump. The neurophysiological presuppositions (most recently by Poeck[19]) or biographical determinants (for example, by Hallen[20]) have been investigated in the genesis of this still puzzling phenomenon. Independently of Hasenjäger and Pötzl[21] we have also arrived at a theory in which the phantom limb is conceived as a mental regenerate.[22]

What has been pointed out in abundantly summative and cursive fashion will *not* be considered in this paper. The details of the phantom limb, its variations and variability, its genesis, and the possibilities of its disappearance, do not constitute our topic. What will concern us principally here is an experimental finding we recently reported in another connection,[23] whose theme has also fascinated Auersperg,[24] Christian,[25] Poeck,[26] and Wunderlich.[27]

Though experiments carried out by these last named authors are very similar in their hypothesis and procedure, their conclusions from the results are much less so, despite the fact that their experimental findings showed scarcely any differences.

The basic experiment requires a mid-forearm amputee who has developed a differentiated and impressive phantom limb to bring the stump of his arm to within one to two centimeters of a wall, say of a room, at an angle of ninety degrees.

If one then unexpectedly asks the subject whether his phantom limb might have penetrated the wall, whether it has become shorter in being compressed by the approach of the stump to the wall, or whether,

pushed out of its original direction, it has been deflected or has disap-
peared, then our experience is that his first, spontaneous, unreflected
expression is one of *perplexity*, at least evident embarrassment, most
usually an affect, in any event an emotion manifesting a clearly negative
attitude toward the experimenter and the experiment itself.

We always received an impression that the patient felt he had been
duped. He felt that what we expected of him was "unfair." He said it
was wrong to expose him to such a situation. He was vexed at being
taken by surprise and usually withdrew himself from the conflict, re-
marking: "After all that's something entirely different."

Christian's[28] patient too and those examined by Wunderlich[29] re-
acted spontaneously in the same way, first with perplexity and embarrassment, then with scornful refusal. The former patient, however, was
an intellectual who pushed away the obvious conflict into which the experimenter had put him by means of apparently supercilious reflections.

From the case material of Poeck,[30] which presents an abundance of
interesting observations of the diverse modes of behavior of phantom
limbs, we are unable to spell out as clearly the perplexity spontaneously
appearing in similarly set up experiments. We surmise that Poeck
directed his attention much more to the "morphological" and "functional" variations of the phantom limb, so carefully recorded by him,
and less to the patient's initial spontaneous reaction. But his protocols
also reveal the *discomfort* that befell the respective experimental subject. Particularly in his experiments with "choc à blanc,"[31] the experiments communicated by Poeck confirm ours in so far as his patients
spontaneously showed perplexity or a negative attitude of being annoyed. From the published protocols it appears that they expressed substantially the same meaning as our subjects: "After all that's something
entirely different." This position is the same as that of Christian's
patient who said in an analogous situation: "Your question is wrong,"
and then digressed into reflection, which we will not pursue here.

For our theme is the perplexity, the conflict into which we put our
patients in our experiment. We placed them in a dilemma which revealed itself through a confrontation of the *reflectively experienced*
spatiality of the phantom limb with geometrically structured spatiality,
through the contraposition of the sensorily unquestionable reality of the
phantom perceived as bodily live to the extensive reality of the nearly
physically definable thing "stump."

For of this there can be no doubt: the amputee lives with his phantom limb *in two realities* at the same time. The phantom limb is undoubtedly his *own arm,* which he *has,* in many cases can move, which he protects and under all circumstances defends.

That this reality is not to be grasped with geometrical and physical concepts demonstrates only that the reality of the phantom limb is another reality, one *non*-physical and *non*-geometric.

Also that the phantom limb of many patients is experienced reflectively as something "husklike," "hollow," "fluid," in any event "inferior" does nothing at all to change the fact that it is a lived and reflectively experienced part of my real live body, *my* hand, *my* leg, consequently a reality.

On the other hand, for the patient his stump as *stump* is likewise a reality. The stump as mutilated limb is no less sensorily perceptible, optically, tactually, kinesthetically. Its form, length, and thing-properties are approximately determinable by physical means.

With our experiment we bring these two realities to the consciousness of the patient, the reality of a pathic spatiality and that of a quasi-thinglike one. We confront him with the absurdity that he lives in two completely disparate realities. Through reflection he is able to keep them apart; he is able to orient himself in the conceptual worlds corresponding to each of these two realities. But in the *contradictoriness* which becomes clear with this experiment he can make no changes. He can shut himself off from the knowledge of this absurdity, can look past it, while he, as it were, "pulls out" of the experiment. But that simply means that he returns from the *reflectively experienced* dilemma back to the *pre-reflective* dilemma out of which we jerked him with our experiment.

Naturally the question immediately arises whether this dilemma plays a role exclusively or at least preferentially in the case of an amputee with a phantom limb, or whether, with our experiment, we have come upon something perhaps characteristic for all human live bodiness.

If the latter should be so, then we would have to acknowledge that in the fulfillment of live bodily existence something paradoxical, anyway contradictory, is hidden as structural principle, of which we notice very little in everyday life, but which becomes apparent in extreme situations.

In this connection it is worth noting the *mode* with which the phantom bearer finds his way back from the *reflectively* lived to the *pre-reflectively* lived dilemma, that is, as no longer dominating his present situation.

As we have seen, the phantom bearer can on the one hand *close* himself to the absurdity experienced in the experiment; i.e., he can as it were "pressure" himself as he returns to unreflected living. On the other hand we have learned from Christian's patient that it is precisely the reflective activity which makes an effort to distinguish cleanly between the two pre-existing realities (stump and phantom limb) that is in a position to allow the two worlds in which he obviously lives to exist, each for itself, alongside one another. Under circumstances this latter mode, that of conceptual resolution, leads out of the perplexity, provided the patient acknowledges the *critical character* of this collision and faces up to it.

But we must further ask whether the realities that have here emerged (stump and phantom limb) are sufficiently described in terms of the confrontation of two *spatialities,* one pathic and one of things?

The mere fact that the experience of the amputated stump as thinglike mediates something almost objectal, thus determinable and often already determined, and that on the other hand the phantom limb presents itself as something living, as something that "emerges" or fades, as something moving or something at rest, as something tacitly available or as an imposition, vexing in its autonomy, thus as something changing in *time,* all this makes clear that these two realities are characterized not only by their spatial diversities, but just as much by *temporal* ones.

To be sure they are generally blended togther by living, are, as it were, "lived together." Their discrepancies scarcely emerge in the action and involvement of everyday life. In our daily encounter and concern with the world the *live bodily* character, i.e., live bodiness as event, mediation, as something continually changing, is predominant. On the other hand, the *physically bodily* qualities, in the sense of something thinglike and objectal and consequently determined, are recessive. They are suspended within movement and perception, in involvement and reference to the world. This condition of suspension, which of course is also one of latency, is what Merleau-Ponty[32] means when he formulates the *role* of the bodily live as mediating in these words: "The mind realizes itself through the body." The character of the *bodily as physical,* as something extensively spatial (*res extensa*), enters into the continual change of our live body in countless different forms. Our extensive physical bodiness conceals itself in the intentionality of our phenomenal live bodiness.

Naturally the amputee *has* his stump; but in whatever he undertakes and does, wherever he becomes engaged and involved in something, his amputated arm often persists as *phantom* arm, as his own "old" arm, much as it always was, i.e., as mental regenerate.

Here we encounter a further aspect of our contradictoriness: we *are* bodily live, but *have* the bodily as physical.

Yet this formulation is but an extremely provisional as well as disputable description of the singular character of our live bodiness. For one could assume from it, as it stands, that the bodily as live and the bodily as physical are opposed to each other or even mutually exclusive.

But that, as we further propose to show, is commonly not the case.

The bodily as live and the bodily as physical are, strictly speaking, not even two *aspects*, say, outcomes of a natural science approach and one that is phenomenological.

One might best speak of *"characters"* which, depending on the situation, can become respectively foreground or background in the appearance of our live body. Just as J. Zutt prefers to treat of the "mundane" live body in his works, and Sartre on the contrary of the "onerous" live body.

But even when we approximate to the apparently dichotomous structure of our live body through a view of this sort, we run the risk of constructing something in which live body and physical body are opposed, and which does not correspond to the facts.

Ruffin[33] has found a very clear and unmistakable formulation when he says that the character of the onerous tends to appear with *failure* of our live bodily performance. This view fits in with the findings of our own earlier work which tried to show that the onerous character of human live bodiness becomes especially evident in *extreme situations,* for example, in fatigue and exhaustion, but even more in pathology, in internal illnesses.

But neither should it be forgotten that the first traces of thinglike characteristics in our live bodiness are found *already in the healthy*. The nursling regards his legs in the first months of life as strange and distant things, until he is able to incorporate them through feeling and kicking.

Even the adult can come near to viewing his feet or his hands as thinglike while they lie motionless in front of him and he gives himself up completely to the contemplation of the morphological details of his members. The older one becomes, the less motile and more unwieldy, the more often one succeeds in being able to contemplate one's own resting limbs, however well known, as nearly objects in their own right.

But the preponderant sphere in which the objectal appears to the point of onerousness is, after all, that of pathology. The occurrence of a pressure of heaviness in the chest, a cramped feeling, or even the mere appearance of something unexpectedly present inside us, a feeling of bloatedness or emptiness in the stomach, etc., introduce into the pre-reflectively lived bodiness—otherwise mere possibility, permissibility, disposition, self-involvement as expressive of harmonious well-being—the character of the thinglike and foreign. The bodily as physical and objectal appears as a sort of *thickening* in the sense of a change in an aggregate state of the otherwise unnoticed live bodiness—much as if I were to suddenly notice the air, which I usually do not feel during respiration, as something thinglike, having consistency. The bodily as physical intrudes as something strange. The *res extensa* emerges phenomenally at the heart of the otherwise unnoticed pre-reflectively lived body.

Earlier we have already pointed out in detail that such an estrangement of an otherwise merely pre-reflectively lived part of the live body is not just reflectively experienced as a thickening in the sense of a displacement in the direction of the objectal. At one and the same time as this uncanny emergence there is an experience of intensified *belongingness* of this altered part. What threatens to estrange itself in us communicates to us *all the more*—under some circumstances even the experience itself for the very first time—that it is actually our own. It belongs to the contradictory character of our live bodiness that the self-conspicuousness, self-estrangement, and simultaneously experienced belongingness of this part within an estrangement from our live bodiness do not exclude one another, but are in fact mutually enhancing. More than this they form *one* single, inseparable event.

If one can legitimately claim that with the development of pathological sensations in our live body, experiencing of the objectal makes its entry into the previously scarcely noticed dimension of the bodily live, it is just as true that the experience of this reification takes on the character of one's most intimate own live bodiness. If my heart weighs like a stone in my breast, I simultaneously reflectively experience all the more that this heaviness is *my* heart, despite the fact that it acts as if it were something independent and autonomous. Here too a having enters with this into the previously unnoticed being. But over and beyond that the experience also of *being had*. In pathology anyway it is a rule that everything which I have also has me.[34]

One need but consider the unexpected discovery of an eruption on one's own body. The very instant I notice this rash on me, it has me in its clutches. This dialectics of having and being had is almost always linked with uncertainty, anxiousness, perplexity, and incipient reflection, and an effort to clarify the meaning of this exanthema.

To the examples thus far given of the contradictoriness of our phenomenal live bodily events, i.e., the singular linkage of live bodily being and having a live body, of having and being had, the intrusion of something virtually objectal into the previously merely unreflectively lived bodiness, i.e., the emergence of "heft" into the previously taken-for-granted freshness, puissance, and volition, its actualization accompanied by intensified belongingness to me and on the other hand too by the experience of its estrangement, the reciprocal intertwinedness of the characters of the one who bears and what is borne, of the egoic and the mundane—to all these examples one more should be added: the frequent instance of the unclear source of a discomfort.

There are countless situations in which I feel ill at ease in a way almost impossible to describe, without being able to clarify whether I am coming down with something or whether I am annoyed because something on which I had planned has not turned out, whether a sudden change of weather is bothering me or whether an impending, probably unpleasant, incident is "on my mind." In such situations we often do not know whence the disturbance comes and what its nature is.

The "uncertainty" or "equivocality" of what "pressures" us is possible only, and explicable only, if we take into account that our live body is always latently mundane and at the same time onerous. My live body and my world are never two separated or even separable things. My world arises of course initially through (*à travers*) my live body; it is linked with the presence of my live body. Our live body belongs factually to both at the same time: to my *I* and to my world. How could uncertainties, ambiguities, and questionable situations not enter into our condition! Man moves about, as Ruffin formulated it, in the mutually confluent, but also mutually enabling, regions of the mundane and the bodily live (in the limited sense of the word). Thus he is often completely unable to distinguish where the source of the current disturbance is to be sought. His live bodiness is of course part of his world, and his world is possible only through his live bodiness.

Here we have demonstrated one more example of the chiaroscuro in which we live both as bodily live and as physical body.

It would seem that we must rest content with these determinations. Evidently we are not going to go beyond this, namely that dual characters distinguish our live bodily existence—whether it is the inseparability of being as bodily live and having a live body, the having and the concomitant being had, the mutually suffusing live bodily characters of the onerous and the bearer, live body as action and as reified, estrangement and enhanced belongingness in one experience, or, finally, the competing realities of stump and phantom limb.

One fact, however, has not been sufficiently appreciated in our presentation. No matter how suspect and contradictory our live bodily existence may be, it is plain that every human being has a *certain* physical body, *this* physical body with *these* hands, feet, fingers, toes, *this* heart, *this* liver, *this* hair; and these morphological and functional characteristics belonging to this physical body not only ground our thus-and-thus constituted live bodiness but also our very own presence, our unique existence.

V. v. Weizsäcker had already made clear in his analysis of performance that our organs and their functions *make possible* our performance, but are also able to make these impossible. For him the organs and their functions were *conditions* of our human performance.[35] Buytendijk considered not only the performance of man, but our integral phenomenon, our existence. He saw that this unique physical body which developed for each human being in a particular way *grounded* his existence. "Grounded' signifies: ground, beginning, $\dot{\eta}$ $\dot{a}\rho\chi\dot{\eta}$, and fatum all in one. But this *"fatalité"*—and here the dual character of human live bodiness appears again—is not one that excludes every other one. For "The human being unites in himself fatalité and élan."[36] That is to say, one's own physical body is under circumstances my fate, but at the same time also simply "the provisional sketch of my existence" (Buytendijk). For as a whole it is not merely a particular thing with particular characteristics, but "The origin of relationships with a world which it chooses and by which it is chosen" (Buytendijk).[37]

All we can do, beyond these determinations, to bring us still a bit closer to the secret of our live bodily existence is to clarify matters *conceptually*.

In this paper we have used continuously changing definitions for the examples given of the contradictory or dual character of our live bodiness. All these formulations were, however, still provisional, merely attempts to suggest the essential.

Merleau-Ponty took a further step, when he introduced the concept of *ambiguïté*[38] to distinguish the singularity of human live bodiness. For him "ambiguïté" is the term most suitable for encompassing all the characteristics of our live body.

Merleau-Ponty sought for a concept to describe the bodily as physical in the midst of the phenomenon of live bodily being, the lived intermingling of *fatalité* and *élan*, the modification of live bodily being through germination within it of the having of the live body, the conjunction of live bodily *I* and mundane live body reflectively experienced as unitary condition. But it was just as important for him to capture those questionable states and possibilities of error given structurally in the live body, the failure of a rational separation of the apparently non-unifiable and contradictory, with the same concept.

He was altogether cognizant of the enigmatic character of the bodily as live, but he sought *one* word for it, i.e., for the indissoluble intertwining of (on the one hand) live bodily *process*, i.e., its mediating role, which constitutes phenomenally the essence of the bodily as live, and (on the other hand) the *objectality* in the live body, for the interwovenness of *action* and *substance*.

This One in the Other (as for example the emergence of the quasi-objectal within the self-transformation of the bodily as live) was termed by Merleau-Ponty "ambiguïté."

In looking into the history of this word, we found it used previously in a similar if not identical sense solely in Pascal's *Pensées*. Pascal uses it to characterize the theory dominating his entire anthropology, namely, that of the two "natures" indissolubly intertwined in man and constituting his being. An example he mentions repeatedly is that of "la grandeur et la misère de l'homme." The *Grandeur* and the *Misère* of man are not alternatives, nor do they describe an ambivalence. It is in no wise a matter of two sides of man each of which, depending on the aspect, becomes alternately visible. The *ambiguïté* in Pascal consists in this, that *with* the *Grandeur* of man his *Misère* is *eo ipso* also given. His *Grandeur* is at the same time his *Misère*. Both *is* one state of affairs.

Perhaps we can show more clearly what we mean through the use of an analogy. The *Trinity* has a fundamentally identical structure. In the "Praefatio of the Most Holy Trinity" are the words: "With your only-begotten Son and the Holy Spirit you are *one* God, *one* Lord. Not, as if you were but *one* person, you are rather *one and one alone in three persons*." Here, in the case of the Trinity, it is a matter of *one being in three*. In the *ambiguïté* which is constitutive of all bodily live human existence it is a matter of one essential being, in which *two* actually non-unitable states of affairs, substance and action, live bodily *I* and human world, etc., are united.

Over the years the word "ambiguïté" has not always been used in the above meaning. The *Dictionnaire alphabétique* of Robert[39] gives an interesting survey of the changes in the sense of this concept. What is important for us is that, in any event, according to Robert, even today what it means is an "accord," a condition "which reunites two opposed qualities, participates in two different natures."

This and nothing else is what Merleau-Ponty wanted to express with his choice of the concept of *ambiguïté*. It was to be a concept valid for the uniqueness of the live bodily structure of man. And it was to make clear his efforts to clarify this structure, the approximation he achieved in his important works to the enigmatic character of human live bodiness.

NOTES

1. Where English has but one word "body," German has two: *Körper*, derived from Latin "corpus," here translated generally as "physical body"; and *Leib*, of Germanic derivation, cognate with English "life," here translated as "live body" and occasionally as "human body." The usefulness of "Leib" for contrasting the body as phenomenally "live" from the physical body as *phenomenon*, or "Körper," should be evident.—*Tr*.

2. Merleau-Ponty, M. "L'oeil et l'esprit." *Les Temps Modernes*, 17 (1961): 193–94.

3. Ibid., p. 194.

4. Lefort, Claude. "L'idée d' 'être brut' et d' 'esprit sauvage.' " Les Temps Modernes, 17 (1961): 277.

5. Merleau-Ponty, op. cit., p. 198.

6. Concerning the concept of ambiguïté, see A. de Waelhens, Une philosophie de l'ambiguïté. Louvain, 1951.

7. "Anthropologist" is used here in the European sense to refer to the philosophical student of man.—Tr.

8. Arzt im Irrsal der Zeit; Festschrift zum 70. Geburtstag V. v. Weizsäcker. Göttingen, 1956, p. 86.

9. The alteration of the bodily as live as described here in the terminally ill and dying resembles to the point of confusion that of aging persons. Even a practiced and perceptive physician will in many cases be unable to decide at the time of the initial observation of his patient whether he is dealing with someone critically ill or sorely beset by old age. For in old age as well everything bodily live becomes onerous: getting up, shaving, washing, dressing, etc. The old man moves differently, more slowly, with greater effort. He inserts pauses where earlier there were none. The bodily live becomes a "job" for him that means toil and trouble. Trouble in so far as his live bodiness is no longer largely unvocal and weightless mediation. Now the world presents itself to him as attainable only with difficulty, a world no longer so interesting or so attractive. The greater and more frequent the hindrances, stresses, and strains which load this live bodily mediation, the more the character of the bodily as physical enters into the bodily as live. Posture and stance become bothersome. Old men move less and more slowly. . . . They have an aversion to haste. And thus their inclination to deliberate. All this expresses itself physiognomically. The "slackening" as an inner stance mirrors itself in the morphology of skin folds, for example in the area of lids, neck, and abdomen. Under circumstances old people see their hands and feet before them as if they were "things." That they belong to their own live body becomes ever less relevant. Consequently hands, feet, nails, etc., are no longer cared for as they were earlier. They are neglected like an old coat to which one is no longer related. Old men often become "sloppy," more and more indifferent in their existence as visible. One must now look for that ambiguity which impressed itself upon us in so many different instances.

10. Hasenjäger, Th. and Pötzl, O. Dtsch. Zschr. f. Nervenheilkunde, 152 (1941): 112.

11. Christian, Geo. Ibid., p. 256.

12. Wunderlich, Chr. Inaug. Diss. Heidelberg, 1948.

13. Plügge, H. Dtsch. Zschr. f. Nervenheilkunde, 154 (1943): 199.

14. For a description of these experiments see pp. 300–2, supra.—Tr.

15. A reference to the creation of man in Genesis.

16. Paré, A. Oeuvres completes, II, 220ff. Paris, 1840.

17. Lhermitte, F. Révue neurologique, 75 (1942): 20; 38.

18. Hécain, H. and Ajuriaguerra, J. de. Méconnaissances et hallucinations corporelles. Paris, 1952.

19. Poeck, K. Nervenarzt, 34 (1963): 241.

20. Hallen, O. Z. Psychother. med. Psychol., 6 (1956): 3.

21. Hasenjäger, Th. and Poetzl, O. *Deutsch. Z f. Nervenheilkunde,* 152 (1941): 112.

22. Plügge, H. *Deutsch. Z. f. Nervenheilkunde,* 154 (1943): 199.

23. Plügge, H. "Über den menschlichen Raum." *Psyche, Stutt.,* 17 (1963–64): 561–603.

24. Auersperg, A. Prinz. *Nervenarzt,* 21 (1950): 425.

25. Christian, P. *Psyche, Stutt.,* 4 (1950): 263.

26. Poeck, K. See note 19.

27. Wunderlich, Chr. *Inaug. Diss.* Heidelberg, 1948.

28. Christian, P. See note 25.

29. Wunderlich, Chr. See note 27.

30. Poeck, K. See note 19.

31. The experiment consists of the experimenter's having the amputee describe the position of his phantom, its size and spatial contours, and then unexpectedly and violently delivering a blow to this (objectively vacant) place. The amputee then usually retracts his stump in fright, at the same time alleging strong pains at the spot where the phantom was "struck." To the best of my knowledge this experiment was first described by J. Abatucci in an "Étude psychologique sur les hallucinations des amputés" (Thèse de Bordeaux, 1904), and recently taken up again by Poeck.

32. Merleau-Ponty, M. *The Structure of Behavior.* Boston: Beacon Press, 1963, pp. 208–09.

33. Ruffin, H. *Nervenarzt,* 30 (1959): 198.

34. Marcel, G. *Being and Having.* Glasgow: Dacre Press, 1949, pp. 163–66.

35. Weizsäcker, V. v. *Der Gestaltkreis.* Leipzig, 1940.

36. Buytendijk, F. J. J. "Die Sonderstellung des Menschen," in: *Handbuch der Neurosenlehre.* Hrsg. von V. E. von Gebsattel. Bd.: Biologische Grenzgebiete, p. 117ff.

37. Buytendijk, F. J. J. "Avant-propos," in: *Situation 1.* Utrecht-Antwerpen: Spectrum Verlag, 1954, pp. 7, 14.

38. Cf. Waelhens, A. de. *Une philosophie de l'ambiguïté.* Louvain, 1951.

39. Robert, P. *Dictionnaire alphabétique.* Paris, 1951, Fasc. II, p. 124.

THE NOBILITY OF SIGHT:

A STUDY IN THE

PHENOMENOLOGY

OF THE SENSES

Hans Jonas

Since the days of Greek philosophy sight has been hailed as the most excellent of the senses. The noblest activity of the mind, *theoria*, is described in metaphors mostly taken from the visual sphere. Plato, and Western philosophy after him, speaks of the "eye of the soul" and of the "light of reason." Aristotle, in the first lines of the *Metaphysics*, relates the desire for knowledge inherent in the nature of all men to the common delight in perception, most of all in vision. Yet neither he nor any other of the Greek thinkers, in the brief treatments of sight itself which we have, seems to have really explained by what properties sight qualifies for these supreme philosophical honors.[1] Nor have the different virtues of the several senses been properly compared and assessed. Sight, in addition to furnishing the analogues for the intellectual upperstructure, has tended to serve as the model of perception in general and

This selection first appeared as an article in *Philosophy and Phenomenological Research*, XIV, No. 4 (June, 1954), 507–19. It was expanded and included in Hans Jonas' *The Phenomenon of Life: Toward a Philosophical Biology* (New York: Harper & Row, Publishers, 1966), pp. 135–56. Copyright © 1966 by Hans Jonas and reprinted with the permission of the author and Harper & Row, Publishers, Inc.

thus as the measure of the other senses. But it is in fact a very special sense. It is incomplete by itself; it requires the complement of other senses and functions for its cognitive office; its highest virtues are also its essential insufficiencies. Its very nobility calls for the support of more vulgar modes of commerce with the importunity of things. In this sense, in which all eminence pays for itself the price of increased dependence, the "nobility of sight" will be considered in the following discussion. As one of its results, we shall find the ancient claims for sight substantiated and at the same time qualified.

The unique distinction of sight consists in what we may provisionally call the *image*-performance, where "image" implies these three characteristics: (1) *simultaneity* in the presentation of a manifold, (2) *neutralization* of the causality of sense-affection, (3) *distance* in the spatial and mental senses. In considering these three characteristics we may hope to contribute not only to the phenomenology of the senses by themselves but also to the evaluation of their role in the higher mental performances based upon them in the case of man.

1. THE SIMULTANEITY OF IMAGE OR THE TIME-ASPECT OF SEEING

Sight is *par excellence* the sense of the simultaneous or the coordinated, and thereby of the extensive. A view comprehends many things juxtaposed, as coexistent parts of one field of vision. It does so in an instant: as in a flash one glance, an opening of the eyes, discloses a world of co-present qualities spread out in space, ranged in depth, continuing into indefinite distance, suggesting, if any direction in their static order, then by their perspective a direction away from the subject rather than toward it. The theme of depth will engage us later under the head of "distance." Sight is unique already in beholding a cotemporaneous manifold as such, which may be at rest. All other senses construct their perceptual "unities of a manifold" out of a temporal sequence of sensations which are in themselves time-bound and non-spatial. Their synthesis therefore, ever unfinished and depending on memory, must move along with the actual progress of the sensations, each of which fills the now of the sense from moment to moment with its own fugitive quality. Any present quality is just a point of passage in the transition from the preceding to the subsequent one, none is closed in itself, and only one is there at a time. Thus the content is never simultaneously present as a whole, but always in the making, always partial and incomplete. These more temporal senses therefore never achieve for their object that detachment of its *modus essendi* from their own, e.g., of persistent existence from the transitory event of sense-affection, which sight at any moment offers in the presentation of a complete visual field. We may illustrate the difference by the cases of hearing and touch, the two senses which in certain respects deserve particular comparison with sight.

a. Hearing

The case of hearing is obvious: according to the nature of sound as such it can "give" only dynamic and never static reality. The wholes which it achieves by the synthesis of its manifold are strictly temporal ones, and their objective time-measure is identical with the time of the sense-activation itself: the duration of the sound heard is just the duration of hearing it. Extension of object and extension of its perception thus coincide. What the sound immediately discloses is not an object but a dynamical event at the locus of the object, and thereby mediately the state the object is in at the moment of that occurrence. The rustling of an animal in the leaves, the footsteps of men, the noise of a passing car, betray the presence of those things by something they do. The immediate object of hearing is the sounds themselves, and then these indicate something else, viz., the actions producing those sounds; and only in the third place does the experience of hearing reveal the agent as an entity whose existence is independent of the noise it makes. I can say that I hear a dog, but what I hear is his bark, a sound recognized as the bark of a dog, and thereby I hear the dog barking, and thereby I perceive the dog himself in a certain way. But this way of perceiving him arises and ceases with his act of barking. By itself it does not reveal anything beyond it, and that there is an agent preceding and outlasting the acoustic act I know from information other than the acoustic one. The object-reference of sounds is not provided by the sounds as such, and it transcends the performance of mere hearing. All indications of existents, of enduring things beyond the sound-events themselves, are extraneous to their own nature.

On the other hand, precisely because of this looseness of external object reference and thus of representative function, sound is eminently suited to constitute its own, immanent "objectivity" of acoustic values as such—and thus, free from other-representative duty, to represent just itself. In hearing music, our synthesis of a manifold to a unity of perception refers not to an object other than the sensory contents but to their own order and interconnection. Since this synthesis deals with succeeding data and is spread over the length of their procession, so that at the presence of any one element of the series all the others are either no more or not yet, and the present one must disappear for the next one to appear, the synthesis itself is a temporal process achieved with the help of memory. Through it and certain anticipations, the whole sequence, though at each moment only atomically realized in one of its elements, is bound together into one comprehensive unity of experience. The acoustic "object" thus created is a time-object that lasts just as long as the act of its synthesis lasts, that is, as the sequence of hearing itself does (or its re-creation in fantasy), with whose progress the "object" part for part coincides. It has no other dimension than that of time.

It is true that hearing, though wholly governed by succession, knows also juxtaposition of simultaneous acoustic content—witness polyphony in music, or the separable voice strands in the vocal babel of a cocktail party. One may even speak of a kind of inner-acoustic "space" in which a manifold can coexist. But this is a metaphor. The "coexistence" is always one of common procession in time, i.e., of strands of movement and change; and their distinction requires qualitative difference (in pitch, timbre, etc.) whose continuation in the sequence lets "strands" be identified: two notes of identical quality sounded together simply reinforce each other and make one (except for the "stereo" effect from the spacing of their sources), whereas real space is a principle of cotemporaneous, discrete plurality irrespective of qualitative difference. Also the "identity" of the single strands in a polyphony, and thus the conservation of discrete simultaneity through time, is a function of certain figural coherences (such, e.g., as make a tune) which come under the "Gestalt" principle and thus make the juxtapositon of plurality not a primary datum of the *now* but a feat of ongoing organization —i.e., a product itself of process. Even so the limits for a simultaneous manifold allowing integrity to its members are narrow in the world of sounds: a strong sound drowns its weaker contemporaries; to relate more than a few at a time to different source-loci in space becomes difficult, and beyond a limited number any multiplicity of sounds merges into a compound noise. There is no "keeping to one's place" in the community of acoustic individuals. The simple fact is that sounds are dynamic events, not just static qualities, and thus trespassers by nature.

This brings us to what is perhaps the most important feature to be considered in our comparison of hearing with seeing: sound, itself a dynamic fact, intrudes upon a passive subject. For the sensation of hearing to come about the percipient is entirely dependent on something happening outside his control, and in hearing he is exposed to its happening. All he can contribute to the situation is a state of attentive readiness for sounds to occur (except where he produces them himself). He cannot let his ears wander, as his eyes do, over a field of possible percepts, already present as a material for his attention, and focus them on the object chosen, but he has simply to wait for a sound to strike them: he has no choice in the matter. In hearing, the percipient is at the mercy of environmental action, which intrudes upon his sensibility without his asking and by mere intensity decides for him which of several qualities distinguishable at the moment is to be the dominant impression. The strongest sound may not be the vitally most important one in a situation, but it simply seizes the attention from among the competing ones. Against this the freedom of selective attention is extremely limited.

In view of these characteristics we understand why for our ears we have nothing corresponding to the lids of our eyes. One does not know when a sound may occur: when it occurs it gives notice of an event in the environment and not merely of its permanent existence: and since an event, i.e., a change in the environment, may always be of vital import, ears have to be open always for this contingency. To have them closed could be fatal, just as it would be useless to open them at arbitrarily chosen moments. With all the initiative left to the outer world, the contingency aspect of hearing is entirely one-sided and requires therefore continual readiness for perception. The deepest reason for this basic contingency in the sense of hearing is the fact that it is related to event and not to existence, to becoming and not to being. Thus hearing, bound to succession and not presenting a simultaneous coordinated manifold of objects, falls short of sight in respect of the freedom which it confers upon its possessor.

b. Touch

The case is different with touch, though it shares with hearing the successiveness of apprehension, while it shares with vision the synthesis of its data into a static presence of objects. A proper analysis of touch is probably the most difficult in the phenomenology of sense-perception, because it is the least specialized and in its physiology and achievements the most compound of the senses. In fact, "touch" serves as a blanket label for a very complex set of functions. The most elementary level in this complexity is the contact-sensation in which the presence of a contiguous body is felt at the point of incidence. I leave for later consideration the important fact that the contact-situation always involves pressure and therefore a modicum of force as part of the experience. Here we deal as far as possible with the mere qualities sensed. The first observation to be made then is that *shape* is not an original datum of touch, but a construct which emerges additively from a serial multiplicity of single or continuously blending touch sensations, and this in conjunction only with proprioceptive motor sensations. The single touch-sensation confined to the point of contact and without correlation to more of its own kind is rather barren of information. Already the simple tactile qualities, such as soft and hard, and even more so rough and smooth, are not really an instantaneous experience but require a series of changing sensations obtained by pressure and by friction, i.e., generally speaking by movement. Thus in their very constitution, a synthesis on the part of the percipient is involved, extending over the time-span of the series and, by a short-term retention, unifying its elements into one impression. Touch and hearing agree in this respect: that their primary objects, the qualities sensed, have process character and are thus essentially time-entities. (This observation, incidentally, disposes of the rather sterile question whether all sentient life is endowed with memory. In the form of immediate short-term retention, memory enters into the very constitution of sensibility, and is thus coeval with it.) But in hearing, the process is purely passive, while in touching it involves bodily activity.

For the tactile situation moves to a higher level when the sentient body itself becomes the voluntary agent of that movement which is required for the acquisition of this serial sequence of impressions. Then touch passes over from suffering to acting: its progress comes under the control of the percipient, and it may be continued and varied with a view to fuller information. Thus mere touch-impression changes into the act of feeling. There is a basic difference between simply having a tactile encounter and *feeling* another *body*. The former may be said to be the atomic element in the more complex totality of the latter, but this totality is more than the mere additive result of such atomic touch-sensations. The *motor* element introduces an essentially new quality into the picture: its active employment discloses spatial characteristics in the touch-object which were no inherent part of the elementary tactile qualities. Through the kinesthetic accompaniment of voluntary motion the whole perception is raised to a higher order: the touch-qualities become arranged in a spatial scheme, they fall into the pattern of *surface,* and become elements of *form.* This is a synthesis of a higher order, superimposed on that already operative in the constitution of the simple sense-qualities, which integrate their own time-series of atomic contact-sensations but now enter as material into the larger unit of spatial order. In this order the manifold concresces into a shape. The higher order of synthesis means also a larger time-span for its performance, and thus involves more of the memory inherent in all perception. But what in hearing results in a time-object, in touch results in the co-presence of a space-object: the data successively registered are entered into a matrix of static simultaneity.

An organ for real shape-feeling exists probably only in the human hand, and there is more than mere coincidence in the fact that in his hand man possesses a tactile organ which can take over some of the distinctive achievements of his eye. There is a mental side to the highest performance of the tactile sense, or rather to the use which is made of its information, that transcends all mere sentience, and it is this mental use which brings touch within the dimension of the achievements of sight. Briefly, it is the image-faculty, in classical terms: *imaginatio, phantasia,* which makes that use of the data of touch. Only a creature that has the visual faculty characteristic of man can also vicariously "see" by touch. The level of form-perception at the command of a creature will be essentially the same for both senses, incommensurable as they are in terms of their proper sensible qualities. Blind men can "see" by means of their hands, not because they are devoid of eyes but because they are beings endowed with the general faculty of "vision" and only happen to be deprived of the primary organ of sight.

c. Comparison with sight

We are engaged in showing the unique position of sight with respect to simultaneity of presentation, the thesis being that all the other senses operate on the basis of time-series in the presentation of their qualities. Hearing, so we found, stays entirely within this dimension in that the results of its synthesis, the extensive acoustic objects (such as a tune), retain the successiveness of elements which the succession of experience itself originally possessed. Melody not only is generated by sequence, it *is* a sequence. The time-measure is an essential aspect in the content of the sound-experience. A visual value, the presence of a color, may have a long or short duration: this may make a difference to the percipient for reasons of his own, but it does not make any difference to the experience-content itself. This color-quality has no intrinsic reference to time. With touch we found that already the single "atomic" sensation includes a time-element as part of the sense-content itself, the time without which such a quality as rough cannot be "generated" for experience and in which alone it presents itself; and moreover we found the composite tactile objectivity to emerge from a successive synthesis of such sensations. But the result of the synthesis itself, in the case of surface- and shape-perception, represents a spatial and not a temporal entity, and we have here presentation of simultaneity through successiveness.

In this presentation the original time-order of the atomic sensations becomes irrelevant and has no voice in the synthesized content now "present." It was merely the accidental order of the acquisition of data, which could be *ad libitum* changed and still procure the same result, whereas in hearing the order of the acquisition of data is the order of the object itself.

Thus it would seem that the three cases can be distinguished in this formula: Hearing—presentation of sequence through sequence; touch —presentation of simultaneity through sequence; sight—presentation of simultaneity through simultaneity.

According to this formula sight retains its unique position even in relation to the most developed case of tactile performance. We may take it that the achievement is at its best in the case of blind people who have learned to glean full information about shape and spatial situation of objects from the tactile data which they collect through their own activity. Yet even the densest distribution of the point-determinants collected and correlated in the course of extensive scanning by touch still leaves areas to be supplied by imagination. Knowledge of the complete form emerges progressively in this series of partial delimitations, and from a certain stage onward it is for all practical purposes "complete." How complete it can be is testified by the work of blind portrait sculptors. But this completeness is the product of an elaborate synthesis of many single perceptions, integrated into the one simultaneous form in whose presentness to the imagination the time sequence of its building-up is forgotten.[2] Thus we have here to distinguish what in the case of sight is identical, namely, the feat of the sense itself and the feat of the image-presentation *on the basis* of this sense-performance. The second is strictly speaking no longer a matter of touch but a kind of seeing by means of the heterogeneous material of touch. But however many data may be registered in succession and entered into the plane of simultaneous presentation, they can never fill a horizon such as is disclosed to one glance of the eyes. There are bound to remain blank spaces in between and an unrealized horizon in depth beyond the proximity of the actually contacted resistant objects.

d. Seeing and time

With sight, all I have to do is open my eyes, and the world is there, as it was all the time. We have shown that the case is different with hearing; and touch has to go out and seek the objects in bodily motion and through bodily contact, and this narrows down the actual object-relation to one particular instance: the realized relation is committed by the previous choice in which it originated, whereas in sight selection by focusing proceeds noncommittally within the field which the total vision presents and in which all the elements are simultaneously available. The particular focus impairs nothing of this simultaneous presentness. It has not committed freedom to this one choice at the expense of all the other possible ones, which remain at its instantaneous disposal without involving the kind of action that would change the situation obtaining between the subject and its vis-à-vis, the environment. Only the simultaneity of image allows the beholder to compare and interrelate: it not only offers many things at once, but offers them in their mutual proportion, and thus objectivity emerges preeminently from sight.

As regards the time-aspect as such, the simultaneity of sight is not only of practical advantage, in that it saves the time needed to collect the manifold data successively, but it introduces the beholder to a whole time-dimension otherwise not disclosed to him, namely, the *present* as something more than the point-experience of the passing *now*. In the case of every other sense, no instant is closed in itself, and no instantaneous datum tells its story. Sensation has to go on, to follow up the beginnings made in the evanescing antecedent, datum has to follow upon datum to let the larger units of experience in process emerge. Sound exists in sequence, every *now* of it vanishing into the past while it goes on: to arrest this flow and "view" a momentary "slice" of it would mean to have not a snapshot but an atomic fragment of it, and strictly speaking nothing at all. Transience is thus of the very essence of the *now* of hearing, and "present" is here a mere following in the stream of onmoving process. The situation is similar with touch, only that here the sequence is one more of active performance than of mere incoming data. In neither case is there a static present; to put it in Platonic terms, they are senses not of being but of becoming. Only the simultaneous representation of the visual field gives us coexistence as such, i.e., the co-presence of things in one being which embraces them all as their common present. The present, instead of being a pointlike experience, becomes a *dimension* within which things can be beheld at once and can be related to each other by the wandering glance of attention. This scanning, though proceeding *in* time, articulates only what was present to the first glance and what stays unchanged while being scanned. The time thus taken in taking-in the view is not experienced as the passing away of contents before new ones in the flux of event, but as a lasting of the same, an identity which is the extension of the instantaneous *now* and therefore unmoved, continued present—so long as no change occurs in the objects themselves. When it does, then time starts rolling visually. Indeed only the simultaneity of sight, with its extended "present" of enduring objects, allows the distinction between change and the unchanging and therefore between becoming and being. All the other senses operate by registering change and cannot make that distinction. Only sight therefore provides the sensual basis on which the mind may conceive the idea of the eternal, that which never changes and is always present. The very contrast between eternity and temporality rests upon an idealization of "present" experienced visually as the holder of stable contents as against the fleeting succession of nonvisual sensation. In the visual presence of objects the beholder may come to rest and possess an extended *now*.

Over these wider issues we must not forget the immense advantage which an instantaneous survey of the whole field of possible encounters represents in the biological situation. In the simultaneous field of vision a coordinated manifold, as yet outside active communication with me, offers itself to my selection for *possible* action. In this connection simultaneity means selectivity, and is thus a major factor in the higher freedom of the self-moving animal.

2. DYNAMIC NEUTRALIZATION

The freedom of choice just mentioned is dependent not only on the simultaneity of presence but at the same time on the fact that in seeing I am not yet engaged by the seen object. I may choose to enter into intercourse with it, but it can appear without the fact of its appearance already involving intercourse. By my seeing it, no issue of my possible relations with it is prejudged. Neither I nor the object has so far done anything to determine the mutual situation. It lets me be as I let it be. In this respect sight differs decisively from touch and hearing. The obtaining of the touch-experience itself is nothing but the entering into actual intercourse with the object: i.e., the very coming into play of this sense already changes the situation obtaining between me and the object. A fuller information then involves further such changes, each of which affects the object and my body at once and so is itself already a phase in my practical commerce with the object, for which on the other hand my sense-information is meant to prepare me. We therefore do not have in touch that clear separation between the theoretical function of information and the practical conduct, freely based on it, that we have in vision. Here again we have in the very constitution of a sense and its physical conditions the organic root of a highly spiritual distinction on the human level: that between theory and practice. While in touch subject and object are already doing something to each other in the very act in which the object becomes a phenomenal presence, the presence of the visual manifold leaves me still entirely free as to actual commerce, as I see without doing and without the object's doing anything.

In hearing, it is true, there is also no doing on my part, but all the more on the part of the object. Things are not by their own nature audible as they are visible; it does not belong to their mere being to emit sound as it belongs to them to reflect light. I can therefore not choose to hear something, but have to wait till something happens to a part of my environment to make it sound, and this sound will strike me whether I choose or not. And since it is an event of which sound informs me and not merely the existence of things in their total configuration, my choice of action is determined for me by the acoustic information. Something is going on in my surroundings, so hearing informs me, and I have to respond to that change, which affects me as an interested party not free to contemplate: I have to strain myself toward what may come next from that quarter, to which I am now bound in a dynamical situation.[3]

Now, it is the complete absence of such a dynamical situation, of any intrusion of causality into the relation, which distinguishes sight. I have to do nothing but to look, and the object is not affected by that: and once there is light, the object has only to be there to be visible, and I am not affected by that: and yet it is apprehended in its self-containment from out of my own self-containment, it is present to me without drawing me into its presence. Whatever dynamic commerce there is in physical fact between source of light, illuminated object, and perceiving eye, this context forms no part of the phenomenal result. This complete neutralization of dynamic content in the visual object, the expurgation of all traces of causal activity from its presentation, is one of the major accomplishments of what we call the image-function of sight, and it results in a subtle balance of gain and loss in the cognitive economy of man, the pre-eminently seeing creature.

The gain is the concept of objectivity, of the thing as it is in itself as distinct from the thing as it affects me, and from this distinction arises the whole idea of *theoria* and theoretical truth. Furthermore, the image is handed over to imagination, which can deal with it in complete detachment from the actual presence of the original object: this detachability of the image, i.e., of "form" from its "matter," of "essence" from "existence," is at the bottom of abstraction and therefore of all free thought. In imagination the image can be varied at will. This is also the case with sound, it is true, of which "imagination" can compose a freely created world of its own: but this has no reference to the world of things and therefore no cognitive function, whereas even the freest exercise of visual imagination retains this reference and may reveal properties or possibilities of the external world, as the case of geometry shows. Only the peculiar causal "indifference" of visual presence provides the material and engenders the attitude for these mental feats.

The loss, on the other hand, consists in the very feature which makes these higher developments possible, namely, the elimination of the causal connection from the visual account. The pure form-presentation which vision affords does not betray its own causal genesis, and it suppresses with it every causal aspect in its objects, since their self-containedness vis-à-vis the observer becomes at the same time a mutual self-containedness among themselves. No force-experience, no character of impulse and transitive causality, enters into the nature of image, and thus any edifice of concepts built on that evidence alone must show the gap in the interconnection of objects which Hume has noted. This means only that we have to integrate the evidence of sight with evidence of another kind which in the exclusiveness of *"theoria"* is all too often forgotten.

Let us consider more closely this causal detachment by which sight is the freest and at the same time the least "realistic" of the senses. Reality is primarily evidenced in resistance which is an ingredient in touch-experience. For physical contact is more than geometrical contiguity: it involves impact. In other words, touch is the sense, and the only sense, in which the perception of quality is normally blended with the experience of force, which being reciprocal does not let the subject be passive; thus touch is the sense in which the original encounter with reality as reality takes place. Touch brings the reality of its object within the experience of sense in virtue of that by which it exceeds mere sense, viz., the force-component in its original make-up. The percipient on his part can magnify this component by his voluntary counteraction against the affecting object. For this reason touch is the true test of reality: I can dispel every suspicion of illusion by grasping the doubtful object and trying its reality in terms of the resistance it offers to my efforts to displace it. Differently expressed, external reality is disclosed in the same act and as one with the disclosure of my own reality—which occurs in self-action: in feeling my own reality by some sort of *effort* I make, I feel the reality of the world. And I make an effort in the encounter with something other than myself.

The effortlessness of sight is a privilege which, with the toil, foregoes also the reward of the lower sense. Seeing requires no perceptible activity either on the part of the object or on that of the subject. Neither invades the sphere of the other: they let each other be what they are and as they are, and thus emerge the self-contained object and the self-contained subject. The nonactivity of the seen object in relation to the seeing subject is not impaired by the fact that, physically speaking, action on its part (emission of light) is involved as a condition of its being seen. The singular properties of light[4] permit the whole dynamic genesis to disappear in the perceptual result, so that in seeing, the percipient remains entirely free from causal involvement in the things to be perceived. Thus vision secures that standing back from the aggressiveness of the world which frees for observation and opens a horizon for elective attention. But it does so at the price of offering a becalmed abstract of reality denuded of its raw power. To quote from our own earlier account (see *The Phenomenon of Life*, p. 31): The object, staying in its bounds, faces the subject across the gap which the evanescence of the force context has created. Distance of appearance yields neutral "image" which, unlike "effect," can be looked at and compared, in memory retained and recalled, in imagination varied and freely composed. Thus becomes essence separable from existence and therewith theory possible. It is but the basic freedom of vision, and the element of abstraction inherent in it, which are carried further in conceptual thought; and from visual perception, concept and idea inherit that ontological pattern of objectivity which vision has first created.

Thus in speaking of the advantage of the causal detachment of sight, it must be borne in mind that this results also in the causal muteness of its objects. Sight, more than any other sense, indeed withholds the experience of causality: causality is not a visual datum. And as long as percepts ("impressions" and "ideas") are taken as just more or less perfect instances of the model case of visual images, Hume's denial of causal information to them must stand. Vision, however, is not the primary but the most sublime case of sense perception and rests on the understructure of more elementary functions in which the commerce with the world is maintained on far more elementary terms. A king with no subjects to rule over ceases to be a king. The evidence of sight does not falsify reality when supplemented by that of the underlying strata of experience, notably of motility and touch: when arrogantly rejecting it sight becomes barren of truth.

3 · SPATIAL DISTANCE

Neither simultaneity of presentation nor dynamic neutrality would be possible without the element of distance. A manifold can be presented simultaneously only if it does not crowd my immediate proximity where each item observed would block out the rest. And causality could not be neutralized if the object invaded my private bodysphere or its closest vicinity. Now sight is the ideal distance-sense. Light travels farther than sound and smell and does not suffer distortion on its way over any distance. Indeed, sight is the only sense in which the advantage lies not in proximity but in distance: the best view is by no means the closest view; to get the proper view we take the proper distance, which may vary for different objects and different purposes, but which is always realized as a positive and not a defective feature in the phenomenal presence of the object. By distance up to a point sight gains in distinctness of detail, and beyond that point in comprehensiveness of survey, in accuracy of proportions—generally speaking, in integration. We consciously stand back and create distance in order to look at the world, i.e., at objects as parts of the world: and also in order to be unembarrassed by the closeness of that which we wish *only* to see; to have the full liberty of our scanning attention. It is different with the other two distance-senses, hearing and smell. Smell never gains, always loses by distance. And as to hearing, though within a narrow range of local vicinity it also may have optimal distance and suffer by overcloseness (e.g., with large volumes of sound sources such as an orchestra), further withdrawal will not disclose new "vistas" to it, as to sight, which would compensate it for the loss of distinctness. Its case then becomes similar to that of smell. Both may bridge distance effectively, i.e., overcome what is in itself a disadvantage, but can only lose from its increase and will always tend to gain better information by closing the range.

Besides this quantitative aspect, the most telling characteristic is the *manner* in which distance is experienced in vision. Sound or smell may report an object as merely distant, without reporting the state of the intervening space: in sight the object *faces* me *across* the intervening distance, which in all its potential "steps" is included in the perception. In viewing an object there is the situation of a "vis-à-vis," which discloses the object as the terminal of a dimension leading from me toward it, and this dimension lies open before me. The facing across a distance thus discloses the distance itself as something I am free to traverse; it is an invitation to forward motion, putting the intervening space at my disposal. The dynamics of perspective depth connects me with the projected terminus.

This terminus itself is arbitrary in each given case, and my glance even if focused on it includes as a background the open field of other presences behind it, just as it includes, as a corona fading toward the edges, the manifold co-present in the plane. This indefinite "and so on" with which the visual perception is imbued, an ever-ready potential for realization, and especially the "and so on" in depth, is the birthplace

of the idea of *infinity,* to which no other sense could supply the ex-
periential basis. Touch conjoined with locomotion certainly also includes
awareness of the potentiality of going on to the next point, and thence
to the next, and so on. But touch does not already adumbrate these
imminent realizations in its perceptual content, as a marginal part into
which the core continuously blends. In the visual field it is this continuous blending of the focused area into more and more distant back-
ground-planes, and its shading off toward the fringes, which make the
"and so on" more than an empty potentiality: there is the co-represented
readiness of the field to be penetrated, a positive pull which draws the
glance on as the given content passes as it were of itself over into further
contents. No such blending of actual and potential content is given in
touch; there is merely the abstract possibility of replacing the present
by a subsequent content, and the whole results only from the progressive
addition of discrete parts. Sight includes at any given instant an *infinite*
manifold at once, and its own qualitative conditions open the way into
what lies beyond. The unfolding of space before the eye, under the
magic of light, bears in itself the germ of infinity—as a perceptual
aspect. Its conceptual framing in the idea of infinity is a step beyond
perception, but one that was taken from this base. The fact that we
can look into the unbounded depth of the universe has surely been of
immense importance in the formation of our ideas.

To revert to the straight phenomenon of distance, it goes without
saying that sight by this mere widening of the horizon of information
confers a tremendous biological advantage. Knowledge at a distance is
tantamount to foreknowledge. The uncommitted reach into space is
gain of time for adaptive behavior: I know in good time what I have
to reckon with. The apprehension of distant objects therefore means
an immediate increase in freedom by the mere increase which remoteness allows in the time-margin for action; just as we found simultaneity
of presentation to mean an increase in freedom by the opportunity of
choice it offers in the presented manifold. It has been said before that
these two aspects of the freedom of sight are closely interrelated. Their
union in one performance is the crowning achievement of freedom in the
sphere of sentience.

It would not be correct to say that in sight the distant is brought
near. Rather it is left in its distance, and if this is great enough it can
put the observed object outside the sphere of possible intercourse and
of environmental relevance. In that case, perceptual distance may

turn into mental distance, and the phenomenon of disinterested beholding may emerge, this essential ingredient in what we call "objectivity," of which we have found another condition in causal neutrality.

We turn back to the beginning, the partiality of classical philosophy for one of the bodily senses. Our investigation has shown some grounds for this partiality in the virtues inherent in sight. We even found, in each of the three aspects under which we treated vision, the ground for some basic concept of philosophy. *Simultaneity of presentation* furnishes the idea of enduring present, the contrast between change and the unchanging, between time and eternity. *Dynamic neutralization* furnishes form as distinct from matter, essence as distinct from existence, and the difference of theory and practice. *Distance* furnishes the idea of infinity.

Thus the mind has gone where vision pointed.

APPENDIX

Sight and Movement

The "Nobility of Sight" has dwelt on the nondynamic quality of the visual world and the "quietive" transmutation by which this distillate of reality is obtained; and reference was made to its need for cognitive complementation from other senses and from the sphere of action. We must add that the latter, or the *motility of our body* generally, is not called in *post hoc* only but is already a factor in the very constitution of seeing and the seen world themselves, much as this genesis is forgotten in the conscious result. Lest our preoccupation with the finished product in its contemplative "nobility" be taken as a similar forgetting on our part, some remarks on the role of *movement* in the production of it are in order. They naturally involve the more general question of the share of *praxis* in the bringing about of so seemingly "theoretical" a thing as the perceived world, or more generally still, the question of our active part in the organization of our sensa. Our particular concern here is with the visual province; but though we do *not* regard vision as a *model* of the other senses, its extreme of aloofness challenges the thesis of a practical dependence of perception more than any other sense, and so what is found of such dependence to inhere even there should hold *a fortiori* for the less privileged rest.

Kant posed the question of the cognitive organization of our percepts as the question of the relative shares of "receptivity" and "spontaneity," of the passive and active components of our being. But by "activity" in this context he understood mental activity alone (the formal articulation of the sense material through the categories of the understanding), not bodily action of the psychophysical person in his practical dealings with the world. It is strange how little the command of our limbs entered into the long history of the problem. To Kant, the "theoretical" subject is self-sufficient for the cognitive task of constructing from primitive data a meaningful perceptual whole called "world"; and the "practical" subject—becoming this under the spur of need or the moral will—acts in and on a world already constituted by the theoretical faculties of sense and reason. Kant only exemplifies a long-dominant trend: the idea of the theoretical subject separable from *praxis*, and more particularly of the passive or receptive nature of "mere" sense and sense knowledge, is deeply ingrained in the philosophical tradition and has decisively determined the course of epistemology. The corrective reactions to this partisanship (they started with Hegel's *Phenomenology of the Spirit* and include Pragmatism as a determined and vocal cause) are in the natural danger of being provoked into opposite partisanship. The following limited observations take "action" in its primary sense of moving, i.e., moving one's body and through it other things; and since the "passive" in this context is represented by sense-affection, they can also be said to deal with the interrelation of sentience and motility.

Since Berkeley's classical *Essay Towards a New Theory of Vision* (1709) it has become almost a commonplace in the theory of perception that visual data acquire their spatial (three-dimensional) meaning only by correlation with parallel tactual data; or more generally, that our object-perception and its spatial framework are the result of a mental integration of the deliverance of these two senses: sight and touch. The account is incomplete, however, so long as "touch" in this combination is taken as just another *sense*, only qualitatively different from sight, hearing, and smell. No mere superimposition of one set of qualities over another, no correlation of them as such, could conceivably yield the new property of space-in-depth. But when we include in "touch" the fact of its being an activity involving *motion*, then we go beyond "mere sensation" (an abstraction of analysis) and add to its "receptivity" that complement of action without which it would be barren of information. Note that the motion, to have this effect, must be my performance, i.e., "intentional" or "directed" motion: only as purposive act does movement vitally contribute to the organization of the perceptual world. Self-movement indeed may be called the spatial organizer in each sense-species, and the synthesizer of the several senses toward one common objectivity.

For the case of touch, the point has been made in the Essay: how, in exploring an object by feeling alone (e.g., in darkness), it is the direction of my own voluntary movements of limb, with my body as reference-system, that furnishes the framework of dimensional coordinates into which the successive contact sensations are integrated. We here merely repeat that without this kinesthetic side of the complex process no unification of the individual local data into a coherent series, and eventually no concrescence of them into a total simultaneous form, would come about in touch.

But what is obvious in the case of touch, seems at first inapplicable to the case of sight: that its cognitive feat should depend on movement. For was not the point of our Essay precisely that sight is the sense of the passive observer par excellence? That to look at things, at the world at large, is compatible with a state of complete rest, which even seems the optimal condition for visual attention and contemplation? Was not even the whole opposition of "theory versus practice," and hence of the *vita contemplativa* versus the *vita activa,* derived from this very aspect of vision? This still stands. Yet we should not be able to "see" if we had not previously moved. We should, e.g., not see the world arranged in depth, stretching away from us indefinitely, if we were not more than seeing creatures: if we were not creatures that also can move into space and have done so in the past.

The basic fact, of course, is that vision is the part-function of a whole body which experiences its dynamic involvement with the environment in the feeling of its position and changes of position. The "possession" of a body of which the eyes are a part is indeed the primal fact of our "spatiality": the body not merely as occupying a volume of space geometrically, but as always interacting with the world physically, even when at rest (e.g., by mere gravity). Without this background of non-visual, corporeal feeling and the accumulated experience of performed motion, the eyes alone would not supply the knowledge of space, notwithstanding the immanent extension of the visual field.

This proposition can be argued on many levels. One might show that the reaching for and manipulating of things by the infant provides the elementary experience of the corporeality of seen objects and of an order of distances correlated to the sensations of sight. Or one might elaborate on the many neuromuscular adjustments participating in the optical act as such (turning of eyeballs, focusing of lens, etc.—involuntary small-scale motor activations), which help to imbue the optical sensation with objective reference. Or one might point to the built-in spatial orientation which the physical "directions" of the body provide with the organic sense of right and left,[5] front and back,[6] up and down —a sense always actualized in some rudiment of motion. The point I wish to comment upon is a further one: the dependence of optical *perspective* on *locomotion*.

It will be agreed that the knowledge of perspective includes an awareness of the potential visual displacements attendant upon a shift of the observer's position, i.e., upon his moving. The ability to preserve the identity of object distribution throughout a sequence of such apparent displacements is a necessary premise for the understanding of perspective distortion. It might seem, therefore, that what is required is the remembered experience of such displacement patterns in connection with motion, i.e., a past of variously having moved in space. But this is not the whole story. For how did motion itself come to be experienced as motion, if its evidence were just visual displacement? The epistemological circle in obvious. It is here where movement *qua performance* becomes crucial. A winged seed sailing on the wind, if it were endowed with eyes, would at most perceive a time sequence of two-dimensional visual manifolds continuously blending into their successors, shapes increasing and decreasing in size, changing in outline, opening and closing their ranks, overlapping and separating—a kaleidoscopic change with a definite but meaningless pattern, lacking reference to position and to dimensions defined thereby. Thus all its travels would not help it to gain a perception of space and to relate the passage of images to a space traversed. The difference between this imaginary case and the real one of the self-moving animal is that the latter changes its place by an exchange of mechanical action with the resisting medium, through or upon which it moves. The muscular effort required means that the relative motion is more than a shift of mutual geometrical position: through the interplay of force the geometrical becomes a dynamical situation which by this very character discloses the geometrical aspect as well. The proprioception of motor activity becomes a guide for the organism in the successive construction of spatial distance and direction out of the phases of the motion it actually performs.

Once in possession of the knowledge bequeathed by these motion-experiences, I can indeed view the world from my fixed standpoint and apprehend it in depth, in perspective, and in the order of its differently extending directions. I may then be the stationary and inactive observer who lets the spectacle of the world pass by his eyes as on a screen. But in this contemplative situation my former activity of actually moving through space, of directing myself toward some goal, of changing my direction, of correlating time used to distance covered, of measuring exertion against the visual results of change, all these and the always present possibility of performing the same acts again, underlie and impregnate that seemingly static presence of space which vision enjoys. We may therefore say that the possession of a body in space, itself part of the space to be apprehended, and that body capable of self-motion in counterplay with other bodies, is the precondition for a vision of the world. We have thus the paradox that it is something dynamic, a process, by which the framework of static experience is constituted, viz., a system of spatial coordinates (directions) with my own body at the "origin." And the example of the sense seemingly remotest from such involvement shows that motility, which itself requires sentience for its operation, in turn enters into the very constitution of sense where this is to be more than the mere registering of irritations from without: in other words, where sensation is to rise to perception.[7]

NOTES

1. Aristotle in the same passage sums up the virtues of vision by stating that it is the sense yielding the most knowledge and excelling in differentiation (*Met.A*, 980 a 25); and he emphasizes that we enjoy vision for its own sake, apart from its utility. This evaluation merely hints at the qualities which elevate sight over the other senses.

2. Cf. the excellent analysis, by Pierre Villey, a blind author, in *The World of the Blind: A Psychological Study*, trans. by Alys Hallard (London: Duckworth, 1930), pp. 187 f.

3. This is not even considering the fact that sound may be specifically *addressed* to me—that its uttering, in outcry, growl, or speech, is meant for

my heeding: in this case, communicative intent reinforces the dynamical claim peculiar to the acoustic situation as such. (Visual signs have not this intrinsic, or natural, power to enforce attention, but only acquire some of it through symbolic convention.)

4. The smallness of the disturbances in which light consists affords all the major advantages of sight over the other senses: the distance of reach, the detachment from the cause-effect situation, its replacement by a quiescent image, the simultaneous representation of a manifold, and the extreme minuteness and precision of point-to-point "mapping" in this representation.

5. Cf. Kant's short essay "Of the first principle of the difference of directions in space" (further elaborated in "What is 'to orient oneself in thought'?"), where he points out that the distinction of identifiable directions in visual space is due to our feeling of a qualitative difference between the right and left sides of our bodies: if God between one night and the next changed the whole aspect of the starry sky into its mirror image, we should have no way of telling the difference without recourse to those qualitative body feelings—the purely geometrical evidence exhibiting no change.

6. Significantly, most free-moving animals (all vertebrates) have an axial direction of their body structure; in most cases this coincides with the main, i.e., forward direction of their locomotion. From the latter rule man's upright posture is the significant exception (for its profound meaning cf. the excellent essay by Erwin Straus, "The Upright Posture," *The Psychiatric Quarterly*, 26 [1952], 529–61).

7. It follows, incidentally, that the Leibnizian monad, "mirroring" the universe "in perspective" from its "viewpoint" (note the visual model!) *without doing something* to this universe in the way of interaction, is a self-contradictory concept: the percipient, by the very nature of perception, *must* be also *agent*.—The last expression prompts a reference to Prof. John Macmurray's admirable Gifford Lectures of 1953 (published in 1957) on *The Self as Agent,* whose many striking agreements in viewpoint and conclusions with portions of the present [work] came as a pleasant surprise to me when my attention was recently drawn to it. Especially his discussion of the relative claims of sight and touch, *op. cit.,* pp. 104 ff., finds close parallels in "The Nobility of Sight" (first published in 1954). It is a coincidence of independent insight, which must be gratifying to either side.

BORN TO SEE, BOUND TO BEHOLD: REFLECTIONS ON THE FUNCTION OF UPRIGHT POSTURE IN THE ESTHETIC ATTITUDE

Erwin W. Straus

I

For an anniversary volume in honor of Karl Bonhoeffer's eightieth birthday I contributed a paper on "The Upright Posture." That was in 1948. Since then I have not let go of the topic, and it has not let go of me. Subsequently, I have looked around in literature and scientific writings for critical remarks, and even more for expressions of agreement. To Richard Jung in Freiburg I owe a reference from Herder's *Ideas on the Philosophy of Human History* where he says, "Man is the first

    The selected article, "Zum Sehen Geboren, Zum Schauen Bestellt," was originally published in Stuttgart by Hippokrates-Verlag in 1963 and appeared in *Werden und Handeln,* Herausgegeben von Eckart Wiesenhütter zum 80. Geburtstag von V. E. Freiherr von Gebsattel, pp. 44–73. This paper was translated by Erling Eng, Ph.D., from the German with the English title: "Born to See, Bound to Behold: Reflections on the Function of Upright Posture in the Esthetic Attitude." The editor expresses his appreciation to the author, Erwin W. Straus, for his kind permission in allowing him to reprint the English translation, which appeared in *Tijdschrift voor Filosofie,* 27e Jaargang, Nr. 4 (1965), pp. 659–88. The editor's appreciation is also extended to the editors of *Tijdschrift voor Filosofie,* Louvain, Belgium.

freedman of creation; he stands upright." C. von Lorck gave me a quotation from Ovid's *Metamorphoses:*

Pronaque cum spectent animalia cetera terram
os homini sublime dedit, coelumque videre
juxit et erectos ad sidera tollere vultus.[1]

In Milton's *Paradise Lost* I found the following words of praise for Adam and Eve:

Two of far nobler shape, erect and tall,
Godlike erect, with native honour clad.

From Goethe's poem "The Bounds of Humanity" I had already used two stanzas in my first paper.

On the whole it seemed to me that I might expect the poets to agree with me more readily than the biologists and physicians. The nobility of the human figure is not always so apparent at the bedside of the sick, and therefore it is not surprising to discover that among the physicians who have spoken on this subject many have been inclined to consider the upright posture as a curse, a source of manifold ills, rather than a blessing. Herder mentions such a misanthrope, a Moskati, who in a treatise "On the essential bodily differences between animals and humans" gave an eloquent recital of a "list of evils": "The blood that must accomplish its circulation in an upright machine, the heart crammed into an oblique position, the intestines that work in a standing container—certainly these parts are more exposed to possibilities of disturbance than in an animal body." Others in the wake of Moskati have extended the list still further.

Zoologists and paleontologists may be divided into two groups. Though all of them agree that the upright posture distinguishes man from other species of the animal kingdom, one group, perhaps a majority, seeks to devalue what is characteristically unique for the human frame, stressing that which is common to both man and the primates, while the other group would presumably agree with Herder: "In the case of man everything is arranged in accord with his present figure. Everything in his history is explicable from it; without it nothing is." The first group emphasizes the transitions; ignoring the question how man, in permanent danger of falling, stands upright in and in opposition to the world, attention is only given to the way in which man has become what he is at present. Such discussions shift the accent more and more from present to the past, from modern man to his hypothetical ancestors. Weidenreich, however, opposing such attempts to identify the upright human posture with its antecedents, has given us a lucid formulation of the anatomical differences.[2]

Using the work of Kamper and of Blumenbach, Herder had similarly compared the orang-utan and man: "The ape is formed so that he can walk almost erect, thereby resembling man more than do any of his brothers; however he is not completely formed for it, and this difference appears to make him deficient in everything. . . . The orang-utan has long arms, large hands, short thighs, large feet with long toes, and with these small limbs he obviously lacks the basis for the firm human stance . . . whence he can never stand up entirely straight, but can only learn to stand bandy-legged, as it were."

Twentieth-century physiologists like Magnus and De Kleijn, as well as Sherrington and his students, have investigated the mechanisms which enable the upright posture and erect gait. The object of their studies, however, is the body as machine in the field of gravity and not man in his world.[3]

In his encyclopedic Gifford Lectures, "Man on His Nature," Sherrington has rather surprisingly failed to do justice to the upright posture. He mentions getting up and standing but once, and then merely to wonder and ask what contribution the mind makes to the integration of thousands of nerve fibers and hundreds of thousands of muscle fibrils. His answer is: "The mind is unaware of how we do our standing, walking, running, and so on. The brain as regards their execution does them without mind."[4] Thus Sherrington clearly did not overlook the phenomenon of the upright posture; for him it was apparently not an essential theme in a review of old and new efforts to understand man's nature. But Sherrington hints obliquely at the reasons for his silence. In a brief foreword to the second edition, long delayed because of the war, the nonagenarian—surely pricked by the criticism of his supposed or actual dualism—sets forth the guiding idea of his exposition in precise terms: "The book stresses the view that man is a product, like so much else, of the play of natural forces acting on the material and under the conditions past and present obtaining on the surface of our planet."[5] That play, however, is the play of chance. Accordingly, his basic tendency is to illumine man's nature as the genetic outcome of accidental changes of material in the course of natural evolution. Perhaps it may seem absurd to compare Ovid, the "frivolous" poet banished from the imperial court at Rome, with Sherrington, the infinitely learned president of the Royal Society. Nonetheless both have in common the theme of metamorphosis. Ovid, at home in Greek poetry and philosophy, a connoisseur of Lucretius, knew quite well that he could offer his readers serious thoughts only in a playful mythological guise. Sherrington, familiar with the ways of thinking and the thoughts of philosophers, with the manner of speaking and the words of poets, is compelled willy-nilly to personify nature in a mythical way. Both tell us that man was made from clay. (Sherrington calls it "material.") From that point on, to be sure, their paths part. The enlightened Romans in the age of Augustus certainly no longer believed in the Titans and their sons, and yet "the gods of Greece" had not vanished. Sherrington, however, writes in an age "where now, as our sages say, but a ball of fire revolves" (Schiller). In Ovid's history of creation, with its many surprising parallels to Genesis I, Prometheus makes man from germinal images received from above; he forms man as a whole in accord with a plan. Sherrington's forces of nature produce man without plan or goal. Thus his problem remains to show how a play of forces without meaning can generate by chance a structure of meaningfully related parts, how blind forces could produce an organism that sees, and even has insight into the working of such forces.

Modern science has outlawed all "why" questions; it wants to confine itself to the "how." The sense of discovery, wonderment and even dumbfoundedness in face of the meaninglessness of the whole cosmic enterprise is not without a comic flavor, since whatever is eventually discovered is only what was sought for at the outset. But this anxious avoidance of all questions of purpose cannot keep the teleological approach (if only in the Kantian sense of a regulative principle) from being indispensable in the biological sciences. Research that proposes to limit itself to questions of "how" serves a purpose itself, namely that of knowledge.

Sherrington emphasizes the opposition of energy and mind. Like Descartes, he strives to understand how they work together. "We called them disparate and incommensurable. Are they then absolutely apart? Can they in no wise be linked together? They have this in common—we have already recognized it—they are both of them parts of one mind. They are thus therefore distinguished, but are not sundered. Nature in evolving us makes them two parts of the knowledge of one mind and that one mind our own. We are the tie between them. Perhaps we exist for that."[6]

In these reflections purposes are hesitantly ascribed to nature. But this supposition is counter to the underlying plan of the book. Sherrington's guiding concept requires him to make use of an analytic method. The final explanations must be found by descending to the elements. "The integration of the body is not the work of its finite mind." It "appears to be grounded in the organization of the brain and this is an organization of cells. . . . The cortex is the region where brain and mind meet." The mind does not steer the boat like the captain from its bridge; his performance is limited to the occasional turning of a wheel in the enginehouse. "The biological usefulness of mind for the concrete individual appears to be the improvement and control of the motor act." The mind, banished to the inner realm of the neural switchboard, is unrelated to the world.

The electron microscope has laid bare regions previously unknown; but it has simultaneously removed old and familiar ones from sight. For example, a recent work on muscle physiology deals only with micro-problems. Muscles as organs of movement, individual muscles as listed in the Basle nomenclature, are left unmentioned, and there is no account of animal movement in terrestrial space. But in the last analysis fibrils and molecular processes subserve the organism as a whole. Its relation to the world cannot be derived from those molecular events. While cells and cell structures, organs and limbs, to be sure, enable the upright posture, they are not upright themselves. The feet of the standing man are horizontally positioned, while his hands and arms hang down from the shoulders; the contractions of back and neck muscles are directed downwards. "Man is the first freedman of creation" because he enters into his own through his upright posture in and over against the world. Upright posture, macroscopic in its dimensions, is a phenomenon of the everyday Life-world (*Lebenswelt*).

Everything in the structural plan of the human body is organized for and by the upright posture. Upright posture enables the development of the fore extremities into the human shoulder, arm, and hand, and the development of the head into the human skull and face. Moreover, to the modification of structure correspond not only the variations of functions and accomplishments; with the upright posture a particular mode of being-in-the-world is simultaneously given. The animal organized to stand erect becomes the *animal rationale;* it takes its stand and wins a stance in the world it makes. Language has expressed this through terms like "upright" and "upstanding" and antonyms like "fall," "stumble," and "collapse." In denoting the freedom and jeopardy of human existence language links the human world with the human figure.

Upright posture characterizes the human being, it elevates him above the animals. But there could be no dispute whether he "in this respect is unique on earth" were the animals not also able to get up from the sustaining ground against gravity. Only when in their motility they have reached a limited autonomy can the specialized senses emerge. As optical instruments human and animal eye are certainly comparable. Sight the animal has in common with man, but in the upright posture seeing is transformed into beholding.

> To seeing born,
> Bound to behold,
> To tower sworn,
> Me likes the world.
> I look afar,
> I see anear,
> Moon and star,
> Forest and deer.

From his lofty lookout which extends the upright posture beyond itself, Lynkeus holds watch, contemplating the world as cosmos.

> So in all I see
> The charm eterne,
> As it pleases me
> I please myself.

The animals also see, but they are not "bound to behold"; they have no inkling of the "charm eterne"; they are bound to earth, to the proximity where, in a dramatic turn of the poem, the dreadful becomes actual before the watcher on the tower.

> Merely not for my delight
> Have I been put upon this height:
> What a strange and fearful fright
> Threatens from the world of night!

Lynkeus, the name of the man appointed to watch, derives from lynx, the sharp-eyed animal. With his lynx eyes he nevertheless stands high above the arena of actual events. Condemned to be a spectator of the flames consuming the cottage of Philemon and Baucis, he mourns his gift and his office:

> Why must you, my eyes,
> Know this, see so afar? (*Faust*, II, Act 5)

The tower opens the view of the human being who, in his upright posture, beholds the world and its happenings from a distance. The upright posture removes man from the ground, things, his fellow men, placing him in opposition to all and everything. He has distance from the ground.

A quadruped animal—the dog for example—raises itself from the ground, while its body firmly supported by four legs still remains closely attached to the ground. Even when in rapid motion its center of gravity remains in a more or less safe equilibrium over a fairly wide basal plane. The back delimits the animal body against the upward direction like a roof or dome. The head, placed "ahead" of the trunk, is, with maw, nose, and eyes, set for what is near. ("Pronaque cum spectent animalia cetera terram.") The eyes, placed behind muzzle, snout, and fangs, along the axis of bodily movement, direct the mouth to the prey. The pointed ears are also pricked up for the presently meaningful sounds. Distant thunder frightens a dog no less than thunder nearby. He is frightened by the storm, but he does not wonder at the rainbow. He is indifferent to rosy-fingered Eos, the moon and stars. Only what is near or next to him matters. Things are seen merely in relation to himself, heading for them, much like a swimmer stretched out, fighting his way upstream. The animal's glance hurries on ahead of his approach and incorporation in the direction of its body's movement. When a dog sights something of interest, he stops suddenly and fixes it in the familiar pose of the pointer whose raised forepaw conveys the suspended movement like the frame of a stop-motion film. The pointing dog is still directed at something particular in front of him.

The animal moves in the direction of its length, of its gastrointestinal tract, with its muzzle as entrance and its anus as exit. Its locomotion is in the service of bodily incorporation. The animal is confined to the limits of its own body. Vertical extension is amputated, as it were, from the cardinal directions: upward-downward, forward-backward, left-right. The animal lifts itself from the ground only to return at once. The space sidewards, which our arms broach, is not opened to its grasp. The "backward" movement of a dog is not back-wards, it is actually tail-wards, just as the forward movement is mouth oriented. The zone termed "behind the back" when referring to the human body (*Leib*) is displaced upwards for the dog, enclosing the entire region above its body. While a human being can re-turn to the field left behind, the animal remains turned away from the "above." The horizon of animal interest is pulled down very low and limited to a narrow territory just ahead.

Upright standing man, on the contrary, is quasi an embodiment of the Euclidean dimensions that extend forwards, backwards, and sidewards into the unbounded. Man looks and moves in a direction perpendicular to the length axis of his body. In the upright posture the skull becomes head, upheld by the trunk. The muzzle, turned mouth, has receded beneath the line of sight; in the human "face" the eyes are directed at the things themselves, no longer exclusively devoted to in-corporation, desire and aversion, approach and withdrawal. "Man is anthropos, a creature who looks above and all about him," says Herder, obviously alluding to the etymology of "-opus." While the surround encloses the animal body, the world is opened up for the human look. The vertical is bounded only as a perpendicular downwards; upwards it rises like a flame beyond the crown of the head.

We can clarify this contrast by means of a thought experiment in which we try to imitate the situation of an animal. Let us imagine we are crawling out of a low tent on all fours. Before getting up, we try to reflect on our situation in this knee-and-elbow position. No mistake, we are down, next to the ground. Our gaze is directed forward-downward, along the axis of the trunk, so that we cannot see the grass for the blades. Though in this position we are more helpless than the four-footed animals, it still gives us a certain insight into the confines of their "world." As soon as we get up in front of the tent, the curtain before our eyes soars up; the horizon opens and expands. For the first time the back is turned backwards; the figure shut in on three sides and pointing downwards becomes a form polarized forwards and backwards, upwards and downwards, striving away from the ground. The cardinal direction points upwards, counter to gravity. But the direction of the gaze is forward, at a right angle to the long axis of the body. Thus vision becomes the distance sense par excellence.

The eye of man, emancipated from the bondage of catching, grabbing, and gobbling, can dwell on the things themselves. The animal sees them only in relation to itself, as alluring or repelling. The human gaze is directed to the things "in themselves." We see them in their own shape, at a distance which simultaneously separates and links us and them. We see things "there," in their own place and their own structure. They stand vis-à-vis, offering themselves as objects to our gaze. Thus we are able to behold things in a plane perpendicular to the direction of our gaze, i.e., in the plane of fronto-parallel *Prägnanz* and of transparent distance. The separate planes of viewer and viewed do not intersect. The two partners remain on this and that side of a dividing hiatus. Light conjoins the planes and the gaze binds them, while the planes themselves do not intersect. The gaze counters the direction of light. The phenomenology of vision is no mere addendum to physiological optics. Yet there is an accord between the gaze turned toward distant objects and the light which illumines natural and artificial scenes, in the sense that the light reflected from the surface of things has no impact on what actually happens—apart from photo-chemical, photoelectric, and photothermic effects. On the contrary, light suffers a reflection, receiving a pattern which after a journey of many thousands of miles ends with an effect of point-for-point correspondence with its beginning.

However characteristic for the human species, upright posture must be acquired by the individual. The contemplative gaze develops during a process of maturation. The conquest of distant space passes through a series of phases. At first the distantness of things is not accepted. The small child approaches the visible, though remote, things until he can put his hand on them. Only in a second phase extending over many years does this "grabbing" compulsion fade away as the upright posture is secured. For a long time, however, the child's interest remains confined to things that lie within his grasp. Perhaps the organization of the visible world into near and far reaches its completion only with sexual maturity and the ardent longing for the embraceable proximity of a partner. The observer in the detached attitude of the adult does not intervene in events yonder; he leaves them to themselves, remaining disengaged even when he sympathizes with them deeply. He is not struck by them, even though they impinge on him. In the attitude of composure we reach the visible and yet leave it as it is. Distance is the condition for seeing the other as other in his uniqueness. We comprehend things without prehending them. We apprehend them in their suchness, in their place, their mutual demarcation, simultaneously and successively ordered within the horizon as a whole. The distant does not set off a region which might be approached and reached in the future. The distant opens itself to our gaze in contemplative regard, not in aggressive action; it opens itself in our looking over there, not in going over there. The first great abstraction of suchness is achieved in the beholding gaze: the *eidos* discerned from the *hyle*. Together with and through the suchness we comprehend what reveals and conceals itself in it. It is the suchness that man can represent in a picture. The picture is an effigy of an original image (*Urbild*) seen in a distance. In the contemplative regard of things, however, the original image has not yet attained full relief. The *eidos* remains attached to the *hyle*. The detaching, the *aphairesis,* is only completed in the creation of an effigy that is at once a post-formation and a re-formation. Beginning and end of this process in which the original image simultaneously gains and loses are rooted in the human regard and therewith in the upright posture.

II

Following Heidegger, who has referred to man as a "being of the distant," Hans Kunz attempted to answer the question: Why is he such a being?[7]

It cannot stem, Kunz answers, from his being a bearer of the distance senses. He believes rather "that the perceptual functions bridging the spatial, temporal, and spatiotemporal distances of what is encountered represent a necessary but insufficient condition of distance receptivity, and that the decisive moment must be seen in the original constitution of the mind as a herald of death as possibility." If I understand Kunz correctly, he assumes that perceptual functions eliminate, as it were, the original distance, i.e., bridge the distance. But the bridges across a river span the chasm only for the one who uses them in leaving one bank and coming to the other. In vision, contrariwise, the "allon" is both accessible and removed. We never leave the one bank; the other reveals itself to us in the distance, and *only* in the distance. While Kunz, who does not distinguish between seeing and beholding, believes "that the experiencing of distance remains attached to the seeing of images and the hearing of tones," we would like to show that the experiencing of distance makes the sight of images possible.

The relation of radical opposition between us is, after all, only apparent, for the images of which I wish to speak and those to which Kunz refers are not the same. By images I understand paintings and drawings for which collectors and museums pay high prices, and also *the* pictorial material in newspapers and magazines that we discard every day. Kunz, on the contrary, speaks of phantasms, presentations, drive-immanent images and dream images. It seems that he also conceives "reality-adequate perception as images (in the broadest sense)," in which "objects of the surrounding world present themselves to the senses in the infinite fullness of their forms."[8]

Perceptual images, conceptual images, and memory images are metaphorical expressions for which the pictures of everyday life have been used as models. The hypostasizing translation to "contents of consciousness" has, however, remained satisfied with a vague analogy without much concern for the structure of the model. In a widespread but primitive form of the doctrine of perceptual images it is assumed that an agent, strictly physically determined, acts on the sense organs— a process supposedly accompanied on the "psychophysical level" by a perceptual image so endowed with subjective, secondary qualities that in the optical sphere, for example, the perceptual image should correspond more or less precisely to the image on the retina. The theorist initially claims for himself a position—no one knows how he got it—in the "outer world." We, however, by a sudden switch of standpoint, are assigned a position within the magic castle whose ground floor is cluttered with perceptual images, its attic with memory images, and its cellar with dream images. Through unconscious inferences or existential judgments, external projection or even animating acts, perceptual images are said to be transformed into what is perceived, appearances of things into things that appear.[9] If this were actually so, how could real pictures be once again distinguished from real objects after the perceptual images had been transformed into objects of perception? Even were this to be made intelligible, how could we understand that real pictures are encountered solely in the visual sphere? The expression "perceptual image" is certainly a generic term that embraces all the modalities without preference. The pictures of the everyday Life-world, however, can only be seen. We can, to be sure, touch, grasp, and handle a picture in the dark, but the feeling hand cannot apprehend it *qua* image. The hand takes hold of the picture-thing in concrete space but not the picture *qua* representation.[10]

In the theory of perceptual images the way leads from image to object. The image is initial; presumably it is the only thing directly given to us in consciousness. In everyday life, however, the way leads from object to picture, a way animals never learn, and the child only in the course of acquiring upright posture. In theory the image changes into an object. In everyday life the picture coexists with the object, separate but related to it, and, in some instances, comparable with it. At this point the further question arises: how can an object be detected as image, though itself a thing—if not one of flesh and blood, nevertheless of canvas and paint? For pictures certainly pass from hand to hand. They are produced in quantity as postcards, are mailed, and occasionally kept as souvenirs. Art treasures, carefully guarded and well lighted, are shown to countless visitors in museums. At home, pictures on the four walls are seen by their owner day after day. The images of consciousness, to the contrary, are strictly private property to which no one else has access; images of imagination do not require lighting, memory images cannot be mailed, and perceptual images cannot be viewed a second time. The eagerly waiting inheritors of a famous collection to whom a wicked uncle would will only his perceptual and memory images might have very little favorable to say about the departed. The images of consciousness are understood through and through or misunderstood through and through as mere image, while the images of everyday life are at the same time material objects and—might we say—immaterial figurations. If pictures consisted only of canvas and colored pigments, paper and daubs, how could a few pencil scrawls, i.e., thinly dispersed deposits of graphite, change a sheet of paper into a drawing, a picture? If pictures are immaterial figurations, how is it that they can be seen? If they are material things, how can they stand for other things, and yet differ from the things they stand for? Pictures are artificial even when they are not artistic human productions. Only man is in a position to understand the pictures of his own making as effigies.[11] For a dog or horse a photograph is something entirely neutral; for man, to the contrary, it is both a something of paper and an effigy which, according to the theme represented, can touch, move, or emotionally shake him.

To explicate this twofold character of the image in everyday life we make a distinction between the image in its material structure as panel (*tabula*), and the image in the genuine sense of the term as effigy (*effigies*). For the composite of the panel and effigy we shall use "picture" (*pictura*). Whenever there is a question of a painting's authenticity or of its attribution to this or that master it always concerns the picture. The picture is authentic when this or that known artist has realized his project on this panel by his own hand. The effigy can be multiplied and so cleverly imitated that the question may arise which of the pictures is *the* original, a question answered either by a critical style analysis of the effigy or a critical analysis of the material of the panel. The devices invented by man for making and multiplying effigies produce only the panels. A photographic film exposed to light suffers photochemical effects just as the retina does. The photograph becomes an effigy only for the human viewer who, at a distance from both, is capable of grasping a visible object as representation of another object. Nature does not produce effigies.

The modes of being of panels and of effigies are fundamentally different. Let us say that someone spreads out ten copies of a photograph on a table in front of him; then looking at ten panels he sees but *one* effigy. This difference does not result from the specific modes of reproduction; on the contrary, the possibility of being reproduced is founded in the mode of being of the effigy. Even in a single picture the mode of being of the effigy is different from that of the panel. The technique, number, and material of the reproductions are all of subordinate importance. Whether a single copy is handmade with material like that of the original or whether millions of copies—as of the enormous editions of American magazines—are made of a material entirely different from that of the original, does not alter the principle of reproduction one whit: the very same effigy is presented over and over again on many panels. In the case of newspaper photography the effigy conveys the same event to the eyes of spectators across the entire country.

The effigy makes reproduction possible. For this reason the phenomenon of reproduction facilitates an understanding of the mode of being of the effigy. Volkswagens too are all alike; they have all been made on the same model, from the same materials. But the single auto does not reproduce the model, nor does it stand for anything else. Its form and material belong to one and the same region of the ontic. An effigy, however, is not the form of the panel; effigy and panel do not go together like form and material. With the Volkswagen the colors belong to the car; it is red, green, black, etc. In representational art, however, the colors of an effigy do not belong to the panel as they occasionally do in abstract painting. The effigy is not a paint brushed onto the panel. Effigy and panel are of different modes of being. The panel has its place in the spatiotemporal continuum of material things, not so the effigy. Thanks to this deficiency—to state the situation accurately—a picture represents something which it is not, something that factually or virtually belongs to the spatiotemporal continuum in which the panel is located.

We shall limit our discussion to the representational image, not from a bias against abstract painting, but because the way from object to effigy appears as the natural one; also it is the route taken by painters in East and West since the earliest days of cave painting. The products of creative phantasy are no exception to this rule. The opposite direction, from effigy to object, does not of course automatically correspond to the direction from object to effigy. It is not necessary for us to compare a portrait with the person portrayed to recognize it as an effigy. Its character as an effigy is not discovered through comparison; an effigy reveals itself as an effigy. It is seen as such, our gaze grasps it as such. Through representation we can "present a picture of an object" to ourselves that we have never seen and never will. Artistic excellence and technical perfection are unimportant. A picture postcard or a drawing by a child are just as good examples as great masterpieces—in a way even better—for two reasons: (1) Great talents are rare in art. But the capacity to recognize and to draw an effigy—at least a crude schema—is universal. The picture book makes its way into the nursery long before the primer. The urge to draw and the pleasure taken in it often disappear with the passage from kindergarten to elementary school, when the autodidact, not yet saddled with rules, changes into a pupil loaded down with homework. (2) In the drawings of children and dilettantes the fundamental discrepancy between object and effigy strikes the eye at once. Even the most faithful reproduction represents the object as transformed. However pejoratively one may use "photographic verisimilitude" in referring to a painting, it is all too easy to overlook the enormous difference between a photograph and its model. The similarity is salient, while the difference goes unnoticed and unconsidered. Seen as a panel, as a flat piece of printed paper, featherlight, the photograph does not resemble the object represented but is radically different from it. The dissimilarity between effigy and object is, however, not a bit less important than their similarity. The object's transformation in the effigy is not a unique contribution of the great artist; the effigy itself is such that it makes the transfiguration both possible and inevitable.

The notion of imitation has, to be sure, played an important role in esthetic theory for centuries. Agreement between effigy and object—the "perfect likeness"—has seemed to determine the character and value of a picture. From antiquity we have Pliny's story of the competition of two Greek painters, Zeuxis and Parrhasius. The winner was to be the one able to most cleverly imitate any object from nature. Zeuxis painted grapes with such faithfulness that birds flew at the picture to peck the fruit. Under circumstances to be discussed later, Parrhasius, however, was successful in outwitting even Zeuxis. He painted a drapery which Zeuxis struggled in vain to open. In this legend neither birds nor painter recognized the picture as effigy. But a picture is not an imitation, it is not a *trompe-l'œil*. A picture represents an object which as a real object has its unique position in the whole of visible space. From this attachment the effigy detaches the suchness as grasped by the contemplative gaze. In this regard both artistically accomplished work and the most awkward drawings of children are alike.

But how is it possible for an effigy, visible as it is, to differ so from an object which it resembles that we take the one as a representation of the other? An effigy represents something else without any shift of sense modality. It does not represent the object like an ambassador representing his country or a salesman his firm, nor does it stand as a sign for anything else. It represents, itself being visible, something else likewise visible. Therefore we are more interested in finding out how effigy and object differ than how they are alike, i.e., how they differ in order that one may represent the other. In the *Magic Flute* Tamino is charmed by the picture of Pamina; he falls in love on the spot, not with the picture in his hand, but with the maiden shown in the picture. In the relationship of the representation to the represented the former is of lesser status, just as a representative stands for another whose place he takes. In political life the representative is named by the one represented, the actual authority. In the same way, what is represented in the picture is the real thing, and not the effigy. This observation marks but one of a number of negative characteristics. Compared with the thing itself the picture is of lesser ontological status, a deficiency more readily demonstrated through the pictures and drawings of dilettantes. Our tendency to think of an esthetically valuable work of art whenever a picture is mentioned prevents us from acknowledging the ontological

deficit of a picture, nay from even registering it. We are justly inclined
to consider the work of a great master as more significant and valuable
than what it represents. All the rabbits in the world—it seems to us—
cannot outweigh Dürer's hare. But the merest bunny that hops around
into Pygmalion's statue. Dürer's hare is after all *but* a painted hare;
any more than Galatea would be willing to be metamorphosed back
into Pygmalion's statue. Dürer's hare is after all but a painted hare;
he doesn't run, nibble grass, breed, nor feel the warm sun. The
ontological deficiency of the effigy is nonetheless at the same time
the condition of the artistic metamorphosis and the enhancement
of reality. To put the truth gently we may say that the reality
lacking in an effigy is just banal everyday reality, without ever entirely
forgetting the fact that it is just the banal everyday within which we
suffer and rejoice, live and die.

III

A picture represents something that it is not. The panel has, like everything else, its place there on a particular spot within space. But its
place on the wall is not the locality of the imaginal representation.
The effigy does not belong to the spatiotemporal continuum of things
into which the panel has been inserted and in which the viewer finds
himself. The panel can be transferred to another place; many pictures
have changed owners and museums. But the locality depicted has not
changed in the course of this odyssey. Whether here or there, in the
new place or the old, the effigy is not located in the spatiotemporal
continuum. Yet a place can only be determined or revealed within a
continuum. Even when pictures unmistakably represent buildings or
landscapes localized in mundane space there is still no spatial kinship
between the effigy, say of Big Ben, St. Peter's Cathedral, the Empire
State Building, and these buildings themselves. The effigy represents
them; but it does not point them out as a road sign points out a
direction. A picture of sunrise is not oriented to the east. Therefore
it is customary to isolate a picture from its surroundings by means of
a frame. The frame separates the picture space from physical space,
but not like a fence which cuts out as property a piece of land from
the spatial continuum. The frame does not effect the separation; it
only betokens a distinction already made in composing the picture
within the unnatural, rigid form of a rectangle. The frame, however,

delimits the effigy from its surroundings within its own representational spatiality. The walls of a museum are continuous, while the pictures appear singly, unrelated to one another; they do not fit into the continuity of one representational picture space. Pictures that hang beside one another are not neighbors, or if so, only mediately through what is represented. Biblical scenes have been represented by the old masters in endless variety. But one effigy is not counter to another. Grünewald does not cancel out Mantegna, Rubens does not clash with Dürer.

The spatiality represented in the effigy does not embrace the viewer. His action space does not extend into the effigy space. The effigy, even a miniature, represents something with which physical contact is suspended, i.e., a picture is visible only at a distance. One can come near the panel and move away from it to find a place for the best view; but it is not possible to approach the effigy space itself. It appears in the sphere of what is counter, open to the gaze but detached from any contact. What is represented, on the other hand, belongs inherently to the spatiotemporal continuum, even in creations of pure phantasy. Mythological and religious pictures do not claim to be historically faithful reproductions, but they are still objective representations. The human beings and scenes in the paintings, be it Aeneas and Dido, Adam and Eve, or Achilles and Hector, David and Goliath, they all are represented as creatures belonging to the field of earth's gravity.

The effigy itself, however, is weightless. A book with pictures of Swiss villages and landscapes will never fail to show a view of the Matterhorn. But this page is as easy to turn as all the others. The effigy showing the giant rock pyramid is itself weightless, and would be so even if it were shown on bronze altar doors. The noble steeds of the sun yoked to Beatrice's chariot in Tiepolo's paintings on the ceiling of the Imperial Ballroom in the Würzburg Palace do not inspire our dread. The horses seen from below are, we say, "true to nature"; they appear to the viewer at the very moment of their rearing up before a morning cloud, their white bellies prominently displayed. A ballroom ceiling is an odd place for steeds and chariot, but there is no apprehension lest they come crashing down from their empyrean heights. A ceiling painting does not give, nor is it intended to give, an illusion of reality. It represents reality as released from all the conditions of heaviness. This liberation opens up for the creative phantasy limitless possibilities of *disencumbered* form. In the ceiling frescoes the ultimate consequences have been drawn from the effigy as para-nature. Yet there is no difference in principle whether horses gallop on ceilings, or mountains, houses, tables and chairs are affixed as pictures to walls. Let us not forget that it is only the panel that hangs on the wall and not the image. The weight of the panel does not increase with the weight of the object represented. In fact the painted table doesn't hang on the wall; it stands in a painted room on a painted floor in an imaginary space that remains visible to the eye.

Effigies are of no size that can be measured. The measurements given in a catalogue refer to the panels which may vary between the size of a medallion and a wall fresco. The dimensions of an effigy cannot be established quantitatively. We understand a photograph as the effigy of an object whose life size is ten, a hundred, or even a thousand times as great as its reproduction. We are unable to condense the object itself, but we can enlarge and reduce its suchness, its visible form. Of course we speak of pictures as being large or small, just as we speak of large or small tables. But in such cases we don't mean the effigies, but the panels in relation to the room available in the continuum of perceptual space. The size of the effigies does not vary with the size of the panels. The effigy is not intermediate in size between what it represents and the panel. The effigy of a large life object doesn't require a large panel. On panels with the dimensions $a \times b$ we may find a house at one time, at another a person, and at still another a landscape. The laws of size constancy are suspended. While we are seeing others beside us in life size, we may view an effigy in which people are represented as tiny figures. If we grant that the artist knows how to select the proper proportions for his representation, it is still to be remembered that effigies can be enlarged and reduced, i.e., reproduced on panels of varying sizes. Effigies have no constant size relation to the panel, to the object represented, to the surround, or to the viewer and his space of action. They are beheld in a space which has been disengaged from the continuum of natural space. Every effigy has its own scale, which cannot be transferred to an adjacent picture. It remains remarkable that we can disengage every effigy in its own way from familiarly experienced relationships and, despite their divergence from conventional invariants, can grasp them as representations of actual magnitudes.

The child's understanding of pictorial representation matures slowly. In the course of this development, which requires many years, the performance flaws are especially revealing. William Stern[12] reported that his daughter Hilde, age 3 years, 6 months, could compare the pictures in her animal book with the creatures seen in the zoo. That the ostrich in the picture was only several centimeters high didn't bother her, but it did bother her that its reproduction wasn't larger than those of the other birds. She said, "Is that the ostrich? But he's bigger!" And since in her animal book the armadillo was of about the same size as the wildcat, she was always startled at the zoo by how small the armadillo was. Obviously Hilde expected a constant relationship between the effigy, panel size, and life size. To grasp effigies as such does not guarantee that a representation or its relation to what is represented will be understood in detail. Thus Eva, age 2 years, 1 month, sees a "large figure of the Madonna and thinks that the unclad figure of the baby Jesus should be covered, and asks for a little shirt which she requests be put over him." In this case the little girl had grasped a "similarity" between what was represented and what was familiar to her, completely ignoring the radical dissimilarity which first makes the effigy an effigy. Even when a child names represented objects correctly or reacts to them with appropriate expressions, its tendency to handle the picture makes us wonder whether the child has recognized it altogether as an effigy. Little Eva behaved toward the effigy of the Madonna as if it were a tangible object. She failed to realize the unique immateriality of the effigy spread out on the panel without tangible substance, depth, or thickness.

Effigies are *on* the surface of the panels, they do not constitute the actual surfaces. A coat of paint belongs to the wall; the effigy does not belong to the panel. It is separated no less from the basis that supports it than from its surroundings. In a drawing the ground also is brought into the effigy itself; yet of itself it is without material depth even while representing depth. Space does not surround the effigy, it doesn't extend into the rear. One cannot approach an effigy from the opposite side. Effigies are without reverse; in very dimension they are detached from the spatial continuum; entering from nowhere, entirely self-contained, they face the beholder's gaze. Nothing is beneath, behind, or beside them.[13] No "perspectival appearances" (*Abschattungen*) accompany the sight given in the effigy. (Perspectival appearances are relative to an individual moving in his action space.) The page of the book that shows the Matterhorn presents another landscape on its back; we can turn the panel but not the effigy.

The "suspension" of place, size, and weight in the effigy gives crea-

tive phantasy the possibility for unlimited invention. Yet those products which we owe to the created phantasy of a gifted few are seen
as effigies even by their many uncreative viewers. The most prosaic
person to whom a masterpiece has little to say understands nonetheless
it is an effigy. He may prefer the work of the house painter to that
of the artist, but he does not confuse them. Pictures, like other
things visible, are seen and distinguished from them by seeing—not
in reflection. The effigy represents the real world in an imaginary space.
Nevertheless this imaginary realm is not grasped in imagination but
is seen with the bodily eyes. The imaginary space of the effigy is
visible, like the surroundings from which it has been cut out. How
can one account for the seeing of effigies? The physics of illumination
and the physiology of visual stimulaton are the same for effigy, frame,
and wall. The myopic person needs his glasses to look at an effigy
as in all his other visual activities. At night effigies and walls alike
are obscured in darkness, to reappear again by day. Van Gogh's painted
suns don't shine. The retina is unable to tell whether the light striking
it has been reflected from the surface of a picture or from the wall on
which it hangs. For just this reason a picture, under certain conditions,
can give the deceptive impression of reality. The distinction between
object and effigy cannot be established physiologically—more precisely,
cannot be so determined as long as one attempts to understand the
relation of the seeing person to what is seen solely from the performance
of the visual organ, from the eye as an optical instrument and not as
an organ of a seeing human being. The distinction between effigy and
object is possible only on the basis of the relation of a human being
to the visible world. Both effigy and object are seen; the seeing of an
effigy reveals two modes of seeing: orienting seeing and objectifying
beholding. Orienting seeing is in the service of corporeal existence, of
locomotion, approaching, fleeing, capturing, and incorporating. In
orienting seeing we are directed to things as objects within a common
field of gravity. In beholding, on the contrary, we are directed to
things as objects, released from the tendency of incorporating. Things
in their suchness we comprehend at a distance and vis-à-vis, without
reference to ourselves. In choosing hors-d'œuvres from a buffet we let
ourselves be drawn from one tray to another; we let our appetite
speak and reach for whatever most appeals to us. There is a relationship
of desire. The hostess and cook who take a quick look to see if everything is in order have switched off their appetence, just as we do when

comparing the size of one circle with that of another. Only in beholding in the distance-preserving gaze is it possible to refer something directly to something else over there without reference to the beholder. Only in beholding can we count and measure, relate replica to original, representation to what it represents. In beholding, made possible by upright posture, vision perpendicular to one's own body axis confronts things as they rise up vertically in a fronto-parallel plane. This orthoscopic attitude, first of all centered on distant things, can be employed voluntarily to a considerable extent in adult life. Only the effigy constitutes the exception; it always requires or compels the contemplative regard, i.e., beholding.

The relationship of effigy and beholder is paradoxical. A painting hanging on the wall right in front of us is, in its representatonal function, more remote from us than the moon. The distance separating moon from earth may, it appears, be overcome technically. An unbridgeable distance lies between us and a drawing we hold in our hand. Every bodily (*leiblich*) contact is suspended; trespassing does not need to be forbidden, since access is impossible anyway.

Effigies are possible only in the sphere of the visible. In no other modality is there, nor can there be, anything comparable to the effigy. An effigy must be grasped in its ontological deficiency in contrast to the visible surroundings. The natural surroundings from which the effigy stands out must be pre- and co-given. The thingness of the effigy is negated; but this is only possible within the horizon of the visible. Consequently, it is one of the artist's tasks to emphasize the negative character of the effigy, to so detach it from its surroundings that it is withdrawn from action space. The artist emphasizes its character as artifact. The effigy, however, is essentially different from other artifacts, for example a trace or an object of use. The trace is an alteration in material; an object of use, a chair for example, is manufactured from this or that material; the effigy, however, is so formed that it can be beheld only as a shape of color, as dematerialized *eidos*. Thus disengaged from the natural continuum it represents for the viewer something that can only be imperfectly accomplished in the original itself.

Pictures painted not with the intention to represent reality, but to counterfeit it—say a painted door in a drape—are consequently inserted into the continuum of a room or a hall without a frame. The legendary Parrhasius played a trick on Zeuxis. He painted a drape in his atelier as if it were part of the furnishings, behind which the picture was hidden. The painted drape gave an illusion of reality, because its character as effigy was skillfully concealed. Thus Zeuxis was misled into approaching the effigy not as a beholder.

If our ideas about the modes of seeing and beholding are valid, then we ought to expect certain disturbances, i.e., a pathology of the seeing of pictures. We are not disappointed. Examples are easy to find. In sleep the effigies of the dream are not lived as effigies; the sleeper, who has temporarily given up his posture counter to the field of gravity, has lost the natural surrounding against which an effigy can be set in contrast. Only on reawakening, with reactivation of the upright posture, are the effigies of the dream recognized as such. Closely related are the dreamlike states of the infectious and toxic deliria. One of Beringer's experimental subjects reported his experience of mescaline intoxication: "The picture of Naples was shown to me. I saw it in colors, saw how the city teemed, how the ocean rocked, how the water roared, in short a living picture was before me so plastic and true to life that I could only believe I was really on the beach at Naples. I was completely gripped by its beauty and at one time expected Vesuvius to appear. I don't know how I could see all that; I didn't understand it, because after all I was in the cellar, and yet it was before me in reality. From the way I talked it must have been clear how fascinated I was by this sight and how it made me all aglow. But whenever for a moment I would—I don't know, it sounds so silly—exert my will, then everything was the same as usual; I had to let myself go, and then I would see something."[14] In depersonalization states also—to give a further example—the relation of seeing and beholding is disturbed. In depersonalization the real world appears like an effigy. It is seen and yet it is removed to an unbridgeable distance. In that effigy things show themselves at a uniform distance reduced to the level of stage scenery. Movement loses the meaning of change. "The faces of persons . . . are flat like pancakes."[15] Spatial depth is relative to a motile being in his action space.

The impression of the third dimension in graphic perspective is represented depth, and is as such essentially different from depth and distance as grasped in the space of action. It is a mistaken assumption that the actual perception of spatial depth is to be understood in accordance with the principles of perspective represented in painting, i.e., that in actual seeing a two-dimensional retinal image is apprehended as a stereoscopic structure on the basis of certain cues (binocular vision, parallax, etc.). While the horizon expands in diverging radii to the view of the observer, in picture perspective the horizontal parallels converge to a vanishing point located on the panel somewhat above the lower edge of the picture. To be sure, parallel lines, like railroad tracks for example, appear to converge at a distant point of intersection, yet they converge within a horizon opening up around them into the indeterminate. In the effigy, on the contrary, the field of vision is forced into a frame delimiting it from its surroundings by fixed boundaries on its four sides.

A picture as such is seen in the transparent depths of lived space. Into the painted depths we do not penetrate; we don't move around in the picture space any more than we can or wish to reach for a depicted object, no matter how well it may be rendered. The depth of the represented space is not an expansion of the distance across which we see the picture. The zero point of this distance to and from the picture is given in our Here, itself invisible. The painted spatial depth, however, is related to the transparent foreground of the effigy. All the technical means of perspectival representation are more than mere additions to two-dimensional composition.

Effigies are rigid and motionless, and yet they represent movements and actions. In Ruisdael's pictures the ocean rages, streams plunge, and trees bow in the wind. A famous portrait by Titian shows Charles V astride his horse. For centuries the emperor has been riding through that hall of the Prado without ever leaving his place. The effigy, like all effigies, is timeless in its non-reality, but represents in its timelessness time-soaked reality enhanced beyond all reality. The emperor will not swerve his gaze, his horse's hoofs will not touch the ground. Nothing moves, and yet the inner life is perfectly represented, though not as movement frozen in a single phase in the manner of a slow-motion picture. In the effigy the emperor is *eternalized* as rider. A few rooms farther on in the gallery, and we stand before Velasquez' "The Surrender of Breda." The vanquished extends, with a respectful bow, the key of the city to the victor who accepts it with a gesture of clemency. The picture shows a historical event. For the one moment represented in the picture the curtain is drawn aside and the personae enter from the obscurity of their history, unfamiliar to the modern viewer. But the picture does not tell who the actors are or were, what city was surrendered, or when it occurred. To find that out we must refer to a catalogue, or learn by word of mouth. Pictures are mute. "No space about them, even less a time" (*Faust*, II). The effigy, spared from the continuum of action space, is also removed from present time. Timeless itself, the picture represents something it is not: temporal happenings in nature or history. The moment represented and the moment of beholding are not simultaneous. The past is arrested in the effigy. Yet it does not need the master's hand to accomplish this transformation. The simplest photograph can do as much. Newspapers and magazines overwhelm us with effigies of events from yesterday or last week. Such effigies are also mute, and need a story, i.e., an explanatory caption to tell their beholders who and what are represented, and when and where it has occurred. Despite their flimsiness these newspaper effigies have, we might say, a magical hold on time. "To hold something fast in a picture" means of course that a past event is brought to the beholder's gaze for actualization in the present as past. In the invention of the cinema this temporal counterpoint may well have reached its limit. In a newsreel even movement sequences are preserved. We see the events as earlier and later—the film image has not changed the order of temporal sequence—but we behold them in our personal present as pictorial display, as happenings which are not simultaneous with the act of seeing. The seeing and the seen do not belong to the same temporal order.

The performances of the cinema are merely a technical amplification of the stage and stage play. Every drama, even one whose action is set in "the present," occurs in an imaginary time which has nothing in common with the time of its spectators. A "piece" performed today can be repeated tomorrow. The time of the performance, beginning at 8 o'clock and ending at 11, is not synchronous with that of the drama.

Just as effigies are set off by a frame, so theater stages are divided from the space of spectators by a curtain, proscenium arch, and podium. The space of the stage is not continuous with the space of the spectators. When the curtain goes up, a transparent fourth wall takes its place, through which we behold the events occurring on the stage. In the ancient open air theater, stage space and audience space were of course not separated by a curtain, but even there the axes of scenic space and audience space were perpendicular to one another. The players emerged from a concealing background, and in mask and cathurn announced the mythical time of the action. A drama naturally shows but "a piece" from the history of its participants, who come to the spectator from an unknown past—out of somewhere. The opening of the play is not the beginning of that drama in which the *dramatis personae* are engaged. It is always a technical problem for the play-wright how he is to tell what has led up to the present conflict, as well as to reveal the passage of imaginary time through the speeches of his characters. In the few hours of an evening at the theater a destiny is decided, a course of action brought to a close, whose begin-ning and end are often divided by much larger periods of imaginary time. As in the effigy the opened spatial horizon of the visible world is condensed spatially int o the confined measure of the panel, so too on the stage events (widely dispersed in their natural lived sequence) are meaningfully compressed and temporally condensed in the few acts of the play. Through the power of word and speech, possibilities are opened to the play which are denied to the mute effigy. But both share this: they call for the attitude of the beholder and spectator, the contemplative gaze. Persons converse on the stage, they act before a public, they speak for the spectator, but not to him. He too has a role—the spectator—to whom insight is allowed into remote events, and for whom it is consequently inappropriate to interfere in the action on the stage.[16]

The theater audience knows—as far as the idea of the play is concerned—more of what is going on than all the *personae* of the play. Only the spectators witness Hamlet's meeting with his father's ghost, which remains hidden from all the other *personae*. The spectator is privy to Hamlet's plans against the king and to Claudius' conspiracy with Laertes. The spectator knows the whole of which every participant in it knows but a part. The purpose of the play "both at the first and now, was and is to hold as 't were the mirror up to Nature—to show Virtue her own feature, scorn her own image, and the very age and body of the time his form and pressure."[17]

But beholding is not limited to visitors in museums and theaters. The marching member of a procession is wedged in between the man ahead and the men on either side. It is the one on the reviewing stand who surveys the procession as a whole. It is the historian who, removed from the pressure of events, writes history in retrospect. It is the observer in nature or the laboratory who comprehends the linkages of physical events and represents them as a rational, intelligible order. The space of action, articulated as Here and There, is never homo-geneous, isometric, isotropic. Only space beheld from a distance, remote space, has the character of Euclidean geometry dominated by the vertical and the right angle.

The "being-with" and "taking by" (Binswanger) both lose and gain in the beholding encounter. For what it loses in immediacy and nearness, it gains as a view of the whole in which the human being, "the first freedman of creation," beholds his own position from there to here, as in a mirror.

NOTES

1. Ovid. *Metamorphoses,* I, 84–86. In translation: "While other animals look bellywards to earth, he gave to man a lofty countenance, bade him behold the sky and, upright, lift his gaze unto the stars." The creator of man from clay was Prometheus, son of Iapetus, who formed man in the "image of the all-ruling gods."

2. F. Weidenreich, *Apes, Giants and Man,* Univ. of Chicago Press, 1946; cf. Straus, E., "The Upright Posture," *Psychiatric Quarterly,* 26, 1952.

3. Cf. F. J. J. Buytendijk's comprehensive treatment: *Allgemeine Theorie der Menschlichen Haltung und Bewegung (General Theory of Human Posture and Movement),* Springer-Verlag, 1956.

4. C. Sherrington, *Man on His Nature,* New York, Cambridge University Press, 1940, p. 177.

5. Sherrington, *Man on His Nature,* New York (Doubleday Anchor Book), 2nd ed., 1953.

6. Ibid., p. 261.

7. Hans Kunz, *Die anthropologische Bedeutung der Phantasie (The anthropological Significance of Phantasy),* Verlag f. Recht u. Gesellschaft, Basel, 1946, Bd. II, S. 297.

8. Ibid., Bd. I, S. 273.

9. "Perceptions are appearances for which there is a concomitant knowledge of their causation through an external stimulus. Conceptions are appearances for which there is concomitant innate knowledge that they are not caused by an external stimulus." *Handwörterbuch der Med. Psych.,* ed. by Karl Birnbaum, Thieme-Verlag, 1934. Reference: "Sinnestäuschungen" ("Sensory illusions").

10. Braille writing is not ideographic. The feeling hand of the blind person is presented with spatial configurations within a restricted area, and which are to be taken as tactile signs of phonemes.

11. Cf. Hans Jonas, "Homo pictor und Differentia des Menschen," *Ztschr. f. philosophische Forschung,* 1961, 15 (2), 161.

12. William Stern, *Psychologie der früheren Kindheit (Psychology of Early Childhood),* Leipzig, Quelle & Meyer, 1928.

13. Cézanne's efforts to make his paintings "perfectly dense" probably corresponds to this basic characteristic of effigies.

14. K. Beringer, *Der Mescalinrausch (Mescaline Intoxication),* Berlin, Springer, 1927.

15. Cf. von Gebsattel, "Zur Frage der Depersonalisation" ("The Problem of Depersonalization"). In: *Prolegomena einer medizinischen Anthropologie,* Berlin, Göttingen, Heidelberg, Springer-Verlag, 1954.

16. Children at times forget their roles as audience members, get carried away, and break into the stage action with shouting and cries. One of our patients was brought into the hospital because he had shot at a television set when irritated by supposed personal references. It is perhaps one of the principal features of the paranoid schizophrenic that he is no longer able to maintain the distance of his regard in the presence of actual events.

17. *Hamlet,* III, 2.

Could a machine think?—Could it be in pain?—Well, is the human body to be called such a machine? It surely comes as close as possible to being such a machine.

But a machine surely cannot think!—Is that an empirical statement? No. We only say of a human being and what is like one that it thinks. We also say it of dolls and no doubt of ghosts too. Look at the word "to think" as a tool.

———

"I believe that he is suffering."—Do I also believe that he isn't an automaton?

It would go against the grain to use the word in both connections.

(Or is it like this: I believe that he is suffering, but am certain that he is not an automaton? Nonsense!)

Suppose I say of a friend: "He isn't an automaton."—What information is conveyed by this, and to whom would it be information? To a human being who meets him in ordinary circumstances? What information could it give him? (At the very most that this man always behaves like a human being, and not occasionally like a machine.)

"I believe that he is not an automaton," just like that, so far makes no sense.

My attitude towards him is an attitude towards a soul. I am not of the opinion that he has a soul.

Religion teaches that the soul can exist when the body has disintegrated. Now do I understand this teaching?—Of course I understand it—I can imagine plenty of things in connection with it. And haven't pictures of these things been painted? And why should such a picture be only an imperfect rendering of the spoken doctrine? Why should it not do the same service as the words? And it is the service which is the point.

If the picture of thought in the head can force itself upon us, then why not much more that of thought in the soul?

The human body is the best picture of the human soul.

—Ludwig Wittgenstein
Philosophical Investigations

SELECTED READING

Aristotle. "De Anima" in *The Works of Aristotle*, Vol. III. Ed. W. D. Ross and trans. John Smith (Oxford: The Clarendon Press, 1963). Reprinted in *The Basic Works of Aristotle*. Ed. Richard McKeon (New York: Random House, 1941), pp. 533–603.

Bertocci, Peter A. "Descartes and Marcel on the Person and His Body: A Critique," *Meeting of the Aristotelian Society* (March 25, 1968), pp. 207–26. See *PAS* (n.s.), LXVIII (1967–8).

Bollnow, O.-F. *Das Wesen der Stimmungen* (Frankfort a. Main: Vittorio Klostermann, 1949), 2nd. ed. revised.

Bultmann, Rudolf. *Theology of the New Testament* (London: SCM Press Ltd., 1952), Vol. I, Pt. II, Chap. IV.

Buytendijk, F. J. J. *Pain: Its Modes and Functions* (1943). Trans. Eda O'Shiel (Chicago: University of Chicago Press, 1962).

————. *Attitudes et Mouvements: Étude functionnelle du mouvement humain* (Paris: Desclée de Brouwer, 1957).

————. "The Body in Existential Psychology," *Review of Existential Psychology and Psychiatry*, Vol. I, No. 2 (1961), pp. 149–172.

Canguilhem, Georges. *Le normal et le pathologique* (Paris: Presses Universitaires de France, 1966).

Chappell, V. C., R. M. Chisholm, and H. Spiegelberg. "Ego and Person: Phenomenology or Analysis," *The Monist*, 49, No. 1 (January, 1965), 1–43.

Chirpaz, François. *Le corps* (Paris: Presses Universitaires de France, 1963).

Coburn, Robert C. "Bodily Continuity and Personal Identity," *Analysis*, XX (1960), pp. 117–120.

Cornman, James W. "The Identity of Mind and Body," *Journal of Philosophy* (1962), pp. 486–492.

Douglas, Andrew H. *The Philosophy and Psychology of Pietro Pomponazzi* (Hildesheim: Georg Olms Verlagsbuchhandlung, 1962).

Duhrssen, Alfred. "Philosophic Alienation and the Problem of Other Minds," *Philosophical Review*, LXIX, No. 2 (April, 1960), 211–20.

————. "The Self and the Body," *Review of Metaphysics,* 10 (1956), pp. 28–34.

Federn, Paul. *Ego Psychology and the Psychoses.* Ed. Edoardo Weiss (New York: Basic Books, Inc., 1952). Available in German, *Ich Psychologie und die Psychosen* (Bern and Stuttgart: H. Huber Verlag, 1956).

Feigl, Herbert. *The "Mental" and the "Physical": The Essay and a Postscript* (Minneapolis: University of Minnesota Press, 1967). The essay originally appeared in *Minnesota Studies in the Philosophy of Science,* Vol. II, 1968.

Feyerabend, Paul. "Materialism and the Mind-Body Problem," *Review of Metaphysics,* XVII (1963–1964), pp. 49–66.

Fisher, Seymour. "Body Image and Psychopathology," *Archives of General Psychiatry,* X, No. 5 (1964), pp. 519–529.

———— and Sidney E. Cleveland. *Body Image and Personality* (New York: Dover Publications Inc., 1968) 2nd. ed. revised.

Geach, Peter. *God and the Soul* (London: Routledge & Kegan Paul, 1969). See essays 1, 2, and 3.

Gerstmann, Josef. "Psychological and Phenomenological Aspects of Disorders of the Body Image," *Journal of Nervous and Mental Disease,* CXXVI (1958), pp. 499–512.

Hengstenberg, Hans-Eduard. "Phenomenology and Metaphysics of the Human Body," *International Philosophical Quarterly,* III (1963), pp. 165–200.

Henry, Michel. *Philosophie et phénoménologie du corps* (Paris: Presses Universitaires de France, 1965).

Humanitas. "The Human Body," Vol. II, No. 1 (Spring, 1966). The entire issue is devoted to the human body. See "Selected Subject Bibliography," pp. 98–104, in which numerous psychological references are listed.

Husserl, Edmund. *Cartesian Meditations.* Trans. Dorion Cairns (The Hague: Martinus Nijhoff, 1960). Sections 44–58.

————. *Ideen zu einer Reinen Phänomenologie und Phänomenologischen Philosophie.* Drittes Buch: *Die Phänomenologie und die Fundamente der Wissenschaften.* Ed. Marly Biemel (The Hague: Martinus Nijhoff, 1952), Band V. Erstes Kapitel, Sect. Z, 5–20, 117–25. Also see *Phänomenologische Untersuchungen zur Konstitution.* Ed. Marly Biemel (The Hague: Martinus Nijhoff, 1952), Band IV, Zweites Buch, Zweiter Abschnitt, Drittes Kapitel, 143–61.

Jaspers, Karl. *General Psychopathology.* Trans. J. Hoenig and Marian W. Hamilton (Chicago: University of Chicago Press, 1963).

Jonas, Hans. *The Phenomenon of Life: Toward a Philosophical Biology* (New York: Harper & Row, 1966).

Laing, R. D. *The Divided Self: An Existential Study of Sanity and Madness* (Baltimore: Penguin Books, 1965).

Lopez-Ibor, J. J. "Existential Psychology and Psychosomatic Pathology," *Review of Existential Psychology and Psychiatry*, I (1961), pp. 140–148.

Lyons, Joseph. *Psychology and the Measure of Man* (Glencoe, Ill.: Free Press of Glencoe, 1963).

Madariaga, Salvador de. *A Portrait of a Man Standing* (London: Allen & Unwin Ltd., 1968).

Marcel, Gabriel. *The Mystery of Being: Reflection and Mystery*, Vol. 1 (Chicago: Henry Regnery, Gateway Edition, 1960). Especially pp. 127–53.

Merleau-Ponty, Maurice. *L'union de l'âme et du corps chez Malebranche, Biran et Bergson*, notes prises au cours de Maurice Merleau-Ponty à l'école normale supérieure (1947–1948), recueillies et rédigées par Jean Deprun (Paris: Librairie Philosophique J. Vrin, 1968).

Muller, Philippe. *De la psychologie à l'anthropologie: À travers l'oeuvre de Max Scheler* (Neuchâtel: Éditions de la Baconnière, 1946).

Pfänder, Alexander. *Die Seele des Menschen: Versuch einer verstehenden Psychologie* (Halle: Max Niemeyer Verlag, 1933).

Plessner, Helmuth. *Conditio Humana* (Pfullingen: Neske, 1964).

Plügge, Herbert. *Wohlbefinden und Missbefinden: Beiträge zu einer Medizinischen Anthropologie* (Tübingen: Max Niemeyer Verlag, 1962).

Pomponazzi, Pietro. "On the Immortality of the Soul," in *The Renaissance Philosophy of Man*. Eds. E. Cassirer, P. O. Kristeller, and J. H. Randall (Chicago: University of Chicago Press, 1948), pp. 255–381.

Puccetti, Roland. *Persons: A Study of Possible Moral Agents in the Universe* (London: Macmillan, 1968).

———. "Brain Transplantation and Personal Identity," *Analysis*, XXIX, No. 3 (January, 1969), new series, pp. 65–77.

Ricoeur, Paul. *Freedom and Nature: The Voluntary and the Involuntary*. Trans. Erazim Kohák (Evanston, Ill.: Northwestern University Press, 1966). Originally published as *Le Volontaire et l'involontaire* (Aubier: Editions Montaigne, 1950).

Sarano, Jacques. *Essai sur la signification du corps* (Neuchâtel, Paris: Delachaux et Niestlé, 1963).

Scheler, Max. *The Nature of Sympathy* (New Haven: Yale University Press, 1954). Trans. Peter Heath.

Schrag, Calvin O. "The Lived Body as Phenomenological Datum," *Modern Schoolman*, XXXIX (1961–1962), pp. 203–218.

Shoemaker, Sydney. *Self-Knowledge and Self-Identity* (Ithaca, N.Y.: Cornell University Press, 1963).

Smith, Norman Kemp. *New Studies in the Philosophy of Descartes* (London: Macmillan, 1963). See Chaps. VI, XIII.

Spiegelberg, Herbert. *Alexander Pfänders' Phänomenologie* (The Hague: Martinus Nijhoff, 1963).

———. "On the Motility of the Ego," in *Conditio Humana* (Berlin: Springer-Verlag, 1966), pp. 289–306.

Straus, Erwin. *The Primary World of Senses: A Vindication of Sensory Experience*. Trans. Jacob Needleman (New York: Free Press of Glencoe, 1963).

Strawson, P. F. *Individuals: An Essay in Descriptive Metaphysics* (London: Methuen & Co. Ltd., 1959). Especially Chap. III, "Persons."

Thomas Aquinas, Saint. *Aristotle's De Anima in the Version of William of Moerbeke and the Commentary of St. Thomas Aquinas*. Trans. K. Foster and S. Humphries (New Haven: Yale University Press, 1959).

Todes, Samuel J. *The Human Body as the Material Subject of the World*, Doctoral Dissertation, Harvard University (1963).

Van Den Berg, J. H. *The Changing Nature of Man* (New York: Norton, 1961).

———. "The Human Body and the Significance of Human Movement," *Philosophy and Phenomenological Research*, XIII (1952), pp. 159–183.

Vesey, Godfrey, N. A. "The Location of Bodily Sensations," *Mind*, LXX (1961), pp. 25–35.

Waelhens, A. de. *Une Philosophie de L'Ambiguïté: L'existentialisme de Maurice Merleau-Ponty* (Louvain: Publications Universitaires de Louvain, 1967).

———. La Philosophie et les Experiences Naturelles (The Hague: Martinus Nijhoff, 1961).

Watts, Alan W. *The Joyous Cosmology* (New York: Pantheon Books, 1962). Especially the Prologue.

Weiss, Paul. *Nature and Man* (Carbondale, Ill.: Southern Illinois University Press, 1965). Especially pp. 81–144.

Wiggins, David. *Identity and Spatio-Temporal Continuity* (Oxford: Basil Blackwell, 1967).

Wittgenstein, Ludwig. *The Blue and Brown Books: Preliminary Studies for the Philosophical Investigations*, 1933–1935 (New York: Harper & Row, 1965).

————. *Philosophical Investigations*. Trans. G. E. M. Anscombe (New York: Macmillan, 1953).

Wolff, Charlotte. *A Psychology of Gestures*. Trans. Anne Tennant (London: Methuen and Co. Ltd., 1945) 2nd ed., 1948.

Zaner, Richard M. *The Problem of Embodiment: Some Contributions to a Phenomenology of the Body* (The Hague: Martinus Nijhoff, 1964), Phaenomenologica 17.

QUADRANGLE PAPERBACKS

American History Since 1865

See our complete catalog for titles in American History to 1865, European History, Philosophy, *and* Social Science.

QUADRANGLE PAPERBACKS

European History

William Sheridan Allen. *The Nazi Seizure of Power.* (QP302)
W. O. Henderson. *The Industrial Revolution in Europe.* (QP303)
Raul Hilberg. *The Destruction of the European Jews.* (QP301)
Richard N. Hunt. *German Social Democracy.* (QP306)
Telford Taylor. *Sword and Swastika.* (QP304)
John Weiss. *Nazis and Fascists in Europe, 1918-1945.* (NYTimes Book, QP305)

Philosophy

F. H. Bradley. *The Presuppositions of Critical History.* (QP108)
William Earle. *Objectivity.* (QP109)
James M. Edie, James P. Scanlan, Mary-Barbara Zeldin, George L. Kline. *Russian Philosophy.*
(3 vols, QP111, 112, 113)
James M. Edie. *An Invitation to Phenomenology.* (QP103)
James M. Edie. *New Essays in Phenomenology.* (QP114)
James M. Edie. *Phenomenology in America.* (QP105)
R. O. Elveton. *The Phenomenology of Husserl.* (QP116)
Manfred S. Frings. *Heidegger and the Quest for Truth.* (QP107)
Moltke S. Gram. *Kant: Disputed Questions.* (QP104)
James F. Harris, Jr., and Richard Severens. *Analyticity.* (QP117)
E. D. Klemke. *Studies in the Philosophy of G. E. Moore.* (QP115)
Lionel Rubinoff. *Faith and Reason.* (QP106)
Stuart F. Spicker. *The Philosophy of the Body.* (QP118)
Paul Tibbetts. *Perception.* (QP110)
Pierre Thévenaz. *What Is Phenomenology?* (QP101)

Social Science

Shalom Endleman. *Violence in the Streets.* (QP215)
Nathan Glazer. *Cities in Trouble.* (NYTimes Book, QP212)
George and Eunice Grier. *Equality and Beyond.* (QP204)
Kurt Lang and Gladys Engel Lang. *Politics and Television.* (QP216)
Charles O. Lerche, Jr. *Last Chance in Europe.* (QP207)
Raymond W. Mack. *Prejudice and Race Relations.* (NYTimes Book, QP217)
David Mitrany. *A Working Peace System.* (QP205)
H. L. Nieburg. *In the Name of Science.* (QP218)
Martin Oppenheimer. *The Urban Guerrilla.* (QP219)
Martin Oppenheimer and George Lakey. *A Manual for Direct Action.* (QP202)
James Parkes. *Antisemitism.* (QP213)
Fred Powledge. *To Change a Child.* (QP209)
Lee Rainwater. *And the Poor Get Children.* (QP208)
The Rockefeller Report on the Americas. (QP214)
Clarence Senior. *The Puerto Ricans.* (QP201)
Harold L. Sheppard. *Poverty and Wealth in America.* (NYTimes Book, QP220)
Arthur L. Stinchcombe. *Rebellion in a High School.* (QP211)
Harry M. Trebing. *The Corporation in the American Economy.* (NYTimes Book, QP221)
David Manning White. *Pop Culture in America.* (NYTimes Book, QP222)

See our complete catalog for titles in American History.